T0214282

Communications in Computer and Information Science 1349

More information about this series at http://www.springer.com/series/7899

Andrei Chugunov · Igor Khodachek ·
Yuri Misnikov · Dmitrii Trutnev (Eds.)

Electronic Governance and Open Society: Challenges in Eurasia

7th International Conference, EGOSE 2020
St. Petersburg, Russia, November 18–19, 2020
Proceedings

 Springer

Editors
Andrei Chugunov ⓘ
e-Governance Center
ITMO University
St. Petersburg, Russia

Yuri Misnikov ⓘ
e-Governance Center
ITMO University
St. Petersburg, Russia

Igor Khodachek ⓘ
North-West Institute of Management,
Russian Academy of National Economy
and Public Administration (RANEPA)
St. Petersburg, Russia

Dmitrii Trutnev ⓘ
e-Governance Center
ITMO University
St. Petersburg, Russia

ISSN 1865-0929   ISSN 1865-0937   (electronic)
Communications in Computer and Information Science
ISBN 978-3-030-67237-9   ISBN 978-3-030-67238-6   (eBook)
https://doi.org/10.1007/978-3-030-67238-6

This Springer imprint is published by the registered company Springer Nature Switzerland AG
The registered company address is: Gewerbestrasse 11, 6330 Cham, Switzerland

Preface

The 7th edition of the EGOSE international conference was held in a mixed face-to-face and online format due to the travel constraints caused by the COVID-19 pandemic. As previously, it was organized in St. Petersburg (Russia) on 18–19 November 2020 by the ITMO University's Centre for e-Government Technologies jointly with the North-West Institute of Management, Russian Academy of National Economy and Public Administration (RANEPA). In addition to EGOSE's traditional set of conference topics, a specific feature of the 2020 event was the inclusion of the participatory budgeting theme, as an invitation to share experiences of the EU project "Empowering Participatory Budgeting in the Baltic Sea Region" (EmPaci). Overall, the conference agenda covered the usual diverse list of topics that makes EGOSE unique in the wider Eurasian region, namely:

- E-Governance and Eurasian Integration
- Open Government Prospects
- Information Society and e-Governance
- Citizen-Centred E-Government
- Building the Smart City
- The Smart City and Quality of Life
- E-Governance and Policy Modelling
- Participatory Governance and Participatory Budgeting
- Social Media: Tools for Analysis, Participation and Impact
- Big Data, Computer Analytics and Governance
- Cases and Perspectives of Government Transformations

59 papers coming from 12 counties were submitted for review by the Programme Committee, whose members selected 23 research papers for publication in this volume. Prof. Dirk Draheim representing the Information Systems Group at Tallinn University of Technology (TTÜ) delivered the keynote plenary speech, followed by three paper presentation sessions. Seven papers were presented and discussed at the first session, which was dedicated to digital government services, policies, laws and practices. The second research session addressed the problematics of the digital society viewed from the perspective of openness, participation, trust and competences, as discussed in eight papers. Another eight papers presented in the third session reported research results in the field of digital data science, with a special emphasis placed on methods and techniques used to build models and algorithms for research in, *inter alia*, Artificial Intelligence (AI) and Natural Language Processing (NLP). Each session was concluded with a discussion.

The trend of the rising prominence of research in the area of machine learning and computational linguistics that emerged a few years back has been maintained at this conference as well. The area of digital government and society has revealed possible new emerging topics of research enquiry into surveillance and the silver economy, in addition to such traditional topics as digital services, policies and comparative studies.

November 2020

Andrei Chugunov
Igor Khodachek
Yuri Misnikov
Dmitrii Trutnev

Organization

Steering Committee

Andrei Chugunov	e-Governance Center, ITMO University, Russia
Igor Khodachek	Russian Academy of National Economy and Public Administration, North-West Institute of Management, Russia
Yuri Misnikov	e-Governance Center, ITMO University, Russia
Dmitrii Trutnev	e-Governance Center, ITMO University, Russia

Program Committee

Artur Afonso Sousa	Polytechnic Institute of Viseu, Portugal
Olusegun Agbabiaka	Softrust Technologies Limited, Nigeria
Luis Amaral	University of Minho, Portugal
Dennis Anderson	St. Francis College, USA
Francisco Andrade	University of Minho, Portugal
Mohammed Awad	American University of Ras Al Khaimah, UAE
Maxim Bakaev	Novosibirsk State Technical University, Russia
Luis Barbosa	University of Minho, Portugal
Radomir Bolgov	Saint Petersburg State University, Russia
Mikhail Bundin	Lobachevsky State University of Nizhny Novgorod, Russia
Christos Kalloniatis	University of the Aegean, Greece
Sunil Choenni	Research and Documentation Centre (WODC), Ministry of Justice, The Netherlands
Andrei Chugunov	ITMO University, Russia
Cesar A. Collazos	Universidad del Cauca, Colombia
Shefali S. Dash	National Informatics Centre, India
Saravanan Devadoss	Addis Ababa University, Ethiopia
Subrata Kumar Dey	Independent University, Bangladesh
Dirk Draheim	Tallinn University of Technology, Estonia
Ruben Elamiryan	Public Administration Academy of the Republic of Armenia, Armenia
Behnam Faghih	Technical and Vocational University, Iran
Olga Filatova	St. Petersburg State University, Russia
Enrico Francesconi	Institute of Legal Information Theory and Techniques (ITTIG-CNR), Italy
Fernando Galindo	University of Zaragoza, Spain
Despina Garyfallidou	University of Patras, Greece

João Luís Oliveira Martins	United Nations University, Portugal
Prabir Panda	Independent Researcher, India
Ilias Pappas	Norwegian University of Science and Technology, Norway
Manas Ranjan Patra	Berhampur University, India
Rui Quaresma	Universidade de Évora, Portugal
Irina Radchenko	ITMO University, Russia
Aleksandr Riabushko	Office of the affairs of the Ulyanovsk region, Russia
Gustavo Rossi	La Plata National University (UNLP), Argentina
Aires Rover	Universidade Federal de Santa Catarina (UFSC), Brazil
Alexander Ryjov	Moscow State University, Russia
Michael Sachs	Danube University Krems, Austria
Adriano Santos	Universidade Federal de Campina Grande, Brazil
Carolin Schröder	Technische Universität Berlin, Germany
Shafay Shamail	Lahore University of Management Sciences, Pakistan
Irina Shmeleva	ITMO University, Russia
Rudrapatna Shyamasundar	Tata Institute of Fundamental Research (TIFR), India
Greg Simons	Uppsala University, Sweden
Evgeny Styrin	National Research University Higher School of Economics, Russia
Neelam Tikkha	Rashtrasant Tukadoji Maharaj Nagpur University (RTMNU), India
Dmitrii Trutnev	ITMO University, Russia
Mario Vacca	Italian Ministry of Education, Italy
Costas Vassilakis	University of the Peloponnese, Greece
Lyudmila Vidiasova	ITMO University, Russia
Vasiliki Vrana	Technological Education Institute of Central Macedonia, Greece
Wilfred Warioba	Commission for Human Rights and Good Governance, Tanzania
Maria Wimmer	Universität Koblenz-Landau, Germany
Sherali Zeadally	University of Kentucky, USA
Kostas Zafiropoulos	University of Macedonia, Greece
Nikolina Zajdela Hrustek	University of Zagreb, Croatia
Hans-Dieter Zimmermann	FHS St. Gallen University of Applied Sciences, Switzerland
Vytautas Čyras	Vilnius University, Lithuania

Blockchains from an e-Governance Perspective: Potential and Challenges – Keynote at EGOSE 2020 (Abstract of Keynote)

Dirk Draheim ⓘ

Information Systems Group, Tallinn University of Technology, Estonia
dirk.draheim@taltech.ee

Abstract. Originally, blockchain technology was coupled to the cryptocurrency vision; but recently, it has broken free from the cryptocurrency paradigm and become productive in more diverse platforms and ICT architectures. In this talk, we aim at understanding the potential and challenges of blockchain technology for e-government and e-governance initiatives. We delve into three cases. First, we consider the usage of blockchain technology in the Estonian e-government ecosystem. Second, we look into the controversial case of the Belarusian cryptohub HTP (High Technologies Park) - known as Decree No. 8. Third, we discuss the European Blockchain Services Infrastructure (EBSI) and its use cases, in particular in service of MyData (Self Data, Internet of Me). Now: what can stakeholders in digital transformation expect from current and emerging blockchain technology platforms? How can they benefit from them most?

Keywords: Blockchains · distributed ledgers · European Blockchain services infrastructure · European self-sovereign identity framework · eIDAS · High technologies park HTP · Decree No. 8 · X-Road · Guardtime

Soon after the cryptocurrency Bitcoin [1] was introduced in 2009, and with the quick rise of several further cryptocurrencies that follow the Bitcoin paradigm, its enabling blockchain technology was perceived by the media (with a peak in 2017) and the public as having an immense disruptive potential, i.e., a potential to democratize financial markets, fundamentally transform entire industries, even whole societies etc. Now, there is no convention of policy makers (and business tycoons likewise) all around the globe not having blockchains and/or cryptoeconomics as a topic on its agenda.

Silently, in the slipstream of the roaring disruptive narrative, blockchain-based technology has altered (and matured?) from permissionless to permissioned platforms that have started to be productive in successful ICT sweet spot architectures. The potential and challenges of blockchain technology as an enabler for organizations has been well described by others: In [2], Mendling et al. provide a thorough analysis and roadmap for the exploitation of blockchain technology in business process management [3]; with [4], Janssen et al. provide a conceptual framework for the analysis of blockchain technology adoption from an integrated perspective (institutional/market/technical).

In this talk, we turn to the potential and challenges of blockchain technology for e–government and e-governance initiatives (digital government). After briefly reviewing the intrinsic technological and socio-economic barriers of blockchain technology [5], we delve into three cases.

First, we look into the usage of blockchain technology in the Estonian e-government ecosystem. We explain the role of the nationwide data exchange platform X-Road [6,7] and discuss how blockchain technology is related to it. We look into the pioneering Guardtime blockchain solution (KSI blockchain [8]) and how it is used to back Estonian state registries.

Second, we look into the controversial case of the Belarusian cryptohub HTP (High Technologies Park) - known as Decree No. 8 (Decree on the development of the digital economy). The circulation of cryptocurrencies gets regulated (introducing roles of cryptographic platform operators, cryptocurrency exchange operators etc.) for the whole economy. But this comes at the price that the HTP creates a detached technocratic/tech-savvy [9] subsociety inside the state.

Third, we discuss the European Blockchain Services Infrastructure (EBSI) and its use cases. In particular, we are interested in EBSI as an enabler of the (eIDAS-compliant) European Self-Sovereign Identity Framework (eSSIF).

Now, we ask the following questions. Where are we heading for in e-governance? Centralized super-applications such as WeChat [10] or de-centralized self-sovereign citizen data (following the approach of MyData, Self Data, Internet of Me etc.) [11]? Is it possible to combine elements of these strands or do they contradict each other fundamentally? And against that background: What can stakeholders in digital transformation expect from current and emerging blockchain technology platforms? How can they benefit from them most (and best serve citizens) to create an ever more open society?

References

1. Nakamoto, S.: Bitcoin: A Peer-to-Peer Electronic Cash System (2008). https://bitcoin.org/bitcoin.pdf. Accessed 21 April 2020
2. Mendling, J., Weber, I., van der Aalst, W., et al.: Blockchains for business process management − challenges and opportunities. ACM Trans. Manag. Inf. Syst. **9**(1), 1–16 (2018).
3. Dumas, M., Rosa, M.L., Mendling, J., Reijers, H.A.: Fundamentals of Business Process Management, 2nd edn. Springer, Heidelberg (2018). https://doi.org/10.1007/978-3-662-56509-4
4. Janssen, M., Weerakkody, V., Ismagilova, E., Sivarajah, U., Irani, Z.: A framework for analysing blockchain technology adoption: integrating institutional, market and technical factors. Int. J. Inf. Manag. **50** (2020)
5. Buldas, A., Draheim, D., Nagumo, T., Vedeshin, A.: Blockchain technology: intrinsic technological and socio-economic barriers. In: Dang, T.K., Küng, J., Takizawa, M., Chung, T.M. (eds.) FDSE 2020. LNCS, vol. 12466, pp. 3–27. Springer, Cham (2020). https://doi.org/10.1007/978-3-030-63924-2_1

6. Kalja, A.: The first ten years of X-Road. In Kastehein, K., ed.: Estonian Information Society Yearbook 2011/2012. Ministry of Economic Affairs and Communications of Estonia, pp. 78–80 (2012).

7. Ansper, A., Buldas, A., Freudenthal, M., Willemson, J.: High-performance qualified digital signatures for X-road. In: Riis Nielson, H., Gollmann, D., (eds.) NordSec 2013. LNCS, vol. 8208, pp. 123–138. Springer, Heidelberg (2013). https://doi.org/10.1007/978-3-642-41488-6_9

8. Buldas, A., Kroonmaa, A., Laanoja, R.: Keyless signatures' infrastructure: how to build global distributed hash-trees. In: Riis Nielson, H., Gollmann, D., (eds.) NordSec 2013. LNCS, vol. 8208, pp. 313–320. Springer, Heidelberg (2013). https://doi.org/10.1007/978-3-642-41488-6_21

9. Draheim, D., et al.: On the narratives and background narratives of e-government. In: Proceedings of HICSS 2020 - the 53rd Hawaii International Conference on System Sciences, AIS, pp. 2114–2122 (2020).

10. Lemke, F., Taveter, K., Erlenheim, R., Pappel, I., Draheim, D., Janssen, M.: Stage models for moving from e-government to smart government. In: Chugunov, A., Khodachek, I., Misnikov, Y., Trutnev, D. (eds.) EGOSE 2019. CCCIS, vol. 1135, pp. 346–359. Springer, Cham (2020). https://doi.org/10.1007/978-3-030-39296-3_12

11. Buyle, R., et al.: Streamlining governmental processes by putting citizens in control of their personal data. In: Chugunov, A., Khodachek, I., Misnikov, Y., Trutnev, D., (eds.) EGOSE 2019. CCCIS, vol. 1135, pp. 346–359. Springer, Cham (2020). https://doi.org/10.1007/978-3-030-39296-3_26

Contents

Digital Data: Data Science, Methods, Modelling, AI, NLP

Digital Government: Services, Policies, Laws, Practices, Surveillance

On the Narratives of e–Government: A Comparison of the Democratic and Technocratic Approach in Post–Soviet States

Sam van Wijk[1]([⊠]), Florian Lemke[1]([⊠]), and Dirk Draheim[2]([⊠]) [iD]

[1] Capgemini Business & Technology Solutions – Public Sector,
Berlin, Germany
sam.van-wijk@capgemini.com,
florian.lemke@capgemini.com
[2] Information Systems Group, Tallinn University of Technology,
Tallinn, Estonia
dirk.draheim@taltech.ee

Abstract. Narratives influence our perception and determine how we look on social phenomena, the society and public politics. Since the introduction of the term e–Government and the usage of technical innovations in the public sector, three narratives seem to have emerged. A review of the 100 most cited papers and publications on e–Government has revealed that at the current state, the focus on narrative in publications on e–Government seem to be the democratic narrative, the technocratic narrative, and the tech–savvy narrative. Combined with a survey of n = 417 participants, consisting of both civil society as well as IT user and IT experts, it turned out that there is a difference between various country groups regarding their perception of e–Government. Three country groups are analyzed, the established European democracies, the post-Soviet states and one overall country group. This paper aims to find out whether there is a difference in the perception of the introduced governmental initiatives between so–called established European democracies and post–Soviet states. The paper aims to find out in which country groups IT innovations that have been implemented by the public administration reflect a more democracy–based narrative compared to a more efficiency–based.

Keywords: Narratives · Democratic narrative · Technocratic narrative · Tech–savvy narrative · Post–Soviet states · e–Government

1 Introduction

The rapid integration of digital technologies is transforming today's societies and economies [1]. That phenomenon is not only characteristic for the economy and thus the private sector, but it remarkably influences how the public sector is working. E–Government has changed and continuously changes the way the administration and public sector are managed since the late 1990s. The term e–Government is used for different characteristics of digital innovations developed for the public sector.

© Springer Nature Switzerland AG 2020
A. Chugunov et al. (Eds.): EGOSE 2020, CCIS 1349, pp. 3–16, 2020.
https://doi.org/10.1007/978-3-030-67238-6_1

E–Government is not just about applying for tax numbers online or saving waiting time at administration offices; it is about the way the public sector functions and how it is organized.

As narratives create our social–political reality and perception, the question emerges of what narratives are used with respect to e–Government, what they consist of, how they are created and which perceptions they reflect in the state they are told. According to Draheim et al. [2], there are basically three predominant narratives in e–Government research: the democratic, the technocratic and the tech–savvy narrative. Each of the three narratives holds a different political, historical and theoretical background.

Within these narratives, the perception of e–Government within the society is reflected. In 2019, Tallinn University of Technology conducted a study with $n = 417$ participants with respect to the perception of ten digital initiatives (Open Data [3], e–Voting, Basic e–Government, Digital Globalization, m–Government [4], Smart Contracts, Smart City, e–Participation, e–Health, Smart Government) and their potential to (a) strengthen the democracy and (b) make the government and economy more effective and efficient. The potential to increase the democracy stands representative for the democratic narrative and the technocratic narrative is interrogated through the question to what extend e–Government innovations are capable to increase the effectiveness and efficiency of the public sector.

Basically, there is a huge amount of research regarding the e–Government and the way it will change democracy and society [5, 6]. E–Government research discusses how the communication between government and citizens, between citizens, government and businesses will look like in the presence of e–Government in the future. E–Government will impact our way of life and the way the public sector is perceived by the public. But there is a lack of research regarding how the public perception is changing in countries where there is a stronger technological transformation of the public sector and how this affects the public's opinion regarding e–Government. In order to create a formation of opinion and an initial impression of the differences regarding the perception of e–Government in different country groups, the survey of Tallinn University of Technology [7] will be taken into consideration. The total participants in the survey will be classified into three different country groups: the established European democracies, the post–Soviet states and one group with the overall average of the answers. The survey as well as the review of research papers convey the impression that there is a difference between the established European democracies and the post–Soviet states looking at their perception of the democratic and technocratic narrative. It is assumed that the technocratic narrative should be perceived stronger in established European democracies, whereas the post–Soviet show a stronger drive towards the democratic narrative, as their transformation character may suggest.

2   The Democratic vs. the Technocratic Narrative

The democratic narrative is converging on the fact that within that narrative, according to Draheim et al. [2], a citizen is seen as a citizen. This is the main distinction from the technocratic narrative. In the field of the democratic narrative a lot of research has been done so far; especially on the question if and how e–Government influences our democracy as well as what positive and negative effects e–Democracy have concerning the relationship between government and citizens.

In times where countries as well as global institutions complain about decreasing interest in politics, represented in low voting turnouts, there is a relatively high demand of improving the relationship between government and citizens [8]. In this field there are a lot of research regarding whether e–Voting could improve communication between citizens and the state and thus increase participation again. This key point can be summarized by the term empowerment and it aims to achieve a better and especially more individual communication and closer connection between the two parties. Through digital innovations, in this manner e–Government and citizens get the opportunity to interact with officials and get individual information from a direct and online approach about government and politics. Through a good user centricity, divided in the extend of online provided service, mobile friendliness and usability, [9] the barrier could be decreased and as a result, citizens could be empowered in their communication with the government. An empowered citizen is able to effectively exercise their rights as well as responsibilities regarding the relationship with its government [10].

In distinction, the technocratic narrative has a different core focus. In regard of the implementation of e–Government innovations, stakeholders seem to have the aspects of that narrative in mind, because they think of e–Government as business driven rather than democracy driven [2]. This narrative seems to be more about finances and the effectiveness or efficiency values rather than a democratic way of thinking. This narrative has a strong technology aspect but does not leave out the understanding of e–Government service as a service provided by the government. By the broad definition of technocracy as having high level experts at the top of an institution, in this case the government combines two aspects: service and expertise of the technocratic way of thinking [2].

The technocratic approach rarely can exist without the democratic approach. One definitely can be stronger than the other but with this example it is shown that although the focus lies on the increase of the planning budget, there is a strong focus on a higher participation of citizen within the decision–making progress as well. Making the public administration more effective and efficient, the main aim of the technocratic approach, always comes from a political background. Direct participation correlates with direct democratic aspects. With empowering people to be part of the decision–making process in order to fulfill the goal to increase the effectiveness of the public administration. This is oftentimes transferred into a greater scheme of progress: the technical developments are seen to potentially transform the whole government as well as society, as changes in the way of living and interacting with each other are seen on both sides.

3 The Case Study on Post–Soviet States and Established European Democracies

For the case study, hereinafter three different country groups will be analyzed. On one side of the comparison, there are the post–Soviet states and their former satellite states and on the other side, the established European democracies. These two paired country groups will be also compared to a country group that holds an average value of all the countries taken place in the survey.

The case study is based on a survey of Tallinn University of Technology [7]. To generate a meaningful result for the research question, the decision was made to compare two rather different types of societies with a different historical background and state systems.

Because of the participants of the study and the numbers of answers, it has been decided to pair Germany (answers given by 90 people) together with Austria (number of answers given is five). In total that makes 95 participants answering the questions and therefore represent the group of established European democracies. It is clear that these states and political systems do not resemble entirely and at core are different states and comparable young democracies when looking at the Republic of France, that has a longer history when it comes to their democratic values. Additionally, there are a lot of researches done regarding the common and comparable Nazi history of both countries. These two countries were selected because of the restricted resources of comparable countries representing the group of established European democracies.

To represent the counterpart with another understanding of the democracy and public perception of government, we decided to take some of the post–Soviet states as the investigation object. Belarus, Estonia, Georgia, Hungary, Kyrgyzstan, Latvia, Russia and the Ukraine will be taken into consideration. This is just a part of the group of post–Soviet states but for this case study, they will be representative for the group in total.

As mentioned above, these two groups for the case study were selected because of their different perceptions of the political system and democracy at first glance. Post–Soviets states are marked and characterized by their transformation process and the democratic process happening in the last 30 years after the fall of the iron curtain and the accession to the European Union for many of the countries in 2004. The other part of the analyzed countries is perceived in public as established members of the European Union with a strong democratic thinking, a long and historical background regarding democracy.

The survey, in which the case study is based on, served as a background to have an impression and the initial meaningful results about the public perception of implemented e–Government innovations. The total number of participants was 417 ($n = 417$) and the survey was open from 20th of May 2019 until 10th of June 2019. The survey was constructed of 30 + 3 questions and designed as single–choice–questions but with a possibility to give an open answer for each of the initiative at the end of the survey. Regarding the open answers, they were never published and were only used for gaining an impression for further detailed research and have been entirely deleted on 20th of June 2020; exactly one year after the closing of the survey. For the publication, the data and answers were fully anonymized. The definition of each of the ten digital initiatives that the questions focused on was given beforehand to avoid misunderstandings.

The survey was accomplished with Google Docs and was designed with the Likert scale, including negative values. In total, 5 answers were possible: two positive values, two negative ones and one answer with a neutral value. Answer -2 means a fully disagreement, -1 represents a somehow disagreement, 0 stands for neutrality, 1 for somehow agreement and 2 for fully agreement. The first question is covered by the democratic narrative and asks: "Do you think that e–Voting will strengthen our democracies? (with elements such as: participation; transparency; open society; anti–corruption; social inclusion; trust in government; privacy)". The second one covers the technocratic narrative and reads: "Do you think that e–Voting will make our governments and economies more effective and efficient? (with elements such as: cost savings; quality of services; responsiveness; citizen–as–customer; citizen–orientation; service innovation; public–private–partnership; economic growth; anti–fraud)" [7].

4   Comparison of the Perception of e–Government Innovations

4.1   Perception of the Digital Initiatives in Total

First, we will look at the survey outcome in general regarding all the countries participated in the survey (number of countries is 47 and the perception of each of the digital initiatives. Figure 1 shows the arrangement and positioning of the ten digital initiatives mentioned in the survey regarding the public perception in the categories of

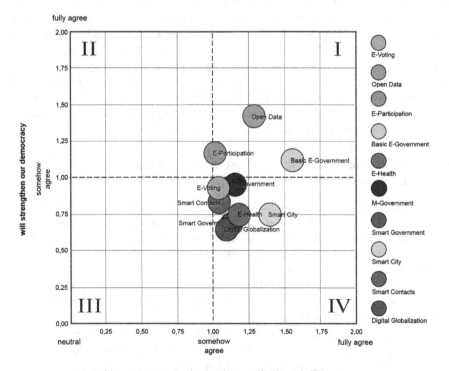

Fig. 1. Survey outcome - overview of overall positioning of the digital initiatives with y-axis democratic narrative vs. y-axis technocratic narrative (based on Draheim. Private Communications, 2019).

the possible strengthening of democracy and the effectiveness gain and efficiency increase of the economy and government.

The y-axis is representative for the democratic narrative whereas the x-axis serves for the technocratic narrative. For this analysis, the average score for each of the narratives was calculated. The first score was calculated for the democratic narrative, the question about the possibility to strengthen democracy and the second one for the technocratic narrative, about the possible increase of effectiveness and efficiency.

All of the digital initiatives are in the quadrants I and IV. The distributions are not the same, as only three of the ten initiatives are in the 1st quadrant. Open Data, e–Participation and basic government have values on the democratic axis as well as the technocratic axis higher than 1. The other initiatives, m–Government, Smart Contracts, e–Health, e–Voting, Smart Government, Digital Globalization and Smart City, all have a lower than 1 score on the democratic axis but a higher than one score on the technocratic axis. One can observe that the initiatives range in a quite small field of values.

Even most of the initiatives on the democratic axis are rated lower than 1 whereas on the technocratic axis, none of the initiative is rated lower than 1. At the first glance one can observe that the responders of the survey see the implementation of all of the 10 implemented digital initiatives as overall making the economy and the government as much more efficient and effective than strengthening the democracy. In total, the people participated in the survey, do not think that the digital initiatives do harm the democracy or making the economy or the government ineffective or inefficient. Combining the focus of the questions and the narratives, the democratic narrative overall is pronounced weaker than the technocratic narrative. By gaining more positive values and having higher results, the technocratic narrative is represented stronger. Other initiatives mark the highest point of the average value. For the democratic narrative, it is Open Data and for the technocratic narrative Basic e–Government.

4.2   Perception of the Digital Initiatives in the Established European Democracies

The values and points for the digital initiatives in Fig. 2 were calculated in the exact same way as they were for Fig. 1. Because the focus for this view was shifted from all of the initiatives and responders of all countries participating in the survey to the countries Germany and Austria representing the established European democracies. In this Fig. 2, the x-axis represents as in the figures before the technocratic narrative and the y-axis the democratic narrative. As in the Figure before, values are illustrated from 0, neutral over 1, somehow agree and 2, fully agree. The field is divided in 4 quadrants starting with quadrant I on the top right.

At first glance the values in Fig. 2 seem to be more scattered than the ones in the digital initiatives in Fig. 3. There is no negative value looking at the responses given in the survey from the countries Germany and Austria. It is noticeable that the digital initiatives are distributed all over the four quadrants.

Comparing the two axes, the digital initiatives overall are seen as way more positive on the technocratic axis than the democratic one. Almost all digital initiatives are perceived as possibility to make the economy and the government more effective and efficient than having the opportunity to strengthening the democracy. If looking at the average value of 0,83 regarding the initiatives rated in the viewpoint of the democratic narrative, it is noticeable that the average is lower than 1. In contrast, the average value of the technocratic narrative is 1,17.

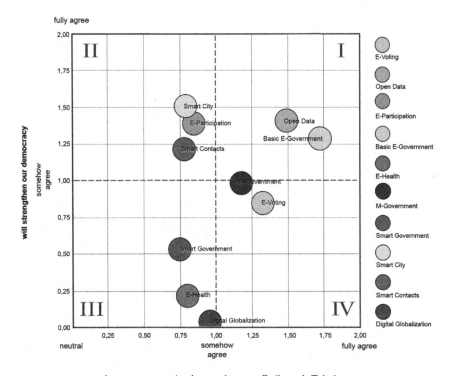

Fig. 2. Survey outcome - positioning of the digital initiatives with y-axis democratic narrative vs. x-axis technocratic narrative for the countries Germany and Austria (Established European Democracies) (based on Draheim. Private Communications, 2019)

Thus, digital initiatives are perceived at least in the countries Germany and Austria, as more technocratic than democratic. The democratic trust of the people participated in the survey seem to be low and especially lower than the trust in the possibilities for the technocratic thinking. Comparing the lowest and the highest score in each of the narrative, the technocratic narrative has the highest score. In contrast, the democratic narrative contains the lowest one.

What is observable is that there are three initiatives (Smart City, e–Participation and Smart Contracts) that rank high, here the highest value, on the democratic axis but does not rank high at all regarding the technocratic value. This is the only case where the democratic perception ranks higher than the technocratic perception.

4.3   Perception of the Digital Initiatives in the Post-Soviet States

Figure 3 illustrates the values of the countries Belarus, Estonia, Georgia, Hungary, Kyrgyzstan, Latvia, Russia and the Ukraine representing the post–Soviet states. Similar to the Figures before, the y-axis is the democratic narrative axis and the x-axis the technocratic narrative.

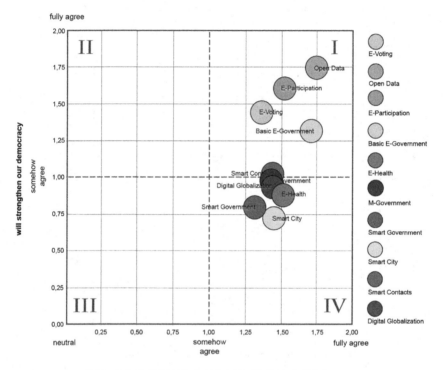

Fig. 3. Survey outcome - overview of positioning of the digital initiatives with y-axis democratic narrative vs. x-axis technocratic narrative for the countries Belarus, Estonia, Georgia, Hungary, Kyrgyzstan, Latvia, Russia and the Ukraine (Post-Soviet States) (based on Draheim. Private Communications, 2019)

The ranking of the digital initiatives is only taking place in the I and IV quadrant with no digital initiatives being located in the quadrants II and III. With no initiative rated with a lower value than 0,5 it can be observed seemingly that the initiatives are located on the right side of the field all positioned closely. Overall, the initiatives are positioned in a rather narrow field. Five of the digital initiatives are located in the I quadrant: Smart Contracts, e–Voting, Basic e–Government and e–Participation. The other initiatives can be found one field beneath that in the IV quadrant.

Comparing the two axes with the democratic and technocratic narrative it is noticeable that none of the values, neither democratic nor technocratic, have a value under 0,5. The technocratic narrative on average is rated higher than the democratic one with a value of 1,5 instead of 1,12. The extreme points and the digital initiatives reaching the highest or the lowest value do not match in this case. For the democratic approach, Smart City reaches the lowest one with 0,71 whereas looking at the technocratic low point it is Smart Government with the value of 1,3. This is somehow surprising as the two points do have a big difference of almost 0,6 value points. Still, the democratic average value is high as well. The difference is big, but it can be basically explained by the extreme points on this focus.

Six of the ten initiatives are, comparing the democratic as well the technocratic values, positioned in a small field. The values vary insignificantly. Excluding the digital initiatives of e–Voting, Basic e–Government, e–Participation and Open Data, all the other initiatives are rated between the values 0,71 and 1,05 on the democratic axis and between 1,30 and 1,44 on the technocratic one. This is observed as a bundle of six initiatives. The highest rated in the democratic focus, Open Data and e–Participation do not fit one hundred percent regarding the highest ones on the technocratic axis. Open Data is thus the overlap if we look at the two extensive values.

4.4 Overall Perception in the Three Country Groups

Figure 4 shows the overall distribution of the average values of all country groups considered in the case study, the average value of Germany and Austria thus what we consider in this case study as the established European democracies and thirdly the average value of the countries Belarus, Estonia, Georgia, Hungary, Kyrgyzstan, Latvia, Russia and the Ukraine thus the post–Soviet states. The third country group contains all the countries participating in the study.

To give a numerical overview, the lowest average value in total is having Germany and Austria thus in this case study the representatives for the established European democracies with the values of the democratic average of 0,83 and in the technocratic focus 1,17. On the middle of the spectrum, the values of the overall countries average with the points at democratic 0,93 and technocratic 1,19 can be found. The post–Soviet states had the highest score with the average value of the democratic axis at 1,14 and for the technocratic one 1,5. Thus it is noticeable that the country group of established European democracies as well as the overall country values are closely linked together within the almost the same spectrum of values. The overall average in both of the narratives shows higher values than the ones from Germany and Austria but compared to the spacing regarding the post–Soviet states, it can be said that the digital initiatives in both of the groups looked at are not far apart.

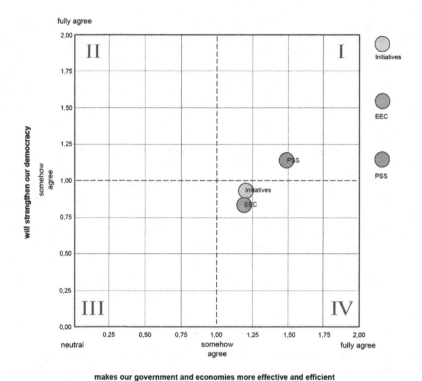

Fig. 4. Survey outcome - overview of positioning of the digital initiatives with y-axis democratic narrative vs. x-axis technocratic narrative with average values for the countries in total, average value of established European democracies and average value of post-Soviet states (based on Draheim. Private Communications, 2019)

The technocratic average value is a quite high one compared to the average values of the democratic focus. In all of the country groups the responders in arithmetic mean more than somehow agree that there is a possibility brought by digital initiatives regarding the technocratic approach. This is higher than the people having trust in digital initiatives to strengthen the democracy. What is interesting is that all of the country groups show similar differences between the average value of democratic and technocratic approach. If we look at the dissimilarity in the group of all the countries participating in the survey, this difference is 0,26 followed by the difference in the established European democracies with 0,34 and the post–Soviet states having the highest one with 0,36. The values are different but located closely to one another. Post–Soviet states with the highest difference is somehow noticeable because they already have the highest value in all of the other categories. They have the highest value for the democratic as well as the technocratic narrative.

In summary one can say that the countries representing the established European democracy have lower values in average than it is observed in all of the countries summed up together. On the other side, there is the figure of the post–Soviet states showing a higher average value in both of the narrative focus and in total a higher average value than the one regarding all the countries in total and the established European democracies.

Comparing all of the three groups and the average values of the ten rated initiatives it is outstanding that there are two initiatives that almost in all countries and in the democratic as well as technocratic narrative have high values. These two initiatives, as mentioned above the highest values in the democratic approach. Comparing to the almost in all average values observed higher technocratic values than democratic values, Open Data and Basic e–Government almost have the same democratic as well as technocratic output. People seem to have faith in these initiatives to have the possibility to strengthen the democracy but also make the government and economy more efficient and effective. One reason for these two to rank as high as they did in all of the three country groups could be that these are two initiatives that play a rather big role in the public perception and political debate.

5 Learnings for the Public Sector

Two main things are outstanding and could lead to a learning for the public sector. Basically, it was shown that the overall feedback on the digital initiatives regarding the topic of e–Government is positive, there is no negative output from the survey looking at the average values. This shows that the initiatives are on a good way to show the positive effects of innovations regarding e–Government, and citizens in general are not perceiving e–Government as something negative. People in average do not think of e–Government initiatives as something that harms the democracy or make the government less effective and efficient [11].

In the country group of the post–Soviet states, it is observable that there is an overall high set of values on all the digital initiatives. Both narratives and therefore the technocratic x-values and the democratic y-values demonstrate a high ranking of the ten digital initiatives. One explanation for that phenomenon could be the situation of the public administration in the post–Soviet countries. Chang and Golden [12] stated that corruption tends to be a higher in authoritarian regimes. Nondemocratic also show a higher corruption rate if looking at the Corruption Perceptions Index. Most of the post–Soviet states still show higher corruption rates among the European Union but still it is quite interesting that they show more and higher aspects of corruption until today. Whereas Germany is ranked 8th from in total 180 countries with a corruption rate of 2% as to the barometer of the Corruption Perception Index published and created by transparency.org, Latvia ranks 14th with a percentage of 14% as to the barometer [13]. The barometer within the Corruption Perception Index shows the "percentage of public service users paid a bribe in the previous 12 months" [13]. Even Estonia with a strong drive towards the European Union and being a member since 2004, has a corruption percentage of 5% and the 18th rank [13].

The corruption index also shows that countries such as Estonia and Latvia have improved their corruption level significantly since the transformation after the fall of the iron curtain. On the other hand, corruption still seems to be anchored in the post–Soviet states. After decades being part of the USSR, it is possible that many countries wish to become more democratic. The high values in both the democratic and the technocratic research seem to show a picture of faith regarding the strengthening of the democracy as well as the effectiveness of the public sector.

Accountability and transparency appear to be the main drives of the trust that citizens are putting into the digital initiatives, at least in the post–Soviet states. Innovations such as e–Voting and the low turnout of that initiative in the established European democracies seems to have an origin in citizens who have faith for better, fairer and corruption–free votes. E–Voting is neither in the overall average nor in the established European democracies ranked as high as in the post–Soviet states. A simple explanation could be that the population in e.g. Estonia are simply used to this initiative as they have been using e–Voting for years. Another aspect could basically be that the people having no or few trusts in public administration. This could still be a relic of the former USSR times but for sure still is an issue in most of the post–Soviet states. Digital initiatives and e–Government should begin with this perspective or start to work on this perspective. The main challenge should be the creation of a stable and trustworthy public sector. Transparency and accountability should be the two main drives resulting in a process of strengthening the democracies in the countries of the post–Soviet states with the help and through innovations of e–Government such as e–Voting and Open Data [14].

The second aspect is the surprisingly low turnout of the votes of the initiatives in the established European democracies. They show a higher technocratic rating of initiatives than the democratic ones but still a rather low average values comparing to the other two groups. Two explanations are convincible and therefore the question arises if citizens of the established European democracies, in the case study Germany and Austria, have a huge amount of trust regarding the status quo of the public administration or have they been afraid towards new digital innovations and e–Government. On average they do not think that the ten digital initiatives are having a huge positive effect or impact on neither the strengthening of the democracy nor the effectiveness and efficiency of the public sector. One explanation could be that citizens of this country group are indeed quite satisfied with the status quo of the public administration. Looking at the kind of initiatives that are ranked higher than the other ones it shows an interesting picture. Not only do they have significant higher values as the other ones, but they are also two initiatives that citizens gotten in touch automatically over the past years. Basic e–Government and Open Data are not new initiatives and it seems that citizens have a basic trust in the two innovations. Regarding the low ranking of Digital Globalization and e–Health this shows that there could be a kind of skeptical thinking of new digital initiatives regarding e–Government. The difference could be that basically citizens in established European democracies have faith in their public sector.

This is another starting point as in the post–Soviet states where the citizens do not have much trust in the public sector. Overall, this presents one big issue regarding the country group established European democracies and their public sector: awareness. Taking the low turnouts, this could be the origin of citizens having a skeptical opinion of digital initiatives. Awareness could surely help to push e–Government along and give digital innovation a better starting point in the field of e–Government and provide a better future perspective through creating awareness within society.

6   Conclusion

The case study and the three country groups showed an interesting picture. The overall country group showed a relatively even picture with the initiatives grouped closely together, whereas the values in the established European democracies seem to be scattered. The country group containing Germany and Austria, show the lowest value of the initiatives. Except for Open Data and Basic e–Government, all the initiatives are ranked lower than in the post–Soviet states.

It is surprising that these happen in both narratives. The second research question asked whether a difference between these country groups can be observed. Not only is there a difference between the groups of established European democracies and the post–Soviet states but the overall country group is somewhat ranked between these two in most of their initiatives. There are indeed differences between the perception of digital initiatives looking at the outcome of the survey in the analyzed country groups.

Looking at the assumption that the established European democracies are perceived to have a stronger drive towards making the government and economy more effective and efficient, it is surprising that this must be falsified. In fact, compared to their votes regarding the democratic values of the initiatives, the values are higher on the technocratic axis, but these are not as high as the one in the country group of the post–Soviet states. On the other hand, the post–Soviet states, as in the hypothesis, actually show higher ranked voting regarding the democratic approach. On the democratic axis the post–Soviet states have the highest values, at least on average. This could correlate with their transformation character and their freshly transformed political system in comparison, but could have other reasons, for example, the faith in digital initiatives to deter corruption. There have been clear limitations to the study as well. Regarding to the sample size and the choice of cases, overall universal statements on the results of the study needs to be considered within its specific setting when making further research. The choice of cases had been limited due to the number of responses within established democracies.

Finally, the main outcome of the analyzed case study is that digital initiatives in the post–Soviet states rank highest, on the democratic as well as technocratic narrative. On the contrary, the established European democracies show a picture of low turnouts in the survey regarding the question whether they think that the ten digital initiatives can strengthen the democracy as well as whether they think e–Government can make the government and economy more effective and efficient. The established European democracies performed under the average compared to all the countries taking place in the survey. It must be stated that this is only a small section of the population. Though there have been respondents with different levels of knowledge regarding e–Government, the amount of people with a total n = 417 cannot represent the society within these three country groups. The case study together with the survey gives an impression on how it might look like and how the perception of e–Government innovations can be. We see a surprisingly different outcome in the end and some new hypotheses that need further verification. Indeed, there seems to be a lack of research regarding the perception of digital initiatives and e–Government innovations. A lot of researches are done on the topic of the perception of e–Government in general. The noticeable differences of the perception found in the case study depending on the country group looked at, could be a possible further research field.

Not all of the population in all of the countries that have been analyzed in the case study seem to have the same level of clarification of facts. The output of the survey and the country group of Germany and Austria adumbrate this. The low trust in the initiatives, besides Open Data and Basic e–Government, may result from excessive demands and a lot of unclear issues within the society regarding the topic of e–Government. One way to raise awareness for and to improve trust in e–Government innovations could be by improving communication with the population, i.e., to talk about the risks and especially the chances brought by e–Government. Strengthening the democracy and increasing effectiveness and efficiency within the public sector are only a small part of the change that e–Government contains. This implies that the communication between the citizens and government, the communication between citizens will change. By rising the digital awareness – the society as well as the public sector can take the chances that e–Government possibly brings.

References

1. OECD. Strengthening digital government. OECD Going Digital Policy Note. OECD, Paris. www.oecd.org/going-digital/strengthening-digital-government.pdf. Accessed 08 July 2020
2. Draheim, D., et al.: On the narratives and background narratives of e–Government. In: 2020 Proceedings of the 53rd Hawaii International Conference on System Sciences, pp. 2114–2122 (2020)
3. Janssen, M., Brous, P., Estevez, E., Barboasa, L., Janowski, T.: Data governance: organizing data for trustworthy artificial intelligence. Gov. Inf. Q. **37**(3), 101493 (2020)
4. Lemke, F., Taveter, K., Erlenheim, R., Pappel, I., Draheim, D., Janssen, M.: Stage models for moving from e-Government to smart government. In: Chugunov, A., Khodachek, I., Misnikov, Y., Trutnev, D. (eds.) EGOSE 2019. CCIS, vol. 1135, pp. 152–164. Springer, Cham (2020). https://doi.org/10.1007/978-3-030-39296-3_12
5. Yildiz, M.: E-Government research: reviewing the literature, limitations, and ways forward. Gov. Inf. Q. **24**(3), 646–665 (2007)
6. Brown, D.: Electronic government and public administration. Int. Rev. Admin. Sci. **71**(2), 241–254 (2005)
7. Tallinn University of Technology Homepage, Survey on the Impact of Digital Initiatives. https://old.taltech.ee/projects/lss/1-7/survey/. Accessed 12 Sept 2020
8. Tuzzi, A., Padovani, C., Nesti, G.: Communication and (e)democracy: assessing European E–Democracy discourses. In: Cammaert, B., Carpentier, N. (eds.) Reclaiming the Media. Communication Rights and Democratic Media Roles, pp. 31–65. Intellect, Bristol (2007)
9. Capgemini; IDC; Sogeti; Poltecnico di Milando (2018): e–Government Benchmark 2018. Securing e–Government for all. European Commission (2018)
10. La Porte, T.M., Demchak, C., Jong, M.: Democracy and bureaucracy in the age of the web. Admin. Soc. **344**(4), 411–446 (2002)
11. Gil-Garcia, J.R., Helbig, N., Ojo, A.: Being smart: emerging technologies and innovation in the public sector. Gov. Inf. Q. **31**(1), 11–18 (2014)
12. Chang, E., Golden, M.A.: Sources of corruption in authoritarian regimes. Soc. Sci. Q. **91**(1), 1–20 (2010)
13. Transparency International, Country Data. https://www.transparency.org/en/countries/estonia. Accessed 08 July 2020
14. Matheus, R., Janssen, M.: A systematic literature study to unvravel transparency enabled by open government: the window theory. Public Perform. Manag. Rev. **43**(3), 503–534 (2020)

E-Government Mechanisms Development: Comparative Analysis of British and Russian Cases

Svetlana Morozova$^{(\boxtimes)}$ ⓘ and Alexander Kurochkin ⓘ

Faculty of Political Science, St. Petersburg State University, Smolny St., 1/3, 191124 St. Petersburg, Russia
s.s.morozova@spbu.ru

Abstract. The main goal of the study is to identify shortcomings in the implementation of e-government mechanisms in Russian Federation and to propose recommendations for improving these mechanisms. Particular attention in the article is paid to current trends and problems in the field of e-government, which are based on high rates of technological development, informatization and digitalization. The relevance of this study lies in the need to improve the state system and its industries in the context of digitalization, as well as its dynamic transformations in order to meet the urgent needs of citizens. In this context, successful development and operation experience of e-government in the United Kingdom is indicative. In order to achieve the goal set in the study, the authors conduct a composite graphical analysis of the UK and Russian e-government websites. As a result of identifying the significant advantages of e-government in the UK, as well as taking into account the current challenges of digitalization and the needs of society, the authors develop recommendations for improving e-government mechanisms in Russia.

Keywords: E-Government · Digitalization · Compositional graphic analysis · E-Participation · Public policy

1 Introduction

The dynamic changes taking place today in all spheres of social life are taking on unprecedented proportions and require an adequate managerial reaction. Over the past 10–15 years, industrial relations, the pace of technological development, the structure of employment, the needs of the labor market, the system of social coordinates, the functions and place of political power and the state in the economy and public relations have radically transformed. It is almost impossible to catch the colossal streams of constantly updated information.

It is even more difficult to manage them, given the extremely intricate global information connections, the decentralized nature of network power, and the ever-changing balance between regional, national, and global components of governance.

Rapidly evolving technologies are transforming traditional ways of doing business within all the functions and fields of the state. At the same time, they provide governments with the opportunity to achieve their sustainable development goals

A. Chugunov et al. (Eds.): EGOSE 2020, CCIS 1349, pp. 17–26, 2020.
https://doi.org/10.1007/978-3-030-67238-6_2

and improve the well-being of their citizens as soon as possible. However, in this vein, the problem of the prevalence of ICT development rates over the quick response of governments to them is manifested.

The state sector in many countries is poorly prepared for digital transformation. In response, governments are developing the necessary services and regulations, but most often the implementation of these tools is very slow. Especially given the need for the permanent adaptation of government services to the changing needs of citizens.

In this context, «electronic government» is of particular relevance, which is designed to improve the quality of state services, ensure transparency and accountability of the authorities at the local level and last but not least, to increase citizen engagement in the processes of governance and control. At the same time, «electronic government» is able to improve the flexibility and sustainability of the political system, as well as properly coordinate the activities of local authorities with national strategies in the field of digital technologies.

Hence, the main research question of this paper is how should e-government mechanisms develop in the new digital reality in order to meet the above objectives? The problem is that the digitalization process is intensive and continuous, so the development of e-government mechanisms should also take place constantly, based on new trends in the field of digitalization and following the demands of modern society. What are the current challenges of digitalization and the needs of society? In this vein, what are the advantages of implementing e-government mechanisms in Great Britain and the shortcomings in the e-government tools development in the Russian Federation?

Today there is a distinct lack of recent interdisciplinary scientific works on the issues being investigated. Thus, the theoretical and applied groundwork presented in this study is especially important.

2 Theoretical Framework

It is believed that the first discussions about the «electronic government» creation appeared in the early 1990s in the United States. Bill Clinton, the current president at that time, attached great importance to the development of information technology. The term «e-government» and its meaning have been actively discussed in scientific circles from different points of view. There are several approaches to its definition:

- Applied, considering the practice of using individual tools of «electronic government»;
- Technical, focusing on the mechanisms of its functioning through the use of ICT.

It is also possible to highlight various approaches to conceptualizing the e-government concept.

In the early 2000s, the first definitions of «electronic government» appeared as a project of a state internet portal [1], «interactive interaction between the state and business using the Internet» [2]. Already in the mid-2000s, Professor Smorgunov L.V. formulated a more detailed definition of this concept: «E-government refers to inter-institutional relations, including political coordination, political decision-making and the provision of public services. E-administration includes policy development, orga-nizational activities and knowledge management. And e-government characterizes relations between citizens, government bodies, public opinion and officials» [3: 183].

Some authors [4] follow the common method of conceptualizing e-government, which consists in the separation of three spheres of technologically mediated interactions:

- Government-to-government interactions (the use of technologies to enhance the internal efficiency of public administration);
- Government-to-business interactions (the use of technologies to increase the rela-tionship between the subject of public administration and the enterprises);
- Government-to-citizen interactions (using the Internet to increase the relationship between the subject of public administration and the citizen; providing public services and transactions online).

Taking into account the Russian experience of the «electronic government» func-tioning, we define it as a public administration system based on the use of ICT.

However, the interpretation of this concept in a broader sense, as an «electronic state» , encompassing all power structures, is most consistent with the «E-government» English version. In the Western scientific tradition, «electronic govern-ment» was originally understood as an online service of the local, regional and federal government for the state services provision and the involvement of citizens in political decision-making [5].

The United Nation [6] and the Gartner Group - one of the largest research and consulting companies specializing in the government and society interaction [7], in their e-government definitions emphasize the quality improvement of public services provided to citizens, based on internal and external communications' enhancing through the optimal use of ICT. E-development study carried out by the World Bank Group highlights such important e-government characteristics as transparency, accountability, responsiveness and usability [8].

Despite the multifaceted definitions of e-government, there are a number of com-mon competencies that unites them. So, «electronic government» involves the use of information technology, especially the Internet, to provide public services to citizens, enterprises and other government agencies, transforming public administration into an open network form. «E-government» allows citizens to interact with federal, regional or local authorities in real time, attracting new actors in this way and expanding citizen participation in governance. The mechanisms of «electronic government» are aimed at improving the transparency and convenience of services for citizens to participate in evaluating government performance.

3   Methods

The main objective of this article is a comparative analysis of one of the most suc-cessfully functioning e-governments – the British Gov.uk [9] and the e-government internet portals of the Russian Federation. Based on the identified advantages of gov.

uk, the authors proposed recommendations for improving various components of e-government in the Russian Federation.

As the main method of analysis, the authors use the compositional graphic method, which allows analyzing in detail the advantages, as well as the disadvantages or problem areas of electronic government services of the both countries.

The choice of the United Kingdom (UK) e-government for this comparative study is based primarily on its high rates in the ranking of the UN e-government development level (first place in 2016 [10], fourth in 2019 [11]). Due to the fact that the e-government of Great Britain is based on one service - Gov.uk, and the e-government system of the Russian Federation on 10 internet portals, we conducted a comparative analysis of 11 Internet resources.

To analyze the compositional and graphic features of the websites, we used a seven-component model [12] that includes the following content elements:

1. «Focus on target groups» - target groups of users on which the website is directed.
2. «Design» - compliance with the website's mission. This is a unified style for all pages of the website, high-quality graphics, significantly supplementing the content, use of previews, professionally selected color palette, matching the font with the background color, the absence of annoying animation and the presence of «tooltips» under the images.
3. The «content» of the website is analyzed by the following parameters: sufficient content of the entire website; informativeness, adequacy of the information presentation (absence of information overload), originality of the plan; readable blocks of text; absence of errors (grammatical, syntactic, etc.); availability of news on the website; availability of language versions.
4. The following indicators are responsible for the quality of navigation: clarity of the basic structure of the website from the main page; website map availability; clarity in the definition of hyperlinks (color, underline); uniformity of semantic organization of pages; the presence of convenient menu links; implementation of the «three clicks» principle; implementation of a convenient search system.
5. «Usability» - the website loading speed should correspond to the speed of the communication line, the page length should not be long, and pages should be adequately displayed through different versions of browsers and at different monitor resolutions. The website should have an RSS feed and a form for applications (questions).
6. «Interactivity» involves registering visitors, conducting polls and voting, organizing forums and guest books, targeted mailing lists, and having an online question-and-answer system.
7. «Search engine optimization» is a set of measures for internal and external optimization to increase the position of the website in the results of search engines for specific user requests, in order to increase network traffic and potential customers and the subsequent monetization of this traffic.

4 Results

We adapted the system described above to the specifics of the study. Websites analysis results for all criteria are presented in the table below (see Table 1), where the following notation is accepted: «1» - satisfactory value of the parameter, «0» - unsatisfactory value of the parameter.

Thus, the obvious advantage of the UK e-government internet portal is its versatility. Citizens should not search for internet portals of necessary services.

The gov.uk resource contains all 25 ministerial departments and 408 other agencies and government bodies. Based on this internet portal, users can get advice, find out detailed information about all relevant public services, as well as evaluate their quality and receive answers to questions of interest.

In addition, gov.uk offers the convenience and ease of use. Being influenced by digital trends, users increasingly pay attention to the availability of electronic services, the use of which will allow to spend a minimum amount of time. The UK was one of the first countries that replaced the complex e-government internet site navigation with a simplified system. Therefore, we can talk about following the UK government to current trends, which led to the use of a behavioral approach in the design of the «electronic government» internet portal.

Table 1. Websites analysis results of «electronic government» of Russia and the UK.

Analysis parameters	Websites										
	gov. uk	gosuslugi. ru	data. gov. ru	gosmonitor. ru	budget. gov.ru	regulation. gov.ru	orv. gov. ru	vashkontrol. ru	bus. gov. ru	zakupki. gov.ru	proverki. gov.ru
Focus on target groups											
Individuals	1	1	1	1	1	1	1	1	1	1	1
Legal entities	1	1	1	1	1	1	1	1	1	1	1
Government bodies	1	1	1	1	1	1	1	0	1	1	1
Job seekers	1	0	0	0	0	0	0	0	0	0	0
Business	1	1	1	1	1	1	1	0	0	1	1
Foreign citizens	1	1	1	0	0	0	0	0	0	0	0
Design											
Consistency	1	1	1	1	1	1	1	1	1	1	1
Uniform page style	1	1	1	1	1	1	1	1	1	1	1
Graphic arts	1	1	1	1	1	1	0	0	1	0	0
Color palette	0	1	1	1	1	1	0	0	1	0	0
Absence of annoying animation	1	1	1	1	1	1	0	1	1	1	1
Font	1	1	0	1	1	1	0	0	1	1	1
Content											
Originality of design	1	1	1	1	1	1	0	1	0	0	0
Sufficient fullness of the entire website	1	1	1	1	1	0	0	0	0	1	0
Informational content	1	1	1	0	1	1	1	1	0	1	0
Absence of information congestion	1	0	0	1	1	1	0	1	1	1	1
News availability	1	1	1	1	1	0	1	1	1	1	1
Absence of errors	1	1	0	0	0	1	1	1	1	1	1
Availability of language versions	0	1	1	0	0	0	0	0	0	0	0

(*continued*)

Table 1. (*continued*)

Analysis parameters	Websites										
	gov. uk	gosuslugi. ru	data. gov. ru	gosmonitor. ru	budget. gov.ru	regulation. gov.ru	orv. gov. ru	vashkontrol. ru	bus. gov. ru	zakupki. gov.ru	proverki. gov.ru
Navigation											
The main structure of the website is clear from the main page	1	1	1	1	1	1	0	0	1	1	1
Clear hyperlink highlighting	1	1	1	1	1	1	0	1	1	1	1
The uniform semantic organization of pages	1	1	1	1	1	1	1	1	1	1	1
The presence on each page of an internet link for the menu	1	1	1	1	1	1	1	1	1	1	1
Site map availability	1	0	1	0	1	0	0	0	0	1	0
Implementation of the «three clicks» principle	1	1	1	1	1	1	1	1	1	1	1
Availability of a convenient search system	1	1	1	1	1	1	1	0	1	1	1
Usability											
Site loading speed	1	1	0	1	0	1	1	1	1	1	1
Adequate display through various browsers	1	1	1	1	1	1	1	1	1	1	1
Adequate display at various monitor resolutions	1	1	1	1	1	1	1	1	1	1	1
Availability of application forms (questions)	1	1	1	1	1	0	0	1	1	0	1
Availability of RSS feeds	1	0	0	0	0	1	0	0	1	1	0
Interactivity											
Visitor Registration	1	1	1	1	1	1	0	1	0	1	1
Surveys and polls	1	0	0	0	1	1	0	1	1	1	0
Forums and guest books	1	0	0	0	1	1	0	0	1	1	0
Targeted Mailing Lists	1	0	0	0	0	0	0	0	0	0	0
Online Question-Answer System	1	1	1	0	1	0	0	0	1	1	0
Search engine optimization											
Site Citation Index	1	1	0	0	1	1	0	1	0	1	0
General site assessment by the analyzing system	1	1	0	0	1	1	0	1	0	1	0
Same word repetition rate	1	1	1	1	1	1	1	1	1	1	1
Number of keywords	1	1	1	1	1	1	1	0	1	1	1

Source: author's own work

In general, the results of the compositional graphic analysis allow us to conclude about the quality design of Gov.uk. However, it seems that a brighter color palette could help users quickly structure the services presented on the internet portal and make the right choice. For the remaining components, on the basis of which the analysis was carried out, Gov.uk has satisfactory values. The exception is the absence of language versions of the site, but this fact should not be attributed to disadvantages. Especially considering that the English language is international.

An important advantage of the internet portal is its orientation to a wide range of users, including citizens who are in search of work. By clicking on one link, you can find detailed information about current vacancies in England, Scotland and Wales. Previously, this information was posted on the Universal Jobmatch website. In addition, the main page of the internet portal contains hyperlinks to constantly updated popular Gov.uk services, which also proves the orientation of «electronic government» to the user's needs.

The completeness of information provided by other states also seems interesting and important. So, choosing one of the 229 countries, for example, the Russian Federation, you can find information about services for the UK citizens who travel, study, work or live in Russia, including information on trade and doing business in the UK and Russia.

It should also mention the presence at Gov.uk components such as RSS-feeds, and targeted mailings, which are not available on most e-government websites of the Russian Federation.

As mentioned earlier, in 2016, the UK was a world leader in the e-government development [10]. To date, the United Kingdom is at the fourth place [11]. The decline in positions is «due to a relative decrease in the ranking of its human capital and online service indices» [11: 91]. The UK Government's Transformation Strategy, published in 2017, is aimed at the further e-government development, digital learning and cultural competence, the development of better tools, technologies and approaches to public management, optimization of data and the creation of common platforms, components and business opportunities [13].

On the contrary, in the case of the Russian Federation an obvious drawback is quantity of e-government internet portals, which, unfortunately, is not compensated by quality. Gosuslugi.ru is the most comprehensive internet portal for the provision of relevant public services. Its advantages are:

- English version availability;
- Providing information depending on the target group, which can be selected in advance (citizens, legal entities, foreign citizens, etc.);
- Successful design, a convenient search system availability, sufficient content of the entire site;
- The ability to pay state fees online at a discount;
- Mobile platform availability;
- The shortcomings include:
- Information overload;
- Absence of RSS feeds, polls, forums and targeted mailings.

We decided to present the results of the analysis of other e-government portals in the form of a rating, in descending order.

1. budget.gov.ru
2. zakupki.gov.ru
3. regulation.gov.ru
4. data.gov.ru
5. bus.gov.ru

6. gosmonitor.ru
7. proverki.gov.ru
8. vashkontrol.ru
9. orv.gov.ru

The advantages of the reviewed internet sites include generally satisfactory indicators for the components «design» , «navigation» and «usability» . Whereas in the significant component of «interactivity» , unsatisfactory indicators clearly prevail, especially with regard to the availability of targeted mailing lists, forums and guest books, as well as an online question-answer system.

In the study of the «content» component, the absence of fullness of most analyzed internet sites, the absence of foreign language versions, as well as technical errors were identified.

The main disadvantages of internet sites on the component «target groups» include the absence of information about vacancies and services for foreign citizens. The disadvantages of «design» are not always successful graphics, color palette and font.

Thus, the «electronic government» of the Russian Federation at the present stage as a whole meets the requirements of «electronic democracy» , but its basic mechanisms still need to be improved.

5 Conclusion

Based on the results of the compositional graphic analysis of the Russian Federation and the United Kingdom e-government websites, as well as the current challenges of digitalization and the needs of society, we developed our own recommendations to improve the effectiveness of the Russian Federation «electronic government» mechanisms.

It should start with the fact that the public sector inadvertently creates digital barriers by implementing new technologies (cloud computing, big data and analytics, blockchain and others) and providing «e-government» services to certain categories of citizens who cannot fully use them, due to the lack of the necessary digital culture of communication and competencies.

A survey conducted by Go ON UK and the British Broadcasting Corporation showed that «one in five, or 21% of the population in the United Kingdom do not have the skills or ability to communicate via email, use a search engine or conduct transactions online» [11: 38; 14]. According to the statistics compiled by the Higher School of Economics «Indicators of the Digital Economy: 2018» , 74.8% of the Russian Federation urban population receive state and municipal services in electronic form. 17.1% of the population lack skills and knowledge in the use of ICTs [15]. As an effective measure to solve this problem, government authorities may use other ways of communication with vulnerable groups, for example, through call centers or community centers.

As correctly noted in the UN report, there is a correlation between open access to ICT and how people use it [11]. Studies of various aspects of digital barriers show that low-income families, less educated people, people with disabilities, rural people and minorities usually lag behind both in terms of adopting digital technology and the availability of necessary equipment.

To solve this problem, as practical experience shows, various partner forms of cross-sector interaction are most effectively applied. Multi-stakeholder partnerships contribute to the state in search of innovative methods for solving the traditional problems in the field of social exclusion and poverty. In addition, they can help to improve access to e-government and develop specialized services targeted at vulnerable groups.

The most important component of the «electronic government» success is a high level of electronic participation, which must be ensured through the widespread provision of information on public affairs to citizens, the possibility of participation in the development and implementation of public policy.

According to the results of compositional graphic analysis, the «electronic government» of the Russian Federation provides citizens with wide opportunities for electronic participation through open forums, voting, discussions, etc., however, from our point of view, it's not enough. It is important to make these mechanisms more convenient for citizens. It is necessary to provide e-government with targeted mailing lists, RSS, etc. Moreover, it is important to stimulate the electronic participation of citizens by reporting on the positive results of active civic participation.

The last necessary component of an effective «electronic government» is the development of a public-private partnership mechanism, especially in high-tech and innovation-oriented industries. These conditions can be used by local authorities as a key to improving e-government mechanisms, as well as provide the basis for a comparative analysis of the worldwide e-government effectiveness.

Acknowledgements. The research is funded by Russian Foundation for Basic Research (project №19-011-00792 «Evaluation of social and political effects of new technologies of urban development in the context of the current stage of the administrative reform of the Russian Federation»).

References

1. Ivanov, V.E.: Government-population: dialogue in the virtual space (2000). http://emag.iis. ru/arc/infosoc/emag.nsf/BPA/e3c6bd2f38bbbf14c3256a330040df12. Accessed 10 July 2020
2. Vershinin, M.S.: E-democracy: Russian perspectives (2002). http://emag.iis.ru/arc/infosoc/ emag.nsf/BPA/953fc8431c107b5ec3256d57003ea7a9. Accessed 10 July 2020
3. Smorgunov, L.B.: Electronic government in the public space of the Internet. In: Internet and modern society: Proceedings of the IX All-Russian Joint Conference, St. Petersburg (2006)
4. Chadwick, A.: E-government. In: Encyclopædia Britannica, inc. (2016). https://www. britannica.com/topic/e-government. Accessed 10 July 2020
5. Sharma, S.K.: Assessing E-government implementations. Electron. Gov. J. **1**(2), 198–212 (2004)
6. United Nations Division for Public Economics and Public Administration. Benchmarking E-government: A Global Perspective - Assessing the Progress of the UN Member States (2002). https://d-russia.ru/wp-content/uploads/2013/04/UN_Benchmarking-E-government-2001.pdf

7. Gartner Group. Key Issues in E-Government Strategy and Management. Research Notes, Key Issues, 23 May (2000). https://www.gartner.com/en/documents/306621/key-issues-in-e-government-strategy-and-management. Accessed 10 July 2020

8. The World Bank Group. E-Development: From Excitement to Effectiveness. http://documents1.worldbank.org/curated/en/261151468325237852/pdf/341470EDevelopment.pdf. Accessed 10 July 2020

9. The official portal of the Great Britain electronic government. Gov.uk. Accessed 10 July 2020

10. The United Nations E-Government Survey (2016). https://publicadministration.un.org/egovkb/Reports/UN-E-Government-Survey-2016. Accessed 10 July 2020

11. The United Nations E-Government Survey (2018). https://www.un-ilibrary.org/democracy-and-governance/united-nations-e-government-survey-2018_d54b9179-en. Accessed 10 July 2020

12. Asharchuk, L.M., Movshovich, S.M.: Compositional graphic analysis of Belcoopsoyuz sites. In: Problems and Prospects of Electronic Business, pp. 11–15. Belarusian Trade and Economic University of Consumer Cooperatives, Gomel (2017)

13. The UK Government Transformation Strategy. https://www.gov.uk/government/publications/government-transformation-strategy-2017-to-2020/government-transformation-strategy. Accessed 10 July 2020

14. Past Projects - Go ON UK. https://www.ageuk.org.uk/london/projects-campaigns/our-projects/info/go-on-uk/. Accessed 10 July 2020

15. The digital economy Indicators: (2018). http://d-russia.ru/wp-content/uploads/2018/08/ICE2018.pdf. Accessed 10 July 2020

Development and Validation of an Assessment Framework for E-Government Services

Sayantan Khanra[1](✉) ⓘ and Rojers P. Joseph[2] ⓘ

[1] Woxsen University, Hyderabad 502345, Telangana, India
sayantan.khanra@woxsen.edu.in
[2] Indian Institute of Management Rohtak, Haryana 124010, India
rojers.joseph@iimrohtak.ac.in

Abstract. A standardized approach to assess e-Government services from a strategic perspective of the service providers is rarely found in the prior literature. The research objective of this study is to address the gap in the literature by developing an assessment framework. We identify the key criteria in the framework from themes of mature e-Governance following a meta-ethnography approach. Findings from this study suggest that key themes of a mature e-Governance are online presence, facilitating interaction, integrated ecosystem, online payments, and participatory e-Democracy. Subsequently, we developed an assessment framework using these themes. Furthermore, we validated the framework by assessing an Indian e-Government service. The framework may help practitioners in assessing e-Government services using a simple yet efficient approach, which may potentially emerge as a powerful tool for rating such services.

Keywords: Assessment framework · BHIM app · E-Governance · Meta-ethnography · Online services · Service rating

1 Introduction

Prior literature on e-Governance suggests that researchers followed different approaches in absence of a standard framework for evaluating e-Government services [1–3]. One such approach is to augment a standard e- Governance maturity model for meeting requirements of a specific purpose. For instance, Rooks et al. [2] modified the e-Governance maturity model proposed by Lee [4] to suit their objective of studying adoption and development of e-Governance among Dutch municipalities. The major drawback of this approach is that it offers limited scope for generalization. Another approach to evaluate an e-Government service is to measure the continuous usage intention from consumers' perspective [3]. To capture a strategic perspective is beyond the scope of this approach. The e-Government Development Index (EGDI) developed by the United Nations (UN) presents a third approach that is reasonably free from the drawbacks of both of the previous approaches. EDGI ranks the UN member states on the basis of how e-Governance strategies are implemented in a country [5, 6]. However, EGDI do not aim to evaluate a particular e-Government service available in a country.

© Springer Nature Switzerland AG 2020
A. Chugunov et al. (Eds.): EGOSE 2020, CCIS 1349, pp. 27–41, 2020.
https://doi.org/10.1007/978-3-030-67238-6_3

Countries across the world are conveying noteworthy measure of assets to more readily convey e-Governance [7, 8]. Thus, evaluation of e-Government services with a strategic framework is critical to aid continuous improvement of e-Governance [9, 10]. However, there exists a research gap in the extant literature that focuses on developing a strategic framework to rate and assess e-Government services. This research gap leads us to the research question: how an e-Government service provider can rate and assess an e-Government service? This study aims to address the research question by developing a comprehensive framework from studying e-Governance maturity models, which guide Government organizations to develop capabilities to accomplish action plans [8]. Both academicians and practitioners have documented numerous attempts to develop e-Governance maturity models [9, 10]. This study summarizes the knowledge available from the e-Governance maturity models with a meta-ethnography study [11].

The findings from the meta-ethnography study helps us identify five key themes of mature e-Governance that leads us to develop an assessment framework. The vertical dimension of this framework incorporates these five themes. The horizontal dimension serves the purpose of reporting the level of accomplishment for each theme on a five-item scale. This framework can potentially emerge as a powerful tool to rate e-Government services, albeit with appropriate modifications and adjustments. Therefore, the present study assumes importance for a pioneering attempt to design a comprehensive framework for evaluating e-Government services from a strategic perspective.

This paper is structured in seven sections. The second section of the paper is dedicated to discourse how we conduct the meta-ethnography study. In the third section, we discuss the development of e-GRAF and assessed an Indian e-Government service to illustrate the working principle of the framework. The fourth section of this paper discusses why this study possibly connects the top-down approach of designing maturity models with the bottom-up one. The fifth section elaborates implications of this study. Next, the limitations of this study are duly acknowledged in and the future scopes for research are recommended in the sixth section discussed, prior to concluding the paper in the seventh section.

2 Meta-ethnography Study

A meta-ethnography study follows a qualitative approach for interpreting knowledge about a topic of intellectual interest [11]. Meta-ethnography is often preferred over other approaches for comprehensive interpretation because of its ability to effectively analyze qualitative data even when the study sample is reasonably small [8, 12]. As this approach is found effective in systematically reviewing extant literature in technology management [12], the application of meta-ethnography is suitable in the current context. The meta-ethnography approach involves seven sequential phases [11], dedicated to identifying an intellectual interest, determining what is germane to the intellectual interest, reading the studies, juxtaposing key concepts, finding analogies, synthesizing translations, and reporting findings.

2.1   Study Sample

We searched on Google Scholar for the phrase 'e-Governance maturity model' is performed to identify similar search terms [13]. A scan of the first 100 search results suggests that e-Government system' and 'e-Government network' are commonly used related terms for e-Governance. A maturity model is also referred to as a 'development model' or a 'stage model'.

Therefore, a total of nine combinations of terms can represent the original phrase. The databases considered appropriate for the exploration of relevant studies in the field of e-Governance are: Science Direct, Scopus, and Web of Science [8, 14]. An exploration of three databases with nine pre-dedicated combinations of search terms was conducted, and a total of 335 documents were downloaded. Many documents were downloaded multiple times as they appeared in different search results.

Full texts of 137 documents were read, among which only 18 papers passed the exclusion criteria: eliminate duplicate studies from different searches, exclude studies not available online, exclude studies not available in English, and exclude studies that do not emphasize on constructing an e-Governance maturity model. Citation chaining searches were performed with the 18 papers selected for further review.

Though the forward citation searches did not add any document to our sample, backward citation searches discovered 14 reports, published by practitioners, that are relevant to our intellectual interest. However, we could include only nine such reports in our study, as five of them are either not available online or not publicly accessible. Therefore, our final sample contained 27 documents, following the paper selection process presented in Fig. 1. Also, a summary of database exploration is reported in Table 1.

Appendix 1 reveals the e-Governance maturity models developed by academicians, meaning, those published in academic journals, academic reports, book chapters and conference proceedings. The e-Governance maturity models available in other reports prepared by corporates, government organizations, and intergovernmental organizations are considered to be offered by practitioners, and are reported in Appendix 2.

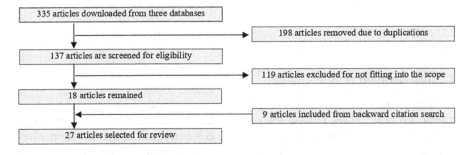

Fig. 1. Selection of documents.

Table 1. Database search summary.

Database	Search terms	Total hits appeared	Abstracts read	Full texts downloaded*
Science Direct	"e-Govenance" AND "maturity model"	225	100	49
	"e-Governance" AND "development model"	757	50	9
	"e-Governance" AND "stage model"	592	50	6
	"e-Government system" AND "maturity model"	227	100	22
	"e-Government system" AND "development model"	174	25	2
	"e-Government system" AND "stage model"	398	50	7
	"e-Government network" AND "maturity model"	208	100	19
	"e-Government network" AND "development model"	437	50	3
	"e-Government network" AND "stage model"	382	50	1
Scopus	"e-Govenance" AND "maturity model"	199	100	26
	"e-Governance" AND "development model"	477	50	16
	"e-Governance" AND "stage model"	285	50	11
	"e-Government system" AND "maturity model"	243	100	29
	"e-Government system" AND "development model"	302	50	10
	"e-Government system" AND "stage model"	211	50	6
	"e-Government network" AND "maturity model"	328	50	8
	"e-Government network" AND "development model"	393	50	1
	"e-Government network" AND "stage model"	638	50	2
Web of Science	"e-Governance" AND "maturity model"	15	15	15
	"e-Governance" AND "development model"	105	50	13
	"e-Governance" AND "stage model"	26	26	18
	"e-Government system" AND "maturity model"	62	50	31
	"e-Government system" AND "development model"	114	50	12
	"e-Government system" AND "stage model"	99	50	17
	"e-Government network" AND "maturity model"	13	13	6
	"e-Government network" AND "development model"	96	50	16
	"e-Government network" AND "stage model"	16	16	10

2.2　Juxtaposition of Key Concepts

The number of stages in the e-Governance maturity models under review ranges between two [15] and six [16]. In this phase of the study, meaning from definition(s) and explanation(s) provided for a total of 115 constructs are interpreted from 27 e-Governance maturity models. Two constructs from different e-Governance maturity models may convey similar meaning. For example, both of the constructs 'Web Presence' [17] and 'Partial Service Delivery' [18] allude to the accessibility of static information with respect to government services. Hence, we translated each construct into other constructs, and vice versa, to pair constructs with similar meaning.

All constructs but 'Basic Capability' [19] are found to be translatable. Consequently, the translation process yielded five clusters, as presented in Table 2.

Table 2. Translation and synthesisation of key concepts.

Cluster	Constructs
Cluster 1	Basic Site [23]; Bill-board [18]; Catalogue [24, 25]; Cataloguing [15]; Electronic Publishing [23]; Emerging Information [26]; Enabling Inter-Organizational and Public Access to Information [21]; Emerging Web Presence [27]; Enhanced Web Presence [27]; Information [20, 28, 29]; Information Interaction [30]; Information Publishing [16]; Initial Conditions [31]; Online Presence [19, 32]; Online Websites [33]; Partial Service Delivery [18]; Presence [28]; Presence on the Web [34]; Presenting [4]; Publish [35, 36]; Service Availability [19]; Simple Information [37]; Simple Website [39]; Web Presence [12, 17, 38]
Cluster 2	Allowing Two-Way Communication [21]; Assimilating [4]; e-Publishing [23]; Enhanced Information Services [26]; Extension [40]; FAQs and Email Systems [33]; Interact [35, 36]; Interaction [12, 17, 28, 29, 32, 38]; Interaction Between the Citizen and the Government [34]; Interactive Web Presence [27]; Official-Two Way Transaction [16]; Online Government [39]; Portal Personalization [16]; Reforming [4]; Two Way Communication [20, 37]; Setting Up an Email System and Internal Network [21]
Cluster 3	Clustering of Common Services [16]; Cultivation [40]; Full Integration and Enterprise Transaction [16]; Fully Integrated and Transformed e-Government [32]; Horizontal and Vertical Integration [37]; Horizontal Integration [25]; Integrated Government [39]; Integration [20, 29]; Joined-Up e-Govemance [23]; Joined-Up Government [21]; Morphing [4]; Multipurpose Portal [16]; One Stop Shop [33]; Portal [18]; Revolution [40]; Seamless/Networked Web Presence [27]; Service Transformation [19]; Transformation [12, 38]; Transformation Citizen Centric [30]; Transformed Government [39]; Vertical Integration [25]
Cluster 4	Allowing Exchange of Value [21]; Complete Transaction Over the Web [34]; Online Services [33]; Service and Financial Transactions [37]; Transact [35, 36]; Transaction [12, 15, 17, 20, 24, 25, 28, 29, 32, 38]; Transaction Efficiency [30]; Transactional [23]; Transactional Services [26]; Transactional Web Presence [27]
Cluster 5	Connected Services [26]; Continuous Improvement [17]; Data Transparency [31]; Digital Democracy [21, 32]; e-Democracy [12]; e-Governance [4]; Forums and Opinion Surveys [33]; Interactive Democracy [18]; Mature Delivery [19]; Maturity [40]; Open Participation [31]; Open Collaboration [31]; Participation [20]; Political Participation [28, 37]

2.3 Synthetization of Key Concepts

In a meta-ethnography study, priority is given to the meaning of a construct rather than its appearance in different stages of e-Governance maturity models. For instance, both 'Integration' [20] and 'Joined-up Government' [21] belong to the same cluster, though they appear in different stages in the respective maturity model, as both of them refer to the requirement of back-end integration in processes of delivering e-Government services. Therefore, summarization of the meaning conveyed by the constructs in a cluster results in the identification of the themes, as discoursed in Table 3.

Table 3. Synthesised findings

Theme	Details
Online Presence (Cluster 1)	• Static information about Government policies and services are available • The information should be updated regularly and organized efficiently • Downloadable forms may be available for certain e-Government services
Facilitating Interaction (Cluster 2)	• A two-way communication channel is established via e-mails and online chat rooms to exchange information between the users and the Government agencies • Advanced services like personalisation options, search options, push notifications, email alerts and uploading documents may be available • The users may provide feedbacks and comment on issues related to a service as well as various rules and regulations concerning the service
Integrated Ecosystem (Cluster 3)	• Vertical integration process involves integration of systems at various levels within an organization • Horizontal integration process refers to inter departmental data sharing • Full integration yields a portal for all e-Government services or an 'one stop shop' for joined-up services • Multichannel integration i.e. a blend of online and offline services is also desirable
Online Payments (Cluster 4)	• Users should be able to perform complete transactions online including receiving payment, if applicable • Online payment gateways are to be included in the e-Government services so that the users can easily perform financial transactions as per the requirements of those services • There may be a possibility of accepting electronic payments by the users, particularly in case of an e-procurement by the Government
Participatory e-Democracy (Cluster 5)	• The users may participate in online discussion within forums that are openly accessible by all • They may take part in anonymous opinion surveys to provide input for policy and legislation proposals • Eligible citizens may cast their votes online

3 The e-Governance Rating and Assessment Framework (e-GRAF)

3.1 Framework Development

The five themes identified from the meta-ethnography study may capture a snapshot of an existing e-Government service. Thus, the status of e-Governance provided by a government division may be assessed on the basis of these themes. In continuation of this argument, we have proposed a two-dimensional framework. The vertical dimension of this framework incorporates the five themes for a mature e-Government ecosystem. For the purpose of simplicity, we assume equal weightage for each of the five criteria. The horizontal dimension serves the purpose of reporting the level of accomplishment for each criterion on a five-item scale. An e-Government service may be examined with respect to each of the criterion to award a score between 0.00 and 1.00, subject to the fulfilment of the requirements of each criterion. The score may fall in one of the five categories: very low, moderately low, medium, moderately high, and very high, separated by breakpoints at 0.2, 0.4, 0.6, and 0.8, respectively. An average of the criterion scores yields the e-GRAF score for an e-Government service.

3.2   Framework Validation

Government authorities in India offer a smartphone-based application named Bharat Interface for Money (BHIM) to foster the adoption of cashless transactions among the citizens [22]. We assess BHIM to illustrate the working principle of e-GRAF. Two authors of this study and three experts have individually assessed BHIM using e-GRAF on September 22, 2019. The first expert is an academician with rich experience in developing conceptual frameworks and deep knowledge on the literature on e-Governance. The second expert is experienced in administering an Indian e-Government service. The third expert is a manager a payment bank that offers service on BHIM. The evaluation is reported in Table 4.

Table 4. Evaluation of BHIM using e-GRAF

Rated by criterion	Author 1	Author 2	Expert 1	Expert 2	Expert 3
Online Presence	0.90	0.90	0.80	0.90	0.90
Facilitating Interaction	0.50	0.40	0.50	0.60	0.60
Integrated Ecosystem	1.00	1.00	1.00	1.00	1.00
Online Payments	1.00	1.00	1.00	1.00	1.00
Participatory e-Democracy	0.20	0.10	0.10	0.00	0.00

The criterion scores for BHIM, as presented in Table 5, is calculated from the scores awarded by five assessors. Consequently, BHIM is awarded with a rating of 3.48 (out of five) by using e-GRAF. This rating signifies that the performance of BHIM is moderately high.

Table 5. Evaluation of BHIM using e-GRAF

Criterion	Score				
	Very low	Moderately low	Medium	Moderately high	Very high
Online Presence					0.88
Facilitating Interaction			0.52		
Integrated Ecosystem					1.00
Online Payments					1.00
Participatory e-Democracy	0.08				

3.3 Subjective Assessment Process

The experts are interviewed post completion of the assessments process to find justifications for the e-GRAF score obtained by BHIM. The interviews capture the psychological processes of the subjective assessments from the experts. A good understanding of the processes may provide insights to the future users of e-GRAF. The excerpts from the interviews are summarized for each criterion, as follows:

First, sufficient static information about BHIM can be obtained from the options available by clicking the collapsed menu icon, that is, the three vertical dots placed at the top right corner of the app. Several of those options open an official website with more information which are regularly updated. Though users may initially face a little difficulty in spotting the specific icon, the app scores very high in the dimension of online presence.

Second, BHIM allows a user to personalize the app, set reminders, raise complaints and send feedback, among other options. However, the app does not facilitate real-time exchange of information between the users and government agencies. Hence, performance of the app is medium in the dimension of facilitating interaction.

Third, almost all major banks in India, irrespective of their license type and ownership structure, have been brought under BHIM to foster seamless interoperability among them. This exhibits unprecedented level of horizontal and vertical integration in the online payment ecosystem in India. Therefore, BHIM scores very high as far as the integrated ecosystem criterion is concerned.

Fourth, BHIM advances the evolution of digital payment ecosystem in India and, hence, deserves to score very high on the dimension of online payments. Moreover, the primary purpose of this app is to facilitate peer-to-peer retail payments without transaction costs, and hence, users do not face any significant value barrier.

Fifth, BHIM fares very low in advocating participatory e-Democracy, probably because it is beyond the scope of the app. However, the service providers may consider opening official forums on social media, where they have very limited presence at present, to improve performance of BHIM in this criterion.

4 Discussion

As nations around the globe are spending noteworthy measure of resources to prolif-
erate the use of e-Government services, concerned administrations may follow a
strategic approach to evaluate the status regarding those services, and consequently,
facilitate ceaseless improvements of those services. One of such strategic approach is a
maturity model that efficiently archives and gives direction to the concerned stakeholders to create and improve capability levels [41]. A maturity model may be characterized as a group of methodically reported stages, organized to manage the
advancement of capabilities so as to accomplish the predefined targets of an organization [42]. The most broadly perceived development model is known as the Capability
Maturity Model [43], that is comprised by five phases: initial, repeatable, defined,
capable and efficient.

Capability Maturity Model exhibited solid impact on the literature extant to
introduction, reliability, characterization, competency and proficiency of projects
related to management of information systems [41, 42]. In the context of e-Governance
Maturity Models, maturity suggests a transformative cycle of exhibiting certain
capacities, and a maturity model is a consistently delineated transformative way [31,
40]. This transformative way is regularly planned with a top-down approach where
every one of the foreordained number of stages is devoted to fuse certain attributes and
meet explicit evaluation destinations or achievements [41]. Notwithstanding, the top-
down approach is frequently condemned for emphatically depending on beginning
suppositions and lacking sound establishment in design method.

Researchers regularly address the condemnation against the top-down approach of
developing maturity models with a bottom-up approach for the equivalent [44]. The
bottom-up approach first identifies required attributes and evaluation criteria and, after
that point, they are grouped into certain focus areas, permitting the groups to follow
their own transformative ways [44]. Generally, the development of e-GRAF followed a
bottom-up approach to the degree of distinguishing key focus areas. Nonetheless, the
criteria in e-GRAF are efficiently gotten from the prior e-Governance maturity models,
which are created following the top-down approach. Along these lines, this study
conceivably goes about as an extension between the literature relating to top-down and
bottom-up approaches of developing maturity models.

5 Implications

E-Government services are committed to conveying public services through electronic
channels, connecting with various stakeholders straightforwardly in the process of
creating policies, and controlling the impacts of such stakeholders, whenever required
[14]. However, there exists a research gap in the extant literature that focuses on
developing a strategic framework to evaluate e-Government services from a point of
view of the service providers. By addressing the research gap, this study offers significant ramifications, as subsequently discussed.

5.1 Theoretical Implications

The present study is a pioneering attempt to develop a comprehensive framework that may be used to rate and assess the e-Government services from a strategic perspective. Therefore, this study assumes importance in addressing an important gap in the literature on e-Governance. A framework named e-GRAF is developed in this study following the meta-ethnographic findings from existing e-Governance maturity models. From a methodological standpoint, this study encapsulates the suitability of the meta-ethnography approach to contribute valuable knowledge to the literature in field of information systems. Furthermore, the study summaries knowledge about e-Governance maturity models, a topic that has arguably saturated post 2012. Therefore, this summarized knowledge may significantly add to the extant literature.

5.2 Practical Implications

The findings of this study potentially offer important implications to government agencies, consultancy firms, and rating agencies, who assess the e-Government services. E-GRAF may emerge as a powerful tool to rate e-Government services and assess the state of e-Governance due to its efficiency and ease of deployment. Furthermore, as the governments across the world continue to put more emphasis on rolling out e-Government services, new business opportunities emerge to software developers. Managers in software developing firms may identify low-rated e-Government services using e-GRAF and develop solutions for improving those services. Consequently, companies involved in business-to-government segments may obtain insights by using e-GRAF to better target their customers.

6 Limitations and Future Scope

Three future research agendas emerge from the limitations of this study, as subsequently discussed. First, the possible influence of gradual advancements post 2012 in the online domain may not be captured in detail by e-GRAF. Therefore, ample opportunities are available for the future researchers to augment e-GRAF, and develop up-to-date e-Governance maturity models. Second, we cannot include five out of 14 practitioner reports that would be suitable for this study, as they are either unavailable online or not publicly accessible. Extensive research may be dedicated to explore government action plans and corporate reports to fetch more insights about technology use in public service delivery to academia. Third, e-GRAF assumes equal weightage for each of the five criteria. However, the importance of different e-Government services may vary, as they differ in complexity and scope. Therefore, the framework may be tested with sufficient training datasets to determine a more sophisticated assignment of weightage.

7   Conclusion

The present study offers an important contribution for theory as a pioneering attempt to develop a comprehensive framework named e-GRAF for rating and assessing the e-Government services from a strategic perspective. The present study found meta-ethnography to be a suitable approach to summarize the knowledge about e-Governance maturity models, a relevant yet saturated topic in the literature. The study findings potentially offer important implications to government agencies, consultancy firms, and rating agencies, who assess the e-Government services. E-GRAF may emerge as a powerful tool to rate e-Government services and assess the state of e-Governance due to its efficiency and ease of deployment.

Appendix 1. E-Governance Maturity Models Developed by the Academicians

Model	Stage 1	Stage 2	Stage 3	Stage 4	Stage 5	Stage 6
Hitler and Belanger (2001) [20]	Information	Two Way Communication	Transaction	Integration	Paiticipation	–
Howard (2001) [35]	Publish	Interact	Transact	–	–	–
Layne and Lee (2001) [25]	Catalogue	Vertical Integration	Transaction	Horizontal Integration	–	–
Wescott (2001) [21]	Setting Up an Email System and Internal Network	Enabling Inter-organizational and Public Access to Information	Allowing Two-Way Communication	Allowing Exchange Of Value	Digital Democracy	Joined-Up Government
Chandler and Emanuel (2002) [29]	Information	Interaction	Transaction	Integration	–	–
Moon (2002) [39]	Simple Information	Two Way Communication	Service And Financial Transactions	Horizontal and Vertical Integration	Political Participation	–
Netchaeva (2002) [33]	Online Websites	FAQs And Email Systems	Forums and Opinion Surveys	Online Seivices	One Stop Shop	–
Reddick (2004) [15]	Cataloguing	Transactions	–	–	–	–
West (2004) [18]	Bill-board	Partial Service Delivery	Portal	Interactive Democracy	–	–
Siau and Long (2005) [12]	Web Presence	Interaction	Transaction	Transformation	e-Democracy	–
Andersen and Henriksen (2006) [40]	Cultivation	Extension	Maturity	Revolution	–	–

(continued)

(*continued*)

Model	Stage 1	Stage 2	Stage 3	Stage 4	Stage 5	Stage 6
Almazan and Gil-Garcia (2008) [28]	Presence	Information	Interaction	Transaction	Political Participation	–
Shahkooh et al. (2008) [32]	Online Presence	Interaction	Transaction	Fully Integrated and Transformed e-Government	Digital Democracy	–
Kim and Grant (2010) [17]	Web Presence	Interaction	Transaction	Integration	Continuous Improvement	–
Lee (2010) [4]	Presenting	Assimilating	Reforming	Morphing	e-Governance	–
Chen et al. (2011) [24	Catalogue	Transaction	Vertical Integration	–	–	–
Alhomod et al. (2012) [34]	Presence on the Web	Interaction between the Citizen and Government	Complete Transaction Over The Web	Integration	–	–
Lee and Kwak (2012) [31]	Initial Conditions	Data Transparency	Open Participation	Open Collaboration	Ubiquitous Engagement	–

Appendix 2. E-Governance Maturity Models Offered by the Practitioners

Model	Stage 1	Stage 2	Stage 3	Stage 4	Stage 5	Stage 6
Deloitte [16]	Information Publish ing	Officiaf Two Way Transaction	Multi-purpose Portal	Portal Personalization	Clustering of Common Services	Frill Integration and Enterprise Transaction
Gartner [38]	Web Presence	Interaction	Transaction	Transformation	–	–
United Nations [27]	Emerging Web Presence	Enhanced Web Presence	Interactive Web Presence	Transactional Web Presence	Seamless/ Networked Web Presence	–
UK National Audit Office [23]	Basic Site	Electronic Publishing	e-Publishing	Transactional	loined-Up e-Govenance	–
Utah CIO [39]	Simple Website	Online Government	Integrated Government	Transformed Government	–	–
Accenture [19]	Online Presence	Basic Capability	Service Availability	Mature Delivery	Service Transformation	–
World Bank [36]	Publish	Interact	Transact	–	–	–
Cisco [30]	Information Interaction	Transaction Efficiency	Transformation Citizen Centric	–	–	–
United Nations [26]	Emerging Information	Enhanced Information Services	Transactional Services	Connected Services	–	–

References

1. Khanra, S., Joseph, R.P.: Adoption and diffusion of e-government services: the impact of demography and service quality. In: Baguma, R., De, R., Janowski, T. (eds.) The 10th International Conference on Theory and Practice of Electronic Governance 2017, pp. 602–605. Association for Computing Machinery, New York (2017). https://doi.org/10.1145/3047273.3047301

2. Rooks, G., Matzat, U., Sadowski, B.: An empirical test of stage models of e-government development: evidence from Dutch municipalities. Inf. Soc. **33**(4), 215–225 (2017). https://doi.org/10.1080/01972243.2017.1318194

3. Veeramootoo, N., Nunkoo, R., Dwivedi, Y.K.: What determines success of an e-government service? Validation of an integrative model of e-filing continuance usage. Gov. Inf. Q. **35**(2), 161–174 (2018). https://doi.org/10.1016/j.giq.2018.03.004

4. Lee, J.: 10 year retrospect on stage models of e-Government: a qualitative meta-synthesis. Gov. Inf. Q. **27**(3), 220–230 (2010). https://doi.org/10.1016/j.giq.2009.12.009

5. United Nations: E-Government Survey (2016). http://tiny.cc/eGDI2016

6. United Nations: E-Government Survey (2018). http://tiny.cc/eGDI2018

7. Khanra, S., Joseph, R.P., Ruparel, N.: Dynamism of an e-Government network in delivering public services. In: Academy of Management Global Proceedings Slovenia 2019, pp. 376. Academy of Management, New York (2019)

8. Khanra, S., Joseph, R.P.: E-governance maturity models: a meta-ethnographic study. Int. Technol. Manag. Rev. **8**(1), 1–9 (2019). https://doi.org/10.2991/itmr.b.190417.001

9. Kassen, M.: Building digital state: understanding two decades of evolution in Kazakh e-government project. Online Inf. Rev. **43**(2), 301–323 (2018). https://doi.org/10.1108/OIR-03-2018-0100

10. Zarei, B., Ghapanchi, A., Sattary, B.: Toward national e-government development models for developing countries: a nine-stage model. Int. Inf. Libr. Rev. **40**(3), 199–207 (2008). https://doi.org/10.1080/10572317.2008.10762782

11. Noblit, G.W., Hare, R.D.: Meta-Ethnography: Synthesizing Qualitative Studies. Sage, Thousand Oaks (1988)

12. Siau, K., Long, Y.: Synthesizing e-government stage models–a meta-synthesis based on meta-ethnography approach. Ind. Manag. Data Syst. **105**(4), 443–458 (2005). https://doi.org/10.1108/02635570510592352

13. Khanra, S., Dhir, A., Mäntymäki, M.: Big data analytics and enterprises: a bibliometric synthesis of the literature. Enterp. Inf. Syst. **14**(6), 737–768 (2020). https://doi.org/10.1080/17517575.2020.1734241

14. Khanra, S., Joseph, R.P.: Adoption of e-Governance: the mediating role of language proficiency and digital divide in an emerging market context. Transform. Gov. People Process Policy **13**(2), 122–142 (2019). https://doi.org/10.1108/TG-12-2018-0076

15. Reddick, C.G.: A two-stage model of e-government growth: theories and empirical evidence for US cities. Gov. Inf. Q. **21**(1), 51–64 (2004). https://doi.org/10.1016/j.giq.2003.11.004

16. Deloitte and Touche: At the dawn of e-government: the citizen as customer. Gov. Finance Rev. **16**(5), 21–24 (2000)

17. Kim, D.Y., Grant, G.: E-government maturity model using the capability maturity model integration. J. Syst. Inf. Technol. **12**(3), 230–244 (2010). https://doi.org/10.1108/13287261011070858

18. West, D.M.: E-government and the transformation of service delivery and citizen attitudes. Public Adm. Rev. **64**(1), 15–27 (2004). https://doi.org/10.1111/j.1540-6210.2004.00343.x

19. Rohleder, S.J., Jupp, V.: E-government Leadership: Engaging the customer. Accenture, New York (2003)
20. Hiller, J.S., Bélanger, F.: Privacy strategies for electronic government. In: E-government Series, The PriceWaterhouseCoopers Endowment for the Business of Government, Arlington, pp. 162–198 (2001)
21. Wescott, C.G.: E-Government in the Asia-pacific region. Asian J. Polit. Sci. **9**(2), 1–24 (2001). https://doi.org/10.1080/02185370108434189
22. BHIM   Product   Overview.   https://www.npci.org.in/product-overview/bhim-product-overview
23. UK National Audit Office. Government on the Web 11. HC 764 2001–2002 Session, House of Commons, Stationery Office, London (2002)
24. Chen, J., Yan, Y., Mingins, C.: A three-dimensional model for e-government development with cases in China's regional e-government practice and experience. In: 5th International Conference on Management of e-Commerce and e-Government, pp. 113–120. Institute of Electrical and Electronics Engineers, Hubei (2011). https://doi.org/10.1109/icmecg.2011.49
25. Layne, K., Lee, J.: Developing fully functional E-government: a four stage model. Gov. Inf. Q. **18**(2), 122–136 (2001). https://doi.org/10.1016/S0740-624X(01)00066-1
26. López, I.P.: UN e-government survey 2012. E-Government for the people, Department of Economic and Social Affairs, United Nations, New York (2012)
27. United Nations: Benchmarking E-government: A Global Perspective. American Society for Public Administration, New York (2001)
28. Almazan, R.S., Gil-García, J.R.: E-Government portals in Mexico. In: Anttiroiko, A. (ed.) Electronic Government: Concepts, Methodologies, Tools, and Applications, pp. 1726–1734. IGI Global, Hershey (2008)
29. Chandler, S., Emanuels, S.: Transformation not automation. In: Remenyi, D. (ed.) Proceedings of 2nd European Conference on E-government, European Commission, European Union, pp. 91–102. St Catherine's College Oxford, United Kingdom (2002)
30. Cisco: E-government Best Practices learning from success, avoiding the pitfalls, Cisco IBSG (2007)
31. Lee, G., Kwak, Y.H.: An open government maturity model for social media-based public engagement. Gov. Inf. Q. **29**(4), 492–503 (2012). https://doi.org/10.1016/j.giq.2012.06.001
32. Shahkooh, K.A., Saghafi, F., Abdollahi, A.: A proposed model for e-Government maturity. In: 3rd International Conference on Information and Communication Technologies: From Theory to Applications, pp. 1–5. Institute of Electrical and Electronics Engineers, Damascus (2008). https://doi.org/10.1109/ictta.2008.4529948
33. Netchaeva, I.: E-government and e-democracy: a comparison of opportunities in the north and south. Int. Commun. Gazette (Leiden, Netherlands) **64**(5), 467–477 (2002). https://doi.org/10.1177/17480485020640050601
34. Alhomod, S.M., et al.: Best practices in E government: a review of some Innovative models proposed in different countries. Int. J. Electr. Comput. Sci. **12**(1), 1–6 (2012)
35. Howard, M.: E-Government across the globe: how will'e'change government? Gov. Finan. Rev. **17**(4), 1–9 (2001)
36. Toasaki, Y.: E-government from A User's Perspective. APEC Telecommunication and Information Working Group, Chinese Taipei (2003)
37. Baum, C., Maio, A.D.: Gartner's Four Phases of e-Government Model. Gartner group (2000)
38. Moon, M.J.: The evolution of e-government among municipalities: rhetoric or reality? Public Adm. Rev. **62**(4), 424–433 (2002). https://doi.org/10.1111/0033-3352.00196
39. Windley, P.J.: EGovernment Maturity. Windleys' Technolometria, USA (2002)

40. Andersen, K.V., Henriksen, H.Z.: E-government maturity models: extension of the Layne and Lee model. Gov. Inf. Q. **23**(2), 236–248 (2006). https://doi.org/10.1016/j.giq.2005.11. 008
41. Becker, J., Knackstedt, R., Pöppelbuß, J.: Developing maturity models for IT management. Bus. Inf. Syst. Eng. **1**(3), 213–222 (2009). https://doi.org/10.1007/s12599-009-0044-5
42. Gibson, C.F., Nolan, R.L.: Managing the four stages of EDP growth. Harvard Bus. Rev. **18** (1), 76–87 (1974)
43. Humphrey, W.S.: Managing the Software Process. Addison-Wesley Longman Publishing Co., Boston (1989)
44. van Steenbergen, M., Bos, R., Brinkkemper, S., van de Weerd, I., Bekkers, W.: The design of focus area maturity models. In: Winter, R., Zhao, J.L., Aier, S. (eds.) DESRIST 2010. LNCS, vol. 6105, pp. 317–332. Springer, Heidelberg (2010). https://doi.org/10.1007/978-3-642-13335-0_22

Algorithmic Panopticon: State Surveillance and Transparency in China's Social Credit System

Viktor Suter[✉]

University of St. Gallen, Blumenbergplatz 9, 9000 St. Gallen, Switzerland
Viktor.suter@unisg.ch

Abstract. This article examines China's Social Credit System to illustrate how information and communication technologies bring forth new forms of inter-action between the state and its citizens. In particular, it asks how the transparency generated by the Social Credit System enables new forms of social control, trust, and self-regulation. The study provides a descriptive account of the Social Credit System's basic design elements and the political intentions behind its implementation. Based on Foucault's model of the panopticon, the study then derives three basic parameters, each of which relate to the system's capacity to create transparency and to reconfigure government-citizen relations. The study finds that the system increases the control of the government over society, likely diminishes trust, and reduces the freedom to act. However, compared to the clientelism and arbitrary decision-making of previous decades, the precise and depersonalized standards of the Social Credit System can be seen as an improvement that enables individuals' capacity to self-regulate. This theoretical and analytical study thus adds to the debate about how government through algorithms rearranges practices of state power and control.

Keywords: Algorithmic governance · Transparency · Social credit scoring

1 Introduction

New information and communication technologies (ICT) provoke widely divergent assessments concerning their effects on systems of government. As Bohman [1] points out, optimistic voices reason that technology creates new possibilities for political participation. Pessimists, however, argue that central features of computer-mediated communication lead to a loss of individual autonomy. In the past decades, this discussion centered around the possibilities put in place by the world wide web, digital news media, or social media. However, as ICT have become more sophisticated propelled by advancements in artificial intelligence (AI), they fundamentally shift how civil society and the state organize and relate to each other.

Emerging big data, facial recognition, and AI technologies have given rise to a series of significant worries. Boyd and Crawford [2] are concerned that big data analytics might reinforce human biases and Tufekci [3] argues that algorithmic decision-making perpetuates inequality. Others allege that personalized search results and website algorithms lead to "filter bubbles".

© Springer Nature Switzerland AG 2020
A. Chugunov et al. (Eds.): EGOSE 2020, CCIS 1349, pp. 42–59, 2020.
https://doi.org/10.1007/978-3-030-67238-6_4

Although the validity of this concept is hotly contested [4], some claim that "filter bubbles" cause social and political polarization [5]. Still others point to unresolved ethical concerns regarding data governance [6], privacy [7], or human self-determination [8].

Few studies, however, address the above challenges in the light of state governments that use algorithms and AI to shape the regulations for and the coordination of entire populations. In this context, some have pointed to ethical and legal issues concerning the lack of accountability and transparency regarding public algorithmic decision-making [9, 10]. More recently, Rahwan [11] introduced the idea of an algorithmic social contract that aims to secure the transparency, accountability, and fairness of intelligent machines that are becoming part of government by and for humans. His approach builds on historical concepts of good governance developed during the enlightenment era. Today, societies are confronted with the prospect of political systems of governance that rely exclusively on automation, surveillance, and artificially intelligent systems of control.

Against this backdrop, this paper studies the Social Credit System in China (shehui xinyong tixi, hereafter referred to as SCS) as an instantiation of technology-led state government. In 2014, the Chinese State Council initiated the SCS project that likely constitutes the most comprehensive and politically driven use of data collection technologies and scoring algorithms by any government. The SCS aims to evaluate the conduct of individuals, organizations, and government officials based on the legality and morality of their behavior. If implemented as envisioned, the SCS would use multi-platform data collection methods to algorithmically evaluate economic, political, and social comportment. Measuring compliance with underlying objectives, the system prompts rewards in case of good behavior and sanctions in case of wrongdoing. The Chinese government plans to launch the system nationwide in 2020, but at the time of writing, it is still under construction. Ultimately, the SCS is supposed to take into account online purchases, content posted on social media, and a plethora of other data points, including analogue behavior. The assessments produced by the system would eventually regulate citizens' access to education, employment, financial services, social security, and means of transport.

By focusing on the concept of transparency, the paper assesses how the SCS conditions the connection between the government and citizens. However, before focusing on transparency the article provides an in-depth description of the SCS to establish a baseline understanding of the system's ambit and of the normative context in which it operates. Based on this description, the same section also includes critical evaluations of the system's implementation and functioning. The paper then provides a general overview of Foucault's concept of the panopticon [12] and its constituent parts. Based on this concept and complementing literature, the article derives three heuristic parameters that problematize the notion of transparency. These parameters encompass directions of transparency, transparency as a social norm, and transparency as social control. Building on a panoptic perspective, the parameters guide the theoretical analysis which shows how the transparency, constant surveillance, and automated discipline generated by SCS rearrange aspects of power, trust, and regulation in the relationship between the state and its citizens.

2   China's Social Credit System

The introduction of the SCS has sparked debate about the link between technology and governmental social control. In popular media, the general thrust of coverage centers on the SCS as a tool for technology-enabled authoritarianism [13]. However, differing voices gradually emerge as the system's implementation moves forward. Li, Chen, and Dharmawan [14], for example, describe the system as a *"vanity project"* that deliberately overplays the Chinese Communist Party's (CCP) capacity for control. In contrast to media reports, the CCP itself articulates the aims of the system primarily in terms of good governance. According to this line of reasoning, the SCS contributes to the diffusion of trustworthy information that strengthens cooperation and collective problem solving [15].

Academic research on the topic is incipient but quickly progressing. Some studies point to the SCS' design as *"state surveillance infrastructure"* [16] and to its potential for *"social management"* [17] as proof of the CCP's intent to expand political control. Other research is more cautious about the SCS' large-scale effects. Creemers [18] depicts the system as part of a larger government effort to improve judicial and administrative enforcement processes and as an emergent practice of governance enabled by new technologies. The same study finds that the SCS' current purview is relatively restricted to the monitoring of markets and, to a lesser extent, of political issues. Furthermore, aspects of social control do not seem to be the most pressing concerns for most Chinese citizens themselves. Public approval of the SCS across regions and socio-demographic groups seems to be high and citizens say they embrace the system because it is able to generate rewards and to promote honesty [19]. Although approval is surprisingly high, this survey study [19] also notes the potential of skewed results because respondents might fear repression if they express critical opinions about politically sensitive topics. Even so, the ambivalence of previous research roughly revolves around two concerns: firstly, around the current ambit of the system and, secondly, around its future potential to complement and modify existing techniques of governing.

2.1   Mapping the SCS

State backed systems that keep civil society under surveillance are not entirely new to China. Historically, the government has made use of a household registration system, known as Hukou, to restrain migration; it has also compiled confidential dossiers about citizens' personal information and political attitudes in a repository called Dang'an [16]. The idea for the SCS developed more recently alongside China's economic liberalization. In the early 2000s, the government identified the absence of trust as an impediment to the efficiency of markets. It therefore announced the construction of a system that increases the availability of reputation information to improve trustworthiness [20]. Similar to FICO scores in the US, initial schemes largely focused on financial information and economic conduct. But declining trust in the state bureaucracy, concerns about immoral behavior, and the spread of smartphones and social media led to a radical reassessment of potential uses for the system [18].

From the viewpoint of the CCP, the system evolved from a tool for economic development into an automated compliance mechanism that governs the day-to-day actions of individuals and organizations.

The *"Blueprint for the Construction of the Social Credit System (2014–2020)"* offers an in-depth description of the SCS ([15] provides a full translation). Issued by the Chinese State Council, China's chief administrative body, the paper explains the project's goals and provides a schedule for its implementation. Overall, its official presentation claims that the system accelerates both the *"socialist market economy"* and *"social governance"* by *"raising the transparency of policymaking"* [15]. In particular, the system would target trust-breaking behavior such as production safety accidents, food and drug security incidents, tax evasion, and financial fraud. The blueprint also directs government and non-government actors to create multiple sectoral SCS to tackle misconduct in government, commercial, social, and judicial sectors. And, unlike implied by some media reports, the SCS is not a coherent, integrated system. Instead, it consists of a patchwork of platforms and data pools run by separate government agencies and private companies. Openness and interoperability of different systems that allow for the choreographed application of disciplinary measures are therefore a major concern.

The institutionalization of rewards and punishments are key to the SCS. The reward and punishment mechanisms applied by the government are called "Joint Sanction and Reward" schemes (JSRs) and are realized in the form of redlists and blacklists [20]. Trustworthy individuals or institutions are recorded on redlists, receive preferential treatment, and simplified procedures vis-à-vis the government. Blacklists register trust-breaking actors who face administrative punishments, public shaming, and marketized sanctions. Surprisingly, numerical scores that the attention of popular media tends to focus on, do not feature in the blueprint.

According to the CCP, JSRs improve the poor enforcement capacities of the judiciary and government departments [15]. In some instances, multiple government agencies jointly develop JSRs that focus on specific regulatory offences or a particular territory. Participating agencies then share data across organizational boundaries, and each is responsible for imposing sanctions against blacklisted actors under its supervision. For that reason, actors that offended in one area might find that sanctions against them expand to other, seemingly unrelated, parts of life. The blueprint condenses this idea into the following formula: *"...those keeping trust receive benefit in all respect, and those breaking trust meet with difficulty at every step"* [15].

Dai [20] points out that JSRs might be relatively ineffective: Intra-agency conflict, local authorities' lack of knowledge, crude technological implementations, and workarounds by local officials often prevent the coordinated application of JSRs. But critics point to a lack of procedural transparency, worries about the proportionality of punishments, and discriminatory treatment. Chen and Cheung [21] also show that existing regulation on the SCS allows for the nearly unlimited secondary use of data, including records that many would regard as private. This lack of effective data protection combined with a legal order that is subservient to the interests of the CCP raise significant concerns about the system's impact on privacy and personal autonomy.

With the blueprint in place, the People's Bank of China (PBoC) issued licenses to eight private companies to operate SCS schemes on a pilot basis in 2015. This marked the end of the state monopoly on credit reporting and granted legitimacy to private credit scoring companies that previously operated in a juridical twilight zone [20]. It also started a two-tier arrangement consisting of systems run by private businesses on one hand and government-backed systems on the other. The following paragraphs explore the differences between private and government systems in more detail.

Private SCS. The eight private licensees were made up of technology companies as well as financial service businesses [22]. The companies Alibaba and Tencent are likely the most well-known among these eight firms. In a change of policy, the PBoC did not extend the licenses but created the so-called National Credit Information Sharing Platform. The government owns 36% of this platform while the businesses involved in the pilot scheme each hold 8% [20]. Officially, the government withheld the licenses because the companies fell short of expectations in the areas of privacy, security, and operational independence. In all likelihood, increased control over the SCS project and improved access to the technological know-how of private firms affected this decision too.

Still, private companies remain essential for the SCS. By spring 2017, 137 private companies were active in the social credit market [23]. These commercial systems are more innovative and more often experiment with controversial features than government schemes [24]. Sesame Credit is a case in point. It is run by Ant Financial, Alibaba's finance arm, and offers a mix of rewards to individuals who decide to opt-in via mobile phone applications. It uses behavioral data gathered online in combination with traditional financial lending information. How exactly Sesame Credit produces scores is unclear. However, the company states that it evaluates five dimensions, including credit history, behavioral preferences, funds available on the Alipay app, identity traits, and connections on social networking services [25].

If and how private companies exchange information with government authorities is uncertain. But anecdotal evidence suggests that Sesame Credit incorporates government data into its scoring system, a practice that significantly decreases scores of blacklisted individuals [26]. The scores are re-calculated every month, not in real-time, and range from 350 to 950 points. Scores of 600 points and above are considered good; those in the 700 to 950 point-range are deemed exceptional. Rewards for good scores range from deposit-free bike, car, and apartment rentals to fast lane service at airport security, shorter waiting times in hospitals, try-out purchases in Alibaba's e-commerce shops, and faster treatment of visa applications in certain countries (for example, Luxemburg and Singapore) [27, 28]. Users with low scores forfeit these potential rewards.

Uncertainty remains about the definite role of privately-run SCS because of the fraught relationship between private companies and the Chinese state. Both parties want to exploit the SCS for their own ends and both mutually cooperate. Baidu works with the PBoC to build a national data platform called Credit China. Alibaba and Tencent signed cooperation agreements with city and provincial governments to develop the necessary local infrastructure [29]. But whereas the CCP envisions a government-owned central system, companies would like to see a private system that permits choice and funnels users into their online businesses. Even if immediate regulatory interference by the CCP seems unlikely, the degree to which the interests of the private and the public sectors align in the long run remains to be seen. The extent to which both systems integrate might fundamentally affect the future configuration of the SCS.

Government SCS. The Interministerial Conference on Social Credit System Construction leads the government's implementation of the SCS. The conference is headed by the National Development and Reform Commission (NDRC) and the PBoC. In addition, the conference includes 46 party and government bodies [24]. This involves among others the Ministries of Finance, of Industry and Commerce, of Public Security as well as the Central Propaganda Department. The number of government actors associated with the SCS is hard to track and the actual figure might be much higher because of the diversity and number of projects involved, especially on a local government level.

Large data platforms are the primary components of the central government's SCS infrastructure. The above-mentioned National Credit Information Sharing Platform collects data from central and local governments, from administrative agencies, from sectoral SCS, and in some instances from private SCS [23]. The platform collects 400 data sets focusing on firms and commerce, individuals, social organizations, and government authorities. It gathers a total of 537 variables linked to each data subject [16]. The data typically contains information to assign incoming data to individuals or organizations. This includes unique identifiers like the 18-digit Uniform Social Credit Code but also names, addresses, phone numbers, and so on. The data additionally incorporates information about trust-breaking and trust-keeping activities such as poor financial credit, crime records, or volunteer services [16].

The central government is constructing at least four other national data platforms besides the National Credit Information Sharing Platform. Three of them (the National Enterprise Credit Information Publicity System, the Credit China Platform, and the Credit Reference Center) gather data about positive and negative activities of actors and publish blacklists. The fourth data platform, called List of Dishonest People, contains information about judgement defaulters; that is, individuals that do not fulfil obligations resulting from court rulings [18]. Tasks vary between platforms. For example, the National Credit Information Sharing Platform plays a key role by focusing on data gathering and evaluation. In contrast, the Credit China Platform concentrates on distributing blacklists to the public, in some instance by using news media, online media, and publicly accessible screens [16]. The exact responsibilities of each platform remain obscure and the procedures for sharing and combining data are opaque.

Apart from national initiatives, the NDRC and the PBoC authorized 43 pilot systems in a number of different cities and provinces [23]. Following the example of the central government, some of these local initiatives apply redlists and blacklists. However, after initial experiences they started implementing their own reward and punishment systems and began testing more idiosyncratic scoring methods. For example, Quingzhen, a mostly rural town in the province of Guizhou, embraced the expansion of social credit scoring early on. Its system Honest Quingzhen makes use of scores generated from community monitoring. The village runs regular peer review sessions to score residents' behaviors as specified by a set of village norms [26]. In Wuhan, Hubei province, a system monitors students in order to punish behavior like cheating on exams, plagiarism, and overdue tuition fees [24]. In a common instance of public shaming, a district court in Zhejiang province resorted to showing a 'surprise' public service announcement before a movie screening in a cinema. The announcement displayed the faces and names of visitors that are blacklisted because their debt payments are in arrears [30]. The NDRC and the PBoC observe local initiatives like these. If well-received and effective, such experiments might influence the future development of the SCS on a national level.

Empirical Findings. At present, the SCS is not the homogenous system it is often made out to be. Instead, it consists of a fragmented and loosely connected network of systems held together by a common ideology and CCP oversight. As Fig. 1 illustrates, the central government aims to concentrate control by establishing a centralized infrastructure of large data platforms that aggregate data from numerous sources. Courts, ministries, local governments, and, to some extent, private companies feed the central government's platforms with information. The data is evaluated and then made available to the public by means of blacklists and redlists that restrict or enable access to certain activities and services. Private companies cooperate with the government in the development of the technological infrastructure and data provision. They also run their own SCS based on the data generated from their business activities. However, whereas government SCS mainly focus on the enforcement of laws and behavioral discipline, private systems function more like *"loyalty schemes"* [18] that aim to boost customer satisfaction with perks.

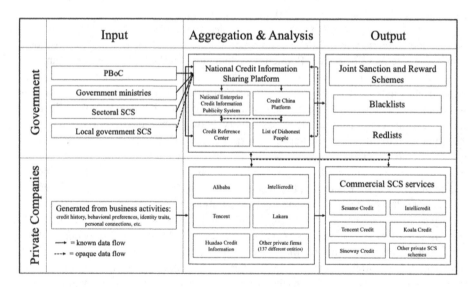

Fig. 1. SCS data sources, repositories, punishment & reward mechanisms, and data flow. Based on [16, 18, 23].

Despite the CCP's considerable progress towards the implementation of a comprehensive reward and punishment mechanism, its efforts face obstacles. First, consider organizational and technological hurdles. It is questionable if joining the fragmented and complex systems of the SCS into a unified infrastructure is practicable. The diverging interests of private companies and state agencies might lead to an unwillingness to integrate. In particular, local governments might hesitate to see their leeway curtailed by submitting to the scrutiny of agencies higher up in the bureaucratic hierarchy. Similarly, private companies might not want to share the data that they rely on for the development of new products and services. Technological difficulties concern questions about the standardization of systems and the ability to automate the exploitation of immense volumes and varieties of data in a way that meaningfully translates into the governance and surveillance mechanisms the CCP envisions.

A second set of obstacles relates to public opinion and the CCP's response thereto. Even if public debate is precarious and dominated by censorship, the CCP is aware of the need to be responsive to widely shared dissatisfaction that might undermine its legitimacy [31, 32]. If large parts of civil society disagree with certain SCS policies, as has happened with worries about data security [23], the CCP might need to adapt to these pressures.

3 Foucaultian Panopticism in China

Foucault employed the concept of the panopticon to describe modern systems of disciplinary power [12]. Initially conceived by Bentham [33], the panopticon is a building with a circular layout that enables a single supervisor to monitor several people at once. Applied to hospitals, schools, or prisons, the design principles require that panoptic 'inmates' can be observed from the watchtower at the center of the building. The guard, obscured from view in the watchtower, can observe the actions of 'inmates' at all times. This architectural arrangement prompts a consciousness of permanent visibility in patients, students, or prisoners. Not knowing whether they are being watched, they are more likely to assume responsibility for their behavior vis-à-vis the guard. Applied to ICT, the panopticon would translate into the automation of constant surveillance that allows for punishment if a person fails to adhere to prescribed standards. In this process, transparency and accountability are equally important tools to obtain the benefits declared by Bentham: *"Morals reformed – health preserved – industry invigorated – instruction diffused – public burthens lightened"* [33].

Foucault [12] uses the panopticon as a metaphor for the emergence of modern disciplinary societies in liberal countries. These societies depend on mechanisms of observation, examination, and judgement, which exercise power over actors by simply monitoring them. The primary concern of this method of control is to modify deviant behavior by creating visibility and imposing detailed norms. Separating actions into analyzable parts and measuring them against precise standards allows for interference and discipline at any point. The effects of observation become permanent even if no actual monitoring takes place because actors assume that they could be watched at any time. As a consequence, disciplinary societies largely render the use of physical force or coercion unnecessary and instead rely on the self-monitoring of those who are watched.

China is markedly different from the democratic context in which Foucault developed the notion of the panopticon. Its political traditions differ from those of democratic countries and its current political institutions have developed under conditions of political and economic reform processes that started in the late 1970 s. Extraordinary changes in virtually every aspect of Chinese society mark this transformation from a planned economy to a socialist market economy. As Lee and Zhang [34] point out, communist state authority used to rest on patron-client ties. In the absence of markets that could ensure the distribution of resources, Chinese society relied on the party-state to organize the allocation of material, political, and social capital. As a result, party officials and citizens exchanged political favors for material rewards. However, the rapid development of a market-oriented economic system has reduced the CCP's ability to engage in this kind of control. Instead, political decision-making has come to increasingly reflect public opinion and calculations of legitimacy that are based on the government's ability to improve the welfare of the Chinese people [35].

Even if Foucault developed the concept of the panopticon based on the history of today's Western European democracies, an application of the panoptic metaphor to non-liberal instances of power and control is still warranted. The CCP governs society through a distinct rationale of planning and administrative control that seem incommensurable with liberal notions of freedom and liberty. But China's emerging system of government combines liberal methods of autonomy and choice with manifestly socialist practices of technocratic command and control [36]. Moreover, Dean [37] notes that liberal and authoritarian forms of power share elements that simultaneously aim at the development of individuals and improve the capacity of the state to govern. Scholars based in liberal countries often rely on exaggerated distinctions between democratic and non-democratic regime types and thereby fail to capture new ways in which governing practices may evolve [38]. More importantly, however, the panopticon is a figure of political technology that sheds light on mechanisms of power detached from any specific use or political circumstances [12]. The likeness between the panopticon and the SCS as techniques to establish discipline make the use of the panoptic concept as a theoretical lens highly appropriate. Both focus on discipline by creating visibility, setting standards, and allowing for interference. A panoptic perspective on the SCS might therefore yield new insights into technology-enabled state surveillance as a governing mechanism, even if Foucault did not foresee the possibilities of today's technology or the political conditions of present-day China.

4   Theoretical Analysis

According to the CCP, the SCS improves governance by rendering actors mutually accountable. Accountability can be understood as a relationship between two actors in which one actor accepts to inform the other, to explain his or her actions, and to submit to pre-determined punishments and rewards the other may impose [39, 40]. Briefly put, accountability encompasses the exchange of responsibilities and potential sanctions between 'the ruled' and 'rulers'. As Davis and Meckel [41] illustrate, transparency plays a major role in this process.

It enables actors to understand and react to the actions of others and, if applied effectively, it also expands the reach of governing mechanisms. To sharpen the focus of this analysis, the following paragraphs are therefore structured around the concept of transparency. Foucault [12] stresses transparency's crucial role for the automatization of panoptic power and control, however, he provides rather limited advice on how to operationalize it. Based on the reading of Foucault [12, 42, 43] and a review of literature on the connection between power and transparency, three heuristic areas of inquiry were derived:

- Directions of transparency: What are the compositional features of the transparency created by the SCS and who observes whom?
- Transparency as a social norm: What are the rationale behind and the consequences of transparency as a behavioral norm?
- Transparency as social control: In what ways does transparency change how government exercises control over society?

Each part of this heuristic framework directs the analysis towards different features of the SCS and its function in the relationship between 'rulers' and 'the ruled'. Because the SCS takes up an unusual position that links transparency and political as well as normative power, the analysis follows a multidisciplinary approach. Concepts from political and social sciences that stem from pragmatist traditions and social theory are brought into dialogue with each other. The study does not blend these approaches to generate novel theory; instead, the different theoretical perspectives are valuable because of the distinct questions they ask and how they guide the analysis. Based on the method of critical discourse analysis [44], the study attempts to better understand the interrelationship of concepts that are usually separately applied.

4.1   Transparency

According to Foucault [12], the increase of power created by the panopticon is unlikely to degenerate into oppression and authoritarianism. To stay with the architectural metaphor, any member of the public should be able to inspect the panoptic watchtower. The public should be free to exercise the surveillance function and to achieve a clear understanding of how punishment is practiced. In this design, transparency provides a control mechanism to supervise the panoptic apparatus itself. In a similar vein, Brin [45] proposes that the continuous advancement of communication technology leads to transparent societies, in which everyone is handed over to visibility. Asymmetrical flows of information that create power relations and domination would then vanish. These claims about the favorable effects of transparency are premised on ideals. They ignore actual differences among actors regarding their ability to access information and the uneven distribution of power that is hardwired into social arrangements and technological systems. The following paragraphs take an analytical look at what kind of transparency the SCS creates to provide insights into the control relationships the system aims to establish.

Directions of Transparency. Questions regarding transparency concern the perspectival optics of transparency or, in other words, the "direction of transparency" [46]. Foucault [12] assumes that the panopticon renders the periphery transparent from a central point of view, allowing for the surveillance of the many by the few. Other authors go beyond this conception to stress *"aperspectival"* transparency [47], i.e. everyone is visible from anywhere, or to highlight watchful transparency from below, i.e. *"sousveillance"* [48]. Analyzing the direction of transparency thus brings into focus who is doing the watching and who is being watched.

Heald [46] distinguishes between four directions to analyze transparency: (1) upwards, (2) downwards, (3) outwards, and (4) inwards. Transparency upwards means that hierarchal superiors can observe subordinate actors whereas transparency downwards (sousveillance) manifests when the 'ruled' can observe their 'rulers'. The former exists in all functioning governments to some degree; it generates knowledge of and access to society that enable central control. The latter is often framed in terms of the rights that protect individuals from government intrusion. Transparency outwards allows actors to observe what is happening outside their organization. This ability allows actors to observe their environment; for example, it is relevant when governments aim to fit policies to specific social patterns or ecosystems. Finally, inward transparency occurs when external actors can observe the conduct and behavior of those inside an organization. On the macro level, transparency inwards is usually understood as freedom of information about government procedures. On a micro level, it also concerns the degree to which the actors of civil society are rendered transparent towards each other.

The SCS' main characteristics are top-down transparency and lateral transparency. This can be interpreted in terms of upwards and symmetrical horizontal transparency. Concerning upwards transparency, the SCS renders individual actors throughout society transparent towards the CCP and, crucially, parts of the party apparatus itself become more visible to the central government. The blueprint for the implementation of the SCS sets out plans for the creation of civil servant dossiers. These contain data points about party officials' personal credit information, records about the violation of laws, and annual performance reviews [15]. The central government thus intends to use the SCS not only as tool to render civil society transparent but also to monitor the activities of party officials who previously escaped its scrutiny. Whether these dossiers are to be made accessible to the public, which would in effect create some degree downwards transparency, or if they are kept confidential is not mentioned in the blueprint. In general terms, however, the SCS focuses on upwards transparency: It renders actors, even those belonging to the party bureaucracy, transparent relative to the central government.

Concerning horizontal transparency, the SCS enables both outwards and inwards transparency. Regarding outwards transparency, the CCP can rely on direct knowledge about society generated through data collected by SCS instead of depending on capricious local elites to relay information. This represents a sizeable leap in the central government's capacity to observe and shape its environment. Inwards transparency is particularly relevant in relation to two aspects. First, it deals with the information that the CCP provides to the public about the rationale and processes on which the SCS rests. The central government is open about the aims of the SCS and explicitly propagates its intent to strengthen honesty and compliance with laws [18]. Private operators of SCS systems usually disclose procedures and scoring methods too. Although, as the case of Sesame Credit shows, precise operational procedures and algorithmic mechanisms remain opaque [25]. Based on the study of two SCS information platforms, Engelmann et al. [49] hypothesize that information disclosure about internal procedures and processes may be kept vague intentionally. Limiting this kind of information, the study argues, might aid behavioral engineering goals and avoids turning norm-guided behavior into a tradeable commodity.

The second aspect about inwards transparency concerns the degree to which individual actors are made transparent towards each other. The CCP intends to distribute blacklists and redlists to the wider public. Similarly, the scores generated by private systems are available to companies and individuals. This creates a highly transparent society in which the conduct and behavior of individual actors are immediately accessible to others. It seems obvious that this kind of uncurbed exposure to public scrutiny creates social pressure that occupies an important role in enforcing behavioral patterns and control.

In general, the SCS is characterized by upwards and symmetrical horizontal transparency. Upwards transparency enables the central government to exercise control by simply making actions visible and by enabling the application of disciplinary mechanisms. In terms of horizontal transparency, the government and private companies publish guidelines that enable actors to understand what kind of conduct is considered legitimate. However, imprecise descriptions of scoring mechanisms limit inwards transparency and thereby make it difficult to contest scoring decisions or to game the system. On the micro level, the SCS creates expansive horizontal transparency that not only renders individuals answerable to the central government but also to the public at large.

Transparency as a Social Norm. The CCP assigns several desirable outcomes to transparency. Positive effects would include enhanced trust, increased market efficiency, and better collective problem solving [15]. But, as the above paragraphs show, the effects of transparency are ambivalent and depend on the specificities of the context in which they occur. Han [47] additionally problematizes transparency by focusing on its role as a cultural norm that drives voluntary information disclosure and openness. The use of normative authority by the Chinese sovereign to engineer the moral outlook of society is not new [50]. In the case of SCS, the CCP justifies extensive transparency on the grounds that it remedies moral decay and dishonesty. As part of this *"civilizing mission"* [51], transparency turns into a social imperative that encourages individual actors to collaborate in raising their own visibility.

Han [47] further outlines that transparency mainly follows an economic logic. This aligns with the CCP's argument that the SCS strengthens economic development. Afterall, credit scoring initially emerged from an effort to help financial institutions assess the default probability of potential customers [22]. The systems thus rests on a rationale that aims to facilitate commercial transactions and to expand the scale and reliability of market mechanisms. If this focus on efficiency actually leads to more trust among actors and if it facilitates collective problem solving is questionable.

Addressing the above points, Han [47] remarks that transparency is often mis-construed as the functional equivalent of trust. Trust occurs if actors override a lack of information about the consequences of actions with learned expectations and experi-ences [52]. In contrast, transparency presupposes a relationship of control to establish a basis for positive interaction [53]. From this point of view, transparency establishes instrumental control over outcomes that limits the freedom to act and reduces uncer-tainty. However, as Han [47] points out, control and the reduction of uncertainty cannot, or only partially, replace generalized trust. Under these circumstances, no strong communities that might prove capable of mutual political action can form. The transparency the SCS creates thus seems ineffective at best and detrimental at worst when it comes to the facilitation of trust and concerted political action by the public.

Transparency as Social Control. On a global level, removed from particular local institutions, Foucault also confronts the issue of governing societies [42]. Here, he distinguishes between the purposes of government, sovereignty, and discipline. Government is exercised with the well-being of populations in mind; it justifies the use of power based on the ability to develop healthy and prosperous populations. In contrast, sovereignty aims at the expansion of its own power that requires no external justification. The sovereign's right to give orders, make decisions, and enforce obe-dience requires no explanation. Discipline concerns the use of punishment and rewards to correct the behavior of actors that the government deems unable to attend to the responsibilities necessary to be part of the population.

On first sight, the SCS seems to combine coercive measures and discipline. It is ultimately effective at governing behavior because it is backed by the threat of pun-ishment and by the possibility of rewards. However, like other methods of government, the SCS is unlikely to rely on coercion and discipline alone. Similar to law, it deter-mines a range of viable actions to encourage or prevent certain activities and, at the same time, shapes the habits, preferences, and beliefs of its target population. The population might perceive the system not as an outside imposition but as an ordinary part of daily exchanges that integrates into life with no apparent ruptures [54]. From this point of view, the SCS is a technological infrastructure that arranges things so that *"people, following their own self-interest, will do as they ought"* [55].

Foucault's concept of *"practices of the self"* [56] allows for a more elaborate analysis of the above-mentioned process of internalization. Actors are not simply subjected to power but they themselves partake in the processes of control to adapt their behavior. The 'ruled' become involved in refining structures of control if they accept the interest of their 'rulers' as their own. Given this situation, supervised actors internalize the aims of their supervisors and encounter claims to control with an attitude of *"betterment"* or *"modernization"* [57]. The explicit exercise of power is no longer required at this point; instead actors self-regulate their behavior in accordance with official expectations. In the case of the SCS, Kostka [19] showed that this alignment of interests occurs because actors perceive the system to deliver direct material benefits (e.g. access to financial credit) or general improvements to life quality (e.g. reducing fraud). The SCS thus not only applies coercion or discipline but it integrates both of these aspects with practices of the self. It institutionalizes self-regulation that grants the members of populations the status of autonomous actors in some areas (e.g. market transactions) and combines them with a system of coercion and discipline in others.

In conclusion, the analysis finds that although the SCS could potentially create transparency that dramatically reduces information asymmetries and power inequalities between the state and society, it in effect does so in a relatively limited fashion. Compared to the clientelism and arbitrary decision-making of the earlier decades, the precise and depersonalized standards of the SCS can be seen as an improvement. However, contrary to the claims of the CCP, the SCS is unlikely to improve trust. It rather replaces trust with control by limiting the freedom to act and thereby restricting the range of possible actions and their outcomes. Additionally, the SCS exposes and judges any actor's behavior for everyone to see, which creates social pressure and aids enforcing social control. The SCS also represents a form of power that departs from direct coercion. Although the state has the ability to control a number of essential opportunities concerning the livelihood citizens, within the categories and standards laid down by the CCP, actors are free to manage their conduct according to their own interests.

5 Conclusion

The SCS gives rise to far reaching dismay about the impact of big data and AI-driven decision-making on the governance of societies. The causes for concern gain urgency in times when the CCP consolidates its authoritarian rule, not least, by pioneering the use of advanced technologies for governing purposes. Despite the Chinese polity's authoritarian leanings, its propensity to change and its openness to institutional innovation cast a light on practices of governing that are relevant beyond China's borders. The governments of countries as different as India, Norway, the United States, or Venezuela employ algorithmic decision-making in criminal justice, social welfare, or tax systems to assess behavioral risks and to grant access to public services. Disregarding the question about political order for a moment, it is perhaps more useful to ask the question about how ICT changes governing practices across different regime types. Here, the SCS illustrates that technology is not only employed to arrive at specific economic or political goals, but its use points towards another form of administration, politics, and governing altogether.

The coordination of society by purely technological means potentially threatens good governance because *"technological management"* [58] is prone to instrumentalism (i.e. means-to-end reasoning). Unconstrained instrumentalism in itself is objectionable because it aims at achieving policy goals without concern for ideals and values oriented towards the common good or public interest [8]. This invites broader questions about the social and political effects of algorithmic governance. Will the choice architecture put in place by algorithms overdetermine human behavior? What happens to notions of human sovereignty? What are the limits of automation and will current political systems eventually be replaced by autonomous AIs that leave humans *"out of the loop"* [9]?

In liberal societies, the willingness to experiment with technology-enabled governing practices on a large scale seems to be relatively low [59, 60]. Reluctance likely centers on worries about the protection of privacy and of citizen's civil rights. Tinkering with unfamiliar governing methods also disrupts long-established and relatively well-functioning state institutions and the rule of law. Still, algorithmic governing proliferates at a gradual pace. To tame the *"techno-leviathan"* [11] governments and citizens need to develop channels that allow for the incorporation of social norms, rights, and values into intelligent computer systems. Political and state institutions also need to actively examine how the benefits of algorithmic governing can be obtained without sacrificing democratic principles and the interests of the public.

Finally, it remains to point out some of the limitations of this paper and avenues for further research. In terms of limitations, this paper relies on secondary literature as empirical material. This might cause issues about the reliability of the data either because of selection effects or because the secondary literature might be flawed [61]. The conclusions should therefore be regarded as preliminary and alternative explanations should be awaited. Moreover, the paper takes a Foucaultian perspective that depends on theoretical categories deemed relevant by the author. These categories might differ according to implicit theories and conceptual frameworks used to produce explanations. Other theoretical Foucaultian [62, 63] lenses might prove similarly productive and might lead to different conclusions. In terms of further research regarding algorithmic governance, an analysis of presumably less well-known but equally powerful algorithmic scoring systems in liberal countries might provide new insight into their effects. At the same time, a multitude of disciplines and perspectives [64–66] suitable for the analysis of these systems present themselves.

References

1. Bohman, J.: Expanding dialogue: the internet, the public sphere and prospects for transnational democracy. Sociol. Rev. **52**, 131–155 (2004). https://doi.org/10.1111/j.1467-954X.2004.00477.x
2. Boyd, D., Crawford, K.: Critical questions for big data: provocations for a cultural, technological, and scholarly phenomenon. Inf. Commun. Soc. **15**, 662–679 (2012). https://doi.org/10.1080/1369118X.2012.678878
3. Tufekci, Z.: Algorithmic harms beyond Facebook and Google: emergent challenges of computational agency. J. Telecommun. High Technol. Law **13**, 203–218 (2015)
4. Rau, J.P., Stier, S.: Die Echokammer-Hypothese: Fragmentierung der Öffentlichkeit und politische Polarisierung durch digitale Medien? Zeitschrift für Vergleichende Politikwissenschaft **13**(3), 399–417 (2019). https://doi.org/10.1007/s12286-019-00429-1
5. Pariser, E.: The Filter Bubble: What the Internet is Hiding from You. Penguin Press, New York (2011)
6. Hummel, P., Braun M., Dabrock,, P.: Own data? Ethical reflections on data ownership. Philos. Technol. 1–28 (2020). https://doi.org/10.1007/s13347-020-00404-9
7. Solove, D.J.: Privacy and power: computer databases metaphors for information privacy. Stanford Law Rev. **53**, 1393 (2001)
8. Hildebrandt, M., O'Hara, K.: Life and the Law in the Era of Data-Driven Agency. Edward Elgar Publishing, Cheltenham (2020)
9. Citron, D.K., Pasquale, F.: The scored society: due process for automated predictions. Washington Law Rev. **89**, 35 (2014)

10. Zarsky, T.Z.: Transparent predictions. Univ. Ill. Law Rev. **2013**, 1503–1570 (2013)
11. Rahwan, I.: Society-in-the-loop: programming the algorithmic social contract. Ethics Inf. Technol. **20**(1), 5–14 (2017). https://doi.org/10.1007/s10676-017-9430-8
12. Foucault, M.: Discipline and Punish: The Birth of the Prison, 2nd edn. Vintage Books, New York (1995)
13. Hvistendahl, M.: Inside China's vast new experiment in social ranking. In: Wired (2017). https://www.wired.com/story/age-of-social-credit/
14. Li, D., Chen, S., Dharmawan, K.: China's most advanced big brother experiment is a bureaucratic mess. In: Bloomberg News (2019). https://www.bloomberg.com/news/features/2019-06-18/china-social-credit-rating-flaws-seen-in-suzhou-osmanthus-program
15. Creemers, R.: Planning outline for the construction of a social credit system (2014–2020). In: China Copyright and Media (2014). https://chinacopyrightandmedia.wordpress.com/2014/06/14/planning-outline-for-the-construction-of-a-social-credit-system-2014-2020/. Accessed 16 Jan 2019
16. Liang, F., Das, V., Kostyuk, N., Hussain, M.M.: Constructing a data-driven society: China's social credit system as a state surveillance infrastructure. Policy Internet **10**, 415–453 (2018). https://doi.org/10.1002/poi3.183
17. Hoffman, S.: Programming China: The Communist Party's Autonomic Approach to Managing State Security. The University of Nottingham (2017)
18. Creemers, R.: China's social credit system: an evolving practice of control. SSRN Electron. J. (2018). https://doi.org/10.2139/ssrn.3175792
19. Kostka, G.: China's social credit systems and public opinion: explaining high levels of approval. SSRN Electron. J. (2018). https://doi.org/10.2139/ssrn.3215138
20. Dai, X.: Toward a reputation state: the social credit system project of China. SSRN Electron. J. (2018). https://doi.org/10.2139/ssrn.3193577
21. Chen, Y., Cheung, A.S.Y.: The transparent self under big data profiling: privacy and Chinese legislation on the social credit system. SSRN Electron. J. (2017). https://doi.org/10.2139/ssrn.2992537
22. Huang, Z., Lei, Y., Shen, S.: China's personal credit reporting system in the internet finance era: challenges and opportunities. China Econ. J. **9**, 288–303 (2016). https://doi.org/10.1080/17538963.2016.1209868
23. Meissner, M.: China's social credit system: a big data enabled approach to market regulation with broad implications for doing business in China. Mercator Institute for China Studies (2017)
24. Ohlberg, M., Ahmed, S., Lang, B. Central planning, local experiments: the complex implementation of China's social credit system. Mercator Institute for China Studies (2017)
25. Ahmed, S.: Cashless society, cached data security: considerations for a chinese social credit system. In: The Citizen Lab (2017). https://citizenlab.ca/2017/01/cashless-society-cached-data-security-considerations-chinese-social-credit-system/
26. China Dail. Chinese courts use technology to tighten noose on debt defaulters (2017). http://www.chinadaily.com.cn/china/2017-10/04/content_32830450.htm. Accessed 22 Jan 2019
27. BusinessWire Alitrip Introduces Credit-based Visa Application Service for Qualified Chinese Travelers (2015). https://www.businesswire.com/news/home/20150603006726/en/Alitrip-Introduces-Credit-based-Visa-Application-Service-Qualified. Accessed 22 Jan 2019
28. Koetse, M.: Insights into sesame credit & top 5 ways to use a high sesame score. In: What's on Weibo (2018). https://www.whatsonweibo.com/insights-into-sesame-credit-top-5-ways-to-use-a-high-sesame-score/. Accessed 22 Jan 2019
29. Lv, A., Luo, T.: Asymmetrical power between internet giants and users in China. Int. J. Commun. **12**, 3877–3895 (2018)

30. Koetse, M.: Zhejiang movie theatre displays blacklisted individuals in avengers movie preview. In: What's on Weibo (2019). https://www.whatsonweibo.com/zhejiang-movie-theatre-displays-blacklisted-individuals-in-avengers-movie-preview/

31. Noesselt, N.: Microblogs and the adaptation of the chinese party-state's governance strategy: microblogs and governance in China. Governance **27**, 449–468 (2014). https://doi.org/10.1111/gove.12045

32. Zheng, Y., Wu, G.: Information technology, public space, and collective action in China. Comp. Polit. Stud. **38**, 507–536 (2005). https://doi.org/10.1177/0010414004273505

33. Bentham, J.: Panopticon Or the Inspection-House. Anodos Books, Dumfries & Galloway (2017)

34. Lee, C.K., Zhang, Y.H. Seeing like a Grassroots State: producing power and instability in China's bargained authoritarianism. In: Shue, V., Thornton, P.M. (eds.) To Govern China, 1st edn. pp. 177–201. Cambridge University Press (2017)

35. He, B., Warren, M.E.: Authoritarian deliberation: the deliberative turn in Chinese political development. Perspect. Polit. **9**, 269–289 (2011). https://doi.org/10.1017/S1537592711000892

36. Sigley, G.: Chinese governmentalities: government, governance and the socialist market economy. Econ. Soc. **35**, 487–508 (2006). https://doi.org/10.1080/03085140600960773

37. Dean, M.: Governmentality: Power and Rule in Modern Society, 2nd edn. London, SAGE (2010)

38. Shue, V., Thornton, P.M.: Introduction: beyond implicit political dichotomies and linear models of change in China. In: Shue, V., Thornton, P.M. (eds.) To Govern China: Evolving Practices of Power, 1st edn., pp. 1–26. Cambridge University Press, Cambridge (2017)

39. Manin, B., Przeworski, A., Stokes, S.C.: Introduction. In: Przeworski, A., Stokes, S.C., Manin, B. (eds.) Democracy, Accountability, and Representation, pp. 1–26. Cambridge University Press, Cambridge (1999)

40. Schmitter, P.C.: Political Accountability in 'Real-Existing' Democracies: Meaning and Mechanisms (2007)

41. Davis, J.W., Meckel, M.: Political power and the requirements of accountability in the age of WikiLeaks. Zeitschrift für Politikwissenschaft **22**, 463–491 (2012). https://doi.org/10.5771/1430-6387-2012-4-463

42. Foucault, M.: Governmentality. In: Burchell, G., Gordon, C., Miller, P. (eds.) The Foucault Effect: Studies in Governmentality, pp 87–104. University of Chicago Press, Chicago (1991)

43. Foucault, M.: Technologies of the self. In: Martin, L.H. (ed.) Technologies of the Self: A Seminar with Michel Foucault. University of Massachusetts Press, Amherst (1988)

44. Wodak, R., Meyer, M.: Methods of Critical Discourse Analysis, 2nd edn. SAGE, London (2009)

45. Brin, D.: The Transparent Society: Will Technology Force Us to Choose Between Privacy and Freedom?. Perseus Books, Reading (1998)

46. Heald, D.: Varieties of transparency. In: Hood, C. (ed.) Transparency: The Key to Better Governance? 1st edn. British Academy Scholarship (2006)

47. Han, B.-C.: The Transparency Society. Stanford University Press, Stanford (2015)

48. Mann, S., Nolan, J., Wellman, B.: Sousveillance: inventing and using wearable computing devices for data collection in surveillance environments. Surveill. Soc. **1**, 331–355 (2003). https://doi.org/10.24908/ss.v1i3.3344

49. Engelmann, S., Chen, M.., Fischer, F., et al.: Clear sanctions, vague rewards: how China's social credit system currently defines "good" and "bad" behavior. In: Proceedings of the Conference on Fairness, Accountability, and Transparency - FAT 2019, Atlanta, GA, USA, pp. 69–78. ACM Press (2019)

50. Thornton, P.M.: Disciplining the State: Virtue, Violence, and State-Making in Modern China. Harvard University, Cambridge (2007)
51. Scott, J.C.: Seeing Like a State: How Certain Schemes to Improve the Human Condition Have Failed. Yale University Press, New Haven (2008)
52. Deutsch, M.: Trust and suspicion. J. Conflict Resolut. **2**, 265–279 (1958). https://doi.org/10.1177/002200275800200401
53. Luhmann, N.: Vertrauen: ein Mechanismus der Reduktion sozialer Komplexität, 5. Auflage. UVK Verlagsgesellschaft mbH, Konstanz (2014)
54. Li, T.: The Will to Improve: Governmentality, Development, and the Practice of Politics. Duke University Press, Durham (2007)
55. Scott, D.: Colonial governmentality. In: Inda, J.X. (ed.) Anthropologies of Modernity, pp. 23–49. Blackwell Publishing Ltd., Oxford (2005)
56. Foucault, M.: The History of Sexuality, vol. 2. The Use of Pleasure, Reprinted. Penguin Books, London (1992)
57. Göbel, C., Heberer, T.: The policy innovation imperative: changing techniques for governing China's local governors. In: Shue, V., Thornton, P.M. (eds.) To Govern China, 1st edn., pp. 283–308, Cambridge University Press (2017)
58. Brownsword, R.: Technological management and the Rule of Law. Law Innov. Technol. **8**, 100–140 (2016). https://doi.org/10.1080/17579961.2016.1161891
59. Araujo, T., Helberger, N., Kruikemeier, S., de Vreese, C.H.: In AI we trust? Perceptions about automated decision-making by artificial intelligence. AI Soc. **35**(3), 611–623 (2020). https://doi.org/10.1007/s00146-019-00931-w
60. Rubio, D., Lastra, C.: European Tech Insights 2019: Mapping European Attitudes to Technological Change and its Governance. Center for the Governance of Change, Mardid, Spain (2019)
61. Lustick, I.S.: History, historiography, and political science: multiple historical records and the problem of selection bias. Am. Polit. Sci. Rev. **90**, 605–618 (1996)
62. Rouvroy, A.: The end(s) of critique: data-behaviorism vs. due-process. In: Hildebrandt, M., De Vries, E. (eds.) Privacy, Due Process and the Computational Turn. Philosophers of Law Meet Philosophers of Technology. Routledge (2013)
63. Berns, T.: Not individuals, relations: what transparency is really about. a theory of algorithmic governmentality. In: Alloa, E., Thomä, D. (eds.) Transparency, Society and Subjectivity, pp. 243–257. Springer, Cham (2018). https://doi.org/10.1007/978-3-319-77161-8_12
64. Bauman, Z.: Liquid Modernity. Polity Press, Cambridge (2012)
65. Haggerty, K., Ericson, R.: The surveillant assemblage. Br. J. Sociol. **51**, 605–622 (2000). https://doi.org/10.1080/00071310020015280
66. Lyon, D.: Surveillance Studies: An Overview. Polity, Cambridge (2007)

Enhancement of the e-Invoicing Systems by Increasing the Efficiency of Workflows via Disruptive Technologies

Hiruni Gunaratne$^{(\boxtimes)}$ and Ingrid Pappel

Tallinn University of Technology, Akadeemia tee 15a, 12618 Tallinn, Estonia
hirunigunaratne@gmail.com, ingrid.pappel@taltech.ee

Abstract. E-invoicing is a rapidly growing e-service in Europe as well as in the world. It is identified as a substantially significant element in progressing towards the goals of 'Digital Economy' in the European Union. This paper focuses on identifying inefficiencies in e-invoicing systems currently in use and the opportunities to apply emerging technologies such as artificial intelligence and robotic process automation, in order to increase efficiency and level of automatization. The study incorporates expert opinions and users' perceptions in e-invoicing systems on the status quo and the necessities for higher automation. We focus on e-invoicing systems in the Baltic region consisting of the countries Estonia, Latvia and Lithuania. Based on the conducted research, the drawbacks in e-invoicing systems were identified related to operational, technological and information security-related. Furthermore, the automation opportunities and general requirements for automation were identified. The functionalities that can be improved are discovered as well discussed in this paper and the advantages of using emerging technologies in the context are explained. Based on research outcomes we propose a conceptual e-invoicing ecosystem and present recommendations for its application along the future work needed in that field.

Keywords: E-invoicing · Artificial intelligence · Robotic process automation · Automatization · Efficiency

1 Introduction

1.1 The Background

Electronic invoicing is defined as "an invoice that has been issued, transmitted and received in a structured electronic format which allows for its automatic and electronic processing" [1]. According to Salmony and Bo Harald, "the e-invoice is a pivotal document in the supply chain whose digitalization will generate savings in its own right, as well as contributing to many other benefits along the supply chain" [2]. Thus, the e-invoices should consist of fully structured data, therefore it can be automatically processed.

E-invoicing was known to be growing rapidly in the world with over 400 e-invoicing service providers active in Europe, transacting 3.3 billion Euros worth of e-invoices globally in 2017, predicted to be 16.1 billion Euros in 2024 [3].

© Springer Nature Switzerland AG 2020
A. Chugunov et al. (Eds.): EGOSE 2020, CCIS 1349, pp. 60–74, 2020.
https://doi.org/10.1007/978-3-030-67238-6_5

Given that e-invoicing is one of the main e-services in e-commerce and e-governance [6], the study revolves around e-invoicing.

In 2014, a directive on electronic invoicing in public procurement was voted by the European Parliament and Council which is known as DIRECTIVE 2014/55/EU. This directive emphasizes on defining a common standard for e-invoicing which will develop interoperability within the European Union [1]. The key target is to process the invoice automatically. As the bigger picture of the above directive, the European Union aims to create a 'digital single market' with no online barriers to flows of goods, services and data with the Europe 2020 ten-year plan [3]. According to the European Union's six strategic priorities for 2019–2024, 'A European Green Deal' (Striving to be the first climate-neutral continent) and 'A Europe fit for the digital age' (Empowering people with a new generation of technologies) [4] directly benefits from the usage of e-invoicing within the member states. Emerging technologies such as Artificial Intelligence (AI), Internet of things (IoT) and Robotic Process Automation (RPA) hold great significance when they are amalgamated with specific systems. Digital revolution is taking place globally enhancing the global markets concerning industries. Business sectors such as industrial manufacturing, healthcare, financial services, food services, automotive etc. are progressively adopting AI, IoT and RPA technologies. The assimilation of these emerging technologies holds the aptitude of generating smarter, safer, efficient, and more secure systems. Solution providers seem to be more confident in applying several technological developments to answer volatile, uncertain, complex, and ambiguous challenges in the systems [9].

The Baltic countries share common features and history similar to each other. According to Aurélien Poissonnier, a quantitative analysis of the economy of three Baltic countries reveals that there is an integrated Baltic economy which consists of a sizable part by common factors and economic links among the three countries [5]. Hence, we decided to scope the research within the Baltic region because study results can be generalized to the whole region. In addition, Estonia is quite well known in terms of both state and local digitalization, where important aspects are related to data sharing, data quality [21] and also understanding of digital capability [22].

In Europe, the initial progress of e-invoicing was driven by the private sector whereas in the present it is being very much supported by the governments [7]. Given that the governments are introducing the initiatives for e-invoicing through moves such as mandates [1] and the businesses are requesting the technologies to be upgraded and the services to be better [7], the requirements and opportunities in a comprehensive e-invoicing platform should be identified. Even though the e-invoicing in Estonia has reached a considerable level of effectiveness which can also be considered somewhere in between digitization and automated e-invoicing, there are many prospects to improve. Rapidly growing emerging technologies which could be used for disruptive innovation also lay a heavy base for strategic drivers. These technologies take a completely new approach for some of the existing problems and can act as a substitution for old solutions [8]. In order to approach this challenge, we have formulated our research question as **how to enhance e-invoicing systems and increase the efficiency of workflows with higher levels of automation?**

Thus the research question aims to find out what kind of inefficiencies are in the e-invoicing systems and process currently, what kind of and to what extent automation is present in the current e-invoicing systems, find out how can emerging technologies help to overcome the barriers and achieve higher levels of automation in e-invoicing.

This paper is structured as follows. The first section gives an understanding about domain and the second section discusses the relevant work along the existing research. In the third section, we present results and discuss them based on findings and analysis. Finally, the fourth section is aimed to present the eco-system that we believe would help application of disruptive technologies for the future work and we summarize our research in Sect. 5 based on the outcome of our research.

1.2   Methodology

The study incorporated a qualitative research approach. To find answers for the research problem, we required subject matter experts' opinions. This data was collected with 6 semi-structured interviews held via Skype. The perceptual feedback from e-invoicing application users were collected via a survey shared publicly among employees of organizations operating within the Baltic region. In pursuance of analyzing interview data, a systematic approach based on thematic mapping was followed after transcribing the interviews. Patterns among the interview data were explored iteratively using NVivo 12 software for qualitative data analysis. For Experts interviews, purposive sampling was used by our own experience and discussions with relevant stakeholders. From the shared survey, 224 employees (varying from different designations) responded based on their thoughts and feedback. There were 114 respondents from Estonia, 54 from Latvia and 36 from Lithuania. In addition to primary data, the secondary data in terms of literature overview has been applied. The questions to measure the user perceptions were carried out under 5 main perceptions namely perceived ease of use, perceived usefulness, perceived risk, perceived trust and perception on information security. The format of the questions were in the Likert scale format, simple 'Yes, No, May be' format and format of 'options selecting'. For the survey results, Microsoft Excel have been used to analyze data with simple excel formulas. For the sampling method, a non- probability sampling method has been used for the survey. The sampling method is a mix of convenience sampling (sample includes individuals who happen to be most accessible to the researcher) and voluntary sampling (sending a survey via e-mail and posting on related LinkedIn forums).

2   Literature Review

2.1   E-invoicing Market in the Baltics

A commercial invoice is the most significant document exchanged between trading partners. Along with the commercial significance, the invoice is an accounting document which has legal insinuations being the basis of calculating VAT (value-added tax) [10]. When we consider market adoption of e-invoices Baltics, Estonia is one of the leaders in the e-invoicing market.

Latvia and Lithuania are in the second-tier with average market penetration [10]. As an example, good e-invoicing practices are currently followed in the Estonian public sector. From 2011, invoicing was transitioned from paper-based management to solely digital. With financial support from the Estonian government, document management systems (DMS) as well as the required APIs and functionalities were developed making the digitalization and automatization of invoicing possible. These projects enabled local municipalities to apply digital workflows in terms of e-invoicing. As a result, since 2017 the whole public sector deals with digital invoices [11]. This process of digitalization has drastically decreased inefficient manual work by eliminating paper-based management. Additionally, the resulting level of automation has laid the foundation needed for the development and application of disruptive technologies.

2.2   Robotic Process Automation and Artificial Intelligence

When we discuss about the emerging technologies, Robotic Process Automation (RPA) is a novel dimension of upcoming technologies. According to Madakam et al., "It is a combination of both hardware and software, networking and automation for doing things very simple". There are examples of usage of RPA such as repetitive processing of transactions in e-invoice processing, rules-based processing in error checking and handling a large number of transaction volumes in orders processing. RPA brings direct cost-effectiveness while enhancing precision across businesses. Software robots who are trained to perform a variety of repeating functionalities can interpret, prompt replies and connect with different interfaces or systems just like human beings. Software robots are known to be "only substantially better: a robot never sleeps, makes zero mistakes and costs a lot less than an employee" [12].

In 2016, at the World Economic Forum, the significance of AI was stressed and the impact of AI on the governments where it makes the governments agile [13]. There are different methodologies and techniques of AI which can be classified as techniques which reply on the mathematical enhancement, network-based approaches wherein represents problems are sets of possible states and transitions in between them, agent-based methodologies and multi-agent system interactions, automated reasoning-based approaches on present knowledge and big data and machine learning analytics [17].

2.3   User Perceptions Towards Using an e-Invoicing System

Jiunn-Woei Lian has described seven "Critical factors for e-invoice service adoption in Taiwan according to Unified Theory of Acceptance and Use of Technology 2 (UTAUT2)" [14]. It was decided that five of those factors to be used to measuring the user perception in this study. Out of the 7 factors, facilitation condition is taken out assuming the users work in a corporate structure where all the facilitation conditions are fulfilled such as internet connections, training on the system etc. Social influence condition is taken out assuming there is no social influence in a corporate environment, as it is a business requirement to use an e-invoicing system at the workplace.

Perceived ease of use or Effort Expectation is "The degree of ease of use with the use of e-invoice" according to Davis. Even it can be defined as 'the degree which the user can effortlessly use an e-invoicing system' where it has an inverse relation with the notion of complexity [15].

Perceived usefulness or Performance expectation describes the degree to which users of e-invoicing systems will consider that its use will improve their performance, also providing advantages in the organizational level. Perceived usefulness can modify user behavior and predict the continuous usage of the service [15].

Perceived risk is known to be "the degree to which people perceived risk when using e-invoice" [18]. Perceived risk is known to be affected by the perceived trust. Then the perception of risk is affecting the actual usage of a technology or a system [15]. There are many different types of perceived risks such as functional, physical, financial, psychological and social. Perceived risk can involve possible social consequences, financial loss, physical danger, loss of time and ineffective performance [19].

Perceived trust is "the degree to which people trust government e-invoice policy and service" [16]. Some researchers have analyzed the role of trust in different stages such as trust before the use of the system (pre-use trust) and after use of the system (post-use trust). In the pre-use the users are not familiar with the technology and the systems, hence trust is based on their tendency to trust. Once the users have used the system or the software, experience and previous perceptions determine the level of trust they have [17]. This study analyses post-use trust since the users is already using some sort of e-invoicing system.

Perceived Security reflects a perception of reliability of the methods of data transmission, storage and access [14]. Deficiencies in security are one of the most noteworthy barriers in the development of e-commerce related software products. If the knowledge of IT systems is low in users, the fears of hackers or a third party will tamper the information is high. E-invoicing must adhere to the requirements imposed by Directive 2011/115/EC in the Baltic region. These requirements include the relationships with other agents in terms of authentication and non-repudiation of transactions. Other requirements of security can be derived from company policies and national level requirements such as archiving digital content for a while [1].

3 Results and Discussion

3.1 Interview Outcomes

We investigated the current inefficiencies in terms of scope and operational gap, performance, security and technology in the e-invoicing systems. Also, the automation requirements related to technological effectiveness and functional effectiveness were investigated. With respect to the inefficiencies in current e-invoicing systems, there were three sub themes identified with the thematic analysis of interview results which are operational, technological and information security (referred to as InfoSec) (Table 1).

Table 1. Thematic analysis of inefficiencies of current e-invoicing systems.

Sub theme	Inefficiencies under the theme	Frequency of references
Operational	Bad e-invoicing model Problems in e-invoicing standards Cost related problems Business logic problems Data quality problems E-invoice receiving problems Difference in businesses and e-invoicing systems Human errors E-invoice roaming problems Less awareness related to e-invoicing No e-invoicing post processing functionalities Not supporting small or micro companies	58
Technological	ERP partner related problems Data extraction from different systems Use of old technologies and legacy systems	10
InfoSec	Relying on e-invoice service providers Less awareness of information security Data integrity Information security problems related to roaming activities In-house built systems and their issues Identification, authentication and authorization problems	13

The nodes for each sub-theme and the frequency (number of occurrences of the sub-theme in dataset) of references to each category (node) of problems are depicted by the above table. Operational inefficiencies are the most category out of all the inefficiencies. One major problem is with the e-invoicing standards which was mentioned in all the interviews. The standards are not strongly imposed for e-invoicing as they are in payments, securities trading or telecom. Some companies are still using older standards and there are compatibility issues with the formats and the data fields. Another standard related issue is that all of the standards do not cater to every type of businesses. Standards can be loosely validated, the receivers might end up interpreting non-mandatory field data in their way, paving the way for larger problems.

There was a lot of instances identified where PDF or images used as invoices which cost a lot to be digitized. They can be erroneous, not validated and inefficient. The above issue could be mostly observed in Latvia and Lithuania than in Estonia. Several functional elements in e-invoicing process are not supported and one of them is not having an approval process in the system after receiving the e-invoice. Quoting an expert opinion on this, "Lithuanian government have their public self-service platform 'eSaskaita' for e-invoicing and e-invoice are sent via the portal. There are many drawbacks such as absence of approval flows. Hence most of the times e-invoices are printed and approvals take place manually". The stakeholders have less awareness about e-invoicing. The information contained in an e-invoice and the structure is not known by users. The awareness in Latvia and Lithuania seems to be lesser than Estonia.

Human mistakes are known to happen in the e-invoicing realm because there is manual intervention in the process such as sending the e-invoice to the wrong party. E-invoicing roaming in the Baltics is built on peer to peer connections with agreements between the operators. Also, this is burdened by different web services for each operator. Regarding the content of e-invoices operators have their own validation rules and standards, even within the standard different versions are used. Most of the times the status of the roaming-invoice is not visible to all the parties while roaming.

E-invoicing receiving has issues such as having to always reconfigure the systems to receive e-invoices from different suppliers especially when the supplier count is high, some suppliers sending e-invoices through a centralized portal (in Lithuania), not having messages delivered upon receiving or not-receiving e-invoices and accepting wrong e-invoices or-invoices with errors.

Businesses are different from each other and it appears to be very hard to maintain one generalized e-invoicing system for all the businesses. e-invoicing operators are only supporting mid and large-sized companies but not small or Micro companies in many instances because they have to customize the solutions. Another major problem is the quality of data in e-invoices. This is a closely related issue with e-invoicing standards. Currently, there is a lot of non-validated data which are erroneous in the e-invoices. Different stakeholders interpret these data in different ways.

There are non-mandatory fields in e-invoices which carry invalid data. There are cost-related problems, especially affecting the small and micro businesses where the cost of connecting to an e-invoice operator and cost per e-invoice is high. This can affect the ERP partners as well, which was identified as a reason for the volume of B2B e-invoicing not developing as expected. Business logic problems were also significant. Some of these are related to wrong tax calculations, lack of information on the e-invoice and erroneous values.

When talking about Latvia and Lithuania, the e-invoicing market model seems unsatisfactory. Centralized portals in Lithuania hinders fully automated e-invoicing processes and also B2B market restrictions. It works well with the B2G market. When compared to Estonia; Latvia and Lithuania do not have a central registry for companies to register for e-invoicing use. And the roaming infrastructure seems to be deficient. Another significant inadequacy in Latvia and Lithuania is the awareness and knowledge distribution compared to Estonia.

One of the main problems identified with respect to technologies and systems is that they are outdated and the technology in the transportation layer seems to be old which makes it very hard to upgrade. Even integrating with customers who has legacy software is a problem. In the e-invoicing realm, the accounting system or ERP system should be connected to the e-invoicing system to achieve automation and other benefits. Some ERPs are quite costly to be connected to an e-invoicing service provider.

Also, ERP systems can be less capable when it comes to integration and fulfilling the requirements of e-invoicing systems still use data entering manually or extracting with digitization services which are not that accurate as stated by the experts. It is mentioned that there are no index files when the information comes through PDF or other formats.

There are several authentication, authorization and identification problems discussed by the interviewees. It is evident that there are problems such as no electronic signing, not having fully automated systems, some still arrive as PDF or Paper and getting extracted to e-invoicing systems and having to manage different channels of access to a system. Also, it was mentioned that there are data integrity problems, that the information can be changed during the transportation layer. Currently, companies just rely on e-invoicing service providers for data integrity. There is another major functionality that the e-invoice operators perform which is e-invoice roaming. This is not controlled by any authority currently. The problem arises when the market grows or broadens outside Estonia or Baltic region respectively. Regarding the small systems built in-house by the companies, they lack information security aspects (Table 2).

Table 2. Thematic analysis of requirements/automation opportunities in e-invoicing systems.

Sub theme	Inefficiencies under the theme	Frequency of references
Automation opportunities	Workflow automation E-invoice sending and receiving automation Rule based automation E-receipt Automation of VAT reporting E-ordering Payment reconciliation automation Payment receival automation	15
General requirements	User friendliness requirement Reuse of components Use of bank infrastructure in e-invoicing systems Information security requirements	9

Currently e-invoice sending and receiving is quite automatic, but the processes around it need more automation. Many of the automation requirements were identified as 'Rule-Based Automation' which were, pre-posting of the documents, matching the invoices with orders, assigning workflows to an e-invoice, and automated journal entries for recursive invoices.

E-ordering was pointed out as an enhancement which proactively contributes to the e-invoicing and real-time economy. As e-ordering has very special benefits, e-receipt was brought out to be the following step after e-invoicing, because it uses the same semantic and technical standards which is also an example from Finland. Experts have stated that payments automation and reconciliations of payments received are also the next steps in automation. E-invoice workflow automation is already available with some e-invoice operators up to some level but some functionalities are yet to be implemented (Table 3).

Table 3. Sentiments analysis of using AI and RPA.

Technology	Positive occurrences	Negative occurrences
AI	11	4
RPA	7	4

The ideas from the experts about using the emerging technologies were both positive and negative. According to the above table of sentiments (made with Nvivo12) expressed about applying emerging technologies where positive sentiments are more than the negative sentiments. The number depicts the number of references which had positive or negative sentiment in the dataset.

Artificial Intelligence (AI) is considered to be implemented by several e-invoicing operators in the Baltics but not yet executed. Most answers were towards using AI in purchase invoices, not sales invoices. And the challenges such as training the AI and making proper data sets for training, cost of implementing AI, trust in AI was discussed by experts. It emerged that AI can be used to analyse the e-invoices and get the necessary information as a solution for e-invoicing standard issues (e-invoice receiving), checking data quality, analyse and compare accounts posting templates, automating accounting entries and data analysis and predictions.

RPA was not implemented by any of the companies currently, but it is considered in future. The uses and challenges of using RPA were discussed. It emerged that RPA can be put to use to insert data into e-invoicing systems, data matching, order matching with e-invoices, e-invoice approval process automation, e-invoicing formats translation, extracting data from several different systems such as banking system, web shop interfaces etc. without integrating all these systems and preparing orders. As per our thoughts, it can be the reason that many stakeholders are not very familiar with the AI and RPA technologies, for them these technologies seem very far away from being implemented in the near future. On the other hand, some of the experts mentioned that the cost of these technologies is high. But when compared with the benefits in the future, this cost may be recovered with time.

3.2 Survey Outcomes

Based on the responds, we looked at the user's perceptions under each element described in Sect. 2 and tried to understand the automation requirement from users' perspective.

Perceived Ease of Use. In Estonia, more than 60% among the respondents have rated 4 and 5 which illustrates that they are considerably happy with how effective and user-friendly their current e-Invoicing system is. In Latvia and Lithuania, 52% and 64% of the respondents respectively have rated 3 which reveals that they neither agree nor disagree with how effectively the current e-Invoicing system performs and 33% and 25% of the respondents respectively have rated 4 and they are somewhat happy with the e-invoicing systems. It is observable that most of the respondents' organizations use minimal labor force to get involved in day-to-day invoicing operational activities in all the countries but it is not zero. Around 64%–71% of the respondents' organizations use a labor force up to 5 people for e-invoicing operations while less than 5% of the respondents represent organizations using over 10 employees for manual invoicing activities.

Perceived Usefulness/Performance Expectation. In Estonia, most of the respondents (above 65%) agree that their current e-Invoicing system covers most of their day-to-day invoicing operational activities while 24% of respondents neither agree, nor disagree with the current functionalities. Only 7% express their disagreements on how useful the current features exist in their invoicing systems. In Latvia, it is observable that around 45% of the respondents vote in favor of current system functional coverage whilst another 40%–45% of respondents neither agree to that statement nor do they disagree. With the 11% of respondents voting otherwise, it is safe to conclude that though a certain population among the respondents disagree with their system functional coverage, yet a considerable set of respondents do embrace the current feature set positively leaving room for further improvements in the current invoicing systems. In Lithuania, most of the respondents (above 70%) neither agree nor disagree. Among respondents, only 20% accept the fact that their invoicing system does provide their expected functional coverage. Only 5% express their disagreements on the usefulness.

Perceived Risk. This was a "Yes, No, May be" type question about the e-invoicing user's perception of risk. There were more than 50% of 'May Be' answers which shows that users have a doubt or they simply do not know. It can be stated as they are not denying the fact that there can be risks related to e-invoicing solutions. Also, about 48% of users said that there are definite risks.

Perceived Trust. When taking the Baltic region in general, more than 50% of answers contain 'maybe' which means the users are not sure where they trust the e-invoicing solutions or not. But when we take the percentage of users who have said 'yes' which is about 40% to the above question, it means they trust e-invoicing solutions. A very few percentages of the users do not trust the e-invoicing systems and in Estonia this number is 0.

Perceived Information Security. More than 60% of the respondents from Latvia and Lithuania think that the e-invoicing system is fairly secure, while about 25% think there is good security. Almost none think either it is very poor or excellent in information security. A majority of Estonian respondents about 60% thinks that information security is good in e-invoicing systems and 27% of the respondents think information security in e-invoicing systems is just moderate. About 10% of the Estonian e-invoicing users think that the information security aspect is excellent in e-invoicing.

Automation Requirement on E-invoicing. 50% of the Estonian respondents would like to have fully automated systems while 50% of them would like to have nearly automated systems. In Latvia again similar to Estonia, 50% of the users would like fully automated systems, where 25% of them would like to have somewhat automated and 25% of them would like lower automated level in e-invoicing systems. In Lithuania, only 25% of the respondents would want to have a fully automated system, and about 39% of the respondents would like to have somewhat automated and 36% of the respondents like to have lower level of automated systems.

There may be various reasons that some users do not like fully automated systems. We think one of them is that they might be that the users think they will lose control over the systems.

4　Suggested e-Invoice Conceptual Ecosystem with AI and RPA

Based on the survey findings and a thorough analysis of the secondary data from literature we propose an eco-system. We see the eco-system as a conceptual view which can be taken for the further development. Suppliers, buyers, trading partners such as financial institutions and government institutions such as tax authorities are the entities that participate in the eco-system. In the diagram only one entity from each supplier, buyer etc. is depicted, but in reality, there are many contact points where many participants can join to the data exchange which is depicted with item 1 (Fig. 1).

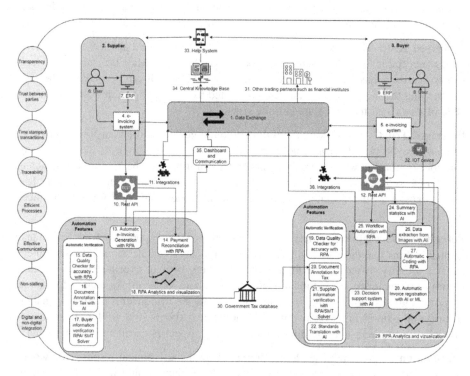

Fig. 1. Proposed ecosystem for e-invoicing.

The items 4, 6, 7 shows how a user from the supplier company is connected to their own ERP/accounting system and the e-invoicing system front end. The items 5, 9, 8 shows how a user from the buyer company is connected to their own ERP/accounting system and the e-invoicing system front-end. A user usually uses the ERP system but there are user interfaces in the e-invoicing system for e-invoicing process related tasks. These two systems are separated because not all the ERP systems have e-invoicing functions available and it is easy to maintain. Just the integration between the two systems is necessary. The e-invoicing system/systems of the users would be connected to the RPA, AI and other components with web services, which is depicted as the Rest API (item 10 and item 12).

With the item 11, 36 - integrations are capable of the e-invoicing systems to be integrated into other software or tools as the requirements arise. Also, these integrations can have transactions stored on the knowledgebase, also under the requirements of each company/ organization.

When describing the item 13-automatic e-invoice generation which is an RPA service, it includes getting necessary data from the ERP of the supplier. 56% of the e-invoice users said they would prefer to have this functionality in an e-invoicing system. RPA is suggested in this case because invoice generation is rule-based, matched with an order. Also, RPA can perform collecting data from different systems and generating one document which answers the problems of using different systems by the company. While the e-invoice is getting generated, the verification on the e-invoice can be done by the sub-module labelled as 'Automatic Verification'. This includes data quality checking with RPA (item 15), especially the syntaxes and semantics according to the required standard. Since different buyers can be using different standards as mentioned in the thematic analysis of this study. The rules for data quality checks should be identified before designing the functionality and could be enhanced with the usage. Another component of the automatic verification is document annotation for tax (item 16). The tax values can be calculated against the government tax database rules and this component should have a connection with the government tax database. The other component is buyer information verification (item 17), which could be done with a simple rule-based matching process with RPA or SMT solvers (Satisfiability Modulo Theories) which includes higher degree verifications [20].

The payment reconciliation of e-invoices (item 14) can be done by matching with payments received against an e-invoice. This is a simple rule-based process.

With RPA analytics and visualizations (item 18), there can be a dashboard of summary statistics of invoices, taxations, goods, buyer related information etc. During the study, 47% of the e-invoicing users stated that they would prefer to have this feature of summary statistics.

Item 26 which is data extraction from images with AI, this can include PDFs and other non-machine-readable formats. In an e-invoicing system, an image or a PDF is not counted as an e-invoice but there is some percentage of non-readable invoices still circulating in the Baltic region. AI is capable of training to read these invoices and convert them to an e-invoice until all the B2B invoices become fully electronic. This can have inputs from an IOT device where the users are out of office scenarios with the integration of item 32.

Summary statistics with AI (item 24) would help to show the buyer a condensed summary of very long invoices such as invoice for electricity in different locations of a huge retail chain. That in turn helps to make decisions without having to read the whole invoice.

Under the automatic verification module of the buyer's side, all the items except standards translation using AI (item 22) are the same as the supplier's automatic verification module. This will be the solution for significant standards related problems emerged in the study, where there is no proper standard to be used and different versions of the standards are being used by companies.

With AI, there is no requirement to have one proper standard for everyone, instead each standard can be analysed and translated into other standards as required.

Item 28 which is automatic invoice registration to the ERP or accounting system that can be based on AI or machine learning. It can be trained with the exceptions for each supplier etc. Also, this feature can include the invoice returning.

E-Invoicing workflow would be automated with RPA (item 25) as it is a rule-based process and this can be complemented with a decision support system with AI (item 23). The decision making can be either the decision to be taken by AI or the decision can be prompt to the user, so that the user can either go ahead or not in the workflow.

Automatic coding is simply another rule-based process which is automated with RPA where the accounting entries are made to the ERP or accounting system. As same as item 18 in the supplier's side, item 29 is RPA analytics and visualization for the buyer concerning all the e-invoices which were again a required feature to make informed decisions.

Dashboard and communication (item 35) would be a common functionality which is integrated into the whole ecosystem to solve the problem of visibility. This is an inefficiency mentioned by many experts during the study that buyers, sellers and e-invoicing operators do not know the status of an e-invoice or the ability to send e-invoices across the Baltic region.

The help system (item 33) which will be connected to a central knowledge base (item 34) is the presence of a chatbot to enhance the communication between trade partners. The main reason it being different from the dashboard is that the dashboard is a dynamic information display related to e-invoices, where the help system is capable of answering queries on trade-related matters. It was brought up by an expert during the interviews that the communication between trade partners regarding e-invoicing capabilities is very hard. As an example, a supplier can ask the help system to retrieve the agreements that need to be re-evaluated at the end of a period. The help system ought to be designed in a way that each participant has their limitations of accessing information.

4.1 Future Work and Limitations

The next stage of this research is to conduct a feasibility study of the proposed ecosystem for the Baltic region. Then it can be prototyped and tested paving the way for a real implementation if the tests bring positive results. It can also be the whole ecosystem or a part of it, which we think to be implemented step by step.

There were some limitations of the research such as the information collected through the survey and interviews may not be representing every e-invoicing user and expert in the Baltics. The data is generalized. Qualitative data gathering and analysis is limitless, where in this study it is limited to 6 interviews and only the data which needs to answer the research questions are studied. For more insights, views of ERP Partners and other integrated systems and stakeholders on e-invoicing can be considered in future work.

5 Conclusion

The study concludes that, in the Baltic region there are inefficiencies in e-invoicing systems and there is room for improvement. With respect our main research question, it can be emphasized that most of the inefficiencies are operational followed by technical and information security related problems. The perceptions of users regarding e-invoicing systems are moderate or fairly positive. Among the three countries, perceptions of Estonian users are generally more positive than Latvian and Lithuanian users. There is potential to use AI and RPA technologies in e-invoicing to minimize identified inefficiencies and introduce more automation to the e-invoicing systems. This benefits to increase the positivity of user perceptions related to all the angles considered in the study. Based on the results of the research, the guidelines and recommendation can be made to increase the efficiency of workflows to bring higher level automatization into existing e-invoice work routines. Consequently, the suggested eco-system can be researched further in the Baltic region as the next step.

References

1. Directive 2014/55/EU of the European Parliament and of the Council of 16 April 2014 on electronic invoicing in public procurement (Text with EEA relevance), https://eur-lex.europa.eu/legal-content/EN/TXT/HTML/?uri=CELEX:32014L0055&from=EN.   Accessed 13 Apr 2020
2. Salmony, M., Harald, B.: E-invoicing in Europe: now and the future. J. Payments Strategy Syst. **4**(4), 371–380 (2010)
3. e-Estonia State of the Future. https://e-estonia.com/e-estonia-state-of-the-future/. Accessed 04 May 2020
4. European Commission – Priorities. https://ec.europa.eu/info/strategy/priorities-2019-2024_en. Accessed 13 Apr 2020
5. Poissonnier, A.: The Baltics: three countries, one economy. European Economy Economic Brief 24 (2017)
6. Pappel, I., Pappel, I., Tampere, T., Draheim, D.: Implementation of e-invoicing principles in Estonian local governments. In: The Proceedings of 17th European Conference on Digital Government, ECDG 2017, p. 127 (2017)
7. Koch, B.: E-Invoicing/E-Billing Significant Market Transition Lies Ahead. https://www.billentis.com/einvoicing_ebilling_market_report_2017.pdf. Accessed 13 Apr 2020

8. Mendling, J., Decker, G., Hull, R., Reijers, H.A., Weber, I.: How do machine learning, robotic process automation, and blockchains affect the human factor in business process management? Commun. Assoc. Inf. Syst. **43**(1), 19 (2018)
9. Daniels, J., Sargolzaei, S., Sargolzaei, A., Ahram, T., Laplante, P.A., Amaba, B.: The internet of things, artificial intelligence, blockchain, and professionalism. IT Prof. **20**(6), 15–19 (2018)
10. Koch,B.: The Einvoicing Journey 2019–2025. https://www.billentis.com/The_einvoicing_journey_2019-2025.pdf. Accessed 13 Apr 2020
11. Pappel, I., Tsap, V., Draheim, D.: The e-LocGov model for introducing e-governance into local governments: an estonian case study. IEEE Trans. Emerg. Top. Comput. (2020). https://doi.org/10.1109/TETC.2019.2910199
12. Madakam, S., Holmukhe, R.M., Jaiswal, D.K.: The future digital work force: robotic process automation (RPA). JISTEM J. Inf. Syst. Technol. Manage. **16** (2019)
13. Simionescu, V.: The impact of artificial and cognitive intelligence on Romanian public procurement. Revista Economica **68**(6) (2016)
14. Lian, J.W.: Critical factors for cloud based e-invoice service adoption in Taiwan: an empirical study. Int. J. Inf. Manage. **35**(1), 98–109 (2015)
15. Davis, F.D.: Perceived usefulness, perceived ease of use, and user acceptance of information technology. MIS Q. 319–340 (1989)
16. Pavlou, P.A., Gefen, D.: Building effective online marketplaces with institution-based trust. Inf. Syst. Res. **15**(1), 37–59 (2014)
17. Hernandez-Ortega, B., Jimenez-Martinez, J.: Performance of e-invoicing in Spanish firms. IseB **11**(3), 457–480 (2013)
18. Bélanger, F., Carter, L.: Trust and risk in e-government adoption. J. Strateg. Inf. Syst. **17**(2), 165–176 (2008)
19. Chen, T.Y., Chang, H.S.: Reducing consumers' perceived risk through banking service quality cues in Taiwan. J. Bus. Psychol. **19**(4), 521–540 (2005)
20. Calvi, A., Ranise, S., Vigano, L.: Automated validation of security-sensitive web services specified in BPEL and RBAC. In: 12th International Symposium on Symbolic and Numeric Algorithms for Scientific Computing, pp. 456–464. IEEE (2010)
21. Tepandi, J.: The data quality framework for the Estonian public sector and its evaluation: establishing a systematic process-oriented viewpoint on cross-organizational data quality. In: Hameurlain, A., et al. (eds.) Transactions on Large-Scale Data- and Knowledge-Centered Systems XXXV. LNCS, vol. 10680, pp. 1–26. Springer, Heidelberg (2017). https://doi.org/10.1007/978-3-662-56121-8_1
22. Pappel, I.; Pappel, I.: Methodology for measuring the digital capability of local governments. In: 5th International Conference on Theory and Practice of Electronic Governance, Tallinn, Estonia, 26–28 September 2011, pp. 357–358. ACM (2011)

eIDAS Implementation Challenges:
The Case of Estonia and the Netherlands

Silvia Lips[1]([⊠])(iD), Nitesh Bharosa[2](iD), and Dirk Draheim[1](iD)

[1] Tallinn University of Technology, Ehitajate tee 5, 19086 Tallinn, Estonia
{Silvia.lips,dirk.draheim}@taltech.ee
[2] Delft University of Technology, Postbus5, 2600 AA Delft, The Netherlands
n.bharosa@tudelft.nl

Abstract. Solid eID (electronic identification) infrastructures form the backbone of today's digital transformation. In June 2014, the European Commission adopted the eIDAS regulation (electronic identification and trust services for electronic transactions in the internal market) as a major initiative towards EU-wide eID interoperability; which receives massive attention in all EU member states in recent years. As a joint effort of Estonia and the Netherlands, this study provides a comparative case study on eIDAS implementation practices of the two countries. The aim was to analyze eIDAS implementation challenges of the two countries and to propose a variety of possible solutions to overcome them. During an action learning workshop in November 2019, key experts from Estonia and the Netherlands identified eIDAS implementation challenges and proposed possible solutions to the problems from the policy maker, the service provider and the user perspective. As a result, we identified five themes of common challenges: compliance issues, interpretation problems, different practices in member states, cooperation and collaboration barriers, and representation of legal persons. Proposed solutions do not only involve changes in the eIDAS regulation, but different actions to develop an eIDAS framework and to improve cross-border service provision - which has recently become an important topic among member states. Eventually, the study provides practical input to the ongoing eIDAS review process and can help member states to overcome eIDAS implementation challenges.

Keywords: eIDAS · Electronic authentication · Electronic identity · Implementation challenges · Identity management

1 Introduction

Digital transformation of countries offers many opportunities, but at the same time reduces control over their operating environment [1]. More and more, public and private sector organisations offer their services online and across borders. To access these e-services, implementation of an accurate and reliable digital authentication procedure together with a digital signature option is essential [2, 3].

© Springer Nature Switzerland AG 2020
A. Chugunov et al. (Eds.): EGOSE 2020, CCIS 1349, pp. 75–89, 2020.
https://doi.org/10.1007/978-3-030-67238-6_6

In July 2014, the European Commission (EC) adopted regulation No 910/2014 [4] on electronic identification and trust services for electronic transactions in the internal market (eIDAS) to enable a secure and seamless electronic data exchange and inter-action of public and private entities and users, not only inside the member states, but also across the European Union (EU). This initiative is part of the EU Digital Single Market strategy [5] and mandatory for all EU member states since September 2018 [4].

The implementation of the eIDAS regulation and its first years of implementation have raised many practical questions and revealed various research gaps. According to the eIDAS regulation Article 49, the EC shall review the regulation by 01.07.2020 latest to evaluate whether the regulation needs to be modified [4]. The EC has already initiated a feedback collection process among its member states. In parallel with the ongoing eIDAS implementation actions, EC progressed further and adopted in October 2018 SDGR regulation, which established a single digital gateway to provide access to information, procedures and for assistance and problem-solving services, also known as the SDGR regulation [6]. The aim of this regulation is to simplify access to cross-border administrative services for citizens and companies [7]. One pre-condition for the SDGR implementation is successful and smooth eIDAS implementation in the member states. Therefore, it is now the perfect time to analyze the implementation practices of different EU countries and to provide relevant feedback to the ongoing evaluation process.

We decided to research the practices of Estonia and the Netherlands. Both of the countries have stable and functional e-government, but at the same time, they have different e-governance models and approaches to the eIDAS implementation [8].

The aim of this research paper is to analyze eIDAS implementation challenges of Estonia and the Netherlands and to propose a variety of possible solutions to overcome them. The research objectives are therefore to:

1) Identify the challenges Estonia and the Netherlands faced during the implementa-tion of eIDAS from the user's, the service provider's and the policy maker's per-spective; and
2) Recommend possible solutions to overcoming identified challenges.

We use a comparative case study research approach [9] together with action learning methodology [10] to analyse above-mentioned research questions.

The paper is organized as follows. Section 2 provides background information about the current eIDAS implementation situation in Estonia and the Netherlands and an overview of important related literature. Section 3 presents the research design and gives insight into the used theoretical framework. Section 4 sums up research findings from the policy maker, service provider and user perspective. In Sect. 5, we discuss the research results and make recommendations to the eIDAS review process. Section 6 provides an insight to the future research perspective followed by Sect. 7 that con-cludes the study.

2   Background

In this section, we provide a brief overview of existing literature on eIDAS implementation. In addition, to understand the results of this paper, it is important to introduce shortly the eIDAS implementation state and situation in Estonia and the Netherlands.

2.1   eIDAS Implementation in the EU from the Literature Perspective

The eIDAS regulation has been in force for more than five years, of which it has been actively implemented and used over the past two years. According to the regulation itself, voluntary recognition of electronic identities were possible since September 2015, rules for trust service providers had to be adopted by July 2016 and cross-border recognition of electronic identities was enabled by September 2018 [5]. First countries notified their eID schemes[1] under eIDAS already in 2017 (Germany) and 2018 (Estonia, Spain, Croatia, Belgium etc.). The implementation process itself is complex and time-consuming. Figure 1 illustrates the steps that member states have to pass to notify their eID schemes.

Fig. 1. eID scheme notification process.

From a research perspective, the topic is quite new; and, so far, it has been handled rather from the angle of a specific country or sector. For example, several studies focus on the academic sector, e.g., on how to build eIDAS-based cross-border services in the education and to enable secure and seamless interaction between different parties [11–15]. The focus is mainly on solving the practical problems: how to transport new data attributes through eIDAS infrastructure solutions [11, 13], how to implement eIDAS-based academic services and create secure connections between academic services and the national eIDAS node [12, 13]. Some studies are even more specific and concentrate on a part of an eIDAS node that member states have to modify independently [14].

Several studies focus on eIDAS implementation challenges in a particular country [16–18]. In case of United Kingdom (UK), it is questionable if the country should notify their eID scheme and does the existing system complies with the eIDAS privacy and data protection requirements [17]. Pelikánová, Cvik and MacGregor analyze and

---

[1] According to eIDAS, an eID scheme is a system for electronic identification under which electronic identification means are issued to natural or legal persons (or to natural persons representing legal persons).

evaluate the eIDAS adoption in the Czech public sector bodies and compare the results with some other EU member states practice. Their research results show a lot of hesitation and passivity in the Czech public sector while adopting eIDAS requirements [18].

Other research projects focus more on different aspects of the regulation, such as security, privacy [19, 20] and data protection issues [21]. From the data protection perspective, Tsakalakis, Stalla-Bourdillon and O'Hara argue that technical architecture of an eID scheme affects the level of data protection. They propose that the use of pseudonyms and selective disclosure help to fulfill the data minimization and purpose limitation principles [21]. Only few studies analyze different identification and trust services compatible with the eIDAS regulation in wider context and do not focus on a particular member state [22].

While conducting the literature overview it became clear that many of the studies focus on specific sectors or solve very concrete data exchange or integration issues in the eIDAS context. We did not find pan-European studies addressing eIDAS implementation practices in various member states with proposals to improve the current environment. Therefore, our research aims to fill this significant research gap and to provide recommendations for the further eIDAS review process.

2.2   Estonia

Estonia has implemented eIDAS according to the EC timetable and notified its eID scheme on assurance level "high" in November 2018. The notification consisted of six different eID tokens: ID-card, residence permit card, digital identity card, e-residency digital identity card, mobile-ID and diplomatic identity card.[2]

The Estonian eID management is based on tight public-private cooperation. Public sector authorities are responsible for personal identification, identity management, eID infrastructure management and supervisory activities. Private sector organization offers eID tokens as well as personalization and trust services [23]. In December 2018, Estonia changed the eID token manufacturer and since then, has issued the fourth generation electronic of identity cards [24].

All previously mentioned electronic identities are in active use and the public acceptance of the eID is high [25, 26]. According to the latest statistics from March 2020, there are more than 1,35 million eID cards and around 234 000 mobile-ID´s issued by the public sector. In February 2020, the total amount of transactions related to eID´s exceeded 37 million.[3]

---

[2] Estonian eID scheme notified under eIDAS, https://ec.europa.eu/cefdigital/wiki/display/EIDCOM-MUNITY/Estonia.

[3] Estonian eID statistics, https://www.id.ee/?lang=en&id=.

In addition to the public sector eID tokens, the local trust service provider SK ID Solutions AS issues QSCD (Qualified Signature Creation Device) certified Smart-ID for authentication and signing purposes.[4] More than 500 000 users also actively use this solution.[5]

2.3   The Netherlands

In 2019, the Netherlands notified its electronic identification trust framework for businesses, also known as eHerkenning, on the assurance levels "substantial" and "high".[6] There are several authentication service providers in the country (i.e., Connectis, Digidentity, KPN, QuoVadis, Reconi, and Unified Post).[7]

In December 2019, the Netherlands pre-notified another authentication service named "DigiD. This solution enables authentication of natural persons in relation with the governmental authorities and organizations that perform public tasks. Logius, an organization operating in the governing area of the Dutch Ministry of the Interior and Kingdom Relations, manages and maintains the DigiD in the Netherlands [27].

Around 80% (14 million people) of the Dutch population use the service. More than 650 service providers are connected to the DigiD service. According to the statistics, DigiD service processes over 300 million authentication requests per year.[8]

The Netherlands is currently working towards the next generation DigiD solution called "DigiD hoog". The solution will be more secure and will base on the Dutch identity card and driving license information [27]. The Netherlands also tries to integrate biometrical features into their national authentication scheme.

3   Research Design

In this research, we conduct a comparative case study on eIDAS implementation in the Netherlands and Estonia. For this purpose, we gathered an expert team and used action learning [10, 28] to compare the eIDAS implementation challenges of Estonia and the Netherlands and to find possible solutions to identified problems. Action learning [10, 28] is particularly well suited to research complex phenomena such as eIDAS [29].

One of the alternative research designs was a world café approach [30], but as the focus of this particular method is more on generating broader range of perspectives than to find answers, we found action learning more appropriate for, this study.

---

[4] Smart-ID's recognition as Qualified Signature Creation Device (QSCD), https://www.smart-id.com/e-service-providers/smart-id-as-a-qscd/.

[5] Estonian eID statistics, https://www.id.ee/?lang=en&id=.

[6] The Netherlands (DTF/eHerkenning) eID scheme notified under eIDAS, https://ec.europa.eu/cefdigital/wiki/pages/viewpage.action?pageId=74091935.

[7] Dutch Trust framework for Electronic Identification, https://ec.europa.eu/cefdigital/wiki/pages/viewpage.action?pageId=74091935.

[8] The Netherlands (DigiD) scheme pre-notified under eIDAS, https://ec.europa.eu/cefdigital/wiki/pages/viewpage.action?pageId=176620999.

The research relies on an international collaboration between researchers, public and private sector experts from the Netherlands and Estonia. The Netherland authority Digicampus[9] coordinated and facilitated the cooperation. The Digicampus is an innovation hub that connects science, government, market players and citizens/users to shape future public services. Figure 2 illustrates action-learning-based collaboration between the Netherlands and Estonia [28].

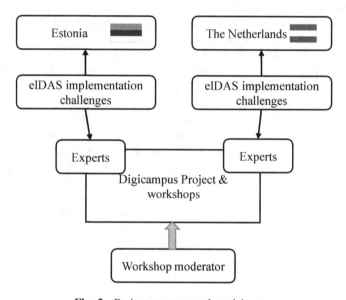

Fig. 2. Project structure and participants.

As a result of the cooperation, two expert workshop sessions on (i) eIDAS implementation challenges and (ii) in service of finding possible solutions have been held at Tallinn University of Technology, Estonia, from November 18 to 21, 2019. Nine experts from Estonia and 14 experts from the Netherlands have been involved. Table 1 provides a detailed overview of the participants and their roles.

During the workshop sessions, we divided all participants into three groups presenting policy makers, the private sector and users. All groups consisted of participants from both countries. The first workshop took place on 19.11.2020, where experts shared their practical experience and challenges with the eIDAS implementation.

On the next day, the same groups continued working together and tried to find solutions to these challenges. After group work on both days, each group presented its result and the other groups had an opportunity to supplement it.

---

[9] Digicampus homepage, https://www.dedigicampus.nl/.

Table 1. Project structure and participants.

Estonia		The Netherlands	
Organization	Role	Organization	Role
Information System Authority	Head of eID department	Ministry of the Interior and Kingdom Relations	Policy officer (digital government)
	Product owner (eIDAS cross-border usage)		Senior advisor (member of the Dutch eIDAS team)
Police and Border Guard Board	Adviser-expert (eIDAS implementation, auditing)		eHerkenning project manager
	Chief-expert (eIDAS SPOC)		Strategic advisor
Ministry of Economic Affairs and Communications	Adviser (SDG national coordination)	Municipality of Den Haag	Advisor (digital transformation)
SK ID Solutions AS	Lawyer (trust services, eIDAS, ETSI EN standards, national law)		Product owner (digitalization and authentication)
TalTech	Full Professor of Information Systems (e-governance and technologies)	TU Delft	Senior researcher Master students (2)
		Agentschap Telecom	Supervision of eIDs
		ICTU	Sr advisor Program manager
	Researcher (eIDAS framework)	Netherlands Enterprise Agency	Product owner (International Access)
	Researcher (public acceptance of eID)	Private sector representatives	Four persons

4 Findings

In this section, we present our research findings from three different perspectives: policy maker, service provider and user perspective. We focus mainly on the eIDAS implementation problematics and do not reflect the discussions regarding other relevant topics more or less related to eIDAS, like applicability of the once-only principle (OOP) [31] or the implementation of the SDGR regulation.

4.1 Challenges and Solutions from the Policy Maker Perspective

From the policy maker perspective, we identified challenges related to the following issues: *implementation, (national) legislation, interpretation, compliance and communication.*

A crucial eIDAS implementation barrier is the lack of the EU common identifier. It is still not possible to use national eIDs and digital signatures for EU services. Particularly problematic is when users would like to act on behalf of others despite of sufficient legal grounds. The experts found that it is important to find a workaround or initiate further discussions on the EU common identifier to overcome this barrier. These challenges concern both natural and legal persons; and the topic should be added to the further research agenda.

The experts found that slight differences in the national laws complicate the uniform eIDAS implementation process in the EU. For example, according to the national laws, the actions that minors are allowed to perform varies from country to country. This affects, in particular, the establishment of cross-border services.

From the legal person's perspective, eIDAS allows for company eIDs without persons attached to it. This raises several practical questions. For instance, how to make it possible that a person is allowed to act on behalf of a company? How to use a legal person eID across borders? It is important to define all the issues related to legal persons separately and provide feedback to the eIDAS review process.

Representatives of the policy maker group considered interpretation of the eIDAS regulation as a crucial challenge. For example, Article 6 (that regulates mutual recognition of eIDs) is ambiguous. In addition, it is not clear how to map existing technologies to eIDAS assurance levels and how to assess their risks.

The experts identified the following shortcomings at the level of compliancy:

- not all member states offer eID;
- lack of supervision;
- the EC executes its supervisory role only weakly;
- the member states do not always accept each other's eIDs (e.g. Germany/Estonia);
- it lacks a framework for conformity assessment on the EU-level;
- There are no common rules for supervisory bodies.

The creation of assessment guidelines for auditors would help significantly to overcome the previously identified issues. Another solution that experts considered was the integration of ethical hacking into the eIDAS framework in order to improve existing requirements.

Finally, the experts agreed that the current SDG (Single Digital Gateway) program should have a stronger link to the eIDAS regulation and implementation activities. They also noted, that communication activities (i.e., why it is important to implement eIDAS) from the EU side should be improved.

4.2   Challenges and Solutions from the Service Provider Perspective

From the service provider perspective, we identified challenges related to the following issues: *collaboration, compliancy, reputation, change management, notification and record matching.*

The experts found a crucial challenge that lies on a co-operational level. It is not clear how to combine different competences in case of incidents (problem ownership issue). Applying EU wide user testing and meta-research on the cross-border collaboration level would help to solve this issue.

There exist no common rules for service providers on how to comply with the eIDAS regulation. Service providers are unsure, how to test their systems, i.e. how to understand whether their systems are compliant or not. Therefore, a standardized test framework with test data would be very helpful (e.g., a standard backward-compatible API).

Different change management issues complicate the eIDAS implementation process. It is not easy to keep up with changing standards and regulations. Often, changes are unpredictable and require remarkable additional investments. Misinterpretation of requirements can cause unnecessary additional work and costs. The experts found that eIDAS could be provided as a service for all public and private authorities (e.g. "spin a node and go"). Exploiting the World Wide Web Consortium (W3C), decentralized identifier (DiD) as a unique identifier (UiD) seems promising, but needs further in-depth research.

The eIDAS regulation provides no guidelines and standards for unique identifiers of persons (i.e., mandatory vs. free attributes, registration of foreign identities, tracking etc.). There is also lack of a common architecture API platform. The experts found that use of decentralized identifiers and identity linking would help to overcome the previously identified issues.

Notification of private sector solutions is a complex topic. Private sector service providers has no access to the data in the scope of the eIDAS regulation. However, fully automated and cross-border services need person related data. In this case, a common understanding of trust and privacy models plays an important role.

The experts found, that reputation is also an important topic, dependent on the reputation of all participants acting inside the eIDAS framework. The eIDAS framework is based on trust, but the meaning of *trust* differs in different cultures.

4.3   Challenges and Solutions from User Perspective

The user perspective covers a variety of challenges starting from usability to security and privacy concerns.

Accessibility and user experience (UX) of cross-border services needs improvement through additional guidelines, templates, examples, UX tests, experience and sharing of best practices. The same service may have a completely different user experience in different countries. This makes it difficult to find the right services abroad. In this case, standardized service portals that direct people to the right place, would be helpful. The experts also discussed language support and semantics problems that can be overcome by organizing learning courses and by describing step-by-step use cases.

From the security perspective, users have to understand whether they are using qualified services to avoid possible "man in the middle" attacks. Security awareness can be increased by developing guidelines, templates, sharing best practices and educating users continuously.

There is also a need for a governance framework and clear role division, as users often do not know whom to contact in case of technical error, usability problems or other relevant questions.

The experts discussed how to avoid errors and how to deal with service continuity when certificates become invalid. A would help solving this issue.

Finally, the experts found the current cross-border roles and mandates are insufficient. For example, users are unable to act on behalf of a legal person that they represent. From that perspective, the experts suggested that the scope of eIDAS regulation should contain the procedures related to the legal persons. They also proposed introduction of an EU common identifier.

5 Discussion and Recommendations

Based on our research results, it is clear that eIDAS implementation process is challenging from various perspectives. Policy makers, service providers and users have different expectations and needs. Based on the workshop results, where experts offered solutions to the eIDAS implementation challenges, we identified five main themes that all groups mentioned during the workshops in one or another way. These five common challenges are:

- compliance issues;
- interpretation problems;
- different practices in member states;
- co-operation and collaboration barriers;
- legal persons and their representation.

Compliance issues include insufficient guidelines (and supervision) for public service providers, private sector service providers and conformity assessment bodies. In this situation, parties start to interpret the requirements according to their practice; and this leads to the problem of different interpretations, starting from the usage of terminology to system usability issues. All identified challenges create additional communication and collaboration barriers between service providers and users as well as between EU member states.

Another interesting finding from the workshops is that most of the challenges are related with cross-border service provision rather than eIDAS implementation inside countries. Existing rules and requirements support the implementation of eIDAS inside member states, but are not sufficient to support the EU-wide implementation.

Table 2 provides detailed summary of eIDAS implementation related challenges and solutions from all three perspectives.

During the workshop, the experts discussed various options to overcome existing challenges and improve the eIDAS implementation process. Therefore, European Commission could consider the following proposals in the upcoming eIDAS review process:

- options to implement a common EU identifier;
- regulate the identification of users so that they can act on behalf of others when legally required;
- specify the regulation with respect to legal persons;
- clarify the terminology of the eIDAS regulation;

Table 2. Summary of eIDAS related challenges and solutions.

	Category	Challenges	Solutions
Policy maker	Implementation	No EU wide identifier	Workaround
		Acting on behalf of others	Workaround
		National eIDs/digital signatures are not usable for EU services	Initiating further discussions on the EU common identifier
	Legislation	Different legal practices in Member States	Creation of assessment guidelines for auditors
	Interpretation	Differences in the interpretation of the eIDAS articles	Creation of assessment guidelines for auditors
	Compliance	Different shortcomings	Creation of assessment guidelines for auditors
	Communication	eIDAS implementation importance	Communication plan
Service provider	Collaboration	Problem ownership issue	EU wide user testing
			Meta-research on the cross-border collaboration
	Compliancy	Compliancy of service providers	Standardized test framework with test data
	Change management	Changing regulations, standards	eIDAS provided as a service
	Notification	Notification of private sector solutions	Common understanding of trust and privacy models
	Record matching	No standards for unique identifiers/lack of common architecture	Common architecture API platform
			Use of decentralized identifiers Identity linking
User	Usability	UI consistence usage	Additional guidelines, templates, examples, UX testing, experience and sharing of best practices
		Accessibility to e-services	
		Different countries have different practices	Standardized service portals
	Helpdesk/ Support	User support in case of errors	Clear role division
		Language support and semantics	Courses, step-by-step use cases
	Security	Possible "Man in the middle" issue	Guidelines, templates, sharing best practices, user education
		"Dirty error" issue when certificates are invalid	Central monitoring service

- clarify often misinterpreted articles in the eIDAS regulation;
- develop common assessment guidelines for auditors;
- develop a standardized testing framework;
- provide eIDAS as a service;
- create a common monitoring system for cross-border transactions;
- develop a framework of standards for cross-border services.

Not all of these proposals and activities presume changes in the eIDAS regulation. Many of these initiatives require further discussion between the member states and more detailed analysis by the responsible organizations.

6 Future Directions

Current research is a part of a larger research project regarding the eIDAS, which aims to improve its compliancy assessment model. To develop this model we analyze and compare the eID schemes of different member states and their eIDAS implementation practice.

During this particular research, we identified various topics and questions that need further in-depth research and analysis. For example: requirements and preconditions for the application of a common EU identifier; creation of assessment guidelines for auditors, implementation of EU wide user-testing environment; cross-border service provision; collaboration between public service providers and private sector service providers. These topics will address in the scope of further research actions.

We hope that the outcome of the whole study is a valuable tool for the public and private sector eID service providers and auditors enabling more transparent and comparable assessment of different eID schemes. Moreover, our research results will be the basis for the further universal applicability analysis of the eIDAS principles while implementing SDGR regulation and establishing secure e-service provision between EU and third countries.

7 Conclusion and Research Limitations

This study showed that different EU member states have faced similar problems in the eIDAS implementation process and that it is important to exchange practical experiences at the expert level.

From the limitations point of view, it is not possible to compile a complete list of challenges based on the experience of just two countries. Additionally, offered solutions and recommendations reflect the knowledge and experience of the experts who participated in the workshops. It means that there can be other alternative ways to overcome the identified challenges. However, we are convinced that the results indicate to major shortcomings and practical problems that member states face during an eIDAS implementation.

Based on our research results, it is possible to say that the focus of the member states (with respect to the implementation of eIDAS and in light of the SDGR regulation) has clearly shifted from a national level to a cross-border perspective. However, before taking this next step in terms of cross-border service integration it is important to ensure stable and interoperable network of eIDs.

We identified five challenging areas (compliance issues, interpretation problems, different practices in member states, co-operation and collaboration barriers, legal persons and their representation) in the eIDAS implementation process, which will inevitably affect the implementation of other related regulations.

This new situation requires a review of the existing EU eIDAS framework and procedures by the European Commission. Our study provides practical input to the eIDAS review process by identifying common challenges of the member states and making proposals to overcome them.

References

1. Vial, G.: Understanding digital transformation: a review and a research agenda. J. Strateg. Inf. Syst. **28**(2), 118–144 (2019)
2. Khatchatourov, A., Laurent, M., Levallois-Barth, C.: Privacy in digital identity systems: models, assessment, and user adoption. In: Tambouris, E., et al. (eds.) EGOV 2015. LNCS, vol. 9248, pp. 273–290. Springer, Cham (2015). https://doi.org/10.1007/978-3-319-22479-4_21
3. Pappel, I., Pappel, I., Tepandi, J., Draheim, D.: Systematic digital signing in estonian e-government processes. In: Hameurlain, A., Küng, J., Wagner, R., Dang, T.K., Thoai, N. (eds.) Transactions on Large-Scale Data- and Knowledge-Centered Systems XXXVI. LNCS, vol. 10720, pp. 31–51. Springer, Heidelberg (2017). https://doi.org/10.1007/978-3-662-56266-6_2
4. European Parliament and Council: EU Parliament and Council regulation (EU) No 910/2014 on electronic identification and trust services for electronic transactions in the internal market and repealing directive 1999/93/EC (2014)
5. The European Parliament: EU Parliament Resolution. Towards a Digital Single Market Act (2015/2147(INI) (2016)
6. European Parliament and Council: EU Parliament and Council Regulation (EU) No 2018/1724 establishing a single digital gateway to provide access to information, to procedures and to assistance and problem-solving services and amending Regulation (EU) No 1024/2012 (2018)
7. Bhattarai, R., Pappel, I., Vainsalu, H., Yahia, S.B., Draheim, D.: The impact of the single digital gateway regulation from the citizens' perspective. Procedia Comput. Sci. **164**, 159–167 (2019)
8. Bharosa, N., Lips, S., Draheim, D.: Making e-government work: learning from the Netherlands and Estonia. In: Hofmann, S., Csáki, C., Edelmann, N., Lampoltshammer, T., Melin, U., Parycek, P., Schwabe, G., Tambouris, E. (eds.) ePart 2020. LNCS, vol. 12220, pp. 41–53. Springer, Cham (2020). https://doi.org/10.1007/978-3-030-58141-1_4
9. Yin, R.K.: Applications of Case Study Research. Sage, Thousand Oaks (2011)
10. Revans, R.W.: ABC of Action Learning. Gower Publishing, Ltd., Farnham (2011)
11. Berbecaru, D., Lioy, A., Cameroni, C.: Electronic identification for universities: building cross-border services based on the eIDAS infrastructure. Information **10**(6), 210 (2019)

12. Maliappis, M., Gerakos, K., Costopoulou, C., Ntaliani, M.: Authenticated academic services through eIDAS. Int. J. Electron. Gov. **11**(3/4), 386 (2019)
13. Klobučar, T.: Improving cross-border educational services with eIDAS. In: Rocha, Á., Adeli, H., Reis, L.P., Costanzo, S. (eds.) WorldCIST'19 2019. AISC, vol. 931, pp. 932–938. Springer, Cham (2019). https://doi.org/10.1007/978-3-030-16184-2_88
14. Berbecaru, D., Lioy, A., Cameroni, C.: Providing digital identity and academic attributes through European eID infrastructures: results achieved, limitations, and future steps. Softw. Pract. Exp. **49**(11), 1643–1662 (2019)
15. Gerakos, K., Maliappis, M., Costopoulou, C., Ntaliani, M.: Electronic authentication for university transactions using eIDAS. In: Katsikas, S.K., Zorkadis, V. (eds.) e-Democracy 2017. CCIS, vol. 792, pp. 187–195. Springer, Cham (2017). https://doi.org/10.1007/978-3-319-71117-1_13
16. Vogt, T.: Die neue eIDAS-verordnung – chance und herausforderung für die öffentliche verwaltung in deutschland. Inf. Wissenschaft Praxis **67**(1), 61–68 (2016)
17. Tsakalakis, N., OHara, K., Stalla-Bourdillon, S.: Identity assurance in the UK. In: Proceedings of WebSci 16 - The 8th ACM Conference on Web Science. ACM Press (2016)
18. Pelikánová, R.M., Cvik, E.D., MacGregor, R.: Qualified electronic signature – eIDAS striking czech public sector bodies. Acta Universitatis Agriculturae et Silviculturae Mendelianae Brunensis **67**(6), 1551–1560 (2019)
19. Engelbertz, N., Erinola, N., Herring, D., Somorovsky, J., Mladenov, V., Schwenk, J.: Security analysis of eidas – the cross-country authentication scheme in europe. In: 12th USENIX Workshop on Offensive Technologies (WOOT 2018). USENIX Association, Baltimore, MD, August 2018
20. Kutyłowski, M., Hanzlik, L., Kluczniak, K.: Pseudonymous signature on eIDAS token – implementation based privacy threats. In: Liu, J.K., Steinfeld, R. (eds.) ACISP 2016. LNCS, vol. 9723, pp. 467–477. Springer, Cham (2016). https://doi.org/10.1007/978-3-319-40367-0_31
21. Tsakalakis, N., Stalla-Bourdillon, S., O'Hara, K.: Data protection by design for cross-border electronic identification: does the eIDAS interoperability framework need to be modernised? In: Kosta, E., Pierson, J., Slamanig, D., Fischer-Hübner, S., Krenn, S. (eds.) Privacy and Identity 2018. IAICT, vol. 547, pp. 255–274. Springer, Cham (2019). https://doi.org/10.1007/978-3-030-16744-8_17
22. Mocanu, S., Chiriac, A.M., Popa, C., Dobrescu, R., Saru, D.: Identification and trust techniques compatible with eIDAS regulation. In: Li, J., Liu, Z., Peng, H. (eds.) SPNCE 2019. LNICST, vol. 284, pp. 656–665. Springer, Cham (2019). https://doi.org/10.1007/978-3-030-21373-2_55
23. Lips, S., Pappel, I., Tsap, V., Draheim, D.: Key factors in coping with large-scale security vulnerabilities in the eID field. In: Kő, A., Francesconi, E. (eds.) EGOVIS 2018. LNCS, vol. 11032, pp. 60–70. Springer, Cham (2018). https://doi.org/10.1007/978-3-319-98349-3_5
24. Lips, S., Aas, K., Pappel, I., Draheim, D.: Designing an effective long-term identity management strategy for a mature e-state. In: Kő, A., Francesconi, E., Anderst-Kotsis, G., Tjoa, A.M., Khalil, I. (eds.) EGOVIS 2019. LNCS, vol. 11709, pp. 221–234. Springer, Cham (2019). https://doi.org/10.1007/978-3-030-27523-5_16
25. Tsap, V., Pappel, I., Draheim, D.: Factors affecting e-ID public acceptance: a literature review. In: Kő, A., Francesconi, E., Anderst-Kotsis, G., Tjoa, A.M., Khalil, I. (eds.) EGOVIS 2019. LNCS, vol. 11709, pp. 176–188. Springer, Cham (2019). https://doi.org/10.1007/978-3-030-27523-5_13

26. Tsap, V., Pappel, I., Draheim, D.: Key success factors in introducing national e-identification systems. In: Dang, T.K., Wagner, R., Küng, J., Thoai, N., Takizawa, M., Neuhold, E.J. (eds.) FDSE 2017. LNCS, vol. 10646, pp. 455–471. Springer, Cham (2017). https://doi.org/10.1007/978-3-319-70004-5_33

27. Roelofs, F.: Analysis and comparison of identification and authentication systems under the eIDAS regulation. Master's thesis, Radboud University, the Netherlands (2019)

28. Pedler, M.: Action Learning in Practice. Gower Publishing, Farnham (2011)

29. Zuber-Skerritt, O.: Action learning and action research: paradigm, praxis and programs. In: Effective Change Management Through Action Research and Action Learning: Concepts, Perspectives, Processes and Applications, vol. 1, p. 20 (2001)

30. Aldred, R.: From community participation to organizational therapy? World cafe and appreciative inquiry as research methods. Commun. Dev. J. **46**, 57–71 (2009)

31. Wimmer, M.A., Tambouris, E., Krimmer, R., Gil-Garcia, J.R., Chatfield, A.T.: Once only principle. In: Proceedings of the 18th Annual International Conference on Digital Government Research. ACM (2017)

Legal Framework for the Use of Drones by Public Entities for Monitoring and Control Purposes in Russia

Mikhail Bundin[1]([⊠]) [iD], Aleksei Martynov[1] [iD], Ekaterina Shireeva[1], and Maria Egorova[2]

[1] Lobachevsky State University of Nizhny Novgorod (UNN),
Nizhny Novgorod 603950, Russia
mbundin@mail.ru, avm@unn.ru,
shireevaekaterina@yandex.ru
[2] Kutafin Moscow State Law University (MSAL), Moscow 125993, Russia
egorova-ma-mos@yandex.ru

Abstract. The International Civil Aviation Organization (ICAO), in its annual report in 2018, noted an unprecedented increase in the use of small unmanned aircrafts (UAS), which represents a serious challenge for regulators in terms of safety and security. Moreover, there is a general trend in the filing of special requests to the ICAO for preparing of harmonizing documents in the field of legal regulation of drones. According to recent research, both in Russia and abroad, drones are used in more than 50 sectors of the economy to solve more than 450 commercial tasks, which allows companies to increase profits, reduce costs, and optimize many processes. The TOP 5 areas of drone use include: medicine & health care; oil and gas industries; protection of nature reserves and forests; urban planning and surveying; delivery of light cargo by transport companies.

At the same time, considering the current practice, many specialists note the limited applicability of the tools provided for by UN Convention on International Civil Aviation and traditional air regulations in case of UAS, and the urgent need for further efforts to create specific rules and regulations.

At present, considering the increasing frequency of drone use, two main areas can be identified: civil (commercial, recreational) and public (state bodies for monitoring and monitoring compliance with legislation, military). The purpose of this study is to analyze the general state of legal regulation on the use of drones for public administration purposes, as well as to determine its main parameters and possible differences/deviations from the rules applicable for commercial use. The authors also formulate the basic principles that should allegedly become the basis for drafting of special rules for the public use of drones to ensure the necessary level of security and the required efficiency – to achieve the public goals by their using.

Keywords: UAS · Drones · Regulation · Control and supervision · Public administration

A. Chugunov et al. (Eds.): EGOSE 2020, CCIS 1349, pp. 90–105, 2020.
https://doi.org/10.1007/978-3-030-67238-6_7

1   Introduction

The broad use of unmanned aerial systems (UAS) or drones in many spheres of modern economy and society drives inevitably to the issue of forming of an appropriate legal framework in general and in some specific domains.

According to the research data obtained by the Russian drone center Armair, drones are used in more than 50 sectors of the economy to solve more than 450 business tasks, which allows companies to increase profits, reduce costs, and optimize many processes. The TOP 5 areas of drone use include:

- medicine,
- healthcare (private clinics, medical institutions use these devices for fast delivery of medicines, professional equipment);
- oil and gas industry (for bypassing overpasses, for monitoring and protecting fuel storage points, for monitoring the environment at production sites);
- protection of nature reserves and forests;
- urban planning and surveying;
- delivery of light cargo by transport companies [44].

According to American analysts - BI Intelligence drones are mostly used for commercial purposes in such areas as:

- Photo (42.9%);
- Real Estate (20.7%);
- Utilities (10.9%);
- Construction (8.6%);
- Agriculture (8%);
- Education (1.9%), etc. [41].

So large use of drones contaminates also the public sector. We can easily name many cases were UAS are used for military purposes with high level of efficiency and for some state control and monitoring purposes. Thus, we can distinguish two main areas of use of drones – civil (commercial and recreational) and public (state bodies for general monitoring and monitoring compliance with legislation).

The purpose of this study is to analyze the state of legal regulation of the use of drones in the public sector, as well as to identify possible principles and areas of their application.

2   Methodology

The authors made qualitative and quantitative analysis of Russian and foreign publications from international and Russian science citation databases. The main emphasis was made on publications concerning legal issues of using UAV and drones indexed in the and ScienceDirect, Scopus, E-library.

The authors also draw special attention to the existing statistical data on using of drones in the world and by country, current practice of the use of drones in Russia and in other countries, considering mostly and exclusively cases of their use for public needs (public control & monitoring purposes). Considering the main purpose of the research great attention was made to the comparative analysis of international and national legal and policy documents regulating or providing general principles for the use of UAS.

3 Literature Review

Currently, there is a considerable amount of research on different issues on the use of drones. Most of them are devoted to the technical requirements for their use [2, 22, 23, 26, 27, 32, 36, 47, 49], requirements to the drone operator (pilot), the possibilities of using drones in various areas of the civil sector (e.g., construction [25], irrigation and land recultivation, transportation of goods [24, 39, 50]) and social impact of them [5], issues preventing the use of drones for illegal activities [6, 7, 28, 45, 48].

However, it should be noted that there is also a serious potential for using drones in the public sector [28]. The effectiveness of their use in the public sector is considered by some of scholars, but these studies do not formulate General approaches to the legal regulation of the use of drones for public purposes [10–13, 31, 36, 40].

The authors, due to their specialization on control and supervision issues, do not aim to consider the specifics of the use of drones for military purposes [6, 23]. The most discussed public areas where drones can be used to monitor compliance with legislation and prevent its violations are selected as the subject of the study [1, 4]. These are:

- traffic transport;
- land;
- ecological safety;
- forest security.

4 Current Use of Drones by Public Entities for Control and Monitoring in Russia

4.1 Traffic Safety Control

In the Russian Federation, drones are used for traffic safety control in two ways:

- road condition monitoring;
- detection of traffic violations [37].

Monitoring the state of roads using drones is one of the most promising. The total length of the Russian network of public roads of federal, regional and local significance is estimated at 1,396,000 km, including 984,000 km of paved roads. According to Rosstat (Russian State Statistics Agency), the length of Federal highways is 50 800 km. all these roads must be monitored and repaired in a timely manner.

Of course, the existing traditional methods of monitoring roads – mobile laboratories equipped with video cameras – are not so effective. First, because of the narrow visual scope.

As an experiment, the Ministry of Transport of the Russian Federation conducted in April 2019 a survey of a three-kilometer section of the M2 "Crimea" highway on the territory of the city district of Podolsk, Moscow region, with the creation of an orthophotoplane and a 3D model of the object. The experiment made it possible to make sure that the use of drones can contribute to the rapid and most capacious collection of information. Moreover, control and supervision in this area can be carried out in two forms:

- monitoring the state of roads – using drones will allow you to solve such tasks that allow you to make the right management decisions, such as: monitoring the city's road network; aerial photography of roads and Railways, roadside conditions; monitoring of roads, roadside infrastructure objects; road condition assessment; creating a digital cartographic basis for road transport infrastructure; creating aerial photographs in the design, operation and construction of roads;
- operational monitoring – the use of drones will allow you to detect threats to the safety of citizens in the shortest possible time in case of emergency situations.

The possibility of using drones to detect violations of traffic regulations embodied in the special Order of the MIA of Russia # 664 concerning the of federal state control and monitoring of traffic and road safety adopted in 2017 [33]. However, there is no detailed regulation of the procedure and rules for their use.

In this regard, on a regular basis, drones for detecting violations of traffic rules in Russia are practically not used. The first projects for testing drones in this area began in 2014 – in the Tyumen region, an unmanned aerial vehicle was tested to prevent driving on the side of the road; in 2015, in the far East, in the Republic of Adygea and in the Sverdlovsk region, on suburban roads, drones detected facts of oncoming traffic and violations; in 2016, the Stavropol region conducted an experiment to launch drones in a dense urban environment, which revealed the impossibility of their safe use; in 2017, the first example of the use of drones on a permanent basis on long-distance routes by the traffic police in Krasnoyarsk region. According to the results of the experiments, it was noted that drones have brought a positive preventive effect on the road traffic.

4.2   Cadaster/Land Management

The use of UAS for land/cadaster monitoring is possible in accordance with article 71.2 of the Land Code of Russia. Scholars and practitioners constantly and repeatedly note that there are "clear advantages of using drones for state land/cadaster monitoring purposes, including reducing the number of on-site inspections, as well as the ability to conduct targeted inspections if a violation is detected" [28].

Drones for fixing the boundaries of land plots, detecting self-seizure of land, unregistered constructions, and determining the use of land plots have been used since 2015. In the Yamal-Nenets Autonomous Okrug in 2015, drones were used for the purpose of territorial planning and surveying of public areas; in the Moscow region in 2016, they were used for cadastral registration of real estate objects, as well as for administrative survey of land relations objects; in the Udmurt Republic, Belgorod region, Tula region, Krasnodar territory, and Sverdlovsk region in 2017 – to detect violations of land legislation, conduct complex cadastral works, obtain cartographic products, control and management in agriculture, conduct state land monitoring, and an administrative control of land relations, planning and surveying public areas; in the Smolensk region in 2018 - for administrative control of land relations; in the Moscow region, Smolensk region in 2019 - for complex cadastral works.

In the summer of 2019, Rosreestr (Russian Real-Estate Rights Register) officially announced the introduction of active use of drones in order to detect violations of land legislation [42]. However, the experiment also reveals some risks of using drones. According to experts, "in some cases, there may be errors when decrypting information received from drones, which are associated with the dimensions of outbuildings: greenhouses, cabins, etc. – too large objects may well be considered housing." Therefore, it is necessary to create such a procedure and rules for the use of drones, which will be aimed at eliminating such cases.

Considering the already existing experience in the use of drones in the field of cadaster and land management, it is possible to identify such possible forms of control and supervision activities using drones:

– taking measures to prevent and/or eliminate the consequences of identified violations;
– systematic observation (land monitoring);
– implementation of inspections (unscheduled and planned).

4.3 Ecological Monitoring

In Russia, drones for carrying out control and supervision activities in the field of ecology have been used since 2015 in such areas as:

– struggle against poaching;
– detection of violations of environmental legislation;
– monitoring of water bodies;
– fight against unauthorized landfills.

4.4 Forest Fire-Safety

In the Russian Federation drones in this area are mostly used on a permanent basis for fire safety:

– for aerial reconnaissance of the edge of an active large fire;
– as a geographically linked aerial observation point ("flying tower") for detecting fires in areas of high (emergency) forest fire danger, primarily for the protection of localities;
– for inspection of existing fires in emergency periods when the use of classical aviation is not possible due to the smoke pollution of the area;
– for monitoring the status of peat fires;

- to track the progress of forest fires and forecast their development taking into account meteorological conditions and pyrogenic factors;
- for patrolling forests to monitor compliance with logging rules by logging companies [43].

However, there is also a possibility of using drones to detect violations of forest legislation (illegal deforestation, presence in a forest zone when visiting forests is prohibited, etc.).

5   General Regulation of the Use of Drones in National Practice

5.1   International Law

The international civil aviation organization noted an unprecedented increase in the use of light unmanned aerial vehicles, which represents a serious challenge for regulators in terms of safety and security. At the same time, considering the current practice, many scholars note that it is impossible to use the tools provided by UN Convention on International Civil Aviation in most cases, and that further efforts are needed to create specific rules in this case.

Remotely piloted aircraft systems (RPAS) that are generally larger were partly included in the existing legal framework of ICAO/UN regulation. The Annex 1 — Personnel Licensing remote pilot license provisions were adopted by ICAO Council in March 2018 [31]. The regulation frames the procedure of obtaining of remote pilot license and requirements for students, pilots and instructors of RPAS.

5.2   USA

Federal Aviation Administration issued in 2016 the Small Unmanned Aircraft Rule (SUAR) as a part of the Federal Aviation Regulation [18]. According to SUAR the unmanned aircraft (UAS) must weigh less than 55lbs. (25 kg). The operating of UA is possible only inside visual line-of-sight (VLOS) in a daylight (30 min. before sunrise and 30 min. after sunset only with anti-collision lighting). Maximum speed – 100 mph, max. altitude – 400 ft., minimum weather visibility – 3 miles from control station. The flights are prohibited over restricted areas or over any person not involved in operation of UAS. For operating an UAS flight an operator must hold a remote pilot airman certificate or to be 'under the direct supervision of a person who has it'. To be qualified as a remote pilot a person must be at least 16 years old, demonstrate appropriate aeronautical knowledge for operating UAS and complete a small online training course to obtain the certificate. All drones that fall under the provisions of SUAR (except very small models without cameras (less than 0.55lbs.)) are to be registered at the FAA. The FAA posts on its web-site information upon restricted for UAS areas (airports, special use airspaces, sporting events, wildfires etc.) and all information how to register drones and obtain or renew remote pilot's certificate. According to the general statistics on the beginning of 2020 about 1.55 millions of drones are registered ($\sim$400 000 commercial drones and 1.1 millions of recreational; $\sim$167 000 remote pilots certified) in the USA. The hot topic about future regulation of drones is the suggested by FAA remote identification system for UAS operating in the US airspace.

5.3   European Union

Initially EC Regulation 216/2008 on safety of civil aviation within Europe in its Annex II contains an exemption for its applicability to UA that weighs no more than 150 kg [34]. The European Commission has worked a lot in recent years to promote UAS integration into the European civil aviation airspace and adopted consequently several steps since 2015 to allow integration of drones. In 2015 European Aviation community issued Riga Declaration on Remotely Piloted Aircraft (drones) [35], where it stated the necessity to treat UAS as a new type of aircraft that needs specific regulation and operation monitoring. In return European Aviation Safety Agency adopted Concept of Operations for Drones: a risk-based approach to regulation of unmanned aircraft. The Concept document outlines 3 categories of operating UAS flights and correlated regulatory regimes: 'open', 'specific' and 'certified'. This approach was finally introduced by Regulations (EU) 2019/947 and (EU) 2019/945 on the rules and procedures for the operation of unmanned aircraft [14]. This document explained and elaborated criteria for each group of operations:

- 'open' – UAS less than 25 kg, operated in VLOS within 120 m from land and not above people or some objects, the drones could be operated freely – without specific authorization;
- 'specified'- other UAS that do not fall in the 'open' category needs special authorization from national safety aviation authority to operate the flight, additionally the flights divided into several categories according to the possible risks they could represent and special requirements for operators and remote pilots (training);
- 'certified' – mostly concerns the cases of the UAS used to operate flights over assemblies of people, for passenger or danger goods transportation and needs certification of UAS, UAS operator and remote pilot licensing.

The Regulation seems to be one of the most sophisticated and well-elaborated documents in the domain of UAS. Its entry into force was planned for 1 July but postponed for 1 December 2020 because of COVID-19 pandemic. The delay and envisaged timeline for its entry into force is explained by the need to obtain necessary certificates and remote pilot license.

5.4 UK

In UK the exploitation of drones is regulated by The Air Navigation Order 2016 and Regulations containing in art. 94 and 95 special rules concerning small unmanned aircrafts ('any unmanned aircraft, other than a balloon or a kite, having a mass of not more than 20 kg without its fuel') [9]. UAS that weight under 250 g are generally excluded from the scope of Regulations. Larger unmanned aircrafts (over 20 kg) fall under the whole UK Air Navigation Order – ANO. Possible exemptions from certain requirements could be made by the CAA (Civil Aviation Authority). The Regulations distinguish several types of use of UA (based on the general purpose): recreational use, commercial use, model aircraft, larger aircraft use. The use of model and recreational UAs by individuals is subject for registration that could be done online and an operator should have an operator ID (under 18 y.o.) and flyer ID (under 13 y.o.). In both cases a person should pass an online theory test to get the required ID. It's prohibited to fly without registration and ID (flyer under 13 may use UA under supervision of an operator). Commercial use of drones also should be declared and registered (permission is issued for 1 year and subject for renewal). The organization that uses commercial UAs is responsible that drones are operated only by a person having appropriate remote pilot competence (pass a flight test). In all cases drones should be labelled by Operator ID (a sticker on the UA). Normally small unmanned aircraft are allowed to fly without special permission under 400 ft. over the land. Restrictions concern the cases of the use over large peoples meeting, control towers, vessels or vehicles not under operator's control. Police can operate generally in the same legal framework that applies to commercial permission holder but may ignore some of them pursuing public interest which won't be achieved by other means and under condition that the appropriate safety measures are taken.

5.5 France

The French Air Navigation Service Provider (DSNA) in 2018 operated about 3 million of IFR flights and the same number of VFR flights [29]. DSNA already supports thousands of drone flights, that makes the French airspace one of the busiest in Europe. France participates in several EU initiatives in regulating and developing drones' navigation two of them are the most promising: CORUS (Concept of Operations for euRopean Unmanned Systems, the project aims to manage safely drones in very low level (VLL) of atmosphere) and USIS (U-space Initial Service, it aims at creating automated assistance to safely operate and control air traffic even in B-VLOS (beyond vision line of sight). All unmanned systems are divided here in three large groups: RPAS (Remotely Piloted Aircraft System, normally the heaviest group of aircrafts, full subject of air navigation rules); eVTOL (electric Vertical Take-off and Landing); UAS (Unmanned Aircraft System, small aircraft systems). In mid-time perspective DSNA seeks to create a unique U-space for all unmanned air systems and envisaged to divide it into for group according to possible altitude of flight and functionality:

- 'Basic services (e-registration, e-identification)' – level U1;
- 'Initial services (flight planning, authorization and tracking)' – level U2;
- 'Advanced services (dynamic airspace management)' – level U3;
- 'Full services (digital, automatized and interconnected operations)' – level U4.

The lowest level of U-space will be operated by U-space providers that will assist DSNA to control the airspace in the whole.

5.6 Germany

According to German Air Regulation [19] the operation of Unmanned Aviation Systems (UAS) is subject to authorization. Special rules should Generally, any operation of unmanned aerial vehicles that is out of sight of the operator or with a total mass of more than 25 kg is prohibited. Unmanned aircraft may not ascend in restricted areas. Responsible for issuing a permit are the lands aviation authorities. The permission (so-called ascension permit) can be granted if the competent aviation authority has determined that the intended use of the unmanned aerial system does not create a risk to the safety of the air traffic or public safety or order. Within the scope of their competence, the federal government and the lands have uniform regulations for harmonization of administrative action. These "common principles of the federal and state governments for granting permission for the rise of unmanned aerial vehicle were included in the Reader for operators. Thus, the permission issued by one of the lands authorities and is valid throughout all the Federation for up to 2 years. The application forms can be found on the websites of the responsible land authority. However, the special requirements and procedures of the to be observed in the respective federal lands. Normally all the flights over 100 m are prohibited.

5.7 Canada

Canada has one of the most advanced legislation in regulating UAS. The operation of the latter is subject to the Part IX – "Remotely Piloted Aircraft Systems" of the Canadian Aviation Regulations (CARs) [17]. These provisions are applicable to drones less than 25 kg. The operating of model UAV by members of the Model Aeronautics Association of Canada (MAAC) could be an exemption to CARs if it meets certain conditions according to the Exemption NCR-011-2019 (the rules mostly concern the requirements organization of MAAC member organization and organization of flight safety). Drone remote pilots must hold a valid certificate and operate only specially marked and registered UAS. A drone that is less than 250 grams, is not subject for registration or getting a drone pilot certificate to operate it. But the owner is recommended to operate this drone responsibly, taking necessary precautions of the safety. Larger UAV that weight more than 25 kg need to get special permission from Transport Canada. For the majority of drones (250 g a - 25 kg) the rules of operation differ from the basic and advanced level of their use. Basic operations include flight that do not exceed 30 m over the land, in an uncontrolled airspace and not above bystanders – otherwise epy flight will be considered as advanced operation of UAS. The operator of the latter must meet some extended requirements not only to have a remote pilot certificate or register the drone but to have a pilot review and get permission for operating the flight in the prescribed time and space limits. The operation of UAV is subject even for criminal liability for violation safety or registration rules or privacy of citizens.

5.8   Singapore

Civil Aviation Authority of Singapore (CAAS) amended in 2019 the Air Navigation Regulations by a special chapter (101 - Unmanned Aircraft Operations) [8]. All UAS exceeding the weight of 250 g are subject for registration. The applicant should be at least 16 years old. The registration includes: the obtaining of registration label with a unique ID that should stickered to the aircraft and completion of the registration form online that differs from the applicant legal status: individuals, organizations and tourists. The person should de-register the UAS in case of its loss, permanent out of service or selling to another owner.

Regulation distinguish at least 3 main activity spheres for UAS operation according to their purpose: Activity 1 – recreation purpose (enjoyment, relaxation, model competition); Activity 2 – education purpose (lecture, tutorial, seminar with demonstration of UAS); Activity 3 – non-recreation and non-education purpose (any business, commercial or over activity). The permission to operate UAS is needed according to the activity type and some other criteria:

– for any activity 3 regardless the mass of UAS;
– for activity 2 if UAS weights more than 7 kg;
– for activity 1 if UAS weights more than 25 kg;
– for any activity in BVLOS.

The permit depends greatly on the activity and the strictest requirements (concerning restricted zones and altitude of flights) are envisaged for activity 3 and BVLOS flights. The most detailed regulation concerns BVLOS operations that are divided into three risk groups depending on the flight conditions and circumstances (mostly high risk – operation over uninvolved persons). For each risk group there are specific hardware and software requirements for UAS systems (failure management, communication, navigation/flight control, detect and avoid).

5.9   Russia

Just recently, presidential Decree No. 490 on 10.10.2019 "On the development of artificial intelligence in the Russian Federation" [16] approved the national strategy for the development of artificial intelligence for the period up to 2030. As one of the priority areas for the development and use of artificial intelligence, the Strategy notes the use of Autonomous intelligent equipment and robotic systems, intelligent systems. Thus, it is assumed that drones can be introduced into various sectors of the economy and public sector.

Currently, the General legal regulation of drone activity is carried out by the Air code of the Russian Federation 1997. The order of use of airspace of unmanned aircraft is regulated by the Federal rules of using airspace of the Russian Federation approved by Decree of the Government of the Russian Federation dated 11.03.2010 No. 138. The issues of registration of drones are fixed in the 'Rules of accounting for unmanned civil aircraft with a maximum take-off weight from 0.25 kilograms to 30 kilograms imported to the Russian Federation or manufactured in the Russian Federation' (approved by the government of the Russian Federation of 25.05.2019 No. 658) [38].

According to current legislation, drones with a maximum take-off weight of 0.25 kg to 30 kg are subject for registration by the Federal Air Transport Agency. To register a drone, the owner must submit an application that specifies information about the drone and its technical capabilities, the manufacturer of the drone, the drone's owner personal data, with a photo of the drone attached within 10 working days from the date of its purchase/import into the territory of Russian Federation. As a result, the drone is assigned a registration number and all the necessary information for its identification is put into the database/register of unmanned aircrafts.

The owner of the drone is to comply with the rules for its flight. The Russian government has established a permissive procedure for the use of airspace for drone flights, regardless the class of airspace. This procedure implies that it is mandatory to send the aircraft flight plan to the operational bodies (centers) of the unified air traffic management system of the Russian Federation, as well as to obtain permission from it to use the airspace. In addition, restrictions are imposed on the use of airspace by UAS through the introduction of temporary and local regimes, as well as short-term restrictions in the interests of airspace users who organize drone flights.

The current rules provide general legal framework for the use of UAV. However, it is obvious that, following the international tradition, mostly cases of use of drones by private individuals for commercial or recreational purposes are well treated. In turn, considering the increasing use of drones for public purposes (not related to military) by state bodies, it is obvious that there is a need to develop special approaches to the regulation of the use of UAS in the control and supervision activities of state bodies. This is primarily due to the fact that the existing licensing system will not allow state authorities to use drones quickly in emergency situations where it is necessary to act immediately, and the use of drones for public purposes by authorities may pose a threat to the security of the rights and legitimate interests of citizens [15].

6 Envisaged Legal Issues on the Use of Drones by Public Entities

6.1 Standardization & Registration

It should be assumed that the use of drones for public monitoring and control/surveillance purposes will require appropriate standardization and registration. Application of the same criteria existed for civilian UAS is likely to be only partially acceptable. Rather, it is worth talking about the need to form a coherent rather specific regulation for the use of drones as special technical means and the justification/legal ground of their necessity to apply for the purposes of state control and monitoring considering as well safety and privacy issues.

Most likely, the best option would be to develop specific standards for the use of drones and formulate technical requirements for their functionality: the duration of the flight (autonomous flight), take-off weight, the possibility to equip them with photo, video recording or other hardware, the reliability of control function, the security of the radio control channel, personal data security, and others. A possible solution would be to develop recommendations/standards for UAS used for the purposes of state control and monitoring and probably to form a recommendation list of drones models that comply with the needed requirements and could be applicable for appropriate tasks (photo-, video- recording, land monitoring, autonomous flight, take-off weight and possibility to carry/deliver goods, etc.).

Envisaged tasks and expected specific features of UAS for public purposes may require a separate registration, probably to form a special register for them. The UAS used for specific state control and monitoring purposes will have special (color) marking, including indication that they belong to the relevant state control body and a unique registration ID number.

6.2 Management and Piloting Issues

A sufficiently large-scale use of drones for public administration purposes will require appropriate organizational decisions, which may be associated with the creation of special units and services (centers) for the use of UAS under the control and supervision bodies. A possible solution would be to create such center under the control and supervision authorities. On the other hand, the question of possible outsourcing is quite open and quite plausible for Russia given the expanding practice of photo and video recording performed by third-party organizations for traffic violation control. The obtained data is transferred to the Russian road police for its examination and taking appropriate decision on the violations detected.

For security reasons, remote pilots for public purposes should be equally competent and receive the necessary training at a level not inferior to pilots engaged for commercial purposes. Considering the public need to monitor the level of necessary knowledge and skills, the suggested solution would be to pass an exam for the right to control UAS with the issue of an appropriate certificate and to introduce the practice of regular updates (once a year) to confirm the needed pilot's skill level.

6.3 Airspace Control and Monitoring

The use of public drones in the common airspace will certainly need monitoring and tracking them like others UAS. Among other issues related to the use of UAS in common airspace could be named:

1. In certain cases, in order to ensure effective control and surveillance measures, it may be necessary to secure exclusive airspace for the operation of such UAS, for environmental control or over national parks.
2. It should be assumed that it is possible to establish special rules and priorities for the use of airspace by drones used for public purposes in comparison with civil ones (commercial or recreational).
3. Probably in some cases mostly of monitoring violations is possible to keep certain secrecy in using drones to achieve control and prevention purposes.

6.4   Privacy & Data Protection

It is obvious that the data that will be collected by public UAV can equally threat to privacy, especially photo and video data [20–22, 30, 46, 47]. Presumably in this case it is necessary to develop the necessary approaches to ensure the rights of citizens and solve such important issues as:

1. Control of access to photo and video data;
2. Duration of data storage and depersonalization/destruction;
3. Access to and transfer of data to third parties;
4. Data security.

This issue was seriously treated by Article 29 Data Protection Working Party. The use of drones by public entities should also fall into the scope of data protection regulation. Consent, minimization, correction, erasure and anonymization of data, transparency, proportionality, security of data, rights of access – all these issues are to be thoroughly addressed by drone producers and operators [3]. The face recognition technology equipment and unaware(secret) data collecting by drones may represent a considerable threat to individual rights considering a possibility of hacking control even over high-level UAVs used by law enforcement agencies or hijacking [15, 31].

7   Conclusion and Further Work

Considering the latest trends in the field of legal regulation of drones and their frequent practice of using them for the purposes of state control and monitoring it seems appropriate to adopt rules and principles that would amend existing general UAV regulation in Russia and establish:

1. Classification of drones, identify basic and promising designs that are suitable for performing state control and monitoring tasks;
2. Technical requirements and recommendations for UAV used for state control and monitoring;
3. The standards of airworthiness;
4. A uniform program of training for remote pilots;
5. A unified system for accreditation of remote pilots;
6. A unified data exchange system for the use of drones in single Russian airspace, integrated with the national flight control system;
7. Clear rules for information security and control over the turnover of data obtained via UAV operations.

Funding. The reported study was funded by RFBR, project number 20-011-00584.

References

1. Anania, E.C., Rice, S., Pierce, M., et al.: Public support for police drone missions depends on political affiliation and neighborhood demographics. Technol. Soc. **57**, 95–103 (2019). https://doi.org/10.1016/j.techsoc.2018.12.007
2. Armmah, S., Yi, S.: Altitude regulation of quadrotor types of UAVs considering communication delays. IFAC-Papers OnLine **48–12**, 263–268 (2015). https://doi.org/10.1016/j.ifacol.2015.09.388
3. Article 29 Data Protection Working Party. Opinion 01/2015 on privacy and data protection issues relating to the utilization of drones. 01673/15/EN, WP 231, 16 June 2015. https://ec.europa.eu/justice/article-29/documentation/opinion-recommendation/files/2015/wp231_en.pdf. Accessed 14 Sep 2020
4. Barmpounakis, E., Geroliminis, N.: On the new era of urban traffic monitoring with massive drone data: The pNEUMA large-scale field experiment. Transp. Res. Part C **111**, 50–71 (2020). https://doi.org/10.1016/j.trc.2019.11.023
5. Bharat Rao, B., Gopi, A.G., Maione, R.: The societal impact of commercial drones. Technol. Soc. **45**, 83–90 (2015). https://doi.org/10.1016/j.techsoc.2016.02.009
6. Boronenkov, V.: Legal regulation of the fight against unmanned aerial vehicles. Mil. Law **6**(58), 57–68 (2019)
7. Burukina, O.: Legal regulation of UAV use in IHL: international perspective. In: Yakovlev, K., et al. (eds.) Law, Economics and Management: Current Issues: Materials of all-Russian. Science. Conference (Cheboksary, 23 Dec. 2019)/editorial Board, pp. 291–298 (2019)
8. Civil Aviation Authority of Singapore. https://www.caas.gov.sg/legislation-regulations/guidelines-advisory/unmanned-aircraft/advisory-circulars. Accessed 14 Sep 2020
9. Civil Aviation Authority. Unmanned aircraft and drones. https://www.caa.co.uk/Consumers/Unmanned-aircraft-and-drones/. Accessed 14 Sep 2020
10. Clarke, R.: Appropriate regulatory responses to the drone Epidemic. Comput. Law Secur. Rev. **32**, 152–155 (2016). https://doi.org/10.1016/j.clsr.2015.12.010
11. Clarke, R.: The regulation of civilian drones' impacts on behavioral privacy. Comput. Law Secur. Rev. **30**, 286–305 (2014). https://doi.org/10.1016/j.clsr.2014.03.005
12. Clarke, R.: Understanding the drone epidemic. Comput. Law Secur. Rev. **30**, 230–246 (2014). https://doi.org/10.1016/j.clsr.2014.03.002
13. Clarke, R.: What drones inherit from their ancestors. Comput. Law Secur. Rev. **30**, 247–262 (2014). https://doi.org/10.1016/j.clsr.2014.03.006
14. Commission Implementing Regulation (EU) 2019/947 of 24 May 2019 on the rules and procedures for the operation of unmanned aircraft (Text with EEA relevance). https://eur-lex.europa.eu/eli/reg_impl/2019/947/oj. Accessed 14 Sep 2020
15. Cybersecurity risks posed by unmanned aircraft systems: Key findings, The Department of Homeland Security (DHS)/National Protection and Programs Directorate (NPPD)/Office of Cyber and Infrastructure Analysis (OCIA), 22 May 2018. https://www.eisac.com/cartella/Asset/00007102/OCIA%20-%20Cybersecurity%20Risks%20Posed%20by%20Unmanned%20Aircraft%20Systems.pdf?parent=115994. Accessed 14 Sep 2020
16. Decree No. 490 on 10.10.2019 'On the development of artificial intelligence in the Russian Federation'. President of Russian Federation. http://www.kremlin.ru/acts/bank/44731. Accessed 14 Sep 2020
17. Drone safety. https://www.tc.gc.ca/en/services/aviation/drone-safety.html. Accessed 14 Sep 2020
18. Federal Aviation Authority. Unmanned Aircraft Systems (UAS). https://www.faa.gov/uas/. Accessed 14 Sep 2020

19. Federal Ministry for Transport and Digital Infrastructure. https://www.bmvi.de/SharedDocs/DE/Publikationen/LF/unbemannte-luftfahrtsysteme.html. Accessed 14 Sep 2020

20. Finn, R.L., Wright, D.: Privacy, data protection and ethics for civil drone practice: a survey of industry, regulators and civil society organizations. Comput. Law Secur. Rev. **32**, 577–586 (2016). https://doi.org/10.1016/j.clsr.2016.05.010

21. Finn, R.K., Wright, D.: Unmanned aircraft systems: surveillance, ethics and privacy in civil applications. Comput. Law Secur. Rev. **28**, 184–194 (2012). https://doi.org/10.1016/j.clsr.2012.01.005

22. Hassanalian, M., Abdelkefi, M.: Classifications, applications, and design challenges of drones: a review. Prog. Aerosp. Sci. **91**, 99–131 (2017). https://doi.org/10.1016/j.paerosci.2017.04.003

23. Kalnoy, A.: Design features of an unmanned aerial vehicle used by military formations of the Ministry of defense. Bull. Mil. Acad. Logistics **4**, 52–58 (2015)

24. Kellermann, R., Biehle, T., Fischer, L.: Drones for parcel and passenger transportation: A literature review. Transportation Research Interdisciplinary Perspectives xxx (xxxx) xxx (Article in presse). http://dx.doi.org/10.1016/j.trip.2019.100088

25. Kramarenko, A., Krasnova, K.: Analysis of the possibility of using drones in modern construction. Sci. Educ. New Time **6**, 313–319 (2017)

26. Kumar Jha, A., Sathyamoorthy, S., Prakash, V.: Bird strike damage and analysis of UAV's airframe. Procedia Struct. Integr. **4**, 416–428 (2019). https://doi.org/10.1016/j.prostr.2019.0

27. Kurdel, P., Novak Sedlakova, A., Labun, J.: UAV flight safety close to the mountain massif. Transp. Res. Procedia **43**, 319–327 (2019). https://doi.org/10.1016/j.trpro.2019.12.047

28. Meschaninova, E., Nikolyukin, V.: Prospects of the use of UAVs for land & cadastral monitoring. Econ. Ecol. Territorial Entities **3**(2), 122–128 (2018)

29. Ministère de la Transition écologique et solidaire. Direction générale de l'aviation civile (DGAC). https://www.ecologique-solidaire.gouv.fr/quelle-place-drones-dans-ciel-francais. Accessed 14 Sep 2020

30. Morrow, S.: Beware of drones! Privacy and security issues with drones, Infosec, 23 April (2019). https://resources.infosecinstitute.com/privacy-and-security-issues-with-drones/. Accessed 14 Sep 2020

31. Motasova, D.D.: International legal regulation of the use of unmanned aerial vehicles: problems and prospects of development. Agrarian Land Law **9**(165), 102–107 (2018)

32. Nelsona, J., Gorichanaz, T.: Trust as an ethical value in emerging technology governance: the case of drone regulation. Technol. Soc. **59**, 101131 (2019). https://doi.org/10.1016/j.techsoc.2019.04.007

33. Order of the Ministry of Internal Affairs of Russia from 23.08.2017 # 664 'About approval of Administrative regulations of execution by the Ministry of internal Af-fairs of the Russian Federation the state function on implementation of Federal state control of observance by participants of traffic of requirements of the legislation of the Russian Federation in the field of road safety'. https://rg.ru/2017/10/10/mvd-prikaz664-site-dok.html. Accessed 14 Sep 2020

34. Regulation (EC) No 216/2008 of the European Parliament and of the Council of 20 February 2008 on common rules in the field of civil aviation and establishing a European Aviation Safety Agency, and repealing Council Directive 91/670/EEC, Regulation (EC) No 1592/2002 and Directive 2004/36/EC (Text with EEA relevance). https://eur-lex.europa.eu/legal-content/EN/TXT/?uri=celex:32008R0216. Accessed 14 Sep 2020

35. Riga Declaration on Remotely Piloted Aircraft (drones) "Framing the future of aviation" Riga 6 March 2015. https://ec.europa.eu/transport/sites/transport/files/modes/air/news/doc/2015-03-06-drones/2015-03-06-riga-declaration-drones.pdf. Accessed 14 Sep 2020

36. Roberts, A., Tayebi, A.: A new position regulation strategy for VTOL UAVs using IMU and GPS measurements. Automatica **49**(2), 434–440 (2013). https://doi.org/10.1016/j.automatica.2012.10.009
37. Rosenfeld, A.: Are drivers ready for traffic enforcement drones? Accid. Anal. Prev. **122**, 199–206 (2019). https://doi.org/10.1016/j.aap.2018.10.006
38. Rules of accounting for unmanned civil aircraft with a maximum take-off weight from 0.25 kilograms to 30 kilograms imported to the Russian Federation or manufactured in the Russian Federation. Government of Russian Federation. http://government.ru/docs/all/122058/. Accessed 14 Sep 2020
39. Shikula, I., Gusenko, N., Simanovich, L.: Civil drones in the legislation of Russia and Japan. Eurasian Advocacy **1**(38), 109–111 (2019)
40. Straub, J.: Unmanned aerial systems: consideration of the use of force for law enforcement applications. Technol. Soc. **39**, 100–109 (2014). https://doi.org/10.1016/j.techsoc.2013.12.004
41. The drones report. https://www.businessinsider.com/drone-usage-is-thriving-in-these-three-us-states-2016-4. Accessed 14 Sep 2020
42. The use of drones for detecting cadastral law violations. https://zen.yandex.ru/media/proned/rosreestr-aktivno-nachal-ispolzovat-drony-dlia-vyiavleniia-narushenii-zemelnogo-zakonodatelstva-5d034334cf474f0da03976ad. Accessed 14 Sep 2020
43. The use of drones for forest monitoring. https://rusdrone.ru/otrasli/primeneniya-bespilotnikov-dlya-monitoringa-lesov/. Accessed 14 Sep 2020
44. Using drones. website of the Armair drone center. https://bespilotnik24.ru/ispolzovanie_bespilotnikov/. Accessed 14 Sep 2020
45. Vardanyan, A., Andreev, A.: Unmanned aerial vehicles as a segment of digital technologies in criminal and post-criminal reality. All-Russian J. Criminol. **12**(6), 785–794 (2018)
46. Volovelsky, U.: Civilian uses of unmanned aerial vehicles and the threat to the right to privacy e An Israeli case study. Comput. Law Secur. Rev. **30**, 306–320 (2014). https://doi.org/10.1016/j.clsr.2014.03.008
47. Watkins, S., Burry, J., Mohamed, A., et al.: Ten questions concerning the use of drones in urban environments. Building Environ. **167**, 106458 (2020). https://doi.org/10.1016/j.buildenv.2019.106458
48. Wright, D.: Drones: Regulatory challenges to an incipient industry. Comput. Law Secur. Rev. **30**, 226–229 (2014). https://doi.org/10.1016/j.clsr.2014.03.009
49. Zhou, Y., Rui, T., Li, Y., Zuo, X.: A UAV patrol system using panoramic stitching and object detection. Comput. Electr. Eng. **80**, 106473 (2019). https://doi.org/10.1016/j.compeleceng.2019.106473
50. Zhu, X.: Segmenting the public's risk beliefs about drone delivery: a belief system approach. Telematics Inform. **40**, 27–40 (2019). https://doi.org/10.1016/j.tele.2019.05.007

Digital Society: Openness, Participation, Trust, Competences

Evaluation and Promotion of M-Learning Accessibility for Smart Education Development

Radka Nacheva[1](✉) ⓘ, Kristina Vorobyeva[2], and Maxim Bakaev[2] ⓘ

[1] University of Economics-Varna, Varna, Bulgaria
r.nacheva@ue-varna.bg
[2] Novosibirsk State Technical University, Novosibirsk, Russia
vorobyeva_kr@mail.ru, bakaev@corp.nstu.ru

Abstract. Young people's involvement with their mobile devices is often considered a problem nowadays. However, with the new "learning on the go approach" it can be used for good: for learning purposes, in particular in higher education. The m-learning tools have the potential to turn learning into a more attractive, interesting and motivating process of acquiring new knowledge and developing competencies. At the same time, m-learning can be inclusive of people with special needs, who used to be detached from traditional educational services. In our paper we purpose an evaluation approach to mobile learning software accessibility based on accessibility guidelines and standards. We suggest a formalization of the approach and reducing it to a controlled process. The dedicated usage of mobile devices and m-learning software can assist in improving mental operations speed, executive control of information selection and decision-making, as well as optimize the memorization system. Such enhancements are particularly important for facilitating effective learning in the elderly and the people with disabilities.

Keywords: Mobile accessibility · Mobile learning · WCAG · Smart technologies · Accessibility evaluation

1 Introduction

In 2020, the COVID-19 crisis challenged education systems around the world. The majority of countries in the world announced the closure of schools for months, which according to UNESCO affected over 67% of the world's student population or more than 1.8 billion learners [1]. In such situations, the most vulnerable groups in society are affected, namely children, disadvantaged people and people with special needs. The World Health Organization reported that 15% of world population have a kind of disability, and the percentage of people 15 years and older with significant difficulties in functioning is between 2.2% (110 million) and 3.8% (190 million) [2]. People with disabilities are often subjected to socioeconomic outcomes compared to people without disabilities, including difficult access to health and education services, information, employment.

The coronavirus pandemic prevented students with disabilities from accessing assistive technologies; access to resource personnel; recreation programs; extracurricular

© Springer Nature Switzerland AG 2020
A. Chugunov et al. (Eds.): EGOSE 2020, CCIS 1349, pp. 109–123, 2020.
https://doi.org/10.1007/978-3-030-67238-6_8

activities, non-adapted means of communication and gaps in service delivery [3]. It is also worrying that 90% of students in developing countries do not have access to education [4].

Global awareness of adequate access to education is increasing. The rights of disabled people are regulated by the Convention on the Rights of Persons with Disabilities (CRPD), which focuses on their full integration into society. By the end of July 2020, 181 countries had ratified the convention [5]. According to Article 24 of the GRPD states disabled persons are able to access tertiary education or other form of adult education (vocational training or lifelong learning) without discrimination and on an equal basis with other people and in the same time they should not be discriminated against because of their disability [6]. On the other hand, the 2030 Agenda for Sustainable Development states that inequality of access to all levels of education for people with disabilities has to be eliminated [7]. The Sustainable Development Goals (SDGs) framework also includes 17 objectives, a fourth on the quality of education and a tenth on reducing inequalities between people [8].

The Internet and its use in social and economic activities extend the traditional market space [39]. Modern education, in addition to being accessible, must be innovative and learner-oriented. In view of the active use of mobile technologies in everyday life – 67% of the world's population has a mobile connection [9, 10], they are used as supporting tools in the learning process. As of Q1 2020, according to the global statistics portal Statista, the Education category in the Google Play store ranks second in popularity among all application categories with a share of 8.94%, behind the Games category with a 13.56% share (Fig. 1) [26].

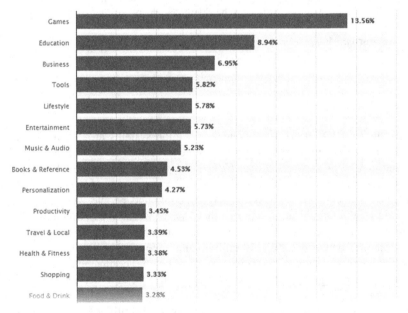

Fig. 1. Most popular Google play application categories in Q1 2020.

In the App Store, the Education category ranks third with a share of 8.69%, yielding to the Business categories – 10.1% and Games – 22.15% (Fig. 2) [27].

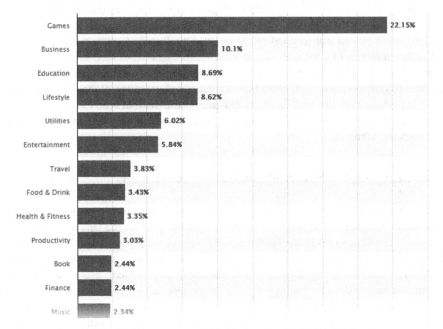

Fig. 2. Top app store application categories in Q1 2020.

According to the data in [28], 249 and 273 million of educational apps were downloaded in Q1 2017, respectively. In Q1 2018, 289 and 321 million of educational apps were downloaded, respectively. In Q1 2019, 322 and 398 million of educational apps were downloaded, respectively. The same source pointed out that the COVID-19 pandemic caused a spike in educational applications downloads in the first quarter of 2020. In the last quarter, 470 million educational apps were downloaded to the Apple App Store. Google Play users have downloaded 466 million educational apps. Both platforms had their highest registered downloads for educational apps this quarter.

Mobile learning is an important education development strategy. According to UNESCO, one of advantages of mobile learning is improving the education and accelerating the realization of the Sustainable Development Agenda [11]. The same source states that mobile technologies have reached the farthest corners of the planet, creating new opportunities for teachers and students, including in communities that do not have access to even traditional educational services. Mobile learning would help students with inability to access educational services, but also to turn the learning process into a more attractive, interesting and motivating process of acquiring new knowledge and competencies. Some authors point out that learning environments should be related as important parts of a city, even in a smart city which provide important supports for implementing a learning city [13]. Investments in the development of smart cities must also be aimed at the development of smart education and, in particular, smart m-learning, so as to ensure access to it for all groups of people.

For smart cities the need for educating all citizens is the basic element of development [14]. This goal is accomplished by analyzing the existing measures used to improve the quality of education through the active use of information and communication technologies [36] based on researched good practices for digitalization [38], including artificial intelligence methods [37, 40, 41].

In view of the above, it can be argued that access to quality education for vulnerable members of our society is a problem that is increasingly exciting global organizations that fight for human rights. In this regard, **the aim of the present study** is to propose an evaluation approach to the mobile learning software accessibility based on accessibility guidelines and standards.

2 M-Learning for Smart Education Development

According to United Nations data, urbanization is growing worldwide and more than half of the world's population lives in cities [18]. One of the goals of the United Nations for sustainable development is related to the development of smart cities [8]. That's goal 11, which advises the cities should be safety, resilient, inclusive and sustainable. According to [19–21], smart cities could provide a better living environment, use environmental information and modern technology to offer better services to citizens and a quality of life so that they can achieve in an innovative way their goals for sustainability. Smart cities facilitate usage of many tools, different types of devices for sensing, capturing, storing, and exploiting from different sources, including mobile.

In turn, this necessitates rapid changes in education, turning it into technology-enhanced learning (TEL). We are already talking about smart schools, which are the result of the socio-technological progress of our time. In [22] they state that smart schools increase computational thinking system and the technical expertise forms from which it derives. Particular data practices can contribute to optimizing education as a social institution.

TEL paradigm is related to providing opportunities for learners' mobility. This requires a change in training approaches, and a new approach "learning on the go" should be applied. It provides the necessary for the new generation of cooperation online and tools to provide a learning-oriented process with Internet of things (IoT), big data, e-learning analytics, wearable technology, etc.

A smart education framework proposed in [23] consists of three core elements: smart environments, smart pedagogy, and smart learner. The former highlights the postulate of developing better education in order to achieve technological progress and the need to apply smart pedagogies (new learning approaches) "as a methodological issue and smart learning environments as technological issue" [23]. The smart learners should have four levels of abilities through which to meet the needs of current society: basic knowledge and core skills; comprehensive abilities; personalized expertise and collective intelligence. These abilities have to be supported by smart learning environments through technologies that include all necessary digital resources and learners could get in touch with the learning systems anywhere and anytime.

The main cognitive functions essential for successful learning are attention and memory. The usage of mobile devices and the developed programs for the training of these functions can improve the speed of mental operations, executive control of information selection and decision-making, and optimize the memorization system, which contributes to the development of learning abilities and further enhancement of its effectiveness. Mobile-based cognitive training is especially important for people with disabilities. Personalized programs for activating the cognitive reserves of the brain make it possible, on the basis of cross-modal reorganization of the functional systems of the brain, to ensure successful learning under conditions of sensory deprivation.

Smart education is education that is based not only on socio-technological development, but also on the inclusion of even vulnerable groups in our society. Mobile learning must use technologies that enable disabled people to access to educational services fully. This requires that the development of mobile learning platforms and applications be developed in accordance with international accessibility standards or guidelines of specific mobile operating system.

A questionnaire has been conducted among computer science students targeted to studying students' attitude towards m-learning. Some of the platforms and applications the students reported: Coursera, Duolingo, freeCodeCamp, Kahoot, Khan Academy, Memrise, Moodle, Quizlet, SoloLearn, Udemy [44].

Duolingo is the world's most popular Android education app among language learners. The software product uses a game technique: the lessons are arranged by levels in order to move to the next one, user must go through the previous one in whole or in part [45]. The number of its installations is over100 million.

SoloLearn is the largest collection of free programming learning materials for beginners and professionals. The application is designed for writing and runing real code by users in a mobile editor for Android [46]. It supports the following programming languages: HTML5, CSS3, JavaScript, Python, Kotlin, C++, C#, PHP and others. The number of its installations is over 5 million.

Moodle is the most popular learning management system worldwide. If the Moodle site is properly configured, the mobile app could be used to [47]:

- view the content of your courses, even when you are not online;
- receive instant notifications for messages and other events;
- quickly find and communicate with other people from your courses;
- upload images, audio, video, etc. files from your mobile device;
- see your grades from the course.

The number of Android app installations is over 10 million. Some of the popular mobile learning platforms are:

- Skill Cup is a universal constructor for organizing mobile learning [48]. They have been on the mobile learning market for 15 year and have 300 completed projects, over 20 million customer employees have increased their efficiency;
- ServiceGuru is a mobile service for personnel training [49];
- We Study is a platform for organizing blended learning [50].

- Nearpod is an integrated multimedia platform that allows the teacher to collaborate with students, as well as assess activities in real time. It is an online platform that allows you to create presentations for your classes and share them with students in real time [51].

Each of the listed applications or platforms has a different practical application - from language learning through programming languages to gamification. Depending on its purpose, different approaches are applied to improve accessibility and usability. The inclusion of disabled people is an important education development strategy.

3 Mobile Accessibility Formalization

The trend towards the use of mobile applications is directly related to the widespread usage of mobile devices. These services provide a wide range of opportunities for education to make more services available to the students. Delivering such an indispensable user experience when working with mobile applications is also related to ensuring their accessibility. It is based on the rules and principles defined in the accessibility standards.

The Web Accessibility Initiative (WAI) offers developers the necessary implementation of websites and mobile applications. The Web Content Accessibility Guidelines (WCAG 2.0) constitute a general standard that provides general principles for accessible development. The document "Mobile Accessibility: How WCAG 2.0 and Other W3C/WAI Guidelines Apply to Mobile" describes how WCAG 2.0 web content accessibility principles, guidelines, and success criteria can be applied to mobile devices, mobile web, native and hybrid apps. It provides informative guidance but requirements are not set.

The standard describes four principles of accessibility: perceivable, operable, understandable, and robust [12], which unite logically connected guidelines and success criteria of WCAG 2.0.

Principle 1: Perceivable is related to ensuring guidelines for: minimizing the amount of information that is put on small screens; using different methods of text resizing; bettering the screen contrast.

Principle 2: Operable is responsible for describing keyboard control for touchscreen devices, touch target size and spacing, touchscreen gestures, device manipulation gestures and placing buttons where they are easy to access.

Principle 3: Understandable is related to guidelines for: changing screen orientation and consistent layout, positioning important page elements before the page scroll, grouping operable elements that perform the same action, providing clear indication that elements are actionable and instructions for custom touchscreen and device manipulation gestures.

The last **Principle 4: Robust** is targeted to setting the virtual keyboard to the type of data entry required, providing easy methods for data entry and supporting the characteristic properties of the platform.

On the other hand, the leading mobile operating systems development companies – Google and Apple, are supporting platform-oriented guidelines that give to developers and designers basic knowledge for main accessibility issues. Google propose some best practices for Android accessibility, targeted to visually impaired people, color blind people, users with impaired hearing, dexterity, cognitive disabled people, and many other disabilities [15]. They include: increasing text visibility (it is related to bettering color contrast); using large, simple controls (each interactive UI element has a focusable area) and describing each UI element (mobile applications include a description that describes the element's purpose). Google propose four basic principles too [16] which every mobile application developer and designer should follow: labeling elements, using or extend system widgets, using cues other than color and making media content more accessible.

Best Practices for Inclusive Design of Apple are part of their Human Interface Guidelines which ensure that everyone can use and understand mobile applications that work on iOS [17]. Apple propose to specialists to Design mobile applications with accessibility in mind that means prioritizing simplicity and perceivability. They relate the simplicity to allowing known, consistent interactions that simplify complex tasks and make them easy to perform [17]. The Perceivability means ensuring that all content can be perceived, regardless of the human senses used - sight, hearing or touch [17]. Apple divides their mobile accessibility principles into following groups: User interactions, Navigation, Text Size and Weight, Color and Contrast, Appearance Effects and Motion and Content.

Standards and principles create a formal framework that guides developers and designers can follow to ensure the accessibility of their applications. There are several intersections between the standard and the Google and Apple guidelines. These are in terms of text, contrast, ways to navigate and maintain standard gestures.

4   An Approach to m-Accessibility Evaluation

CEN, the European Committee for Standardization, developed a standard EN 17161:2019 "Design for All – Accessibility following a Design for All approach in products, goods and services – Extending the range of users" which is based on Design for All approach [24]. The purpose of the standard is to assist companies, regardless of their size, in developing accessibility-oriented products. Figure 3 shows the stages of the design process for all. The interrelations between the processes, procedures and activities are shown that are used to achieve accessibility outcomes based on the application of a Design for All approach.

Defining design objectives and approaches to achieve them takes place during the planning phase. At the next stage (Operation) it is observed whether these goals are compatible with the requirements of users, including people with disabilities, accessible products and services are developed. And at the last stage (Performance Evaluation) is performed monitoring, measuring, analyzing and evaluating the effectiveness and correctness of the Design for All approach and its accessibility outcomes [24].

Based on the formal framework set by EN 17161: 2019, we would like to propose an evaluation approach to the mobile learning software accessibility. We suggest to use process approach defined in ISO 9001 that can be applied to any organization and any management system despite of type, size or complexity [42, 43]. It should assist companies in evaluating m-learning accessibility in a coordinated manner, with clearly

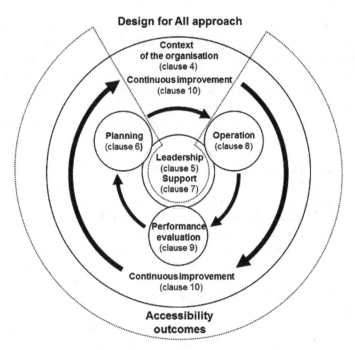

Fig. 3. The scheme of the design for all approach [24].

defined input parameters, constraints, and output artifacts. We propose that accessibility assessment be considered as a business process that takes place in the following phases: Planning, Testing, Analyzing and Reporting (see Fig. 4). The main points in defining the process are related to the correct description of its implementation, related to the determination of the input parameters, constraints, stages of implementation and generated output artifacts.

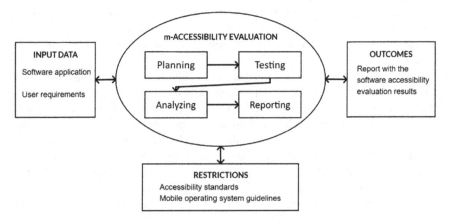

Fig. 4. An approach to m-accessibility evaluation.

The *input data* that the business process receives is the software application that will be evaluated, as well as the requirements of the users.

The *restrictions* that affect the implementation of the process relate to the formal frameworks imposed by the mobile accessibility standards, the specifics of developing mobile applications for a mobile operating system and the rules and principles for ensuring their accessibility.

Each of the phases of the m-accessibility evaluation process is a sub-process. As stated in EN 17161: 2019, *planning* is the first phase during which the objectives of the evaluation and the deadlines for implementation are defined. As is well known, a well-designed plan reduces the cost of implementing the next phases. It simultaneously covers the needs of several teams that participate in software development: designers, developers, managers. The plan needs to be reviewed, approved and adjusted as necessary by each team that is directly affected by the results of the evaluation. The goal is for the relevant team to get the feedback from users that it needs.

The second phase is *testing* the software application accessibility. Accessibility testing tools based on WCAG 2.0 can be used for this purpose. Examples are WCAG Accessibility Checklist for Android or for iOS, Accessibility insights for Android, UBKAccessibilityKit for iOS, A11y Ally by Quittle, Ax for Android, etc. [25] Such tools would increase productivity in the business process.

The next phase of the m-accessibility evaluation process is the *accessibility analysis*. Based on the above-mentioned standard, best practices and principles, *we could propose some basic mobile applications accessibility evaluation criteria*. They are as follows:

- **Ensuring better contrast** – people must be able to distinguish objects from the interface and be able to communicate with them correctly. It is necessary to consider color combinations that are suitable for people with color blindness. When there is sufficient contrast between UI objects, readability and recognizability are improved.
- **Appropriately formatted text content** – due to the specifics of mobile devices, textual content in mobile applications is kept to a minimum, but still needs to be designed to be accessible. It is necessary to provide opportunities for increasing the size of the text, thickening the names of important functionalities or groups of such, highlighting links.
- **Consistent navigation support** – the content of mobile applications is located on multiple screens, between which meaningful navigation must be maintained. UI elements should be ordered and linked so that sighted users can understand the connections between them. It is necessary to emphasize whether the elements are navigable or not. Mobile operating systems'default manipulation gestures must also be maintained. From the point of view of blind users, mobile applications should support accessibility features that provide access to Apple iOS VoiceOver or Google Android TalkBack.
- **Accessible Media Content** – if the mobile application includes multimedia content, such as audio or video, additional functionality must be supported that allows content control, subtitle inclusion, or alternative text content.
- **Compatibility with m-accessibility standards** – these can be specific for certain mobile operating system or international accessibility standards.

The results of the analysis are summarized and we move on to the last phase of the business process – *reporting*. The reports include the final assessment of the software product m-availability and recommendations for its improvement. They are usually made in free form, as there is no single established format. It is advisable to refer to the first phase, indicating whether the project is completed on time and the criteria for success of the project are met.

As *output artifacts* of the process it is expected to receive reports with the results of its implementation and recommendations for improving the m-accessibility of the specific mobile application.

5   Results

Mobile platforms aim to provide the customer with the ability to make changes to the application in accordance with their requirements, aesthetics and ease of access. For example, most mobile platforms have accessibility features that make it easier for the user to access information. These functions include: changing the screen size, color and font size, increasing text, changing the brightness and contrast, and others. The extensive personalization options of the application make the educational process more individual.

To install mobile applications, Google Play and App Store services are used for Android and iOS, respectively. The following characteristics of mobile education applications can be considered: app rating; number of ratings; number of installations; user reviews. Based on some researches [29–32], we decided to test the accessibility of Moodle (Modular Object-Oriented Dynamic Learning Environment) mobile application as one of the most popular learning management systems used in e-learning [33]. A mobile application is available in the Google Play and Apple App Store, with more than 10 million installations in Google Play [34]. The mobile application can be used after entering the address of the e-learning platform of the respective university, school or institution. The user then logs in with his e-learning system username and password and gets access to all available learning materials.

We made the test under the Android OS. We used the Axe for Android mobile application for the testing procedure. It is built to enable WCAG 2.1 conformance. It includes following accessibility rules: Color Contrast Analysis; Control Labeling; Image Labeling; Focus management [35]. The University of Economics – Varna teaching profile has been used. The home page test (Fig. 5) results 9 accessibility violations and 86 passes.

There are problems with search icon which touch target size does not meet the WCAG requirements. There are UI elements that have no text equivalents, which prevents people with visual impairments from using the application adequately.

We tested the accessibility of all of the courses in the platform of the teaching profile. The results are the same as home page results – some of the UI elements' (mainly text links) touch target size does not meet the WCAG requirements and other have no text equivalents. Courses that use multimedia content report errors for not maintaining adequate alternative content. This would create problems for people with visual impairments to use it.

In conclusion, the mobile application of Moodle meets for the most part the requirements for accessibility. It fully meets our accessibility evaluation criteria: Ensuring

Fig. 5. Mobile home page of e-learning platform of University of Economics – Varna.

better contrast; Appropriately formatted text content and Consistent navigation support. Moodle mobile application implements in itself the advantages of the mobile, namely:

- expanding learning opportunities at a convenient time and in any place;
- personalization and individualization of training;
- availability of tuition fees;
- gamification of the learning process;
- instant feedback and evaluation of learning outcomes;
- efficient use of time;
- increasing the quality and cost of teacher services;
- helping students with disabilities.

With the application of mobile technologies, learning becomes truly flexible: mobile devices can be used anytime and anywhere.

6   Discussion and Conclusions

Educational programs that are available online should both meet the needs of students and lead them to the goal, and comply with modern trends and technologies. Smart education development is dependent on the socio-technological progress. Its main element is transforming students to smart learners. The usage of mobile devices allows chunked short-term perception of information, which contributes to its better memorization. The assimilation of educational material can be facilitated due to the combination of the educational process itself and training of attention and memory (particularly with elements of gamification that can relieve the overall cognitive load), both tailored to the individual needs. Thus, the release of an educational product will turn out to be less popular and more unreasonable if it is not adapted for mobile devices - potential customers who value convenience and keep up with the times will prefer more advanced competitors. For a modern education system, a mobile application is almost a prerequisite. Potential clients will appreciate the ability to complete the program from any device.

In most publications on this topic, the evaluation of the accessibility of mobile applications is carried out manually. For example, in [52] the authors conduct a manual app accessibility evaluation using a Samsung S4 running Android 4.4 with TalkBack screen reader, iPhone 5 running iOS and VoiceOver screen reader. The disadvantage of this approach is the possibility of missing some of the problems of the tested product. On the other hand, many tools need to be combined, such as screen readers, color scheme testers, and more. That is why in our study we propose the use of automated tools to detect the mobile applications accessibility problems. These tools should implement international standards or recommendations that provide formal guidance for accessibility evaluation.

This paper examines the formal framework for m-accessibility, on the basis of which we have defined basic criteria for accessibility of mobile applications evaluation. In our opinion, it should be done as a controlled business process that has four phases: Planning, Testing, Analyzing and Reporting. We base our approach on the process approach defined in ISO 9001, as we take into account its advantages as horizontal management, controlling processes, understanding the stakeholders in the process, understanding and consistency in meeting requirements and achieving effective process performance.

The limitations of our current study are manifold: the small sample of tested application. We decided to concentrate on Moodle mobile app which is general purpose platform and it is used as a e-learning platform in University of Economics. Other limitations are related to requirements of some of the above-mentioned apps for corporate or paid login.

Still, we believe that our results can contribute to improving m-education applications accessibility evaluation and choice of appropriate testing tools.

Acknowledgment. The reported study was supported by project NPI-36/2019 "Contemporary Approaches to The Integration of Mobile Technologies in Higher Education" and by RFBR according to the research project No. 19-29-01017.

References

1. UNESCO: Education: From disruption to recovery. https://en.unesco.org/covid19/education response. Accessed 21 July 2020
2. World Health Organization: Disability and health. https://www.who.int/en/news-room/fact-sheets/detail/disability-and-health. Accessed 21 July 2020
3. World Bank. https://www.worldbank.org/en/topic/disability#1. Accessed 21 July 2020
4. United Nations. https://www.un.org/development/desa/disabilities/resources/factsheet-on-persons-with-disabilities.html. Accessed 21 July 2020

5. United Nations: Convention on the Rights of Persons with Disabilities (CRPD). https://www. un.org/development/desa/disabilities/convention-on-the-rights-of-persons-with-disabilities. html. Accessed 21 July 2020
6. United Nations: Convention on the Rights of Persons with Disabilities (CRPD), Article 24 – Education. https://www.un.org/development/desa/disabilities/convention-on-the-rights-of-persons-with-disabilities/article-24-education.html. Accessed 21 July 2020
7. United Nations: Transforming our world: the 2030 Agenda for Sustainable Development. https://sustainabledevelopment.un.org/post2015/transformingourworld. Accessed 21 July 2020
8. United Nations: Sustainable Development Goals. https://www.un.org/sustainabledevelopment/sustainable-development-goals/. Accessed 21 July 2020
9. We Are Social. Digital 2020. https://wearesocial.com/digital-2020. Accessed 21 July 2020
10. GSM Association: The Mobile Economy 2020. https://www.gsma.com/mobileeconomy/#key_stats. Accessed 21 July 2020
11. UNESCO: Mobile learning. https://en.unesco.org/themes/ict-education/mobile-learning. Accessed 21 July 2020
12. W3C: Mobile Accessibility: How WCAG 2.0 and Other W3C/WAI Guidelines Apply to Mobile. https://www.w3.org/TR/mobile-accessibility-mapping/. Accessed 22 July 2020
13. Zhuang, T., et al.: Smart learning environments for a smart city: from the perspective of lifelong and lifewide learning. Smart Learn. Environ. **4**, 6 (2017)
14. Dumančić, M.: Smart education in smart city and student model. In: Proceedings of the International Scientific Conference eLearning and Software for Education; Bucharest 2, pp. 64–71 (2019)
15. Google Developers: Make apps more accessible. https://developer.android.com/guide/topics/ui/accessibility/apps. Accessed 22 July 2020
16. Google Developers: Principles for improving app accessibility. https://developer.android.com/guide/topics/ui/accessibility/principles. Accessed 22 July 2020
17. Apple Developer: Best Practices for Inclusive Design. https://developer.apple.com/design/human-interface-guidelines/accessibility/overview/best-practices/. Accessed 22 July 2020
18. United Nations: Goal 11: Make cities inclusive, safe, resilient and sustainable. https://www.un.org/sustainabledevelopment/cities/. Accessed 22 July 2020
19. ISO: ISO 37106:2018(en) Sustainable cities and communities — Guidance on establishing smart city operating models for sustainable communities (2018)
20. ISO: ISO 37120:2018(en) Sustainable cities and communities — Indicators for city services and quality of life (2018)
21. ISO. ISO 37122:2019(en) Sustainable cities and communities — Indicators for smart cities (2019)
22. Williamson, B.: Educating the smart city: schooling smart citizens through computational urbanism. Big Data Soc. **2**(2), 1–13 (2015)
23. Zhu, Z., et. al.: A research framework of smart education. Smart Learn. Environ. **3**, 4 (2016)
24. CEN: New CEN standard: EN 17161:2019 on Accessibility. https://www.cen.eu/news/brief-news/Pages/NEWS-2019-014.aspx. Accessed 22 July 2020
25. Peri, R.: 17 Free Mobile Accessibility Testing Tools. https://www.digitala11y.com/free-mobile-accessibility-testing-tools/. Accessed 22 July 2020
26. Satista.com: Most popular Google Play app categories as of 1st quarter 2020, by share of available apps. https://www.statista.com/statistics/279286/google-play-android-app-categories/. Accessed 24 July 2020
27. Satista.com: Most popular Apple App Store categories in June 2020, by share of available apps. https://www.statista.com/statistics/270291/popular-categories-in-the-app-store/. Accessed 24 July 2020

28. Satista.com: Worldwide mobile education app downloads from 1st quarter 2017 to 1st quarter 2020, by platform (in millions). https://www.statista.com/statistics/1128262/mobile-educat ion-app-downloads-worldwide-platforms-millions/. Accessed 24 July 2020
29. Poulova, P., et. al.: Which One, or another? comparative analysis of selected LMS. Procedia – Soc. Behav. Sci. **186**, 1302–1308 (2015)
30. Nichols, M.: A comparison of two online learning systems. J. Open Flex. Distance Learn. **20**(1), 19–32 (2016)
31. Oliveira, P., et. al.: Learning Management Systems (LMS) and E-Learning management: an integrative review and research agenda. J. Inf. Syst. Technol. Manage. **13**(2), 157–180 (2016)
32. Al-Samarai, L., et. al.: An analysis of accessibility in learning management system in the context of higher education institution. Int. J. Comput. Sci. Mob. Comput. **8**(3), 261–268 (2019)
33. Moodle App. https://moodle.com/app/. Accessed 24 July 2020
34. Moodle. https://play.google.com/store/apps/details?id=com.moodle.moodlemobile&hl=en_ AU. Accessed 24 July 2020
35. Accessibility Engine (axe) for Android. https://play.google.com/store/apps/details?id=com. deque.axe.android. Accessed 24 July 2020
36. Todoranova, L., Penchev, B.: A conceptual framework for mobile learning development in higher education. In: Proceedings of the 21st International Conference on Computer Systems and Technologies '20 (CompSysTech '20). Association for Computing Machinery, pp. 251–257 (2020). https://doi.org/10.1145/3407982.3407996
37. Sulova, S., Bankov, B.: Approach for social media content-based analysis for vacation resorts. J. Commun. Softw. Syst. **15**(3), 262–270 (2019)
38. Stoyanova, M.: Good practices and recommendations for success in construction digitaliza- tion. TEM J. **9**(1), 42–47 (2020). https://doi.org/10.18421/tem91-07
39. Czaplewski, M.: Asymetria informacji w handlu elektronicznym. Ekonomista **5**, 727–751 (2016)
40. Panayotova, G., Dimitrov, G.P., Petrov, P., Os, B.: Modeling and data processing of informa- tion systems. In: 2016 Third International Conference on Artificial Intelligence and Pattern Recognition (AIPR), Lodz, pp. 1–5 (2016). https://doi.org/10.1109/icaipr.2016.7585229
41. Polkowski, Z., Zajac, D., Vasilev, J., Florina, A.L.: A content analysis of existing educational portals for teaching data warehouse and business intelligence. In: 2016 8th International Conference on Electronics, Computers and Artificial Intelligence (ECAI), pp. 1–6 (2016). https://doi.org/10.1109/ecai.2016.7861146
42. International Organization for Standardization. The Process Approach in ISO 9001: 2015. https://www.iso.org/files/live/sites/isoorg/files/archive/pdf/en/iso9001-2015-process- appr.pdf. Accessed 24 Aug 2020
43. International Organization for Standardization. ISO 9000 Introduction and Sup- port Package: Guidance on the Concept and Use of the Process Approach for management systems. https://www.iso.org/files/live/sites/isoorg/files/archive/pdf/en/04_con cept_and_use_of_the_process_approach_for_management_systems.pdf. Accessed 4 Aug 2020
44. Todoranova, L., Nacheva, R., Sulov, V., Penchev, B.: A model for mobile learning integration in higher education based on students' expectations. Int. J. Interact. Mob. Technol. (iJIM) **4**(11), 171–182 (2020). https://doi.org/10.3991/ijim.v14i11.13711
45. Duolingo: Learn Languages Free. https://play.google.com/store/apps/details?id=com.duo lingo. Accessed 24 Aug 2020
46. SoloLearn: Learn to Code for Free. https://play.google.com/store/apps/details?id=com.sol olearn. Accessed 24 Aug 2020
47. Moodle.   https://play.google.com/store/apps/details?id=com.moodle.moodlemobile. Accessed 24 Aug 2020

48. Skill Cup. https://www.skillcup.ru. Accessed 24 Aug 2020
49. ServiceGuru. https://www.service.guru/. Accessed 24 Aug 2020
50. We Study. https://we.study/. Accessed 24 Aug 2020
51. Nearpod. https://nearpod.com/. Accessed 24 Aug 2020
52. Serra, L.C., et al.: Accessibility evaluation of e-government mobile applications in Brazil. Procedia Comput. Sci. **67**, 348–357 (2015)

Implementing Open Government:
Lessons from Germany

Charlotte Lydia Bock[1(✉)] and Hasnain Bokhari[2]

[1] Willy Brandt School of Public Policy, University of Erfurt, Erfurt, Germany
charlotte.bock@uni-erfurt.de
[2] University of Erfurt, Erfurt, Germany
hasnain.bokhari@uni-erfurt.de

Abstract. Open Government encourages transparent, collaborative, and participatory governmental and administrative actions to promote a public administration that is effective, responsive and innovative. Germany signed up for Open Government Partnership in 2016 and since then it has promulgated two national action plans. Through its grass-roots level initiatives targeted at municipality and regional level German government wishes to enhance relation with its public. This paper aims at examining the German experience of initiating Open Government by reviewing the policy instruments at play and lessons that are involved in the implementation of this broadly government shaping movement. The paper first attempts to analyse the building blocks of German strategy that led to the first and later second National Action Plan for Open Government implementation. It also looks at important initiatives for enhanced citizen participation at the regional level, providing a best practice example. The paper concludes by sharing some important lessons that can not only be learnt for Germany itself but also for aspiring fellow Eurasian states and municipalities pursuing Open Government.

Keywords: Open Government implementation · Regional labs · Citizen participation · Model municipalities · Germany

1 Introduction

In 2017 when Germany went to polls for its 19th post-war federal election, Christian Democrats' (CDU/CSU) leader Angela Merkel was tipped to comfortably win a fourth term as German chancellor. The election results, however, brought Merkel's CDU/CSU and the other mainstream party Social Democrats (SPD) into a historic electoral embarrassment. Both parties posted their worst electoral performance since 1950s and lost more than 5% of their previous voters [1, 2]. For six months following September 2017 the mainstream parties went through hard bargaining as Merkel's CDU/CSU alone could not form a majority government. All sorts of electoral arithmetic were at play to form a coalition that could take Germany forward to form the 19th legislative assembly, and Merkel her fourth term. Even though Angela Merkel managed to stay in power by forming a grand coalition with SPD but 2017 left a deep scar on German electoral history. It provided à time for introspection as to what caused, among several

© Springer Nature Switzerland AG 2020
A. Chugunov et al. (Eds.): EGOSE 2020, CCIS 1349, pp. 124–138, 2020.
https://doi.org/10.1007/978-3-030-67238-6_9

other reasons, German public's displeasure and dissociation from mainstream parties, where this political apathy stemmed from and why the otherwise centre-right voters in Germany tried to find solace in parties with far-right mandate [2]. 2017 is also a significant year in German political history because early that year federal government gave its go-ahead to develop first National Action Plan (NAP) for Open Government. Germany joined Open Government Partnership (OGP) initiative in 2016. Open government as an administrative, political and social construct advocates for increased transparency in public policy formation, enhanced collaboration and improved citizen engagement [3]. If 2017's general elections in Germany serve as any proof then all the three open government promises were among the first causalities. The drop in mainstream parties' voters in German federal elections hints at growing public disengagement with politics and national political parties also seem disconnected from their public [4]. Open government as a concept in this regard offers an opportunity to address this disconnect [5]. In 2021 the OGP initiative will celebrate its tenth commemoration and since its inception in 2011, 78 countries have so far joined this initiative. Regardless of 2017 elections in Germany, the promise of open government initiative requires a bit of introspection. With 78 countries on board, can it be said that civil society can now co-create public policies by means of enhanced collaboration and citizen participation? Based on the transparent and reliant Open Data, do people have more trust in their government now and are more likely to participate in Open Government initiatives because they know their voices will be heard? After almost one decade of shoutout, loud promises, are citizens now more satisfied with their governments? Or how far have we come?

As a reaction to the perceived growing disenchantment with politics [6] co-creation of public policies with the civil society should be the answer to politics which largely neglected its roots of representing people and their needs [7]. OGP is a work in progress and follows an iterative process in which citizens and civil society organisations can be integrated into political processes by the means of modern information and communication technologies to shape this multilateral, political, and social process. Based on transparent, collaborative, and participatory governmental and administrative actions [8] it shall promote a public administration that is effective, responsive, transparent, participatory and innovative [9]. Based on that norms Open Government aims to enhance public and citizen value and make government action more comprehensible to citizens, thus increasing acceptance of decisions through their involvement [6]. At the same time it supports monitoring the public sectors' performance, improving its effectiveness and efficiency [10]. Open Data should foster the potential for innovation [6] and create social and economic value by disclose and reuse public open datasets.

The past one decade has witnessed an increased global interest in open government and the significance and regular roll-out of Open Data is continuously and positively influencing the public sector integrity. However, the benefits of Open Data, to a large extent, also depends on its transparency and reliability. Thus Open Data regulation and policy is vital to increased transparency [10]. Transparency in turn can be a prerequisite to reach new levels of citizen participation in government, one objective the global summit of Open Gov week is striving for. Higher transparency can further strengthen the relationship between government and third actors like citizens, civic society organisations (CSO) and enterprises [10] which can be a crucial factor considering the economic potential. For Germany it is estimated to be at 12.1 to 131.1 billion euros, assuming either a conservative or a proactive approach. Which approach can and will be taken depends tremendously on the way in which the opening of public administration data is pursued [11]. Transparent and non-manipulated Open Data are one of the prerequisites for the functioning of Open Government, which in turn is one tool to disclose and reuse Open Data for the inherent aim of Open Government to create added value. Added value thereby could be defined as social, political, economic and commercial added value.

Such a relationship can foster the debate about drawbacks of transparency and degrees of openness but also opens a plethora of enquiries. To begin with, what are possible consequences of the first out of five G8 Open Data Charter principles to provide all public data "open by default"? What is the degree of transparency that a state can pursue without compromising its sovereignty? Similarly, if governmental data is available across the borders, who owns that data? Regulation and law can play a fundamental role in this debate, resulting in that Open Data might not anymore be a purely technological debate. Having the power to question state sovereignty and simultaneously bearing immense economic potentials, it should become a public policy debate of highest priority.

The German government acknowledges the demands by civil societies for more participation and co-determination, especially since today's governments and societies are faced by numerous structural changes such as migration, energy, or digitalisation, causing disconcertion and distrust towards governmental institutions [5]. There are growing demands by the general public about more clarity on government objectives, its activities as well as decisions. The public would like to be engaged in local politics as an equal partner and also actively involved in implementation process. Additionally, the interest in Open Government from a municipal perspective appears to be very high, the expectations of the impact of Open Government got stated as higher transparency of municipal decisions and public acceptance, increased service quality for citizens and better solutions for municipal tasks [12].

The primary goal of this paper is to examine the German experience of initiating Open Government by reviewing the policy instruments at play. It attempts to show possibilities on where and how to begin with the implementation of this broadly government shaping movement. The paper follows a qualitative approach to review the German strategy and experience by analysing respective international, governmental and municipal strategy and policy papers. In its pursuit of assessing the strategic steps and policy measures taken for implementation of Open Government, this paper first attempts to analyse the building blocks of German strategy that led to the first and later second National Action Plan for Open Government implementation. Acknowledging the regional uptake of Open Government in Germany the paper also looks at a case study that may function as a framework for aspiring fellow Eurasian states and municipalities pursuing Open Government other countries' implementation efforts, followed by lessons learned from the realisation of two National Action Plans as well as two national Open Government project initiatives. Additionally, the paper explores Open Data as a vital component of Open Government and discusses its aspects in the light of its potential threats and benefits. The authors conclude by discussing Germanys implementation efforts within its existing frame and provide possible future research directions and prospective.

2 State of Open Government Implementation in Germany

To meet the publics' need of comprehensive participation in decision making, Germany made several efforts to come up with an approach that could bring majority of stakeholders together, including civil society organisations, academic experts as well as administrative and governmental staff, to initiate an Open Government implementation. After joining OGP in 2016, since 2017 Germany started working towards its first National Action Plan (NAP) for Open Government implementation [3]. Post September 2017 federal election, the mandate of Open Government moved from Federal Ministry of Interior to Federal Chancellery [9]. The core idea was to develop the IT planning commission within the chancellery that could supervise Open Government implementation and more importantly open government implementation should be made a responsibility of federal states. Germany's strategy was to establish a grass-roots level approach by empowering the municipalities in 16 federal states and giving them autonomy on the implementation of Open Government. The motivation of open government's trickle-down effect led to the launch of "Model Commune Open Government" initiative that aims at enhancing citizens' participation in local decision making and to be the starting point of lived administrative cultural change [12]. After the end of the first NAPs period and the comprehensive evaluation of its activities and supporting project, a second NAP was rolled out in 2019. The second NAP was accompanied by a novel initiative of "Open Government labs" that aim to create a sustainable local platform for regular Open Government activities. Both strive for an in-depth understanding of how to implement Open Government at the grass-roots level and close the perceived gap between the local population and their administrative bodies.

Although the concepts of digitalisation have been recently floated in media and public, however, Germany has been making a gradual progress towards eGovernment implementation since early 2000. This progress was also strongly backed by three important components, the European academia, private sector and EU's directives. Since 2001 the European academia has been regularly hosting annual eGovernment conferences which provides a useful repository of not only case studies but also eGovernment's development chronology in Europe. Similarly, the private sector's creative web solutions have continued to inspire the public sector for an uptake of web solutions for electronic public service delivery. Germany's public sector organisations such as Deutsche Post/DHL, banks or German railways were among the initial subscribers of technology uptake. More importantly, the foundations of Open Government in Germany were also supplemented by European Commission's active support for the spread of electronic public service delivery and eGovernment implementation.

Within the German context, Germany undertook three important steps for the adoption and implementation of open data programmes [13]. First, Germany went through an initial exploration of open data in early 2000 when an interest towards transparency and open access to government data started to emerge. This curiosity eventually led to the legal cover in January 2006 when Germany passed Freedom of Information Act that provided German citizens with the right to request information held by federal authorities [3]. The second step determined by experimentation and consolidation efforts to help elaborate and establish Open Data activities. The third step in this regard is the strengthening of international collaboration on common principles. As a testimony to the global relevance of Open Data and the important role it can play for improvements in government and governance as well as in growth stimulation, fostered by innovation in data-driven products and services, the G8 Open Data Charter was enacted in June 2013 at the G8 summit in Lough Erne in Northern Ireland. The five principles adopted are Open Data by Default, Quality and Quantity, Useable by All, Releasing Data for Improved Governance and Releasing Data for Innovation [14].

In 2013, the German Bundestag also passed the eGovernment Act, its first law on eGovernment (EGovG), setting the regulatory framework for digitisation in the federal administration [14]. On 12th July 2017, the eGovernment Act of 2013 got complemented by Sect. 12a, obliging the members of the direct federal administration to make unprocessed data available via publicly accessible networks [15]. This data was collected in the fulfilment of public law tasks or have had collected by third parties on government's behalf [16]. Section 12a was adopted on behalf of the announcement of the Federal Open Data Act of 18th May 2017 [16]. It was seen necessary due to the present risk that Germany might not be able to benefit from the opportunities offered by the provision of administrative data as open data. All federal states especially Baden-Wuerttemberg, Bavaria, Lower Saxony and North Rhine-Westphalia are currently developing their own open data regulations [9]. Since 2015 the national data portal GovData.de has been in operation used by federal, state and local authorities to publish their respective data. These initiatives have led to Germany climbing in the European benchmarking ranks. In 2019, EU28 + open data maturity reported Germany at the 12th position whereas the trend-setters include Ireland as the leading force, followed by Spain and France [17]. A German Open Data strategy is not introduced yet but considered to be in process at federal level [17]. Moreover, the federal government recommends the establishment of an own "Open Data Officer" throughout all public agencies, discussing Open Data policies and coordination issues every second month [18].

Backed by the data provided on the GovData.de portal and aiming to prove the local levels' potential on behalf of the eGovernment Act from 2013, the pilot project "Model Communes E-Government" was conducted in a few municipalities between 2014 and 2016 by the Association of German Cities, the Association of German Counties and the Association of German Cities and Municipalities [19]. Collected valuable experiences while stating advancements in the field, eGovernment remained a matter of high priority which among others led to Germany's announcement of participation at the OGP in December 2016. With its formal membership in OGP, Germany subsequently launched the first National Action Plan (2017–2019) in August 2017. Though ambitious, but as per the first NAP, Germany wishes to become a pioneer in the field of open data [3]. Germany's first NAP stated as prior commitment the implementation of Open Data in administrative practice by the Federal Ministry of the Interior until June 2019, aiming for more transparency and innovation as well as strengthening the common knowledge of the administrative bodies of the direct federal administration for an effective implementation. The first milestone in this respect was to elaborate an evaluation and implementation plan of pending commitments of the G8 Open Data Action Plan by December 2017. A second commitment on Open Data was made by the effort to foster the Open Data environment. Another commitment states the establishment of reliable open-data ecosystem by the identification and reduction of existing deficits as well as constructive dialogue with stakeholders to promote the use and quality of Open Data.

During the implementation period of the first NAP, three major changes influencing the action plans' framework took place. First, post-September 2017's federal election, the 19th legislative assembly headed by a grand coalition between CDU/CSU and SPD reassured their strong support towards OGP commitments. The second change was the transfer of OG mandate. Till 2017, the OGP activities and coordination were supervised by the Federal Ministry of the Interior led by Thomas de Maizière. This mandate was transferred from Ministry of Interior to the Federal Chancellery [9]. The third change refers to the IT Planning Council's' decision to involve all the 16 federal states and municipalities into the next NAP and to be presented in their own chapter. In November 2018 the interim report noted the achievement of 25 of the 68 milestones, 31 running on schedule, and 11 milestones running behind planned time schedule. Similarly, some of the milestones stated to be delayed due to government formation process and the transfer of responsibility.

To gain experiences in the implementation of the novel concept of Open Government from 2017 to 2019, the project "Model Communes Open Government" as part of the first National Action Plan was conducted in nine model municipalities, piloting Open Government establishment in local authorities [12]. The project also worked out how citizens can use the services offered and whether their participation promotes municipal innovation. Within the framework of the model project, various workshops were held with the participating municipalities to identify the practical challenges faced by actors in the municipal sphere when dealing with issues relating to the implementation of open government. A total of six strategic fields of action were identified: Municipal policy, information and data management, organisation and cooperation, administrative culture and change management, human resources management, leadership and steering [12]. Building on the predominantly positive experience of the first NAP and its accompanying project, the second NAP 2019-2021 commits Germany for further development in Open Government implementation and promotion of the Open Data environment. Its objectives are aimed at strengthening the common knowledge base and the development of coherent criteria for the implementation of Open Data in the federal administration in order to achieve a common understanding in the implementation of the Open Data concept and to promote cultural change in public administration. Within the context of implementation of the G8 Charter, the second NAP states commitment on the promotion of transparency and participation also in international development cooperation. In this regard, as one of the milestones in second NAP also wishes to consolidate the coordination of strategic steps with ministries and civil society that may assist in implementation of the principles of Open Data by December 2020 [5]. Germany as one of the most active and important partnering countries in global development cooperation should also aim to be the guiding light by the application of Open Data, bearing huge potentials for reformed approaches in how development cooperation gets conducted.

Even though the Federal Chancellery took over the responsibility for Open Government in Germany in 2017/18, the Ministry of the Interior still supports this initiative because of the involvement of civil society, the aim to increase civil participation and the creation of local social added value. Additionally, the funding has also been shifted out of this Ministry's budget. Building up more local capacities, the Federal Ministry of the Interior supports an initiative for Regional Open Government Laboratories (regOGL) as part of the second NAP. In the timeframe from between 2020 and 2022, 16 municipal laboratories are expected to conduct trials of regional Open Government. Even though the Federal Chancellery took over the responsibility for Open Government in Germany, the Ministry of the Interior will support this initiative because of the involvement of civil society, the aim to increase civil participation and the creation of local social added value. Also the funding is out of this Ministry's budget [20]. With the Regional Open Government Laboratories, citizens are expected to be more involved in local decisions. The rationale behind local participation is to empower people to actively shape their community and their living environment. At the same time, this shall strengthen the citizens' tie to their region and social cohesion in towns and communities as a form of homeland politics [21].

The shift of Open Government mandate from federal level to states and municipal level has the potential for increased citizen participation, particularly through the open data projects. In this regard few of the federal states in Germany have shown sustainable commitment particularly the state of North Rhein Westphalia and Baden Württemberg seem to be at the forefront of Open Government implementation. The launch of regOGL can work as a game changer. A number of regional initiatives have already been started in Germany. One such initiative comes from the German state of North Rhein Westphalia (NRW) that has been a part of both first and second NAP in Germany. NRW is perhaps among the advanced federal states of Germany with regard to digitalisation, Open Government and eGovernment development. It has set up their OG commitments, projects and Open Data on a dedicated webpage "open.nrw". Since the first NAP, the city of Moers in NRW has been participating in the project "Model Commune Open Government". Moers got accepted to be part of the follow-up project "Open Government labs" that aims to create a sustainable platform for regular Open Government activities.

Inspired by a study published in 2012 by the Fraunhofer Fokus Institute [22], four different institutions from the city of Moers came together to form a cooperation agreement between the administration of the city of Moers, the local high school, the Rhine-Waal University of Applied Sciences and the Open Knowledge Lab Niederrhein [6]. This cooperation resulted in a project "data goes school" in 2017. The project was funded from the "Pilot Municipality OpenGovernment NRW" programme of www. open.nrw and aims at a new educational design (Open Educational Resources) and derives its roots from Open Data principle.

The "data goes school" project started as a voluntary university project offered within the graduate course on 'New Public Management' in the eGovernment module at the Rhine-Waal University of Applied Sciences. Its goal was to elaborate a project reflecting the interests of school children, students, teachers, administrative employees and civil society actors, which simultaneously can sustainably be used and further elaborated in school and university education. As of 2020 the joint activities concluded in a local election results portal and a budget visualisation for the municipality of Moers as well as an energy consumption data portal for high schools in Moers. A number of questions raised in the portal included among others, "How can the election results be explained?", "What is our tax money spent on and why?", and "How can buildings be made more energy efficient?" [23].

Through a common ambition to utilise Open Data for the purpose of creating social added value, four different parties of public life have come together in a superordinate community of interests. The initial idea did not come from the state official, but was the result of a brainstorming among students and their professors who, in the course of their conviction, brought other volunteers on board. No financial reward was in prospect but the aim to create social added value individuals and social groups can sustainably benefit from. Moreover, for cross-regional learning effect, this project has made its guide available for download free of charge, thereby sharing its recipe of successful implementation into an open and transparent tool for the implementation of Open Government and the use of Open Data. To maintain and further enhance the triggered developments, in winter semester 2020–2021 the degree programme eGovernment will be offered in an additional, dual-vocational mode of study in collaboration with the State Government of North Rhine-Westphalia [24]. Open Government as such and also as the above example has showed, is a work in progress. It builds upon iterative process by engaging several stakeholders in particular the citizens and municipalities. Open government as acknowledged in Germany is not an end rather it is a tool that can assist in improving mutual interactions where the civil society has to take a lead.

3   Lessons Learned

Since joining the Open Government Partnership in 2016, so far Germany has rolled out two action plans. The first National Action Plan (NAP) completed its mandate from 2017 to 2019 whereas the second NAP (2019–2021) is still in progress. The first NAP as such focused on the initiative of Model Commune Open Government that has brought the OG mandate right at the municipal level. It is at the municipality level where citizens engage with, conduct their day to day business and it is at this level which fosters the open cooperation between administration and citizens. Similarly, the second NAP whereas has built upon the lessons learnt from municipal level engagement and extends this by fostering additional initiative that aims to launch regional Open Government laboratories.

By conducting administration-focused initiative (Model Commune Open Government) and citizen-focused initiative (Regional Open Government Laboratories), Germany has so far made a variety of experiences. A number of lessons can be learnt from this implementation which may be useful for those Eurasian municipalities that are deliberating about the uptake of Open Government. Similarly, these lessons may also be useful for German municipalities itself. The following sections wish to elaborate these lessons that might be most useful and important to pass them on.

3.1   Personal Capacities of Citizen and Administrative Staff

Starting with positive experience, the regional Open Government lab Niederrhein presents an example of an Open Government collaboration. This collaboration of four institutions to build up personnel future key capacities envisions how future generation can be taught to use Open Data and in particular to create social added value by its means. Data literacy gets actively approached as part of school education, aiming to include this practice into the school education system, pointing out current debates and increasing creativity to find appropriate and feasible solutions. Implementing grass-roots Open Government in NRW bore fruits and the federal state continues to work towards the education of eGovernment experts by offering university studies like at Rhine-Waal University, as well as dual courses of study in eGovernment in cooperation with the state agency IT.NRW, combining theoretical semesters with practical training modules.

However, to train administrative staff in this field is a measure that should have been taken a few years earlier. In view of the current shortage of specialists in administrative professions in Germany and the increasing average age of local administrative officials, the ambitious reform of the administrative apparatus must be pursued in the upcoming years mainly with existing personnel capacities and structures. A lack of willingness and competence for open working methods on the part of both managers and employees also seem major hurdles. The competencies required for the implementation of Open Government, such as data literacy, are often not yet developed at especially the municipal level. When external, supposedly more competent people are recruited and higher-rated positions are created, there is a risk that the willingness and acceptance of new administrative concepts may decrease. Matching the above a critical success factor can also be seen in the development of Open Government competencies in the current workforce, as well as strategic personnel planning with the aim of further developing existing requirement profiles. In order to promote and experience digital work, it seems advisable to use it as a tool for routine activities and to offer home office. In this way, on the one hand, personnel capacities are gained and on the other hand, digital work can be used as an accepted basic building block for Open Government activities [12].

3.2   Open Data Policies and Platforms

Being supported by the EU and national law to create own Open Data policies, federal states should make use of it to adapt them to their local necessities and circumstances. Hence, federal agendas can be pushed forward. The creation of Open Data platforms at federal and municipal level have the potential to promote transparency and are fundamental to Open Government activities. By supporting those actively the local government underlines their effort to reach out and cooperate with their citizens, which in turn seems to enhance trust towards the administrative bodies and enhance willingness to participate in the offered initiatives. As seen from the case of Germany, Open Data leads to multi-layered debates and contains many aspects which need to be approached for successful implementation of Open Government. Thereby information and data management contain the aspects of Open Data, interoperability, free software and digital volunteering. Open Data as a concept and the state website GovData depends essentially on the willingness and ability of municipal administrations to make data and information available. Digital volunteering includes the activities of supporting digitisation projects with the aim of making data and information available to the public and using it, as well as voluntary efforts to use open source software, reflecting the will to detach from expensive software. This concept of voluntary participation is not yet fully developed at the municipal level [12], but could be a key component on the way towards a digital society. This engagement could possibly be promoted within the higher education curriculum.

3.3   Participation and Inclusion

The first NAP of Germany had set a priority on the inclusion of civil society. In this regard, 103 representatives of foundations, associations, initiatives and universities were invited to a first workshop at the Federal Ministry of the Interior in February 2017 that resulted in total 265 ideas. The federal webpage verwaltung-innovativ.de notes the implementation of the workshop in February 2017, but it would have been interesting for the growth of OG to clearly put out the participating institutions, civil society groups and the list of agendas. Similarly, as per the interim report, the consultation period of two weeks with the civil society resulted in only one response. Regarding time schedules and considering that high quality responses do need time to be elaborated, the consultation period seem too short. At least four weeks for internal organisation and elaboration of valuable comments should have been provided. These flaws, however, have been improved in the second NAP. An online consultation period to comment on the second NAP before its release in September 2019 lasted four weeks, from end of March until end of April 2019. Also, a participation list as well as a result document including a workshop minute is available on verwaltung-innovativ.de. A detailed look at the participants' list reveals that out of the 80 participants, 28 stem from governmental agencies, 7 from a consultancy firm, 11 from foundations, 7 from the OGP and OG Network Germany. On one hand, Germany wishes to invest big effort to include civic society into the elaboration of the NAPs but on the other hand, the involvement of those municipal actors seems low. The enhanced dialogue and inclusion of the local implementing actors may help to make the iterative process of Open Government implementation efforts more effective.

3.4   Cooperation, Coordination and Organisation

Interdisciplinary and cross-organisational coordination and cooperation within the local government is essential for open government implementation. Based on the project report of model municipality project, there seems to be a lack of integrated and cross-sectional administrative thinking. The iterative process that is characteristic of and necessary for implementation is contrasted with rigid administrative organisational and coordination structures. Another challenge is also the lack of cooperation between neighbouring local authorities. Developing meaningful vertical divisions of labour, for example in the area of digital infrastructures or the development of technical and functional service approaches could be one possibility. In this regard, it is recommended to establish a central management of administrative development that is legitimate throughout the administration and to establish task-related project structures to ensure a systematic strengthening and consistent promotion of networking and cooperation in the public administration system. In terms of internal organisation, Open Government requires the creation of numerous opportunities for experimenting with new approaches, between and outside the administrative structures [12].

3.5   Bureaucratic Cultures

In highly bureaucratic and administrative set-up Open Government is not seen as a strategic cross-cutting issue, but rather as approaches to selective administrative development. This is due to the fact that most of the leadership roles are organisational or status-related, and that administrations are hierarchically structured. Instruments such as checklists, guidance in the form of practical examples for designing the implementation process and argumentation templates help to better clarify and reflect on opportunities and approaches in open government. In this respect, it seems helpful if the administrative leaders themselves communicate necessities transparently and promote them in everyday life, in order to be able to promote corresponding motivations and added value more strategically as well as to "translate" them consistently [12]. Demands for more transparency in many administrations can still be perceived predominantly negatively as a pressure to justify oneself. The establishment of a culture of trust and error within the organisation seems capable of counteracting the issues mentioned above. Therefore, the personnel basis should be systematically expanded and new team structures with procedural innovations should be created [12].

3.6   Political Participation

Amidst widespread political discontent and detachment, political participation and the role of civil society is of prime importance [25]. Open Data offers a unique opportunity to be an alternative tool to illustrate the economic and social impact of current and past political agendas and goals. Open Data can be used to illustrate reliable and impartial analyses that can promote active understanding of political debates within the general public. The dissemination and inclusion of such impartial political analyses among the general population can be an important task for regional Open Government Laboratories. Civic and political education can, for instance, be fostered through a cooperation between a regOG Lab and the local newspaper(s), which could introduce a weekly column in its op-ed section. The analyses reflected in these newspaper columns can not only reflect the status of political debates but there are also various possibilities to create and use synergy effects with civil society. A possible example is of the regOG Lab that can take every political party as its focus of political analysis for one month. Similarly, with the help of Open Data it is more convenient to undertake complex comparison of current government agendas with the previous election manifestos. The weekly newspaper columns can provide the space to present data-driven scenarios in comprehensive and narrative-based formats. This can be further supplemented by hosting a panel discussion at the regOG Lab with the respective political party along with the civil society representatives. These efforts lead to a constructive political dialogue where civil society is included and involved in the deliberative space and can also better relate to political decisions. Similarly, the government can also better deal with the political disconnect by offering a platform for political participation that is supported through the network of regOG Labs. It can in fact also enable the regOG Labs to function as independent political think tanks.

4 Discussion

Governments must now address "how to institutionalise open data as an integrated practice" [13]. Potential threats could arise in the challenge to steer operational and administrative systems in the framework of expanding Open Data policies. Due to its inherent complexity Open Data policies should be shaped and led within an overarching governmental strategy, also to clarify responsibilities. Communicating policy frameworks transparently may foster public trust in government. Nevertheless, governments still lack knowledge on the governance of Open Data, therefore "we do not just need governance of open data; we also need open governance of data" [13]. In an international comparison, Germany ranks 27 in the open data index in 2015. Two years before Germany was found on rank 11, indicating a significantly increased velocity of Open Data sector developments in 16 other countries. "Germany is accepting the risk of losing touch with developments in the open Data sector" [11]. In the course of the institutionalisation of Open Data and the necessity of interministerial coherence and convergence of actions, Open Data creates a platform, a new form of open-source governance, enabling governments to explore new types of collaboration and partnership with each other [13]. Increasing the potential for innovation in between governments Open Data could also turn out to be an important foundation for a growth and opportunity-oriented country [15]. Taking the economic potentials into consideration the systematic publication of administrative data in a uniform and machine-readable standard can create broad possibilities for start-ups and small and medium sized enterprises (SMEs). Publishing raw data material provides various opportunities for data-driven business models.

Some of the potentials of Open Data still need to be unearthed. The study conducted by Konrad Adenauer Foundation concludes that Open Government implementation can lead to the development of new business modelsand scientific community and work can be exponentially accelerated and more importantly the processed data can improve decision making [11]. As stated in the introduction, the economic potential depends on Germany's approach towards Open Data. A realistic estimation for Germany seems to be the election of an ambitious, proactive approach over a conservative or optimistic one. Therefore, to achieve a minimum economic potential of 43.1 billion euros per year and the creation of 20,000 new jobs, Germany would have to follow the G8 Charter's intended strategy of "open by default".

Germany has a tendency to be mostly a policy follower instead of a guiding force when it comes to novel developments in Open Data and Open Government. The projects within the regional Open Government labs and at municipality level show that a proactive and optimistic approach can most likely benefit both government and citizen to become a leader in Open Data. Tackling the implementation efforts of Open

Government down to the municipality level and desiring a cultural change in municipal administrations, the federal level has to go ahead as a visible and strong role model.

Politics should pave the way for civic action, because changes in a society still have to trigger from within. If civilians come up with promising ideas like at Rhine-Waal University of Applied Sciences, then it is the task of the local government to perceive those efforts and to pave the way for the implementation of these ideas. As illustrated in the case, each party involved takes the part they are best in, working with comparative advantages on a Pareto optimal solution. Benevolent participation makes no party worse off without making oneself worse off, therefore civil engagement gets rewarded by the social added value created, tying in with the basic ideas of solidarity system and welfare state.

5 Conclusion

This paper has tried to examine the complicated path peppered with a complex web of political intricacies that has led to the initiation of Open Government in Germany. One of the important lessons that this paper has highlighted is the implementation of Open Government as a trial and error process that finds its roots in its societal strengths and national essence, in line with policy making efforts and digital capacity building. Such an indigenous effort to carry out an implementation process for Open Government into an individual national context not only holds an importance but also bears best-practice approach for fellow Eurasian governments and municipalities. The primary prerequisite for participating in Open Government initiatives, as this paper has tried to argue, is knowledge and education for citizens and bureaucracy alike. School and university curricula require immediate improvement for building future human resource capacity. In order to be able to read and use Open Data, citizens need appropriate, moreover, specific data literacy. These much-needed capacity building measures will impact the future course of not only Open Government in general but the digital age in particular.

Without these capacity-enhancing measures, it could possibly lead to Germany's societal regression in the context of economic, political and social comparison at international front. As the two National Action Plans adopted by Germany have shown, the Open Government carries the strong potential to play an intermediary between citizens and their government. A decisive factor in this regard is the essential data skills for the majority of citizens, which could also form the basis for the digital society. Germany has the long-standing tradition of civic volunteering and participation, especially at the municipal level. This national strength, along with the reformed curricula, has the potential to create comprehensive social added value and to promote constructive and fact-based political debate. Civic engagement in Open Government initiatives would more likely increase if citizens are actively engaged in political debate and are also able to use Open Data with the tools provided by civil society organizations such as the regional Open Government laboratories.

References

1. German Bundestag. Bundestagswahlergebnisse seit 1949 – Zweitstimmen In: Deutscher Bundestag (2017). https://www.bundestag.de/parlament/wahlen/ergebnisse_seit1949-2446 92. Accessed 02 July 2020

2. Brenke, K., Kritikos, A.: Wohin die Wählerschaft bei der Bundestagswahl 2017 wanderte, DIW Wochenbericht **87**(17), 300–310 (2020). https://www.diw.de/de/diw_01.c.761730.de/ publikationen/wochenberichte/2020_17_1/wohin_die_waehlerschaft_bei_der_bundestags wahl_2017_wanderte.html. Accessed 10 July 2020

3. Federal Ministry of the Interior, "Erster Nationaler Aktionsplan 2017–2019," Berlin (2017). https://www.bmi.bund.de/SharedDocs/downloads/DE/veroeffentlichungen/themen/moderne-verwaltung/ogp-aktionsplan.pdf?__blob=publicationFile&v=1. Accessed 02 July 2020

4. Decker, F., Best, V., Fischer, S., Küppers, A.: Vertrauen in Demokratie Wie zufrieden sind die Menschen in Deutschland mit Regierung, Staat und Politik? (2019). https://www.fes.de/ studie-vertrauen-in-demokratie. Accessed 02 July 2020

5. Federal Chancellery. Zweiter nationaler Aktionsplan (NAP) 2019 – 2021 im Rahmen der Teilnahme an der Open Government Partnership (OGP), Berlin (2019) https://www. bundesregierung.de/resource/blob/997532/1667398/d3a4e7a0597be1d49dc37237a3849aca/ 2019-09-04-nationaler-aktionsplan-ogp-data.pdf. Accessed 02 July 2020

6. Konrad Adenauer Foundation. Open Government und Open Data: Tranzparenz, Partizipation, Kooperation (2017). https://www.kas.de/c/document_library/get_file?uuid=5f2bfe6c-d3f1-7e13-b1b8-9d025c0e29a9&groupId=252038. Accessed 02 July 2020

7. DeLeon, P., DeLeon, L.: What ever happened to policy implementation? an alternative approach. J. Public Adm. Res. Theory **12**(4), 467–492 (2002)

8. Wirtz, B.W., Birkmeyer, S.: Open government: origin, development, and conceptual perspectives. Int. J. Public Adm. **38**(5), 381–396 (2015)

9. Federal Chancellery: Interim Report by the Federal Government on the Implementation of the First National Action Plan (NAP) for 2017 – 19 in the Framework of Germany's Participation in the Open Government Partnership (OGP) (2018). https://www.verwaltung-innovativ.de/SharedDocs/Publikationen/Internationales/Zwischenbericht_OGP_engl_ Fassung.pdf?__blob=publicationFile&v=2. Accessed 02 July 2020

10. Wirtz, B.W., Weyerer, J.C., Rösch, M.: Citizen and open government: an empirical analysis of antecedents of open government data. Int. J. Public Adm. **41**(4), 308–320 (2018)

11. Dapp, M., Balta, D., Palmetshofer, W., Krcmar, H.: Open Data. The Benefits. Das volkswirtschaftliche Potential für Deutschland (2016). https://www.kas.de/documents// 253252/7_dokument_dok_pdf_44906_1.pdf/3fbb9ec5-096c-076e-1cc4-473cd84784df? version=1.0&t=1539650934955. Accessed 02 July 2020

12. Beck, J., Stember, J.: Modellkommune Open Government Projektbericht (2019). https:// www.bmi.bund.de/SharedDocs/downloads/DE/veroeffentlichungen/themen/moderne-verwaltung/projektbericht-modellkommune-open-government.pdf?__blob=publicationFile& v=2. Accessed 03 July 2020

13. Ubaldi, B.-C.: Governments. In: Davies, F., Walker, T. (eds.) The State of Open Data: Histories and Horizons. Cape Town and Ottawa: African Minds and International Development Research Centre, pp. 381–394. Cape Town and Ottawa: African Minds and International Development Research Centre (2019)

14. G8, "G8 Open Data Charter: Annex," (2013)

15. European Data Portal, "New Open Data Act in Germany," European Data Portal, (2017). https://www.europeandataportal.eu/en/news/new-open-data-act-germany. Accessed 03 July 2020

16. Federal Government: Erster Bericht der Bundesregierung über die Fortschritte bei der Bereitstellung von Daten (2019). http://dipbt.bundestag.de/dip21/btd/19/141/1914140.pdf. Accessed 03 July 2020
17. Blank M.: Open Data Maturity Report 2019 (2019). https://op.europa.eu/sv/publication-detail/-/publication/5f6a8a5f-36a6-11ea-ba6e-01aa75ed71a1. Accessed 06 July 2020
18. Federal Office of Administration: Prozessbeschreibung zur Veröffentlichung von Daten, Berlin, (2018). https://www.verwaltung-innovativ.de/SharedDocs/Publikationen/eGovernment/open_data_prozessbeschreibung.pdf?__blob=publicationFile&v=2. Accessed 03 July 2020
19. Stember, J., Klähn, C.,: Projektbericht E-Government-Modellkommunen (2016). https://www.bmi.bund.de/SharedDocs/downloads/DE/veroeffentlichungen/2016/projektbericht-e-government-modellkommunen.pdf?__blob=publicationFile&v=1. Accessed 06 July 2020
20. Federal Ministry of the Interior: BMI fördert Regionale Open Government Labore, Press Release Federal Ministry of the Interior (2019). https://www.bmi.bund.de/SharedDocs/pressemitteilungen/DE/2019/09/open-government-labore.html. Accessed 06 July 2020
21. Federal Ministry of the Interior: BMI fördert Regionale Open Government Labore, Press Release Federal Ministry of the Interior (2019)
22. Fraunhofer Fokus Institut: Open Data Köln, Köln (2012). https://cdn0.scrvt.com/fokus/dda1fb903648a/bba9049ebe8373d17749e816c6269c72/open_data_koeln_120918_mit_anhang.pdf. Accessed 05 July 2020
23. Open Knowledge Lab Niederrhein: Daten machen Schule (2020). https://okfn.de/en/projekte/datenmachenschule. Accessed 10 July 2020
24. Hochschule Rhein-Waal: Verwaltungsinformatik - E-Government, B.Sc. (2020). https://www.hochschule-rhein-waal.de/de/fakultaeten/kommunikation-und-umwelt/studienangebot/bachelorstudiengaenge/verwaltungsinformatik-e. Accessed 10 July 2020
25. Harrison, T.M., Burke, G.B., Cook, M., Guerrero, S.: Open government and e-government: democratic challenges from a public value perspective. Inf. Polity **17**(2), 83–97 (2012)

Potential for Increasing the ICT Adaption and Identifying Technology Readiness in the Silver Economy: Case of Estonia

Sidra Azmat Butt[✉️] [ID], Ingrid Pappel[ID], and Enn Õunapuu

Information Systems Group, Tallinn University of Technology,
Akademia Tee 15a, 12618 Tallinn, Estonia
{sidra.butt, ingrid.pappel, enn.ounapuu}@taltech.ee

Abstract. Silver economy is dedicated to catering to the needs of the ageing population with innovative and technological solutions. The paper encompasses a de-tailed overview of the technology readiness and challenges of the silver generation towards ICT adaption. A hybrid approach is employed using the questionnaires and workshops to collect data. The main outcome creates the understanding of the hindering factors to ICT adaption for elderly people which if addressed can serve as the basis for new entrepreneurial opportunities. The present case is part of a larger set of research activities that will be conducted throughout the entire Baltic Sea Region in the coming years. The results of the research activities are aimed to be scale-able to serve the needs and requirements of other interested regions that are tackling similar matters regarding the ageing society.

Keywords: Silver economy · Silver generation · Technological readiness · ICT

1 Introduction

Silver economy is dedicated to the ageing population with production, distribution and consumption of goods and services targeted to the elderly people according to their purchasing power to satisfy their living and health needs. It is the third-largest economy in the world, which generates the biggest opportunities in public and consumer markets. The silvery economy is referred to as "the sum of all economic activity serving the needs of over 50 and including both the products and services they purchase directly and the further economic activity this spending generates" [1]. It has been estimated that by 2060, one out of three Europeans will be over the age of 65 which poses a threat to economic growth [2]. It is, therefore, imperative to ensure that elderly people lead a healthy and active lifestyle for them to contribute back to society. It is possible to increase their productivity by enabling the ageing population to manage their own health which will not only boost their confidence but also help them lead a quality life [30]. European Commission has already devised an action plan that incorporates ICT solutions at the workplace, in society and at home to increase their productivity, reduce isolation and maintain their independence respectively [31]. However, it leads us to the question: how do we make it possible?

© Springer Nature Switzerland AG 2020
A. Chugunov et al. (Eds.): EGOSE 2020, CCIS 1349, pp. 139–155, 2020.
https://doi.org/10.1007/978-3-030-67238-6_10

There are numerous e-services, digital portals, e-health platforms, smart devices, etc. already existing in the market to help the elderly people in their daily routines but adaption to these ICT solutions remains low. For instance, a research conducted in the US found out that only 42% of the elderly population over 65 own a smartphone and 32% own a computer while a whopping 49% does not have a broadband connection at home [36]. This leads us to our main concern: what are the factors that hinder the ICT adaption among elderly people?

ICT plays a significant role in the modern world which has revolutionized the way of living. Paperless management [35], X-road [3], eID [4], digital signature [4], e-voting [5], e-invoicing [6], e-prescriptions [7], e-tax [8], e-school [9], and e-residency [10] are some of the examples of ICT based services that have completely changed the dynamics of the fast-paced society in developed countries such as Estonia. Communication, socialization as well as information retrieval and archival are only a few clicks now. ICT infrastructure is already in place and well established, in these developed countries. Cyber security and cyber hygiene are religiously practiced as it "is inextricably linked to the development and management of state information systems and data" [32]. It has, therefore, become essential to use these resources in order to facilitate the major part of the country's population. ICT, without any doubt, can help develop systems that provide limitless benefits for the silver economy. ICT integration in the silver economy, however, may face several barriers mainly because this segment of the population is the last one to adapt to changes and are more likely to be dependent on others both physically and emotionally [11].

There have been limited research conducted on the silver economy and it is witnessed that innovative technology is being created for the masses especially youth who are tech-savvy and well-equipped with ICT knowledge. However, this research identifies the main obstacles that are faced by the elderly people with respect to technology adaption so that these can be addressed and future projects can bring innovation and technology solutions specifically for the elderly people to help them live an independent and comfortable life.

For research purposes, this study is a part of a larger project called 'Supporting the Smart Specialization Approach in the Silver Economy to Increase Regional Innovation Capacity and Sustainable Growth' – OSIRIS. The project consortium is made up of partners from Latvia, Lithuania, Estonia, Denmark, Russia and Finland representing the business, governmental and academic actors of the Triple Helix model for economic growth and regional development. This transnational partnership unites expertise, resources, and knowledge to share practices and learning on how to apply the smart specialization approach for exploiting silver economy opportunities in the Baltic Sea Region.

1.1 Methodology

The main objective of this paper is to explore the main problems that the silver generation faces when adapting to ICT solutions. In order to cater to the purpose of the study, a hybrid approach was applied which employs two survey questionnaires and two workshops.

First questionnaire was targeted to the elderly people to understand the problems they face when adapting to the ICT solutions. On the basis of the outcomes, second questionnaire was designed which was targeted to the experts who deal with IT solutions for the elderly people. To validate the results derived from the questionnaires, two carefully designed workshops were conducted that involved experts from various walks of life.

As the first step of the research, a survey was conducted by sending out questionnaires to 55 members of the elderly population in Estonia. All the candidates were selected randomly and were aged above 50 belonging to diverse segments of the population in Estonia. The questionnaire was designed to integrate closed-ended and objective questions keeping in mind the convenience of the aged candidates. The questions were aimed at understanding the mindset of the elderly population regarding technology solutions to everyday living. Therefore, the questionnaire included questions like if they were willing to use IT solutions in their daily routines, if they needed help in using smart devices, if they would chose a smart service over a traditional one etc. This helped in creating a better understanding of where elderly people struggled with technology, if either it was difficult to use, or expensive or if they just have a wrong perception about technology altogether.

The second questionnaire was sent to 19 experts working in the following organizations:

- Tallinn University of Technology.
- Tallinn University.
- Ministry of Social Affairs (Sotsiaalministeerium).
- Estonian Association of Pensioners' Societies (Eesti Pensionäride Ühenduste Liit).
- NGO Estonian Village Movement Kodukant.

Questionnaire included a combination of both, open as well as close ended questions to get an even deeper understanding of the obstacles faced by the elderly people when using technology solutions. IT experts who deal with elderly people were contacted because of their experience and understanding of the silver generation. They were asked more in-depth questions like the reasons behind elderly people unwillingness to adapt IT solutions, how pro-active services can help elderly people and which existing services can be transformed to proactive services etc. These experts had already conducted years of research to innovate IT solutions to help elderly population live an independent and comfortable life therefore, their valuable input aided in developing a thorough understanding of the problems and causes behind silver generation's low technology adaption rate.

The data thus gathered contributed towards the quantitative analysis of the responses from the candidates. Quantitative research methods enhance the objectivity of the study and are a form of empirical studies that require statistical analysis to understand various variables in research design [25].

The second phase of the research consisted of two workshops. These workshops encouraged the participation of field experts from the quadruple helix sectors of Estonia to further the research aims and objectives. These sectors include the four domains of ICT stakeholders comprising of the private sector, public sector, academic institutions and the end-users. Qualitative research designs in the social sciences stem from traditions in anthropology and sociology; where the philosophy emphasizes the phenomenological basis of a study, the elaborate description of the "meaning" of phenomena for the people or culture under examination [16]. For this particular phase of the study, the qualitative techniques were applied to understand the belief systems, behavioral aspects, and general attitudes of the population under consideration.

The initial workshop was fashioned in a manner to address the validity of the survey results of the first phase. Experts from the quadruple helix sectors contributed to determining the problems associated with e-solutions for the elderly. Through rigorous discussions and analyses, the experts identified their version of factors hindering ICT adaption. The second workshop attempted to undertake the task of devising recommendations to address the problems identified in the first workshop. The first workshop consisted of 12 participants including end users which were elderly people aged 50+ as well as experts from science, business and government sectors. The workshop was initiated with an introduction to the subject at hand with briefings on silver economy and ICT integration. Participants were then divided into 4 groups and were asked to have an open discussion within the groups about the main factors that hinder the ICT adaption in the silver economy. The second work-shop was dedicated to address the issues faced by the silver generation for ICT adaption identified in the first work-shop. There were 18 participants again from the quadruple helix sectors and lasted for a fair three hours. The same format as first work-shop was used with dividing the participants into 6 groups this time and discussing the possible solutions and measures that can be taken to increase the technological readiness of the elderly people. The workshops ended in open discussions and the results and findings were completed.

The main advantages of a hybrid approach to research include a high level of detailed analysis, and the ability to combine both the objective and the subjective data to gain a thorough understanding of the subject [26].

The remainder of the paper is organized as follows. In the next section, we provide a literature review. In Sect. 3, we provide the results which are discussed along with recommendations in Sect. 4. We proceed with a possible future direction in Sect. 5 and we finish the paper with a conclusion in Sect. 6.

2 Literature Review

2.1 The Silver Economy

The term silver economy is used to identify the needs of the ageing population as an economic opportunity. Silver Economy in today's world is not just a market but across "economy", where it caters to the elderly population of the society. It is imperative to understand that the ageing process of the population is a genuine issue and has real impacts on the markets and industry [12]. The European Commission describes the silver economy as a set of economic activities pertaining to older people that incorporate the production, utilization and exchange of related goods and services [1]. Cornet (2015) considers the Silver Economy to encompass a great diversity of individuals concerning status, income, health, social and cultural context. He suggests that it includes the "50+ markets for wealthy baby boomers, active retirees, as well as poor and frail older adults, mostly lonely women at risk of dependency and social isolation" [13]. It also includes the challenges and opportunities that arise with catering to the requirements of the" greying" generation [13].

The developed countries especially the European region is witnessing a profound demographic change in terms of the ages of its population. Research shows that the proportion of older people is higher in developed countries as compared to the developing countries [1]. This is one of the reasons why in developed countries such as Estonia it is of eminent importance to take into serious consideration the support and welfare of elderly people. It is estimated that by 2060, one out of three Europeans would be above 60 years of age. The ratio of inactive to working citizens is also expected to change from 2:1 today to 4:1 in 2060 [14]. Other studies suggest that by 2025, the percentage of citizens above 60 years of age in the Baltic Sea countries would increase from 25% to 50% [2]. Many consider the evolution of the ageing society as an indicator of prosperity in a region [13]. This has impacted strategic policy development across several sectors especially in the EU nations. The Silver Economy is a cross economy that influences markets such as transport, healthcare, social services, e-health solutions, home accommodation, robotic assistance, public services, and many more [14]. Research suggests that the ICT sector has the potential to cater to the dependency needs of the elderly to support healthy and active ageing [15].

2.2 Existing ICT Services in Estonia

Estonia is an active member of the European Union with strong digital foundations. ICT is a distinguishing feature of the country, sometimes also referred to as "e-Estonia" [15]. It encompasses a wide array of realms including e-health, e-governance, data analytics, cybersecurity, and many more. Research suggests that over the past 20 years Estonia has thrived to become one of the most technologically developed countries in the world [2]. Tambur states that digital public services are a part of everyday life in Estonia. It ranks third in the index of Economic Freedom in the EU and second in Internet Freedom [2]. Internet access is declared as a human right with highly developed telecommunications and the fastest broadband networks all across the country [1]. The country also ranks amongst the top five countries in the cybersecurity index [16]. The ICT infrastructure is quite advanced in the country since the leadership in Estonia had assessed the value of a strong digital base at the beginning of this century. Therefore, it is already on its way towards a paperless and technologically advanced society [34]. For efficiency and security reasons, Estonia has conducted technical [37], policy and legal [38] environment analysis for e-government services migration to cloud servers.

According to Smart City Hub, almost all schools (97%) in Estonia had an online presence in 1997. All the inhabited areas have had a publicly constructed Wi-Fi network since 2002. All the citizens have a state-issued digital identity accessible through the Estonian ID card. They have had digital access to voting since 2007 and can file their taxes and sign documents online [17]. Furthermore, they can get prescriptions from the comfort of their homes with e-health services and almost 100% of bank transfers happen online. By 2017, Estonian citizens could file their taxes digitally in just three minutes [15]. Estonia is home to Skype and TransferWise with advanced digital support for entrepreneurs. Businesses can register online in less than 18 min through the online portal [18].

A country report by Empirica for the European Commission states: "Estonia is number one in the world concerning the use of e-services based on e-identity cards: Estonia holds a leadership position in using, developing and adopting of electronic ID in Europe and sports a center of competence in this field. The Estonian educational system makes strong use of ICT; e-tools and e-learning tools are becoming very common and at least 40% of the working-age population have participated in ICT training/retraining." [18] In 2011, the Estonian Government launched its Competitiveness Strategy for 2020. Its vision was to proactively raise the competitiveness of the economy through effective implementation of ICT across all sectors of the economy with participation from all population groups [19].

2.3   Obstacles for ICT Adaption in the Silver Generation

E-solutions can be of great use for the elderly as there are many belonging to the group who may have issues and inconvenience in being mobile and moving from one place to another easily [14]. Literature suggests that senior citizens face certain inhibitions in accepting and adopting the latest technologies, as compared to the younger generation [20]. Buccoliero et al. (2013) imply that the elderly have been wrongly considered a homogeneous segment and very little efforts have been put in understanding their needs according to their unique characteristics [21]. They believe that the silver generation needs to be evaluated based on their health conditions, financial situation, family status, education and skills into several target segments. These factors can predict their acceptance of ICT innovations. The ICT solutions can be tailored according to the requirements of each target segment [21]. There has been a lot of research to gain perspective into the factors that influence ICT adaption with reference to the elderly. Choudrie et al. (2014) investigated that observability, compatibility, social influence, facilitating conditions, effort expectancy and enjoyment are significant factors in ensuring the adaption of new technologies like smartphones within the silver generation [22]. Other literature highlights the role of individual external variables in developing attitudes of senior citizens towards technology adaption. Social norms, perception of usefulness and the perception of ease are some of the factors that may impact ICT implementation for the elderly [19].

Jensen & Mahan (2008) conducted a study and they have attempted to go beyond physical access to technology or the legal and regulatory framework to include factors like political will, affordability, human capacities, local content and trust in technology to consider for ICT adaption frameworks [23]. Although a large number of ICT solutions are available for a transition towards a digital economy, the adaption of these solutions needs serious thought and effort [20]. It is imperative to mold the technology according to the needs of the elderly to bridge digital divide and disseminate technology skills to the silver surfers [24].

3   Results

3.1   Results from Questionnaires

A total of 55 elderly people were randomly chosen in the age bracket of 50–85 years old and were asked to fill in the questionnaire to help understand the main problems that hinders the ICT adaption in their daily life routines. Majority of the respondents claimed that they did not use computer nor internet mainly because they did not have the required knowledge or skills for using them. When they were asked if they'd be willing to learn IT skills, a whopping 90.9% of respondents mainly above 85 years of age showed unwillingness. The same response was witnessed when they were asked if they'd be willing to use smart services over traditional services such as booking an appointment online. Most of the respondents claimed that they took help from their kids and were mainly dependent on their peers for caretaking. Majority of the respondents also complained about feeling isolated mainly because of the lack of communication.

On the basis of these outcomes, the second questionnaire was designed for experts who deal, communicate, research and/or provide services to the elderly people. Their experiences with elderly people provide a detailed insight to the factors that may hinder ICT adaption in the silver generation. 63.2% (12) of the respondents stated that the elderly people usually find the ICT services difficult to use with 31.6% stating that elderly have privacy concerns and that the websites for these e-services usually have misleading information as shown in Fig. 1. Moreover, 58% also claimed that silver generation did not have the means of using these e-services, such lack of internet-connected devices also contributes to low technology readiness amongst the elderly people. However, when asked about which digital devices elderly people used, 94.7% (18) confirmed that they owned a smart phone and 63.2% also used desktop computers. While the popularity of smart watches (26.3%) and tablets (42.1%) remained low, 8 respondents stated that elderly used laptops, indicating that they preferred using digital devices at the comforts of their homes and unlikely to use them on the go. When asked how often elderly were concerned about privacy when using ICT services, 31.6% agreed that they often did not trust the websites while only 5.2% of them were able to maintain cyber hygiene.

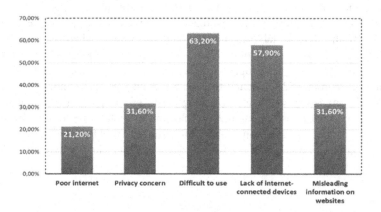

Fig. 1. Challenge when using ICT services.

Experts were asked which services could be turned into proactive services[1] meaning that the state already has the necessary information and provide predictive services to the elderly people. 73.7% stated population registry and 63.2% medical prescription and job search can be made proactive services which will not only save time for elderly but also optimize costs for the service providers. If elderly people were given an option of choosing either consulting an online doctor or physically visiting a doctor, 21.1% of the respondents that they are likely to choose the latter elaborating that they felt more comfortable and confident that they were being heard out in the face-to-face communication. When they were asked how likely are elderly people to be comfortable to use innovative technology over the traditional methods in their daily routine, for e.g. using a smart device for checking blood pressure and pulse rate, only a 10.5% of them chose the former option for the elderly people (see Fig. 2) as the rest of them stated that elderly believe that the digital methods are not always accurate neither convenient.

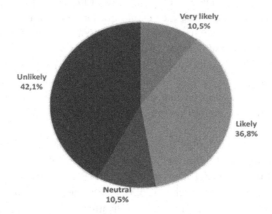

Fig. 2. Likely to use smart device over traditional methods.

When experts were asked how the elderly population can be trained to use digital devices to avail e-services, they pointed out that training workshops (73.7%), community tutoring (84.2%) and peer teaching (63.2%) are the best possible solutions. Moreover, to create awareness amongst the ageing population, 63.2% agreed that print advertising is the most suitable mean of promotion. Lastly, when respondents were asked what are the main limitations associated with the introduction of smart technology in the homes of older people who may be experiencing declining health due to age related conditions, 52.6% stated that elderly dislike using technology because of the lack of confidence and fear of making mistakes, 42.1% confirmed that silver generation could not afford to continue to maintain or replace the technology so they did not want to get dependent on it and 78.9% stated that elderly people were happy with the traditional ways and did not want to adapt to new technology as it was difficult to use.

---

[1] https://e-estonia.com/proactive-services-estonia/.

3.2   Results from Workshops

The results from both the questionnaires were then validated in two workshops which included group activities and open discussions. Silver generation and the obstacles they face in ICT adaption were discussed in immense detail and subsequently, appropriate solutions were provided as shown in Table 1.

Table 1. Results from workshops.

Problem	Description	Solution
Internet penetration	Unfamiliar with using the internet or might not even have it available to their premises	Awareness creation Internet subsidiary packages for elderly
Internet-connected devices	Elderly might not have means to use the internet for e.g., smart phones, tablets, laptops etc.	Peer teaching
Digital incompetency	Elderly population might be fearful and incompetent to learn new things compared with the younger population	Competence centre for digital skills Customer support involvement
Structure of digital application forms	Illogically structured. Lack of easy user experience that is necessary for the elderly users	Review existing forms Pre-filled forms
Lack of awareness	Aware of the existence of the e-service such as e-health but might not be aware of how it could make their lives easy	Community-based workshops Print advertising
Security	Lack of understanding of how to be safe online and how to maintain cyber hygiene	Cyber-security practices: • Notifications • Warnings
Lack of experts	Lack of specialists and trainers particularly for elderly people to cooperate with them and teach them ICT skills	Unified Platform Special training sessions
Inability to learn	Weak cognitive skills and capabilities at an elderly age leading to prolonged learning cycle requiring more repetition regularly	Chatbots One-size-doesn't-fit-all solution

Different age-groups have different needs which requires further research. If there is a logical cooperation between RIA (Information System Authority) and subsequently, solutions are created, it wouldn't have to duplicate systems that we already have.

This means that Estonia already has various training centers that help build digital competencies but for them to be useful for the silver generation, they should know where to find them and how to access them. Moreover, teaching digital skills requires user to already have some basic knowledge and skills. This can be achieved by involving peers and caretakers in the process just to give it a push start. It was suggested that we should follow the 'Hierarchy of skills' model[2] when teaching digital skills to the elderly people (see Fig. 3).

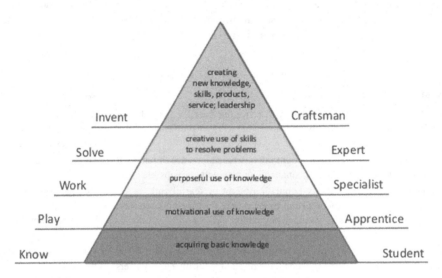

Fig. 3. Hierarchy of Skills.

We always need to keep in mind that automatic solutions are not able to replace real human contact that becomes vital the older we get. Elderly people need more explaining and have questions that programs are just not able to solve so we always need to involve customer support who can also help. Moreover, to create something new or maybe adding them to Facebook elderly-group doesn't mean that they are going to use it. Elderly people are using the same platforms like younger people (they are the ones who teach them how to use it). Therefore, we need to create solutions on a unified platform that are suitable and accessible to as many as possible. Existing application/e-services forms are also needed to be reviewed, we need to make the interface easy-to-use or silver generation will continue to use the traditional ways e.g. call their doctor to make an appointment. When elderly people are using computer and new pop-up windows of information open they can get easily distracted. We need to critically review all existing templates and forms and analyze if it could be possible to automate their execution. State already has all the information and 'once-only' principle can be very beneficial for the elderly people when they have to fill in applications online. This will help them realize that online forms are more convenient and less time consuming and eventually, increase motivation.

Digital guidance on how to use these platform such as "point and click" principle is not suitable for elderly people because this will distract their attention. The ability to pay attention decreases with age therefore, we should make more targeted and

---

[2] I. Kokcharov: Hierarchy of Skills © 2015 Craftsman Expert Specialist Apprentice Student.

personalized videos and use tools that are modern like chatbots which can guide them and help them stay focused. In addition to this, notifications about risks should be in different places (e.g. flashing) and warnings should be displayed. However, it should be done in a way that it doesn't create fear for the elderly people as they would then not be willing to use the digital devices or e-services.

We need more physical tutors who have gone through special training about how to teach elderly and should be community-based. Family members and peers should be included initially in the training process to make the elderly people feel more comfortable. Measure should be taken to increase awareness about ICT solutions and their benefits to the elderly people. E-mails, news, via local government, newspaper and direct mail are some of the best possible ways to distribute information to this age group. Elderly people need information on paper therefore the most effective way is to send a direct mail into their mailboxes. In addition to this, word-of-mouth is also considered useful to create awareness about e-services and ICT solutions as they find it more reliable when they are informed by their acquaintances.

Lastly, one-size-fits-all solution does not seem plausible for the needs of different elderly age groups, for example the groups of age 60+ and 80+ constitute of different challenges and basic needs. A matrix should be created, where different needs, events and cases are mapped. It would include: age groups (60+, 70+, 80+ and 90+), the needs and necessary vital services of the elderly (health, social need/welfare, safety, labor market and financial livelihood) and the sources of problems, where help is needed.

4 Discussion and Recommendations

The silver generation includes people who spent their youth in an era where digital technology was at its inception stage. As stated in the literature, we now know that for the elderly to adopt new technologies, their perceptions about the ease of use and its overall usefulness need to be factored in. 57.9% of the respondents agreed that they do not have the means to access e-services. Therefore, a great contributor to their low technology readiness is the fact that they do not use digital devices very frequently. Since the elderly prefer to follow a set pattern of habits, they find it difficult to add the use of digital technology to their daily activities. Although the survey results confirmed that most of them have access to the internet, computers/laptops, and even smartphones (tablets and smartwatches being less popular), yet their use of those devices was very limited.

Limited technology readiness of the elderly is also a by-product of their suspicion and lack of trust towards ICT solutions. Most of them prefer a face to face mode of interaction as opposed to online communication. When asked about their inclination towards e-health services, the elderly participants of the workshop proclaimed that they preferred to visit their physician physically instead of opting for the more convenient e-health portals. This attitude depicted the underlying trust issues of the silver generation with digital services. Field experts in the workshops also confirmed that people belonging to the elderly segment find it difficult to depend upon e-services. Jensen & Mahan (2008) have also stated a lack of trust as a major obstacle towards ICT framework implementation [23]. A considerable percentage of the survey participants also showed concerns about their privacy while using websites and e-services. They felt more comfortable using traditional methods for measuring blood pressure and pulse and were reluctant to depend upon high-tech devices.

Another major obstacle that was identified as a result of this study, was the limited awareness of the elderly about digital services. Secondary research suggests that senior citizens are less likely to adopt technological innovations since they are not tailored according to their needs. Discussions during the workshops also highlighted that the elderly have limited information about the ICT services and this might affect their confidence to use these services accordingly. It was also found out through the workshops that very few had received any kind of training or guidance on using tech devices, either by their organizations or by peers or family. While literature suggests that about 40% of the working-age population has received tech-trainings [19], it is very clear that the silver generation has been neglected in this respect.

Secondary research has also highlighted the role of individual variables like compatibility, social influence, facilitating conditions, effort expectancy, and enjoyment to improve technology readiness in the elderly [22]. The survey results and the workshops also indicate a general unwillingness of the aged population to learn new IT skills. This is understandable because the human capacity to learn is expected to reduce with age.

This calls for the triple helix actors (the public sector, the private sector, and academia) to come up with community-based solutions to impart tech-based knowledge and skills to the elderly. Based on their mistrust of online transactions and websites, they need to be educated systemically about their cyber rights and cybersecurity practices. As suggested in the Cyber Security strategy 2019–2022, "a small and cohesive cybersecurity community and good interpersonal communication are prerequisites for responding effectively to salient problems." [33] The approaches towards this training need to be user friendly and tailored according to the comprehension abilities of various age brackets amongst the silver generation. Websites for e-services must be designed with the ease of use and perceptions of senior citizens in mind. For examples, pre-filled forms for tax filing or e-health access will improve their reluctance to utilize these services online. Estonia needs to develop the digital competencies of its elderly population since the country has a strong digital infrastructure that can provide smart solutions to the problems faced by this segment. Once, the silver generation is engaged through digital technologies, there is a great scope for them to improve their quality of life.

5   Future Work

As mentioned earlier, this study is a part of a larger project and many fruitful outcomes are expected to be achieved in the future. The results from the study will serve as the basis for future endeavors of discovery, design and implementation process.

This in-depth analysis on the factors influencing the uptake of the technology can help in each of the stages of the project as shown in the Fig. 4.

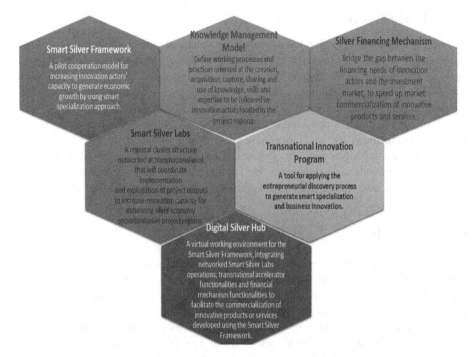

Fig. 4. Project Roadmap(https://www.osiris-smartsilvereconomy.eu/).

However, in terms of Tallinn University of Technology research area, main focus will be on Knowledge Management Model and Digital Silver Hub.

5.1 Knowledge Management Model

The in-depth analysis of the current trends amongst the elderly and issues that they face due to their inability to access to technologically advanced services in general and e-services, in particular, serves as the basis of the larger scope of a study. It is important to understand the current situation and facilities being utilized by the elderly or for the elderly to make sure that the future comes with advancements and ideas that provide support and assistance to them in their daily routines.

The findings from the current research will serve as a basis to develop the Knowledge Management Model for the silver generation of the country in times to come. A knowledge Management System can be defined as an IT system or infrastructure which is developed to improve the collaboration while locating knowledge sources and enhancing the process of Knowledge Management [28]. It helps in archiving, collaborating, and ensuring that all of the related processes are in alignment [27]. Knowledge Management Model will serve as the main instrument for handling the connection between smart specialization approach, industry and knowledge assets. The model will synthetize and integrate knowledge at the regional level for creating a common process for exploiting silver economy growth opportunities.

5.2   Digital Silver Hub

This study will set the cornerstone to realize the technical and operational analysis for developing a virtual collaborative platform known as the Digital Silver Hub that will serve as a virtual ecosystem where different stakeholders can collaborate in innovation processes using a methodology based on "knowledge exchange, co-creation/co-production techniques, and participatory methods" [29].

The aim is to create a conceptual and technical model that bridges companies and research organizations for generating new innovative solutions to tackle ageing challenges and to exploit silver economy opportunities. This study will help to build system specific requirements and design of the virtual collaborative platform to support learning process and knowledge diffusion between innovation actors and regions.

6   Conclusion

Silver economy is the third largest segment of the market where the major consumers belong to the elderly age group which suggests that they require and deserve more attention than it is being given at the moment. The results achieved so far help us to develop an understanding of the main factors that influence the ICT adaption in the elderly people which are lack of use of digital devices (internet, computers, smartphones etc.), lack of digital trust, lack of awareness regarding smart solutions and unwillingness to learn IT skills. The paper helps to build foundation to create a collaborative platform specifically for the elderly people. The collaborative platform will be aimed at innovative solutions to help elderly in their daily routine so they can perform activities independently. Therefore, the findings from this study will be helpful to build system requirements and design specifications of the platform.

It is important to note that this study suggests that the elderly are not very keen in taking up new technological trends and services; one of the reasons being the difficulty they encounter in operating advanced and sometimes even simple technology. This is because the elderly have not evolved with the latest trends and need support in developing an understanding. Hence, it is suggested to ensure that these services are easy-to-use and convenient. We should initiate a trend where elderly people start getting actively involved in IT solutions while learning new trends and skills.

Finally, the study urges the development of technological solutions that are in parallel with the requirements and demands of the silver generation ecosystem.

Acknowledgement. The authors acknowledge the contribution of Edi Kiviniemi and Merilin Liutkevicius from Tallinn University of Technology in data collection for the primary research in the study. They were involved in conducting questionnaires and organizing and participating in the workshops which laid the foundation for the research analysis.

References

1. Technopolis Group and Oxford Economics: The Silver Economy – Final report, Publications Office of the European Union, Luxemburg (2018)
2. Tambur, S.: Digital Economy Estonia: From IT Tiger to the World's Most Pre-Eminent E-State, New European Economy. https://neweuropeaneconomy.com/fdi/digital-economy-estonia/. Accessed 11 June 2020
3. Tepandi, J., et al.: The data quality framework for the Estonian public sector and its evaluation: establishing a systematic process-oriented viewpoint on cross-organizational data quality. In: Hameurlain, A., et al. (eds.) Transactions on Large-Scale Data- and Knowledge-Centered Systems XXXV. LNCS, vol. 10680, pp. 1–26. Springer, Heidelberg (2017). https://doi.org/10.1007/978-3-662-56121-8_1
4. Pappel, I., Pappel, I., Tepandi, J., Draheim, D.: Systematic digital signing in Estonian e-government processes. In: Hameurlain, A., Küng, J., Wagner, R., Dang, T.K., Thoai, N. (eds.) Transactions on Large-Scale Data- and Knowledge-Centered Systems XXXVI. LNCS, vol. 10720, pp. 31–51. Springer, Heidelberg (2017). https://doi.org/10.1007/978-3-662-56266-6_2
5. Drechsler, W., Madise, Ü.: Electronic voting in Estonia. In: Kersting, N., Baldersheim, H. (eds.) Electronic Voting and Democracy, pp. 97–108. Palgrave Macmillan, London (2004). https://doi.org/10.1057/9780230523531_6
6. Pappel, I., Pappel, I., Tampere, T., Draheim, D.: Implementation of e-invoicing principles in Estonian local governments. In: Borges, V.J., Rouco, J.C.D. (eds.) Proceedings of the 17th European Conference on Digital Government (ECDG): Military Academy, Lisbon, Portugal, pp. 127–136. Academic Conferences and Publishing International Limited (2017)
7. CEF Digital Connecting Europe: Estonian Digital Prescription. https://ec.europa.eu/cefdigital/wiki/display/CEFDIGITAL/2019/07/26/Estonian+Digital+Prescription. Accessed 11 June 2020
8. E-Estonia, e-tax: https://e-estonia.com/solutions/business-and-finance/e-tax/. Accessed 11 June 2020
9. E-Estonia, ekool and stuudium: https://e-estonia.com/solutions/education/e-school/. Accessed 11 June 2020
10. Särav, S., Kerikmäe, T.: E-Residency: a cyberdream embodied in a digital identity card? In: Kerikmäe, T., Rull, A. (eds.) The Future of Law and eTechnologies, pp. 57–79. Springer, Cham (2016). https://doi.org/10.1007/978-3-319-26896-5_4
11. Czaja, S.J., Lee, C.C.: The impact of aging on access to technology. Univ. Access Inf. Soc. 5, 341–349 (2007). https://doi.org/10.1007/s10209-006-0060-x
12. Gordon, C.: A silver economy: The value of living longer (2017)
13. Cornet, G.: Europe's 'Silver Economy': a potential source for economic growth? Gerontechnology 13, 319–321 (2015)
14. Zsarnoczky, M.: Innovation challenges of the silver economy. Vadyba J. Manag. 28, 105 (2016). 1648-7974
15. Kitsing, M.: Political Economy of Government Venture Capital in Estonia, pp. 115–124 (2017)
16. Kitsing, M.: Success without strategy: e-government development in Estonia. Policy Internet 3, 1–21 (2011)
17. Arets, M.: How Estonia became the most digital country in the world. Smart City Hub (2017). http://smartcityhub.com/governance-economy/how-estonia-became-the-most-digital-country-in-the-world/. Accessed 11 June 2020

18. Laurits, M., Mägi, E.: E-skills in Europe: Estonia Country Report/ Empirica for European Commission. European Commission: PRAXIS Center for Policy Studies (2014)
19. Gichoya, D.: Factors affecting the successful implementation of ICT projects in government. Electron. J. E-Government **3**, 175–184 (2005)
20. Chatfield, K., Iatridis, K., Stahl, B.C., Paspallis, N.: Innovating responsibly in ICT for ageing: drivers, obstacles and implementation. Sustainability **9**, 971 (2017)
21. Buccoliero, L., Bellio, E., Ishmatova, D.: "Silver" technology acceptance model: a first research framework. In: Aging Society and ICT: Global Silver Innovation, vol. 5, p. 137 (2013)
22. Choudrie, J., Pheeraphuttharangkoon, S., Zamani, E., Giaglis, G.: Investigating the adoption and use of smartphones in the UK: a silver-surfers perspective. In: Proceedings of the 22nd European Conference on Information Systems, pp. 0–19 (2014)
23. Jensen, M., Mahan, A.: Towards better measures of global ICT adoption and use. In: Global Information Society Watch, p. 47 (2008)
24. Fors, M., Moreno, A.: The benefits and obstacles of implementing ICTs strategies for development from a bottom-up approach. Aslib Proc. **54**(3), 198–206 (2002)
25. Brannen, J.: Mixing methods: the entry of qualitative and quantitative approaches into the research process. Int. J. Soc. Res. Methodol. **8**, 173–184 (2005)
26. Vanderstoep, S.W., Johnson, D.D.: Research Methods for Everyday Life: Blending Qualitative and Quantitative Approaches, vol. 32. Wiley, Hoboken (2008)
27. Maier, R.: Knowledge Management Systems: Information and Communication Technologies for Knowledge Management. Springer, Heidelberg (2007). https://doi.org/10.1007/978-3-540-71408-8
28. Davenport, T., Prusak, L.: Working Knowledge: How Organizations Manage What they Know. Harvard Business School Press, Boston (1998)
29. Baccarne, B., Mechant, P., Schuurman, D.: Empowered cities? An analysis of the structure and generated value of the smart city ghent. In: Dameri, R.P., Rosenthal-Sabroux, C. (eds.) Smart City. PI, pp. 157–182. Springer, Cham (2014). https://doi.org/10.1007/978-3-319-06160-3_8
30. Zhou, J., Salvendy, G. (eds.): ITAP 2015. LNCS, vol. 9193. Springer, Cham (2015). https://doi.org/10.1007/978-3-319-20892-3
31. European Commission: Ageing well in the Information Society: Action Plan on Information and Communication Technologies and Ageing. https://eur-lex.europa.eu/legal-content/EN/TXT/?uri=LEGISSUM%3Al24292. Accessed 12 June 2020
32. Republic of Estonia, Information System Authority: Cyber Security in Estonia 2020. https://www.ria.ee/sites/default/files/content-editors/RIA/cyber_security_in_estonia_2020_0.pdf. Accessed 12 June 2020
33. Republic of Estonia, Ministry of Economic Affairs and Communication: Cyber Security Strategy 2019–2022. https://www.mkm.ee/sites/default/files/kyberturvalisuse_strateegia_2022_eng.pdf. Accessed 12 June 2020
34. Pappel, I., Pappel, I.: Methodology for measuring the digital capability of local governments. In: Proceedings of 5th International Conference on Theory and Practice of Electronic Governance, Tallinn, Estonia, pp. 357–358. ACM (2011)
35. Pappel, I., Tsap, V., Draheim, D.: The e-LocGov model for introducing e-governance into local governments: an Estonian case study. IEEE Trans. Emerg. Top. Comput. (2020)
36. Anderson, M., Perrin, A.: Tech adoption climbs among older adults. Pew Research Center (2017). http://www.pewinternet.org/2017/05/17/tech-adoption-climbs-among-older-adults/. Accessed 07 Sept 2020

37. Kotka, T., Johnson, B., Cebul, T., Lovosevic, L., Liiv, I.: E-Government services migration to the public cloud: experiments and technical findings. In: Kő, A., Francesconi, E. (eds.) EGOVIS 2016. LNCS, vol. 9831, pp. 62–76. Springer, Cham (2016). https://doi.org/10.1007/978-3-319-44159-7_5
38. Kotka, T., Kask, L., Raudsepp, K., Storch, T., Radloff, R., Liiv, I.: Policy and legal environment analysis for e-Government services migration to the public cloud. In: Proceedings of the 9th International Conference on Theory and Practice of Electronic Governance, pp. 103–108 (2016)

Specifying Spatial and Temporal Characteristics of Increased Activity of Users of E-Participation Services

Sergei Kudinov$^{(\boxtimes)}$, Aleksandr Antonov , and Ekaterina Ilina

Institute for Design and Urban Studies, ITMO University, Birzhevaya Liniya 14,
199034 Saint Petersburg, Russia
{sergei.kudinov,asantonov,ilinaer}@itmo.ru

Abstract. Electronic participation data has a great potential for its application in studies of urban processes and systems. The popularity of e-participation services, which citizens use to report problems of urban improvement, housing and communal services, led to formation of massive datasets describing civic activity and subjective evaluation of urban environment quality. E-participation data has certain features that create distortions in the results of some research, e.g. when indirect evaluation of environmental or socioeconomic characteristics is concerned. One of the sources of such distortions are superusers. They are a small group of users whose activity is abnormally high. This abnormal activity has a significant impact on the distribution of messages. The fact that activity of e-participation service users is not equally distributed is well-known, however, a universal method of excluding the abnormal activity of superusers has never been proposed. This paper studies the distribution of activity of e-participation service users and proposes several methods of identifying and excluding peaks of increased activity of superusers in different territories and time intervals. The proposed methods were tested on data from the Russian portal "Our Saint Petersburg". As a result, we have defined the optimal approaches to processing e-participation datasets for studies which are sensitive to the unequal distribution of subjective data.

Keywords: Electronic participation · Electronic appeal · Civil society · Civic activity · Urban improvement · Superuser · Participation inequality

1 Introduction

Electronic participation services are a popular mechanism of communication between citizens and authorities via Internet. E-participation plays the role of a special type of feedback in the process of city management [1]. Online portals that citizens use in order to report various problems concerning the urban environment are a typical example of such services. Since sending an electronic message about a certain problem does not require any major effort, these portals' databases contain a noticeable amount of information created by numerous users. This information is well-structured, has spatial and temporal characteristics and, in some cases, even a multi-layered categorization.

© Springer Nature Switzerland AG 2020
A. Chugunov et al. (Eds.): EGOSE 2020, CCIS 1349, pp. 156–171, 2020.
https://doi.org/10.1007/978-3-030-67238-6_11

Moreover, some of such services offer public access to user names or IDs. Together these factors create opportunities to use e-participation data in different studies of urban environment and its socioeconomic characteristics.

Like most urban data that was not collected specifically for scientific research, e-participation data has certain features that should be considered in the analysis. In particular, there is such a significant factor as the existence of superusers. Superusers are a small group of citizens, who, due to their high activity, have a greater influence on the final structure of message array than the more passive majority. Groups of this sort were discovered on various portals which are used for reporting city problems, and on certain social media that focus on posting data with geolocation. Because of their existence, a diagram of sent messages or check-ins, ranked by the number of messages, is well approximated by a truncated power law [2]. Distribution of this kind can be often encountered among the data collected with crowdsourcing [3].

Since high contributors significantly impact data composition while being statistically outliers [4], it is necessary to consider the presence of superusers and filter the data they generate before analysis in order to maintain data representativeness and reduce potential deviations in studies. Such preliminary filtering of datasets is advisable when studying socioeconomic characteristics of a city or civic activity of residents.

This article proposes methods for identifying superusers based on spatial and temporal characteristics of their activity, and for reducing the effect of this activity on the distribution of messages. The methods are tested on the example of data on citizens' messages from an e-participation service in Saint Petersburg, Russia.

2   Related Work

Research on volunteered geographic information sources and e-participation systems shows that unusual activity of individual users has a significant impact on special and temporal data distribution. Therefore, their actions may describe specific urban processes linked to people's activity, and, at the same time, distort some indirect characteristics that depict the urban environment.

It was assumed in "The Promises and Pitfalls of 311 Data" [5] that the identified high correlation between message distribution and such a highly expensive doing as funding a political campaign might be linked to the existence of superusers, who have sufficient resources to maintain a high political activity in a service.

Various methods for identifying superusers have been presented in articles describing predicting the level of public misconduct [6], studying custodianship [7], determining increased civic activity at the level of individual houses [8], and studying noise pollution in a city [9]. They used data from service 311.

Unequal distribution of user activity was also found in other e-participation services. In particular, a research based on FixMyStreet data analyzed user activity [10]. As a result, researchers marked out a number of accounts that formed only 0,8% of all users and have sent 10% of all messages. They were defined as super contributors according to Stewart's classification [3].

A similar group of superusers was also found in a Russian service called "Our Saint Petersburg". A closer examination of user activity has revealed [11] that there is a certain disproportion between the number of messages sent and the number of accounts. The research has shown that 2% of the most active users sent 62% of the total number of messages.

A similar distribution can also be noticed in other services that rely on crowd-sourced spatial data, i.e. social media and Foursquare in particular. Various studies based on check-in data from certain cities (New York [12], Cardiff [13]) and worldwide [14] mention groups formed by 1 to 10% of users whose activity makes up to 10–20% of the total. Thus, researchers often encounter the superuser factor while studying this type of data, therefore, this factor must be taken into consideration in studies, especially in ones concerning the correlation between e-participation data and other city-related information [15, 16]. One of the methods for solving this problem is to delete such data [17]. So, for example, to analyze the activity of the main part of Twitter users, it was proposed to delete messages from the top 1% or 5% of the most active users [18].

The difficulties of this approach are associated with justifying the choice of a specific proportion of users who are highly active, with a significant loss of dataset volume in case superusers create most of the messages, and with uneven activity over time.

3   Detection of Superusers

3.1   The Structure of E-Participation Data

Messages on urban problems, aggregated by e-participation services, form structured datasets. They include information on a problem's location and category, the message submission timestamp, and sometimes anonymized information on its sender.

The spatial distribution of the messages' geographic points does not always precisely represent the actual position of problems in physical space, but in general it characterizes the location quite accurately. The data on the time the message was posted can differ from its actual creation time as well. Many e-participation services have a multi-level categorization of problems. Such a thorough classification of problems not only simplifies the delivery of the message from a citizen to the responsible public authority, but also opens up an opportunity for a detailed analysis of e-participation data.

Some e-participation services offer public access to anonymous data on message authors. This data might include a user ID assigned by the service and/or a nickname or a real name that the users entered themselves. This data allows tracking the activity of individual users and assessing their influence on the overall message distribution in space and time.

3.2   Users of E-Participation Services

Researchers take a particular interest in models of users' behavior in e-participation services. As we have mentioned before, having a small group of abnormally active users, or so-called superusers, who send a major part of messages, is very common for such services. Activity of e-participation service users is distributed unequally and generally follows the 90-9-1 Rule [19].

One can assume that superusers report most problems of the urban environment due to their activity and expertise, but as they are few in number, their influence is not equally distributed across all the areas of the city. This is the reason why in some locations where superusers are active the concentration of messages on certain types of problems or in general is significantly higher than in those locations where superusers are absent.

It was previously shown that superusers pay more attention to problems of public spaces, such as city streets and parks, more rarely yards [11]. Moreover, the presence of superusers in certain locations may be related to the activity of local communities [16].

Time factor should also be considered when analyzing the activity of e-participation service users. First, reported problems remain relevant for a limited period of time. Secondly, periods of citizens' activity are not regular, i.e., a user may collect messages on problems he/she notices for several days and then post them to the service all at once. There are also cases when a user may post messages regularly for several weeks in a row and then become inactive for months.

3.3 Signs of Increased User Activity

Even though behavioral patterns of superusers can be well traced generally, there is no strict classification which could help to identify one or another user as a superuser. Sometimes the services themselves rate the users by their activity, assigning them certain ranks of the portal's inner classification [20].

However, when we consider leveling the inequality of distribution of e-participation data, which is a result of the abnormal activity of individual users, taking into account only the total number of messages sent by them may be insufficient. In the study we have mentioned before [11], superusers were identified on the basis of a dataset which covered a year of e-participation service's work. Using such a dataset was sufficient for the analysis of general traits of superusers' behavioral patterns.

However, users' activity is uneven in time and space. Some users actively report problems only in their neighborhood. Therefore, even if these users do not send an outstanding number of messages compared to the number of messages sent by the most active users, their activity level is significantly different from the other users' level in that particular location. The situation is similar when we are talking about temporary activity.

Therefore, if the subject of the analysis is a set of data collected for a long period of time in a big city, it is possible to suggest that the status of superuser is not a permanent feature of an account, rather, it characterizes user's activity at a certain time and in a certain place.

3.4 Methods of Identifying Superusers and Leveling the Data Distortion Caused by Their Abnormal Activity

This study develops several methods, which can be used to identify superusers and/or to adjust the dataset so that the messages sent by users would be equally distributed.

These methods are applicable to those sets of e-participation data which contain at least the following data fields: a unique message, a unique sender ID, message submission timestamp, coordinates, belonging to a territorial unit, category of the problem.

3.4.1 Defining the Threshold of Increased Activity

Whether the traits of superusers are detected in the whole dataset or only in certain time periods and locations, we should define the criteria for identifying a user as a superuser.

The 90-9-1 Rule describes participation inequality in multi-user web communities. According to it, 1% of users (Heavy Contributors) are the most active on a regular basis, 9% (Intermittent Contributors) participate from time to time, and 90% (Lurkers) are passive observers [21]. Stewart et al. [3] proposed a model of a more equal distribution — the SCOUT (Super Contributor, Contributor, and OUTlier) model. According to it, 33% of users, who are the least active, are the Outliers. They may be compared to those users of e-participation services who reported a problem only once and never did it again. Contributors, who constitute 66% of all users, are moderately active. The remaining 1% of users are the Super Contributors, who provide key input and may be compared to superusers of e-participation services.

We have proposed two methods of establishing the threshold of increased activity based on different approaches. These methods yield threshold values that are similar to the key points of the rules mentioned above.

The ML2S (middle of the log2 scale) method. It follows the same principle that was proposed in the study of "Our Saint Petersburg" [11]. In that study we divided the users into several groups depending on the number of messages they sent and placed them onto a horizontal axis of activity, which has a base-2 logarithmic scale. The groups that belong to the second part of the scale (the users who sent more than 2^6 messages) were clustered together into a group of superusers.

This study refined this method in order to establish a more precise boundary for classifying a user as a superuser. This boundary is defined as the middle of the log_2 scale, where the maximum value is the highest possible number of messages sent by an individual user during the period in question. Thus, all users who sent more messages than S_{ML2S} (1) become superusers.

$$S_{\mathrm{ML2S}} = 2^{\left(\log_2 \max_{1 \leq u \leq \mathrm{UC}} MC_u / 2\right)} = \sqrt{\max_{1 \leq u \leq \mathrm{UC}} MC_u}, \tag{1}$$

where UC is the number of users in the dataset being considered,

MC_u is the number of messages that the u-th user sent.

Superusers defined by this method correspond to Super Contributors of the SCOUT model or to Heavy Contributors in the 90-9-1 Rule.

The SBPO (Standard Boxplot Outliers) Method. This method is based on the standard boxplot, which is used to identify atypical observations [22]. Even though this method is mostly used to search for potential outliers in continuous and unimodal data, the highest extremity of the whiskers may be treated as the boundary for classifying superusers, i.e., the users who sent more than S_{SBPO} (2) messages are identified as superusers.

$$S_{SBPO} = Q_3 + 1.5 IQR = Q_3 + 1.5(Q_3 - Q_1), \tag{2}$$

where Q_1 is the first quartile of distribution of all the messages sent by all users MC_u, $1 \leq u \leq UC$; UC is the number of users in the dataset being considered,

Q_3 is the third quartile of this distribution,

IQR is the interquartile interval.

Superusers identified by this method correspond to Intermittent Contributors and Heavy Contributors of the 90-9-1 Rule.

3.4.2   Selection of Data

We propose three methods of processing a dataset, which include its preliminary division into spatial and temporal fragments.

The Fulldata Method. This method is applicable when the initial dataset covers a small territory and is collected over a relatively short period of time comparable with the periods of user activity. Otherwise there is a high risk of missing out temporally and spatially localized superusers and losing a massive part of the dataset when trying to exclude the activity of superusers. This is what is done when this method is applied:

- a list of unique users is made;
- each user is linked to the total number of messages sent by them;
- the threshold of increased activity is defined using the method chosen;
- the users who sent more messages than the threshold value are identified;
- if the impact of superusers needs to be excluded, messages that were sent by the identified users are deleted from the dataset.

The Spatial Method. This method considers the spatial aspect of users' activity. It is applicable only to those datasets in which messages are linked to territorial units, e.g. administrative districts, municipalities, or cadastral units. In this case local activity of individual users will clearly differ from the activity level of their neighbors, even if the number of messages sent by a particular user is not so big on a citywide scale. The dataset is divided into spatial fragments, then lists of individual users are formed within these fragments during the work of the algorithm. In this case, if there is a need for excluding superuser activity, messages of those individual users will be deleted only on those locations where their number exceeded the threshold value. The dataset is processed the following way:

- in a cycle for each territorial unit:
    - a list of unique users in this territory is made;
    - each user is linked to the total number of messages sent by them in this particular territory;
    - the threshold of increased activity in this territory is defined using the method chosen;

- the users who sent more messages than the threshold value in this territory are identified;
- IDs of messages created by superusers in this territory are identified;
- if the impact of superusers needs to be excluded, messages that were sent by local superusers are deleted from the dataset.

The Spatio-Temporal Method. This method considers both spatial and temporal distribution of activity. In this case a superuser is not an individual, but a characteristic of activity of a certain user in a certain territory during the given period of time. If superuser activity needs to be excluded, this method allows us to exclude messages sent by users during the periods of their abnormal activity and preserve their messages sent during all the other periods. The dataset is processed the following way:

- time interval by which user activity will be discretized on a time scale is specified;
- in a cycle for each territorial unit:
    - a list of unique users in the territory is made;
    - in a cycle for each user in the territory:
        - the total number of messages sent by this user in the territory during each time interval is calculated;
    - an array of numbers of messages in all nonzero intervals of activity of all the users in the territory is put together;
    - the threshold of increased activity in this territory during all the intervals of activity is defined using the method chosen;
    - in a cycle for each user in the territory:
        - intervals during which the users sent more messages than the threshold value in this territory are identified;
        - IDs of messages created by superusers in this territory during the intervals of increased activity are identified;
- if the impact of superusers needs to be excluded, all messages that were sent in different territories during different intervals of increased activity are deleted from the dataset.

3.5   Assessment of the Effectiveness of Detecting Increased Activity

We propose to verify the correctness of superuser identification and the choice of the optimal method of considering their impact on distribution of messages on urban problems with help of two indicators.

The first of them, "the completeness of data", represents the share of messages from all territories t (3) that were kept when excluding superuser activity.

$$C = 1 - \frac{\sum_t MC_{\mathrm{SU}_t}}{MC_{\mathrm{ALL}}}, \tag{3}$$

where MC_{ALL} is the initial number of messages in the dataset, MC_{SU_t} is the number of messages in t territory which were identified as sent by a superuser or during a period of increased activity, depending on the method used.

The second indicator, "the balance of interests", is based on the following hypothesis which was suggested during the study of "Our Saint Petersburg" users [11]: superusers and regular users pay attention to different kinds of problems. The most popular category groups, which concern both private and public places, can be used in the evaluation of the balance of interests.

In order to calculate an indicator for a specific method of evaluation of increased activity, we need to do the following:

- divide the dataset into two parts by message sender: superusers' messages (p_1) and regular users' messages (p_2);
- evaluate the share of messages of each problem category group in comparison with the number of messages of all categories for each dataset part p_k and each problem category group g_n: $M_{p_k g_n} = MC_{p_k g_n} / MC_{p_k}$.

B_n determines the balance of interests in each category group g_n: $B_n = M_{p_1 g_n} - M_{p_2 g_n}$. The higher is the indicator of balance of interests in a category group which concerns public spaces, the more prominent is the participation of superusers in this category. Vice versa, the higher is the indicator of balance of interests in private space categories (house, apartment, etc.), the more prominent is the participation of regular users.

4   Experiment

4.1   Data Collection and Initial Processing of the Dataset

We have used "Our Saint Petersburg" data for approbation of the methods developed. We have obtained the dataset by crawling message webpages from March 2014 to March 2020. The initial dataset included a total of 2 million messages. An important feature of "Our Saint Petersburg" is that messages can be posted not only by citizens, but also by service workers, who use dispatcher accounts and receive messages on urban problems on the phone. Because dispatcher accounts aggregate activity of multiple citizens and therefore cannot be analyzed on the same basis as accounts of individual users, we excluded messages by dispatcher accounts from the dataset.

The final dataset prepared for the analysis included a total of 1,296,239 messages and had the following data fields: ID (the number assigned to the message at the time of registration), LATITUDE, LONGITUDE, CATEGORY (the category of the object to which the problem relates), SUB_CATEGORY (subcategory refining the subject of the problem), NAME (a typical description of the reason or nature of the problem), AUTHOR_ID (message author's account number), D_NAME (the administrative area of the city), MO_NAME (the municipal district), RAISED_DATE (message creation date).

4.2 Detecting Superusers and Excluding Their Activity

In order to analyze and refine the dataset, we have developed separate scripts in Matlab R2017b for each of the three methods of dataset processing. Each script implemented the corresponding algorithm of detecting superusers and excluding their activity on the portal. The threshold of increased activity was established with both methods in each script. We also used Tableau. Desktop 2018.3 and Microsoft Excel 365 (ver. 2006).

4.2.1 Analyzing the Full Dataset

The first step was the analysis of the whole dataset of 1,296,239 messages from all users except from dispatcher accounts without sorting by territorial units. The total number of user accounts was 95,165. 40,580 of them (42.46%) sent only one message (which made up 3.13% of the total number of messages), the median value of the number of sent messages equals 2. Using the ML2S method of establishing the threshold of increased activity, we calculated the following value: $S_{ML2S} = 151.9$. Thus, all portal users who sent at least 152 messages during all the time of using the service were classified as superusers. There turned out to be 874 such accounts (0.92%), which sent a total of 732,178 messages (56.49% of all messages), $C_{ML2S} = 0.4351$.

Then we calculated the threshold of increased activity using the SBPO method. The value of S_{SBPO} equals 13.5. According to this method, all users who sent at least 14 messages were classified as superusers. There were 10,058 (10.57%) of such accounts who sent 1,057,464 messages (81.58% of the total number of messages), $C_{SBPO} = 0.1842$. The calculated values of user activity are summarized in Table 1. The results are presented visually in Fig. 1.

The results clearly demonstrate the contribution of superusers to the total number of messages on the portal and confirm the 90-9-1 Rule. In case of the whole "Our Saint Petersburg" dataset (except for messages from dispatcher accounts) approximately 1% of users posted more than a half of all messages and 10% of users sent more than 80% of all messages in the dataset.

Table 1. Share of activity of different user groups

	Share of users in the dataset	Share of the total number of messages in the dataset
Users who sent only one message	42.64%	3.13%
Superusers calculated by ML2S method	0.92%	56.49%
Superusers calculated by SBPO method	10.57%	81.58%

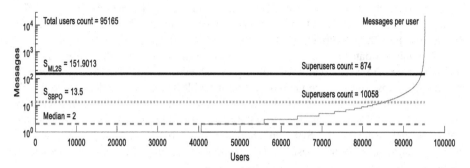

Fig. 1. Diagram of user activity

4.2.2 Data Analysis at the Level of Separate Territories

At this step of our research we separately analyzed data from 18 administrative districts and 111 municipalities in Saint Petersburg. We also calculated median values of activity (i.e. the number of sent messages in the territory) and threshold values of increased activity S_{ML2S} and S_{SBPO}.

Almost all of the 18 districts occupy quite large territories. Median values and S_{SBPO} value correlate with the values calculated on the basis of the whole dataset, but the S_{ML2S} value dropped 2.6-fold (the median value equals 58.5) compared to the city-wide value (Fig. 2). This led to redistribution of user shares. The median value of users who sent only one message did not change drastically: it increased by 6.68% to become 45.49%. The median value of superusers calculated by the SBPO method decreased by 11.5% to become 9.48%. The median value of superusers calculated by the ML2S method increased significantly by 227% to become 2.09%.

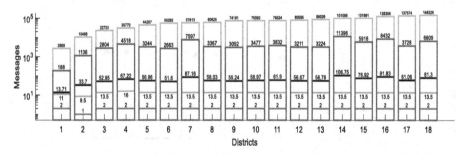

Fig. 2. Diagram of activity values for districts; values are marked inside the bars in ascending order: green line – median value, yellow line – S_{SBPO}, black line – S_{ML2S}, blue bar – the maximum activity of an individual user, grey bar – the total number of messages sent by all users in the area (Color figure online)

The total share of superusers' messages was 77.75% (decreased by 4.7%), C_{SBPO} = 0.222 by the SBPO method, and 58.19% (increased by 2.92%), C_{ML2S} = 0.4181 by the ML2S method.

We analyzed data from 111 municipalities of Saint Petersburg the same way. The median value and S_{SBPO} value of activity remained constant. The S_{ML2S} threshold decreased almost five-fold compared to the city-wide value (the median value equals 30.39). The median value of users who sent only one message in a municipality increased by 11.05% compared to the whole dataset and became 47.35%. The median value of superusers by the SBPO method decreased by 16.41% to become 9.08%, which is similar to district results. The median value of superusers by the ML2S method increased drastically by 430% to become 3.96%.

The total share of municipal superusers' messages was 73.75% by the SBPO method (decreased by 10.62% in comparison with the whole dataset), C_{SBPO} = 0.2625, and 59.7% by the ML2S method (increased by 3%), C_{ML2S} = 0.403.

Thus, both methods of evaluating superuser activity are applicable at the level of city districts or municipalities, but filtering out territorial superusers from the whole dataset doesn't bring significant benefits.

4.2.3   Spatio-Temporal Analysis

In this method we divided all user activity into equal time intervals for each of the 18 districts and 111 municipalities. We chose a fortnight as an interval. This value was chosen experimentally. It was also chosen due to the need to consider weekly periods of citizen activity. In fact, this method divides the dataset into virtual users who are active in the service for a fortnight and have sent at least one message during this period.

The median value of messages sent in one time interval equals 1 for all districts. The S_{SBPO} value for all districts except for a single less active one equals 6. S_{ML2S} threshold, as expected, declined significantly to the median value of 17.33 (Fig. 3).

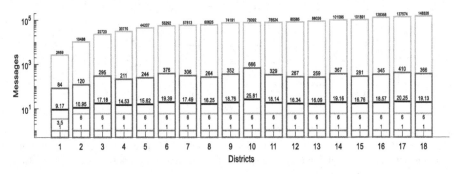

Fig. 3. Diagram of activity values for districts during a fortnight; the following values are marked inside the bars in ascending order: green line – median value, yellow line – S_{SBPO}, black line – S_{ML2S}, blue bar – the maximum number of messages sent during a single interval, grey bar – the total number of messages sent by all users in the area (Color figure online)

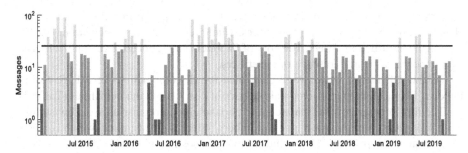

Fig. 4. An example of user activity distribution in one of the districts, each bar represents a fortnight; yellow line is the $S_{SBPO} = 6$ threshold, black line is the $S_{ML2S} = 25.81$ threshold, dark grey bars are periods of increased activity by the SBPO method, light grey bars – by the ML2S method (Color figure online)

Figure 4 demonstrates an example of user activity distribution in district #10 ($S_{SBPO} = 6$, $S_{ML2S} = 25.81$). Applying such a method allows us both to keep the periods of low user activity for analysis and to exclude the periods of increased activity with help of either the SBPO method or the ML2S method.

As only such short periods of activity were considered, the share of users who sent only one message per period was not evaluated. The total number of messages sent in districts during the periods of increased activity equals 54.58% by the SBPO method (decreased by 49.47% in comparison with the share of superusers' messages in the analysis of the full dataset), CSBPO = 0.4542, or 38.95% by the ML2S method (decreased by 45.03%), CML2S = 0.5497.

Similar calculations were made for the 111 municipalities. The median value of the number of messages during an interval equals 1, the median value of S_{SBPO} equals 6, like in districts, the median value of S_{ML2S} threshold decreased to 11.31. The total number of messages sent in municipalities during the periods of increased activity equals 48.86% by the SBPO method (decreased by 66.97% compared to the share of superusers' messages in the analysis of the full dataset), $C_{SBPO} = 0.5114$ or 37.02% by the ML2S method (decreased by 52.59%), $C_{ML2S} = 0.6298$.

Thus, applying this method allows us to target the periods of abnormally increased activity of users and eliminate them without affecting their background activity. Excluding user activity allows us to keep nearly half of the messages from the initial dataset by the SBPO method and almost two thirds of them by the ML2S method.

4.3 Verification of Results

In order to evaluate the effectiveness of detecting increased activity with the balance of interests method, we processed data on seven most popular category groups on "Our Saint Petersburg". The same categories were analyzed in the previous research where the specificities of balance of interests were studied [11]. The first three (Apartment, House, Yard) concern more private spaces, where regular users participate more. The last three (Construction, Street, Territory of St. Petersburg) concern more public spaces, where there is a strong presence of superusers.

Balance of interest values were calculated for all combinations of ML2S, SBPO, Fulldata, Spatial, and Spatio-temporal methods in districts and municipalities (Table 2).

The first three groups, which are more popular among regular users, show shifting of the balance values towards negative numbers, whereas the last three, which are more popular among superusers, show shifting towards positive numbers. Category groups that concern green spaces show values close to zero, i.e. demonstrate parity of popularity among both user groups. Therefore, these values cannot be used to evaluate effectiveness of detection of superusers.

Thus, application of the ML2S method to the full dataset using Fulldata method has shown the highest effectiveness for almost all category groups. A diagram of balance of interests calculated for this method combination is presented on Fig. 5. However, it is important to mention that excluding superuser activity with the Fulldata method results in a significant loss of dataset's completeness. Therefore, it is vital to work on the compatibility of Spatio-temporal and ML2S methods in the future, as the Spatio-temporal method is capable of keeping the most messages in the dataset.

Table 2. Comparison of balance of interests values for popular category groups; the highest absolute value (the light green part of the color gradient) reflects the best suitability of the method for the problem of detecting superusers.

	FULLDATA		SPATIAL (DISTR.)		SPATIAL (MUNICIP.)		SPATIO-TEMPORAL (DISTR.)		SPATIO-TEMPORAL (MUNICIP.)	
	ML2S	SBPO	ML2S	SBPO	ML2S	SBPO	ML2S	SBPO	ML2S	SBPO
Apartment	-0,0414	-0,0666	-0,0411	-0,0572	-0,0395	-0,0486	-0,0305	-0,0393	-0,0293	-0,0347
House	-0,1423	-0,0883	-0,1097	-0,0651	-0,0653	-0,0412	-0,0959	-0,0968	-0,0763	-0,0734
Yard	-0,0742	-0,0459	-0,0525	-0,0348	-0,0302	-0,0194	-0,0464	-0,0536	-0,0238	-0,0301
Park, Garden	-0,0043	-0,0042	-0,0043	-0,0048	-0,0044	-0,0055	-0,0040	-0,0043	-0,0034	-0,0040
Construction	0,0381	0,0310	0,0328	0,0299	0,0278	0,0266	0,0306	0,0337	0,0266	0,0289
Street	0,1234	0,0984	0,0961	0,0721	0,0599	0,0453	0,0778	0,0867	0,0557	0,0578
Terr. of SPb	0,1008	0,0814	0,0833	0,0691	0,0611	0,0558	0,0739	0,0795	0,0587	0,0643

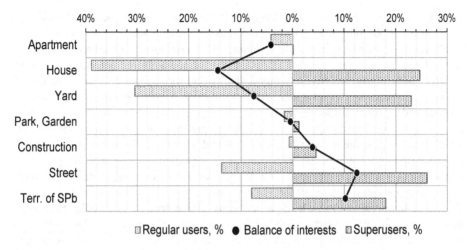

Fig. 5. Diagram of popularity of categories among regular users and superusers and the balance of interests between them.

5 Discussion and Future Work

This study suggests approaches to detecting and excluding abnormal activity of users of e-participation services in order to correct the unequal distribution of messages on urban problems. The methods described in this paper provide an opportunity to evaluate socioeconomic features of urban territories with help of e-participation data which is evenly distributed and cleared of distortions caused by individual overly active users. We have demonstrated the specificities of each method of identifying superusers on the example of "Our Saint Petersburg" data over the past six years which includes about 1.3 million messages.

On the full dataset, the ML2S method classified about 1% of all users as high contributors. They sent more than half of all messages. The SBPO method identified about 10% of users. In this case, superusers sent over 80% of all messages. Analysis of separate districts and municipalities instead of the entire urban area did not show any drastic changes in these values. Obviously, the approach proposed in previous studies, which implies deletion of superuser data, leads to serious data loss in this situation.

The spatio-temporal analysis of messages allows us to break down the activity of all users in each territory into fixed time intervals. In this case, the data of users who were identified as superusers during the analysis of the full dataset will not be deleted for periods when their activity did not stand out against the background of the activity of other users. This approach has shown very high effectiveness of keeping the dataset complete. The ML2S method has shown the best results for the analysis of municipalities: in this case, the data loss after filtering periods of high user activity is 37%. This shows that it is more correct to view the superuser phenomenon not as individual people who generated a large amount of data within the full dataset, but as a special status of a user in a certain location at a certain time of activity. These locations and times may alternate with regular background activity, therefore the method allows us to target and exclude only the peaks of local activity while leaving the rest intact.

Verification of effectiveness of processing the dataset using the balance of interests method has proven the potential of using special methods for detecting increased activity, particularly the ML2S method. However, the intensity of the balance of interests decreases in case of spatio-temporal analysis of municipalities, which means this method requires further refining.

Using the developed approach requires the presence of user IDs in the dataset, which make it possible to analyze their individual activities. This data is not available for all e-participation services. However, it is important to note that the proposed method does not require personal data of users or access to message content, only a system ID. Another limitation of the approach is the criticality of the amount of data for the spacio-temporal method. The e-participation service needs to be popular enough so that many residents in each municipality of the city post regularly. However, the method is flexible, and it is possible to divide the city into larger districts and use longer intervals of activity for small towns and unpopular services.

In the future, it is advisable to test the proposed approaches on similar data from other e-participation services and social media. The question of motivation and behavioral patterns of those citizens that act as superusers most of the time still remains. In further works on evaluating urban environment with help of e-participation data, methods of modelling synthetic superusers might be developed, which would help to predict environmental parameters in conditions of local deficiency of e-participation data.

Acknowledgment. This research is financially supported by The Russian Science Foundation, Agreement №17-71-30029 with co-financing of Bank Saint Petersburg.

References

1. Chugunov, A.: Smart-city concept: functioning of feedback mechanisms in the context of e-participation of citizens. Inf. Resour. Russia **6**, 21–27 (2019). (in Russian)
2. Li, M., Westerholt, R., Fan, H., Zipf, A.: Assessing spatiotemporal predictability of LBSN: a case study of three Foursquare datasets. GeoInformatica **22**(3), 541–561 (2016). https://doi.org/10.1007/s10707-016-0279-5
3. Stewart, O., Lubensky, D., Huerta, J.M.: Crowdsourcing participation inequality: a SCOUT model for the enterprise domain. In: Proceedings of the ACM SIGKDD Workshop on Human Computation, pp. 30–33 (2010)
4. Haklay, M.: Why is participation inequality important? In: European Handbook of Crowdsourced Geographic Information, pp. 35–44. Ubiquity Press, London (2016)
5. White, A., Trump, K.: The promises and pitfalls of 311 data. Urban Aff. Rev. **54**(4), 794–823 (2018)
6. O'Brien, D., Sampson, R., Winship, C.: Ecometrics in the age of big data: measuring and assessing "broken windows" using large-scale administrative records. Sociol. Methodol. **45**(1), 101–147 (2015)

7. O'Brien, D.T.: Custodians and custodianship in urban neighborhoods: a methodology using reports of public issues received by a city's 311 hotline. Environ. Behav. **3**(47), 304–327 (2015)
8. Kontokosta, C., Hong, B., Korsberg, K.: Equity in 311 reporting: understanding sociospatial differentials in the propensity to complain. In: Bloomberg Data for Good Exchange Conference, New York (2017). arXiv:1710.02452
9. Hong, A., Kim, B., Widener, M.: Noise and the city: leveraging crowdsourced big data to examine the spatiotemporal relationship between urban development and noise annoyance. Environ. Plan. B Urban Anal. City Sci. (2019). https://doi.org/10.1177/23998083
10. Solymosi, R.: Exploring spatial patterns of guardianship through civic technology platforms. Crim. Justice Rev. **44**(1), 42–59 (2019)
11. Kudinov, S., Ilina, E., Antonov, A.: Analyzing civic activity in the field of urban improvement and housing maintenance based on e-participation data: St. Petersburg experience. In: Chugunov, A., Khodachek, I., Misnikov, Y., Trutnev, D. (eds.) EGOSE 2019. CCIS, vol. 1135, pp. 88–102. Springer, Cham (2020). https://doi.org/10.1007/978-3-030-39296-3_7
12. Li, M., Sun, Y., Fan, H.: Contextualized relevance evaluation of geographic information for mobile users in location-based social networks. ISPRS Int. J. Geo-Inf. **4**(2), 799–814 (2015)
13. Colombo, G.B.: You are where you eat: foursquare checkins as indicators of human mobility and behaviour. In: 2012 IEEE International Conference on Pervasive Computing and Communications Workshops, pp. 217–222 (2012)
14. Noulas, A.: An empirical study of geographic user activity patterns in foursquare. In: Fifth International AAAI Conference on Weblogs and Social Media (2011)
15. Wang, L., Qian, C., Kats, P., Kontokosta, C., Sobolevsky, S.: Structure of 311 service requests as a signature of urban location. PLoS ONE **12**(10), e0186314 (2017). https://doi.org/10.1371/journal.pone.0186314
16. Kudinov, S., Ilina, E., Grekhneva, E.: Exploring the connection between the existence of local web communities and civic activity: St. Petersburg case study. In: Chugunov, A., Misnikov, Y., Roshchin, E., Trutnev, D. (eds.) EGOSE 2018. CCIS, vol. 947, pp. 334–347. Springer, Cham (2019). https://doi.org/10.1007/978-3-030-13283-5_25
17. Gulnerman, A.G., Karaman, H., Pekaslan, D., Bilgi, S.: Citizens' spatial footprint on Twitter—anomaly, trend and bias investigation in Istanbul. ISPRS Int. J. Geo-Information **9**(4), 222 (2020)
18. Tsou, M.H., Zhang, H., Jung, C.T.: Identifying data noises, user biases, and system errors in geo-tagged twitter messages (Tweets). arXiv:1712.02433 (2017)
19. Solymosi, R., Bowers, K.J., Fujiyama, T.: Crowdsourcing subjective perceptions of neighbourhood disorder: interpreting bias in open data. Br. J. Criminol. **58**(4), 944–967 (2018)
20. Portal User statuses. https://gorod.gov.spb.ru/statusp/. Accessed 10 July 2020. (in Russian)
21. The 90-9-1 Rule for Participation Inequality in Social Media and Online Communities. https://www.nngroup.com/articles/participation-inequality/. Accessed 12 July 2020
22. Dodge, Y.: The Concise Encyclopedia of Statistics. Springer, New York (2008). https://doi.org/10.1007/978-0-387-32833-1

Communication Channels in Public Policy Development and Implementation: Online or Offline? (The Case of Separate Waste Collection in St. Petersburg)

Anastasia A. Golubeva⬤ and Evgenii V. Gilenko$^{(\boxtimes)}$⬤

Graduate School of Management, St. Petersburg State University,
3 Volkhovskiy per., St. Petersburg 199004, Russia
e.gilenko@gsom.spbu.ru

Abstract. In recent decades, the development of information and communication technologies has led to expansion of the range of communication channels used by the society. Cheaper, faster and more user-oriented communication channels, such as the Internet and social networks, have proven effective in implementing strategies for promoting goods and services in the private sector. They also demonstrated their popularity in the interaction of public authorities with citizens. Government websites, public services portals, and platforms for electronic public participation now largely determine the nature, quality, and areas of interaction in the public sector. But are the electronic channels a panacea, and will they replace completely the offline channels? The issue of choosing the optimal communication strategy becomes especially relevant when solving complex multidimensional issues of development and implementation of a public policy in any area. At different stages of the communication strategy life cycle, the tasks of interaction are different. The success in their completion is determined, in particular, by selection of the correct communication channel. This article discusses the attributes of different communication channels (online and offline) and using the example of the separate waste collection policy in St. Petersburg (Russia) provides recommendations on the usage of the most effective communication channels for the policy development and implementation. A formal procedure of the conjoint analysis is used as a way to analyze citizens' preferred attributes of communication channels. The results of a survey conducted among the residents of St. Petersburg allow to conclude that online channels are not always the most preferable and effective ways of such communication.

Keywords: Electronic communication · Separate waste collection · Conjoint analysis · Citizens' preferences

1 Introduction

From January 1, 2019, the "waste reform", which formally introduced amendments to the law "On production and consumption waste" (#89-FZ, as of 31.12.2017), entered its active phase in most regions of the Russian Federation. The actual purpose of this

A. Chugunov et al. (Eds.): EGOSE 2020, CCIS 1349, pp. 172–183, 2020.
https://doi.org/10.1007/978-3-030-67238-6_12

reform of the solid household waste (SHW) management system is reduction in landfill disposal and increasing the volume recycled waste. This, in turn, means elimination of illegal landfills and transition to a more transparent system of waste management.

Thus, today we witness an example of yet another "milestone" of one of the prominent public policies – the waste collection policy. But can this "milestone" efficiently be passed without active communication with the society itself? The answer is, obviously, no, because in this specific case the people of the country play an integral role in operating of the whole waste management system.

According to the targets of the Russian national project "Ecology", from 2019 to 2024 the share of recycled SHW should increase from 3% to 36% [1]. But, at the same time, according to the recent results of a national survey conducted by the Russian Public Opinion Research Center (WCIOM, [2]), 74% of Russians have only heard about the "waste reform" in general, but only 24% of respondents are aware of various aspects and details of the reform.

It should also be noticed that St. Petersburg, as one of the three Russian cities of federal importance, has the right to postpone the launch of the reform, which was actually used by the St. Petersburg authorities in order to make all the necessary preparations. The situation with waste processing in St. Petersburg is better than the national average, but still far from ideal. In St. Petersburg, only about 20% of SHW is processed, the rest is transported to landfills in the Leningrad region. The "waste reform" is expected to change the situation: the share of recycled SHW in the total volume of the generated waste in St. Petersburg in 2025 should reach 69.2% [3]. Thus, the "waste reform" virtually implies a much wider implementation of the separate waste collection (SWC) format of waste processing.

Unfortunately, as of now, as Krasimir Vranski, the principal coordinator of the "Beautiful St. Petersburg" social movement, puts it, one of the main obstacle to achieving significant progress in improving of the SHW management, at large, and implementation of separate waste collection, specifically, is the inability to bring the problem to the proper attention of the St. Petersburg officials and deputies [4].

At the same time, as this kind of policy is hugely dependent on partnering with citizens, this implies the need for working together (co-working) to successfully implement the new waste collection policy. And the authorities are expected to develop an effective communication strategy with the citizens, which, in turn, implies detection and creation of various communication channels accounting for the corresponding preferences of the citizens.

The **purpose** of the current research is to discuss the optimal communication strategies between the St. Petersburg authorities and the citizens, and to analyze the optimal communication channels for them, in the context of the "waste reform". So, the **main research hypothesis** of this research that different groups of people require different channels of communication with, and, thus, the authorities have to identify what these channels are in order to conduct an efficient communication strategy (specifically, in the context of the "waste reform").

The theoretical foundation for the research comprises the recently proposed OECD model (adjusted by the authors of this study) of the life cycle of a strategy of communication between people and authorities when implementing and developing a public policy implying co-working of the people and the authorities. This model is specifically suitable for the "waste reform" in St. Petersburg which is discussed further in the text.

The empirical calculations of this study are based on a survey conducted among the residents of St. Petersburg on their preferences and attitudes towards different communication channels with authorities. The obtained results of the survey were processed with a modern technique of the conjoint analysis to reveal the most preferred attributes of such channels.

The rest of the paper is organized as follows. Section 2 illustrates the theoretical model for the current research, while Sect. 3 gives the research methodology. In Sect. 4, based on the obtained calculation results, the discussion and the corresponding recommendations are provided. Section 5 concludes.

2   Separate Waste Collection Communication Strategy: Objectives and Participants

In this section, we consider the recently proposed theoretical OECD model of the life cycle of a strategy of communication between people and authorities in the case of the "waste reform" in St. Petersburg (Russia). Thus, the separate waste collection communication strategy (SWCCS), at large, and the current situation with waste collection in St. Petersburg, specifically, are discussed.

2.1   The Life-Cycle of the SWCCS

In general, *communication policy* is the process of interaction of authorities with citizens, which allows to form a stable idea of the subject of communication and is implemented to achieve a specific purpose [5]. In the studied case, such communication policy is to be conducted in order to increase the level of involvement and awareness of St. Petersburg citizens in the process of separate waste collection. *Communication strategy* is an integral part of such a process, which allows the authorities to organize and conduct the communication policy in the form of various stages described below in the framework of the OECD model.

In the process of interaction at different stages of the communication strategy, authorities can use specific communication methods and channels to achieve the best possible results. Thus, the result of such communication should be not only raising of the awareness of citizens about the problem in focus, but also providing the people with the most convenient ways to receive quality public services at every stage [5] (Fig. 1).

At the *first stage*, the main purpose of communication is to *increase awareness* of the population – in our case, about the possibility of passing the accumulated waste to recycling. It is impossible to build a constructive dialogue and involve citizens in this process without elaborating the existing and developing new communication channels that transmit information about the existence of such a service as separate waste collection. Moreover, at this stage it is the communication itself that is a very important "detail" which triggers the entire mechanism of co-working of the state, citizens, public organizations and business on waste collection.

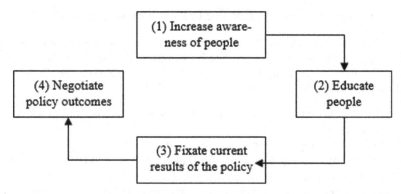

Fig. 1. The life cycle of a communication strategy for implementation of a public policy (composed by the authors based on the OECD model [5]).

The *second stage* in the implementation of the SWCCS is informing/educating the population that, in order to improve the convenience of citizens, there are special bins or organized collection sites, as well as special rules of pre-processing for sorted waste. As a result, the general perception and awareness of the need for citizens' participation in the separate waste collection process will be brought to a principally new level. Interaction with and educating of the population should be done in conjunction with various non-profit organizations (NPOs) that, as the evidence shows, sometimes have considerably more experience in it than the authorities. Besides, in Russia, actually being the founders of the separate waste collection movement, non-profit organizations have practical experience of interacting with citizens in effectively informing them, for example, about the installed containers for separate waste collection.

The *third stage* consists in fixating the current results of the policy (of separate waste collection, in our case) and continuing supporting of the already established trends among the population. This means that at this stage the role of communication will be in consolidation in the people's minds of the important role of complicity in the SWC process, that is, with the help various information resources, lectures, seminars, booklets, posters, the authorities should support the idea of the policy and justify the role of each person involved in its implementation.

At the *fourth stage*, citizens should be informed about the outcomes of the implemented policy. They should know about the value of the efforts made, and the level of satisfaction of citizens increases due to the activities of the authorities.

In particular, the level of confidence in the SWC policy carried out by the state is also expected to increase.

So, despite the fact that careful creation and implementation of an elaborate communication strategy implies certain costs – time, financial resources, and efforts on the part of the authorities, – the value of such system is undeniable in reaching the underlying policy objectives. In the case of the "waste reform" and the process of separate waste collection, such strategy will allow to actually solve the problem of low involvement of citizens in the SWC process.

2.2 The Current Situation with Waste Collection in St. Petersburg

Unfortunately, the implementation of the "waste reform" faced substantial obstacles right from the beginning. This is why the St. Petersburg authorities used the right to postpone the full-fledged realization of this reform. Among such obstacles, can be named the following (see also [6]).

1. The scheme of the regional waste management system does not reflect the needs of the "waste reform".
2. The absence of a single regional waste operator.
3. The current city waste-processing infrastructure is very outdated and unable to implement the reform.
4. It is the society, not the St. Petersburg authorities, that has the initiative in the separate waste collection process.
5. The citizens of St. Petersburg are poorly informed about the waste collection issue.

The original initiative of the St. Petersburg authorities was to postpone the implementation of the "waste reform" as much as possible – till 2022. But due to the interference of the federal authorities, this it was decided to "mildly" start the implementation of the reform in 2020 (see [7]).

Thus, actually, today the St. Petersburg authorities have a quite severe need for launching the first stage of the above-discussed model – the stage of increasing awareness of people about the on-going processes in the sphere of waste collection in order to ultimately be able to organize efficient co-working with the citizens in this sphere. This correspondingly raises the question of the most effective and efficient communication channels with people.

3   Research Methodology

In this section we describe the methodology of the conducted research aimed at revealing the most comfortable for people communication channels with the authorities. The research started with a focus group to identify, on the one hand, the main parties in the waste collection process, and, on the other hand, the key attributes of potential communication channels. Using this information, a questionnaire was developed and a survey was conducted among the citizens of St. Petersburg that allowed to find out the attributes of the most preferable communication channels for different age groups, using the technique of conjoint analysis.

3.1   The Focus Group

At the first step of the current research, we conducted an exploratory focus group. Focus group is a research methodology which "collects data through group interaction on a topic determined by the researcher" [8]. Focus group methodology is considered to be able to generate complex information, to gain a wide range of insights of participants' attitudes, opinions, and perceptions about the research issue, through natural social interaction among the participants in a permissive and non-threatening environment (e.g., [9, 10]).

The conducted focus group consisted of 6 experts (both genders) – 2 young, 2 middle-aged, and 2 aged persons. Due to the COVID-19 situation, the discussion was organized online. Besides the general discussion of the issue of SWC communication strategy, the focus group was organized to identify the following: (1) the main participants of the SWC process; (2) the principal channels of communication between the citizens and the authorities and their important attributes.

As a result of reaching the first of the objectives, the following list of participants was composed:

- producers of consumer goods;
- households and firms (consumers of goods);
- waste collecting companies;
- waste recycling companies;
- non-profit organizations (ecoactivists);
- municipal/state authorities.

Among these participants, of crucial importance for the current research are, of course, households (citizens) and municipal/state authorities.

As we discussed above, the communication process for these two parties is still to be launched in full in St. Petersburg, thus, it is important to identify the most effective channels for such communication. So, as a result of achieving of this goal, the focus group summarized the following communication channels and their main attributes, as provided in Table 1.

Table 1. Communication channels and their main attributes.

Channel	Online	Possibility of feedback	Targeted	Multiformat support	Demographic spread
Web sites	yes	yes	no	yes	high
Social networks and messengers	yes	yes	yes	yes	high
Web media	yes	yes	no	yes	high
Email distribution lists	yes	no	yes	no	medium
Mobile applications	yes	yes	yes	yes	medium
Street activism	no	yes	no	no	high
Conferences	no	yes	yes	yes	medium
Public discussions	no	yes	yes	no	medium
Press	no	no	no	no	low

The given channels and their attributes are quite self-explanatory. So, for the sake of space saving, we now switch to the description of the sample collection process.

Extra comments on the communication channels can be provided upon an email request.

3.2 Sample Collection and Description

Due to the COVID-19 situation, the poll of respondents was organized as an online survey with several blocks of questions, such as socio-demographic questions, the questions on the attitude towards the identified communication channels, and some other. The full questionnaire can be provided upon an email request.

In total, 250 full responses were collected. The principal characteristics of the sample are provided in Table 2. The full list of sample characteristics can be provided upon an email request.

Table 2. The percentage structure of the sample.

Characteristic	Group	%
Age (years)		
	<28 (young)	39.6
	28–45 (middle-aged)	34.0
	>45 (elderly)	26.4
Gender		
	Male	47.2
	Female	52.8
Experience in separate waste collection		
	no experience at all	24.4
	little experience	35.2
	regular participation	**40.4**
Knowledge about the "waste reform"		
	know nothing	26.0
	know very little	53.6
	know in detail	**20.4**

As it can be seen from Table 2, although the age and gender groups are not uniformly represented, the actual peculiarity of the structure of this sample lies in a different thing: although more than 40% of the respondents regularly participate in the separate waste collection process, only about 20% of the respondents know the details of the "waste reform".

3.3 Methods

As the main attributes of the selected communication channels were identified at the previous step, this allowed to apply the modern technique of conjoint analysis to find out their most influential attributes.

As related to each of the identified channels, questions on the likeliness of usage of these channels were posed to the respondents and the answers were collected on a 5–grade Likert scale. The corresponding average values (both for the whole sample and for principal age groups) can be found in Table 3. Cronbach's alpha was used to check the consistency of the answers (also given in Table 3). As it can be seen from the table, the values of Cronbach's alpha are always above 0.7 which speaks in favor of the acceptable internal consistency of the answers in all cases.

Table 3. Average values of the 5-grade Likert scales for the communication channels.

Channel	Whole sample	Young	Middle-aged	Elderly
Web sites	4.22	4.23	4.27	4.04
Social networks and messengers	3.91	4.18	3.59	3.15
Web media	3.38	3.39	3.43	3.23
Email distribution lists	3.36	3.58	3.26	2.31
Mobile applications	2.02	1.88	2.07	2.73
Street activism	2.39	2.4	2.33	2.5
Conferences	2.44	2.31	2.41	3.27
Public discussions	2.81	2.8	2.69	3.23
Press	1.93	1.81	2.03	2.38
Cronbach's alpha	0.72	0.74	0.77	0.71

We applied the technique of *conjoint analysis* that allows to identify the relative importance of the levels of the attributes of the studied communication channels. As a marketing technique, conjoint analysis (CA) is aimed at revealing characteristics of products which are most appealing to the customers – which of the characteristics have the highest utilities (part worths) to the customers [11]. CA is a very popular quantitative technique being used for studying a wide range of applied questions.

The traditional conjoint analysis is based on estimation of a linear regression function of the following kind:

$$Y = pw_0 + pw_1X_1 + pw_2X_2 + pw_3X_3 + \ldots + pw_nX_n, \tag{1}$$

where Y is the dependent variable showing the overall rating/ranking of the various combinations of attribute levels; and pw_i are the part-worths of each attribute X_i.

As a result of estimation of Eq. (1) using the OLS routine, we get estimates of part-worths. The largest positive part-worth on each attribute is the most preferred level on that attribute for the respondent. The results of application of this technique are given in the following section.

4 Results and Recommendations

In this section we briefly discuss the obtained results of conjoint analysis and provide relevant policy recommendations.

4.1 Empirical Results and Discussion

As revealed by the conjoint analysis, most valued attribute levels of the communication channels (for the corresponding age groups) are summarized in Table 4. These findings also allowed to identify optimal channels of communication with these groups of the St. Petersburg population.

Table 4. Preferences of the respondents towards the attributes of communication channels.

Age group	Online	Possibility of feedback	Targeted	Multiformat support	Demographic spread	Optimal channel
Young	yes	no	yes	yes	high	*Social networks*
Middle-aged	yes	yes	no	yes	high	*Web media*
Elderly	no	yes	yes	no	medium	*Public discussions*

These results are in line with the extant literature. As proper policy implementation still remains a challenge to the authorities, the authors of [12] demonstrate that choosing the most effective set of communication channels at various stages of developing and implementing a waste management policy becomes the number one task.

Of course, traditional channels of communication are now comparatively less popular due to their interactivity limitations. Still, while stakeholder engagement is needed at all stages of policy development and implementation, the public perception needs to be taken into account early in the decision making process [13]. Therefore, new electronic channels are more convenient for such close cooperation between citizens and government.

Yet, it has to be kept in mind that the traditional (offline) communication channels are still preferred by the elderly people. So, these channels are still to be used by the authorities in order to extend the population coverage.

In general, our findings actually allow to have an in-depth look into the structure of preferences of the corresponding citizens. By using such approach, the authorities can better understand the fine preferences of the citizens to better adjust the communication strategy for them.

4.2   Policy Recommendations

According to the theoretical model discussed in Sect. 2, and in line with the obtained empirical results, here we can speak about two major recommendations to the authorities of St. Petersburg.

1. To effectively realize the *first step* of the separate waste collection communication strategy (SWCCS), the authorities should take into account that the process of communication with the citizens of St. Petersburg should cover both the online and offline format. So, the relevant information within implementation of the "waste reform" should be equally presented both through the online (social networks, messengers, web media) and offline (public discussion) means.

   In general, the significant positive effect of public education on the willingness of urban residents to classify household waste was proved in [14]. Different governments actively promote public education to popularize the knowledge of the separate waste collection and to enhance the sense of responsibility and environmental-friendly behavior [15]. Educational programs provided through different media channels in Japan, United States (television and the Internet) resulted in various positive effects [16, 17].

2. Understanding of the more in-depth structure of the citizens' preferences towards the different attributes of communication channels can actually help the authorities prepare for the *second step* of the SWCCS which is aimed at educating the citizens.

For example, from Table 4 we can see that the group of young respondents is not very fond of providing feedback. Thus, the authorities should:

(1) understand why this happens – probably, young citizens do not think that there feedback will be of value and influence;
(2) educate the young population of St. Petersburg on the importance of feedback provision.

Also, as it can be seen from Table 4, the elderly people prefer not to use the online format of communication. This means that the authorities should explain to the elderly people the advantages of the online format and educate them on how to appropriately use it. Such education turns out to be quite successful (see [18, 19]).

5   Conclusion

In this research the questions of organization of effective communication channels between citizens and authorities are studied in the context of the introduced changes to the waste collection policy (the "waste reform") in Russia (for the case of St. Petersburg). The conducted analysis clearly demonstrated that online communication channels are not always the most preferable and effective ways of such communication, while a more in-depth studying of the preferences of citizens may let better understand and organize other steps in such communication.

Although the analysis was conducted on a comparatively limited number of citizens' responses (which is definitely one of the limitations of this research), still, the proposed approach can be extended to a wider population to obtain a better understanding on the directions of communication with people in the framework of the "waste reform". This presents room for further research.

References

1. The Russian Ministry of Natural Resources, The "Ecology" National Project Homepage. https://www.mnr.gov.ru/activity/directions/natsionalnyy_proekt_ekologiya/. Accessed 12 July 2020
2. The Russian Public Opinion Research Center (WCIOM). The Ecologic Situation in Russia: Monitoring. https://wciom.ru/index.php?id=236&uid=9544. Accessed 12 July 2020
3. Peterburg, D.: Best practices. About 20% of SHW is processed in St. Petersburg, but the reform will change the situation. https://www.dp.ru/a/2019/09/02/Luchshie_praktiki. Accessed 12 July 2020
4. Krasimir Vranski Interview. https://paperpaper.ru/photos/krasimir-vranski-sem-let-borolsya-za-b/. Accessed 12 July 2020
5. OECD Together for Better Public Services: Partnering with Citizens and Civil Society. OECD Public Governance Reviews, OECD Publishing (2011)
6. RBC.: The main document of the "waste reform" has been published in St. Petersburg. https://www.rbc.ru/spb_sz/20/01/2020/5e256a429a79476ad76775f2. Accessed 12 July 2020
7. Kommersant: Cleaning at the Federal level. The "waste reform". https://www.kommersant.ru/doc/4233194. Accessed 12 July 2020
8. Morgan, D.L.: Focus groups. Ann. Rev. Sociol. **22**, 129–152 (1996)
9. Liamputtong, P.: Focus Group Methodology: Principles and Practice. SAGE, New York (2011)
10. Lamberti, L., Benedetti, M., Chen, S.: Benefits sought by citizens and channel attitudes for multichannel payment services: evidence from Italy. Gov. Inf. Q. **31**(4), 596–609 (2014)
11. Gatignon, H.: Statistical Analysis of Management Data, 3rd edn. Springer, Boston (2014). https://doi.org/10.1007/978-1-4614-8594-0
12. Kala, K., Bolia, N., Sushil, P.: Waste management communication policy for effective citizen awareness. J. Policy Model. **42**, 661–678 (2020)
13. Kirkman, R., Voulvouli, N.: The role of public communication in decision making for waste management infrastructure. J. Environ. Manage. **203**, 640–647 (2017)
14. Ramzan, S., Liu, C., Munir, H., Xu, Y.: Assessing young consumers' awareness and participation in sustainable e-waste management practices: a survey study in Northwest China. Environ. Sci. Pollut. Res. **26**(19), 20003–20013 (2019). https://doi.org/10.1007/s11356-019-05310-y
15. Vicente, P., Reis, E.: Factors influencing households' participation in recycling. Waste Manage. Res. J. Int. Solid Wastes Public Clean. Assoc. ISWA **26**(2), 140–146 (2008)
16. Grodzińska-Jurczak, M., Tomal, P., Tarabuła-Fiertak, M., Nieszporek, K., Read, A.: Effects of an educational campaign on public environmental attitudes and behaviour in Poland. Resour. Conserv. Recycl. **46**, 182–197 (2006)
17. Wen, X., Luo, Q., Hu, H., Wang, N., Chen, Y., Jin, J., Hao, Y., Xu, G., Li, F., Fang, W.: Comparison research on waste classification between China and the EU, Japan, and the USA. J. Mater. Cycles Waste Manage. **16**(2), 321–334 (2013). https://doi.org/10.1007/s10163-013-0190-1

18. Golubeva, Anastasia A., Gilenko, Evgenii V.: Creating public value through public e-services development: the case of landscaping and public amenities in St. Petersburg. In: Chugunov, A., Misnikov, Y., Roshchin, E., Trutnev, D. (eds.) EGOSE 2018. CCIS, vol. 947, pp. 249–264. Springer, Cham (2019). https://doi.org/10.1007/978-3-030-13283-5_19
19. Golubeva, A., Gilenko, E., Dzhedzheya, V.: Enhancing Public Value of Local Public Services Through Electronic Interaction. Russ. Manage. J. **17**(2), 159–178 (2019)

The Interaction Between ICT
and Authoritarian Legitimation Strategies:
An Empirical Inquiry

Yury Kabanov[(⊠)] iD

National Research University Higher School of Economics,
St. Petersburg, Russia
ykabanov@hse.ru

Abstract. Legitimacy is a vital source of stability in authoritarian political systems, and non-democracies are developing various tools to sustain it. The Internet is said to be one such tool, offering a variety of legitimizing effects, but the main discussion in this paper is around the referent object and the type of legitimation. This study attempts to explore how the diffusion of online tools is associated with different legitimation strategies of authoritarian countries, as measured by the *Varieties of Democracy* project. The analysis suggests that IT – tools diffusion is strongly and positively correlated with the *rational-legal* and *performance* types of legitimation. While the data is subject to variation, the results support an earlier claim that the proliferation of online tools is legitimation-driven and is applied to specific forms of legitimacy. This initial analysis will be further developed by including legitimation strategies into the causal Internet diffusion models.

Keywords: Authoritarian stability · Legitimation · ICT · Varieties of Democracy

1 Introduction[1]

The research on the sources of authoritarian stability is growing nowadays [13, 29], together with the variety of tools, institutions and strategies governments utilize to stay in power. In this context the digital domain is becoming an important part of non-democratic politics and governance. A growing number of autocracies implement ICT into their authoritarian consolidation and capacity-building strategies [4, 15], combining active Internet promotion with increasing control over the cyberspace [20, 26]. An example of this shift is the *Networked Readiness Index* 2016, where countries such as the UAE, Singapore, Qatar, Rwanda, Saudi Arabia, Azerbaijan and Bahrain

---

[1] An earlier draft of this paper was presented at 19th Annual Aleksanteri Conference, 23–25 October 2019, Helsinki, Finland.

© Springer Nature Switzerland AG 2020
A. Chugunov et al. (Eds.): EGOSE 2020, CCIS 1349, pp. 184–194, 2020.
https://doi.org/10.1007/978-3-030-67238-6_13

surprisingly occupied leading positions according to the "Importance of ICTs to government vision of the future".[2]

Within the repertoire of authoritarian stability strategies – *legitimation, cooptation,* and *repression* [4, 15] – ICT seem to reinforce all of them, providing technological and communication basis for propaganda, surveillance, control etc. [12, 19, 22]. Yet, many scholars tend to consider the quest for legitimacy to be one of the major factors of ICT diffusion, especially when it comes to citizen- or governance-oriented online tools [2, 27]. As argued by Stier, the Internet is an important driver of legitimacy that "can generate support for an authoritarian government within the two most critical groups for authoritarian survival: regime elites and the masses" [31, p. 7].

While the legitimation hypothesis is becoming more commonplace, its definition requires further refinement because the notions of legitimacy and legitimation are not straightforward [13]. Legitimation strategies of autocracies vary from a traditional authoritarian to a more democratic style [9, 33, 37]. Hence it is useful to know, what kind of legitimation is meant when Internet promotion in relation to online tools is discussed. The empirical answer to this challenge has, so far, been complicated by a lack of measurements. The recent data [6, 33] help to address this gap by associating legitimation strategies of autocracies and their effort in developing Internet tools.

This study deals with the research question, 'are the development of selected online tools associated with legitimation strategies of non-democracies?' And, if so, what are the temporal dynamics of this association? To answer these questions, we ran a preliminary correlation analysis, using data on legitimation strategies from the *Varieties of Democracy* project [6, 33] and the indicators of the *UN E- Government Survey*. For the definition and classification of authoritarian regimes we apply the approach and the data developed by Wahman, Teorell and Hadenius [38]. As this is a preliminary inquiry, the goal of the research is to assess the potential of the new data to be used in further causal analysis. We then outline the future avenues of research that would include legitimation as an explanatory variable of the Internet diffusion.

2 ICT for Legitimation: A Review

When it comes to social media and e-governance, in the literature there are two intertwined explanations on why autocrats support ICT development. The first argues that this helps them to improve the quality of governance by acquiring information about citizens' attitudes towards the regime [7, 25]. Other scholars claim that legitimation is the main imperative, and here autocrats tend to signal their up-to-datedness to the international community [2, 21] or to the citizens [27], and thus to mimic a competent government [18].

Although both incentives might reinforce each other [9, 17], it seems that despite a few examples of particular countries, e.g. China [7, 25], the quest for ICT is rather "an aim in itself" [3]. In most cases there are no signs that online tools have a visible

---

[2] Networked Readiness Index. World Economic Forum. URL: http://reports.weforum.org/global-information-technology-report-2016/networked-readiness-index/.

positive impact on the quality of governance [24], however they nevertheless allow the creation of an image of transparent and accountable governance [34] and generate a certain level of regime support [29, 35]. At the same time, the meaningful input of citizens to public policy are constrained by institutional designs of online channels [5, 39] or restrictive Internet-policies [20, 26, 30]. Particular examples of such countries include the monarchies of the Middle East [23, 31], where oil revenues usually hinder the incentives of seeking information to adjust policies [10].

Of course, using the legitimation effects of ICT should not be taken for granted, as such initiatives may result in legitimacy crises [8] and decrease of institutional trust [40], or their impact on legitimacy will be limited to particular social groups [35] or types of social media citizens use [29]. However, here we need to distinguish between the output of such efforts, and the strategies of autocrats, i.e. what they have in mind, when they promote IT-enabled innovations. In this regard, it is important to find out what legitimation claims [37] are more likely to be connected with these decisions.

Previous studies on IT-enabled legitimation in autocracies tend to take the regime type as an explanatory variable, as different regimes have different institutional incentives and legitimation strategies. For instance, Stier [31] has revealed a higher level of the Internet penetration in monarchies, concluding that they are the most successful in converting oil-revenues into "economic and legitimizing effects of the Internet" (p. 30). Monarchies, on average, are also higher on e-government (e-participation) development [23]. Within e-participation research, scholars tend to focus either on the international [2] or internal [27] legitimation concerns.

Both regime type and competitiveness do not seem to fully answer to the question of whether legitimation is important, and if so, which type exactly. The lack of measurable data, which forced the scholars to use proxies for various legitimation types, contributes to the complexity of the analysis. For instance, though the level of economic globalization can be considered a measure of international legitimation [2] it can also indicate the mechanisms of the policy diffusion [1], which may nevertheless have internal concerns in the core. Furthermore, the functions of Internet tools differ, and so might do the legitimation strategies behind their implementation [2, 12, 17, 27, 32].

Thus, while the legitimation hypothesis seems to be a plausible explanation of the drive to develop ICT based governance tools in autocracies, further work is needed to provide more empirical evidence on what is meant by legitimation in this context.

3   Legitimation Strategies of Authoritarian Countries

The research on legitimation in authoritarian regimes is still in an emerging stage [13, 14], and the question of how to measure this phenomenon is of pivotal importance. Recent studies suggest that the line between democracies and autocracies here is blurred: both in the importance of legitimacy for survival [13], and in the repertoire of the legitimacy claim they make. For instance, Dukalskis and Gerschewski [9] propose four major mechanisms of legitimation: *indoctrination, passivity, performance* and *democratic-procedural.* The latter two are those resembling democratic legitimation and obtaining salience in autocracies. Von Soest and Grauvogel [37], using the expert survey technique, have revealed and measured six types of legitimacy claims:

foundational myth, ideology, personalism, procedures, performance, international engagement. Their findings suggest that though some types of regimes are more likely to use particular claims (e.g. competitive authoritarian regimes usually rely more on *procedures*), certain legitimation strategies (e.g. *performance legitimacy*) are equally popular. The survey results have already been successfully used to explore the variety of non-democratic regimes in the Post-Soviet Space [36], as well as the array of strategies they use to stay in power [28].

This methodology has been refined by the *Varieties of Democracy* project [6, 33]. Here the classification includes four types of legitimation strategies: *performance, rational-legal, ideology* and *the person of the leader*. Though the range of legitimacy claims here is limited in comparison to the previous methodology [37], the data are available for a longer period of time, and there is an opportunity to compare most of the countries, both democracies and authoritarian states. The analysis of the data suggests that, indeed, countries of similar regime types usually have somewhat common patterns, and, importantly, measurements of legitimation strategies "are not mere proxy measures of democracy [and] carry additional information" [33, p. 13].

In understanding the importance of legitimation in ICT development, these measurements are promising and valuable, not only because the data appears to be more straightforward in comparison to the proxy based data but because it also allows a deep look at the differences between the regime types and within them. This may become an important refinement of the previous studies.

4 Methods and Data

In this pilot study we are not aiming to establish causal mechanisms between legitimation strategies and ICT diffusion in autocracies, neither are we claiming that legitimation is the only possible factor explaining the variation in online tools development across regimes. Rather, we test the association between the intensity of particular legitimacy claims and development of Internet enabled policies: in general, and in certain time periods, and estimate the value of these measurements for further rigorous causal analysis.

Here we are focusing on the two popular tools – e-government, which is mainly related to provision of public services, and e-participation that is designed to provide citizens' participation in public policy. These two cases are taken because of their widespread analysis in relation to authoritarian legitimation [e.g. 2, 27], and because data is relatively easily available. Here the development of the tools is mainly taken as a proxy for importance of ICT policies to authoritarian governments.

To measure the legitimation strategies, we use the data from the *Varieties of Democracy* project, taking four variables measuring the extent to which countries justify the regime by: (1) *Ideology*, (2) *Person of the Leader*, (3) *Performance*, and (4) *Rational – legal* [6, 33]. Also, we calculate the average score of the *Performance* and *Rational – Legal* legitimation strategies, to grasp a certain "democratic" type of legitimation.

The data on e-government and e-participation is taken from the *UN E-Government Survey*, namely the *Online Service Index* (OSI) and *E-Participation Index* (EPI). Both indices are biannual and based on the expert analysis of the national web-portals and aim at exploring the extent to which the governments provide citizens with e-services, as well as online tools for information, consultation, and decision-making.[3]

Furthermore, to estimate the association between the development of online tools and regime types, as well as to distinguish between democratic and non-democratic countries, we use the methodology and the data developed by Wahman et al. [38], namely the binary indication of regimes (robust).[4]

The period of analysis is limited to the availability of the data in the *UN E-Government Survey*, which has rankings for 2004, 2005, 2008, 2010, 2012, 2016 and 2018, but the actual year of analysis is lagged for one year (that is, the survey of 2004 contains data for 2003). Other variables are taken with a one-year lag from the actual period of the UN data. Since the data on regime types is available only till 2010, the data for 2012–2016 were created by extrapolation and should be taken cautiously. To estimate the association between the variables, we use Pearson's correlation.

5 Results

In general (Table 1), the development of the selected ICT tools seems to be significantly and positively correlated with performance and rational-legal types of legitimation strategies, while there is a significant negative correlation between online tools and ideological or personalistic legitimation. The patterns of associations differ between democracies and non-democracies: the progress of the former in terms of e-government and e-participation is less associated positively with any of the legitimation strategy. In the latter, however, there is a positive link with all legitimation strategies, especially to performance and rational-legal ones, which is in line with previous studies [27, 32].

Yet, the picture is more complex, when the correlation analysis is conducted for each year, when problems of panel data are minimized. For democracies (Tables 4–5), the legitimation claims appear to be insignificant in each particular year (expect for the negative correlation with the person of the leader). For non-democracies (Tables 2–3) only performance and rational-legal legitimation claims keep being important, but this significance has been changing overtime.

Initially, when few authoritarian countries had advanced e-government and e-participation (e.g. Singapore), the legitimation by performance and norms was significantly associated with this process, but in 2008 onwards it lost significance in comparison to the regime type, as monarchies like the UAE, Bahrain, Jordan etc. took over the *UN E-Government* indices. As there is a low correlation between performance (rational – legal) legitimation and the monarchy regime type, they might indicate two

---

[3] UN E-Government Survey. United Nations. URL: https://publicadministration.un.org/egovkb/en-us/Reports/.

[4] Authoritarian Regimes Data Set, version 5.0, by Axel Hadenius, Jan Teorell, & Michael Wahman. URL: https://xmarquez.github.io/democracyData/reference/wahman_teorell_hadenius.html.

different incentives to introduce online innovations: to socialize internationally in case of monarchies, in line with [2], and to strengthen the claim that the regime aims at providing better governance for citizens, as well as more transparency and participation [27]. From 2016 onwards the monarchy regime type has been fading away as the significant correlate, and internal legitimation considerations (and rational-legal especially from 2018) are getting higher significance.

There are also two notable observations. First, e-government and e-participation, though are meant to be different in their functions and relation to performance and "democratic" participation, have similar connections with the legitimation strategies. This may be due to measurement problems, as the EPI have encountered criticism for estimating technological, rather than participatory aspects [16]. It may also be due to the view of e-participation as a tool for better governance and performance, rather than citizens empowerment. Secondly, there is a high volatility of scores on the rankings, especially among non-democracies, which may be due to particular focus points [23], as well as problems with policy implementation [11].

Table 1. Correlation matrix for OSI and EPI (All Years and Countries). Source: Author's calculations

Variables	Ideology	Leader	Performance	Ration-Legal	Perf_Rat
OSI (All)	−.239**	−.365**	.257**	.293**	.323**
EPI (All)	−.203**	−.296**	.199**	.236**	.256**
OSI (Non-Dem)	.116**	.093*	.266**	.184**	.266**
EPI (Non-Dem)	.056	.050	.211**	.162**	.220**
OSI (Dem)	−.215**	−.388**	.145**	.184**	.195**
EPI (Dem)	−.151**	−.277**	.096*	.133**	.136**

* - significance at .05 level; ** - significance at .01 level (here and in Tables 2–5)

Table 2. Correlation matrix for OSI (Non-Democracies). Source: Author's calculations

Survey Year	2004	2005	2008	2010	2012	2014	2016	2018
V-Dem Year	2002	2003	2006	2008	2010	2012	2014	2016
Ideology	.031	.064	.139	.087	.156	.203	.178	.136
Leader	.019	.067	.078	.135	.150	.213*	.153	.094
Performance	.311**	.289**	.247*	.195	.298**	.313**	.259*	.335**
Rational-Legal	.263*	.221*	.024	.141	.104	.182	.197	.376**
Perf-Rat	.347**	.306**	.165	.200	.235*	.292**	.266*	.408**
Military	−.049	−.202	−.110	−.244*	−.267**	−.248*	−.202	−.207
Multiparty	.091	.106	−.156	−.010	−.192	−.142	−.052	−.025
Monarchy	.112	.237*	.382**	.268*	.424**	.463**	.370**	.333**
Oneparty	−0.94	−.079	−.033	−.041	−.051	−.029	.018	−.044
Noparty	.042	−.086	.246*	.247*	.224*	.255*	.205	.201

Table 3. Correlation matrix for EPI (Non-Democracies). Source: Author's calculations

Survey Year	2004	2005	2008	2010	2012	2014	2016	2018
V-Dem Year	2002	2003	2006	2008	2010	2012	2014	2016
Ideology	−.065	−.027	.087	.024	.052	.151	.158	.126
Leader	−.009	−.005	.109	.103	.148	.199	.087	.080
Performance	.291**	.303**	.143	.205	.172	.352**	.241*	.303**
Ration-Legal	.284**	.230*	.044	.123	−.004	.237*	.221*	.372**
Perf-Rat	.347**	.319**	.143	.195	.097	.347**	.270*	.387**
Military	−.083	−.132	−.110	−.207*	−.167	−.241*	−.225*	−.226*
Multiparty	.216*	.215*	−.172	−.012	−.165	−.079	−.024	−.010
Monarchy	−.099	−.083	.277**	.150	.407**	.364**	.316**	.302
Oneparty	−.108	−.062	.068	.009	−.108	.027	.053	−0.47
Noparty	−.086	−.086	.205	.207*	.177	.206	.167	.201

Table 4. Correlation matrix for OSI (Democracies). Source: Author's calculations

Survey Year	2004	2005	2008	2010	2012	2014	2016	2018
V-Dem Year	2002	2003	2006	2008	2010	2012	2014	2016
Ideology	−.275*	−.217	−.275	−.261*	−.236*	−.187	−.157	−.225*
Leader	−.351**	−.341**	−.413**	−.414**	−.482**	−.487**	−.428**	−.422**
Performance	.071	.139	.198	.181	.138	.129	.184	.169
Ration-Legal	.160	.159	.250*	.177	.183	.225	.193	.182
Perf-Rat	.139	.180	.264*	.208	.190	.208	.224	.209

Table 5. Correlation matrix for EPI (Democracies). Source: Author's calculations

Survey Year	2004	2005	2008	2010	2012	2014	2016	2018
V-Dem Year	2002	2003	2006	2008	2010	2012	2014	2016
Ideology	−.187	−.190	−.085	−.214	−.156	−.214	−.167	−.246*
Leader	−.226	−.244*	−.190	−.373**	−.312**	−.459**	−.411**	−.447**
Performance	.013	.044	.112	.166	−.008	.160	.191	.169
Ration-Legal	.070	.080	.163	.119	.123	.252*	.145	.194
Perf-Rat	.049	.074	.161	.167	−.067	.243	.200	.209

6 Discussion and Conclusion

This paper is a preliminary attempt to estimate the association with the data that is available at the moment, hence the findings should be treated as such. However, in principle, the study contributes to the studies on authoritarian stability, authoritarian legitimation, and *ICT in Politics* research in several respects.

First, though many studies have developed the legitimation hypothesis in the context of ICT diffusion [e.g. 2, 17, 27], this study to attempts to specify and refine it by using the new data. The association of the development of electronic tools with the legitimation strategies seems to be quite significant. It shows the plausibility of the legitimation hypothesis on a large sample of data. The analysis has also helped to indicate exactly what legitimation strategies are related to these tools' development. It has also demonstrated some temporal and cross-regime dynamics, which may give a clue to understanding nuances of ICT diffusion.

Secondly, the study has provided some insights into the survival strategies of authoritarian regimes, which are becoming more dependent on their connection between their citizens [13, 14] and new forms of legitimation [9, 33, 37]. The development of IT-enabled tools of governance seem to be a part of this trend, and our analysis has revealed the association between the new technologies and new methods of legitimation. In general, it contributes to our understanding of the modern technologies role in maintaining authoritarian survival, as well as to the conceptualization of the new types of authoritarian regimes [18].

This study has several limitations, of course. Firstly, the data we use can reflect the supply side of both e-government (e-participation) provision and legitimation. These data may give us some understanding of how important particular IT-tools and legitimation strategies are for the governments. Unfortunately, the data does not allow us to see how the IT-tools are used and whether they have any impact on legitimation, and if so, what kind of legitimation is boosted as a result. The answer to this question requires further in-depth analysis of particular countries, for instance, using the survey methods [35] or experimental designs [39].

Secondly, the method used cannot tell us anything about the causation, and there might also be the case that this correlation is based some third latent variables. Thirdly, the data we use can reflect the supply side of both electronic tools provision and legitimation. These data may give us some understanding of how important particular IT-tools and legitimation strategies are for the governments. Unfortunately, the data does not allow us to see how the IT-tools are used and whether they have any impact on legitimation, and if so, what kind of legitimation is boosted as a result. The answer to this question requires further in-depth analysis of particular countries, for instance, using the survey methods [35] or experimental designs [39]. Thirdly, this topic should be further explored in relation to other online tools autocrats use to sustain their rule, e.g. digital economy, or big data policies [19].

In this regard, our next step is to build causal models that would test the relationship between variables when controlled to other factors and define the role of legitimation in the development of the authoritarian Internet-policies.

Acknowledgement. The study was implemented in the framework of the Basic Research Program at the National Research University Higher School of Economics (HSE University) in 2020, project "Multilevel political systems: problems of management, reform and strategies of actors".

References

1. Ambrosio, T.: Constructing a framework of authoritarian diffusion: concepts, dynamics, and future research. Int. Stud. Perspect. **11**(4), 375–392 (2010). https://doi.org/10.1111/j.1528-3585.2010.00411.x
2. Åström, J., Karlsson, M., Linde, J., Pirannejad, A.: Understanding the rise of e-participation in non-democracies: domestic and international factors. Gov. Inf. Q. **29**(2), 142–150 (2012). https://doi.org/10.1016/j.giq.2011.09.008
3. Bershadskaya, L., Chugunov, A., Trutnev, D.: e-Government in Russia: is or seems? In: Proceedings of the 6th International Conference on Theory and Practice of Electronic Governance, 22–25 October 2012, pp. 79–82. ACM, New York (2012). https://doi.org/10.1145/2463728.2463747
4. Christensen, B.: Cyber state capacity: a model of authoritarian durability, ICTs, and emerging media. Gov. Inf. Q. **36**(3), 460–468 (2019). https://doi.org/10.1016/j.giq.2019.04.004
5. Chugunov, A.V., Kabanov, Y., Zenchenkova, K.: Russian e-petitions portal: exploring regional variance in use. In: Tambouris, E., Panagiotopoulos, P., Sæbø, Ø., Wimmer, M.A., Pardo, T.A., Charalabidis, Y., Soares, D.S., Janowski, T. (eds.) ePart 2016. LNCS, vol. 9821, pp. 109–122. Springer, Cham (2016). https://doi.org/10.1007/978-3-319-45074-2_9
6. Coppedge, M., et al.: V-Dem [Country–Year/Country–Date] Dataset v10. Varieties of Democracy (V-Dem) Project (2020). https://doi.org/10.23696/vdemds20
7. Dimitrov, M.K.: Internal government assessments of the quality of governance in China. Stud. Comp. Int. Dev. **50**(1), 50–72 (2014). https://doi.org/10.1007/s12116-014-9170-2
8. Distelhorst, G.: The power of empty promises: quasi-democratic institutions and activism in China. Comp. Polit. Stud. **50**(4), 464–498 (2017). https://doi.org/10.1177/0010414015617960
9. Dukalskis, A., Gerschewski, J.: What autocracies say (and what citizens hear): proposing four mechanisms of autocratic legitimation. Contemp. Politics **23**(3), 251–268 (2017). https://doi.org/10.1080/13569775.2017.1304320
10. Egorov, G., Guriev, S., Sonin, K.: Why resource-poor dictators allow freer media: a theory and evidence from panel data. Am. Polit. Sci. Rev. **103**(4), 645–668 (2009)
11. Gel'man, V., Starodubtsev, A.: Opportunities and constraints of authoritarian modernisation: Russian policy reforms in the 2000s. Europe-Asia Stud. **68**(1), 97–117 (2016) https://doi.org/10.1080/09668136.2015.1113232
12. Gerschewski, J., Dukalskis, A.: How the internet can reinforce authoritarian regimes: the case of North Korea. Georgetown J. Int. Aff. **19**, 12–19 (2018). https://doi.org/10.1353/gia.2018.0002
13. Gerschewski, J.: Legitimacy in autocracies: oxymoron or essential feature? Perspect. Polit. **16**(3), 652–665 (2018). https://doi.org/10.1017/S1537592717002183
14. Gerschewski, J.: The three pillars of stability: legitimation, repression, and co-optation in autocratic regimes. Democratization **20**(1), 13–38 (2013). https://doi.org/10.1080/13510347.2013.738860
15. Göbel, C.: The information dilemma: how ICT strengthen or weaken authoritarian rule. Statsvetenskaplig tidskrift **115**(2013), 367–384 (2013)
16. Grönlund, Å.: Connecting egovernment to real government - the failure of the un eparticipation index. In: Janssen, M., Scholl, H.J., Wimmer, M.A., Tan, Y.-h. (eds.) EGOV 2011. LNCS, vol. 6846, pp. 26–37. Springer, Heidelberg (2011). https://doi.org/10.1007/978-3-642-22878-0_3

17. Gunitsky, S.: Corrupting the cyber-commons: social media as a tool of autocratic stability. Perspect. Polit. **13**(1), 42–54 (2015). https://doi.org/10.1017/S1537592714003120
18. Guriev, S., Treisman, D.: How modern dictators survive: an informational theory of the new authoritarianism (No. w21136). National Bureau of Economic Research (2015). https://doi.org/10.3386/w21136
19. Kabanov, Y., Karyagin, M.: Data-driven authoritarianism: non-democracies and big data. In: Alexandrov, D.A., Boukhanovsky, A.V., Chugunov, A.V., Kabanov, Y., Koltsova, O. (eds.) DTGS 2018. CCIS, vol. 858, pp. 144–155. Springer, Cham (2018). https://doi.org/10.1007/978-3-030-02843-5_12
20. Karlsson, M.: Carrots and sticks: internet governance in non–democratic regimes. Int. J. Electron. Gov. **6**(3), 179–186 (2013). https://doi.org/10.1504/IJEG.2013.058405
21. Katchanovski, I., La Porte, T.: Cyberdemocracy or Potemkin e-villages? Electronic governments in OECD and post-communist countries. Int. J. Pub. Adm. **28**(7–8), 665–681 (2005). https://doi.org/10.1081/PAD-200064228
22. Keremoğlu, E., Weidmann, N.B.: How dictators control the internet: a review essay. Comp. Polit. Stud. 0010414020912278 (2020). https://doi.org/10.1177/0010414020912278
23. Kneuer, M., Harnisch, S.: Diffusion of e-government and e-participation in democracies and autocracies. Glob. Policy **7**(4), 548–556 (2016). https://doi.org/10.1111/1758-5899.12372
24. Linde, J., Karlsson, M.: The dictator's new clothes: the relationship between e- participation and quality of government in non-democratic regimes. Int. J. Pub. Adm. **36**(4), 269–281 (2013). https://doi.org/10.1080/01900692.2012.757619
25. Lorentzen, P.: China's strategic censorship. Am. J. Polit. Sci. **58**(2), 402–414 (2014). https://doi.org/10.1111/ajps.12065
26. MacKinnon, R.: Liberation technology: China's "networked authoritarianism". J. Democr. **22**(2), 32–46 (2011). https://doi.org/10.1353/jod.2011.0033
27. Maerz, S.F.: The electronic face of authoritarianism: e-government as a tool for gaining legitimacy in competitive and non-competitive regimes. Gov. Inf. Q. **33**(4), 727–735 (2016). https://doi.org/10.1016/j.giq.2016.08.008
28. Maerz, S.F.: The many faces of authoritarian persistence: a set-theory perspective on the survival strategies of authoritarian regimes. Gov. Oppos. **55**(1), 64–87 (2020). https://doi.org/10.1017/gov.2018.17
29. Placek, M.: Social media and regime support in Russia: does it matter which website is used? East Eur. Polit. 1–21 (2019). https://doi.org/10.1080/21599165.2019.1658078
30. Rød, E.G., Weidmann, N.B.: Empowering activists or autocrats? The Internet in authoritarian regimes. J. Peace Res. **52**(3), 338–351 (2015). https://doi.org/10.1177/0022343314555782
31. Stier, S.: Internet diffusion and regime type: temporal patterns in technology adoption. Telecommun. Policy **41**(1), 25–34 (2017). https://doi.org/10.1016/j.telpol.2016.10.005
32. Stier, S.: Political determinants of e-government performance revisited: comparing democracies and autocracies. Gov. Inf. Q. **32**(3), 270–278 (2015). https://doi.org/10.1016/j.giq.2015.05.004
33. Tannenberg, M., Bernhard, M., Gerschewski, J., Lührmann, A., Von Soest, C.: Regime Legitimation Strategies (RLS) 1900 to 2018. V-Dem Working Paper, 86 (2019). https://doi.org/10.2139/ssrn.3378017
34. Toepfl, F.: Innovating consultative authoritarianism: internet votes as a novel digital tool to stabilize non-democratic rule in Russia. New Media Soc. **20**(3), 956–972 (2018). https://doi.org/10.1177/1461444816675444
35. Truex, R.: Consultative authoritarianism and its limits. Comp. Polit. Stud. **50**(3), 329–361 (2017). https://doi.org/10.1177/0010414014534196

36. von Soest, C., Grauvogel, J.: How Do Non-Democratic Regimes Claim Legitimacy? Comparative Insights from Post-Soviet Countries. GIGA Working Paper No. 277 (2015). https://doi.org/10.2139/ssrn.2641749
37. von Soest, C., Grauvogel, J.: Identity, procedures and performance: how authoritarian regimes legitimize their rule. Contemp. Polit. **23**(3), 287–305 (2017). https://doi.org/10.1080/13569775.2017.1304319
38. Wahman, M., Teorell, J., Hadenius, A.: Authoritarian regime types revisited: updated data in comparative perspec-tive. Contemp. Polit. **19**(1), 19–34 (2013). https://doi.org/10.1080/13569775.2013.773200
39. Wallin, P.: Authoritarian collaboration: unexpected effects of open government initiatives in China, Doctoral dissertation, Linnaeus University Press (2014)
40. You, Y., Wang, Z.: The internet, political trust, and regime types: a cross-national and multilevel analysis. Jpn. J. Polit. Sci. 1–22 (2019). https://doi.org/10.1017/S1468109919000203

Institutionalization of C2G New Communication Forms: Trends and Dynamic in Saint Petersburg

Evgenii Vidiasov⑩, Iaroslava Tensina⑩,
and Lyudmila Vidiasova⁽᎐⁾⑩

ITMO University, Saint Petersburg, Russia
vidyasov@lawexp.com, tensina.yaroslava@mail.ru,
bershadskaya.lyudmila@gmail.com

Abstract. Research has been proposed to determine trends and dynamic of citizen's trust in new C2G communication forms. The survey sheds a light to trust concept and its evidences in IT performance in public sector. A representative survey was conducted using a SCOT approach. From the 800 respondents to this survey, the sampling error was no higher than 4%, the level of reliability reached 95%. The questionnaire contained variables to evaluate the experience of use and the level of trust in new technologies in the interaction with the government. The study revealed an increase in citizens' trust in communicating with government authorities via the Internet and in receiving state and municipal services in electronic form.

Keywords: Social trust · Public sector · Information technology · Survey

1 Introduction

Information technologies have been used for more than 20 years in government bodies, including for interaction with citizens. However, modern realities show that the conditions and motivation for using technologies are changing, and the feeling of trust among users in new types and channels of communication is beginning to play an important role. The popularity of new means of communication, their diversity and updates lead to an increase in the feeling of uncertainty and mistrust in the reliability of the information content. Most of the studies are aimed at studying trust in the field of individual social institutions, while the issue of trust in the use of new technologies remains insufficiently studied. Modern research also demonstrates the complexity and multidimensionality of the concept of «trust» in relation to new technologies. Trust here is not constant: it varies not only from one area to another.

This paper investigates a category on trust in IT communication between government and citizens through the analysis of citizens' perceptions of such construct as far as the experience of St. Petersburg, Russia is concerned. In order to explore the extent to which citizens trust the new forms of C2G communication and to define the main tendencies in trust, a comparative analysis of survey in 2019 and 2020 was conducted. A survey and interview with 800 hundred citizens of St. Petersburg is used to define the

© Springer Nature Switzerland AG 2020
A. Chugunov et al. (Eds.): EGOSE 2020, CCIS 1349, pp. 195–204, 2020.
https://doi.org/10.1007/978-3-030-67238-6_14

level of trust in government and new means of communications via Internet. The key research findings as well as discussion on them are given at the last part of the paper.

2   Literature Review

In scientific literature, issues of trust in communication between citizens and authorities are associated with the topic of e-government, e-public services and e-participation.

Modern countries strive to improve the efficiency of public administration by integrating its main links and processes into a single system, improve the quality of public services, and transform hierarchical and bureaucratic structures into horizontally integrated systems. All of the above should make it easier for the consumer to receive the necessary public services, increase the level of transparency and accountability, and, most importantly, reduce institutional barriers that prevent citizens from being included in the decision-making process.

The issues of political and electronic governance in Russia are discussed in the research of I.A. Bykov [1], S.V. Volodenkov [30], Y.A. Kabanov [12], A.V. Kurochkin [14], I.V. Miroshnichenko [16], M.Y. Pavlyutenkova [17], A.V. Porshnev [20], N.K. Radina [21], L.V. Smorgunov [24], A.V. Sokolov [25], E.M. Styrin [5], A.D. Trachtenberg [26], O.G. Filatova, A.V. Chugunov [8].

Despite many scientific publications on electronic civic participation, there is no single approach towards this concept.

E-participation research was preceded by a significant amount of research devoted to e-government. The features and socio-economic effects of e-administration, i.e. implementation and use of information technology in bureaucratic processes (J. Fontaine [22], A. Gronlund [10], L.V. Smorgunov [24], A.D. Trachtenberg [26], O.G. Filatova, A.V. Chugunov [8], D.R. Trutnev [27]).

In its initial meaning e-government is a component of administrative reforms of the new public management (H. Ates [1], P. Frissen [9], S. Bozali [1], Y.V. Irkhin [11], A. V. Pavroz [18], V.A. Vertlib, M.V. Farkhadov, N.V. Petukhova [28]), then it was considered within the context of interaction between e-government and good governance and network approach in public policy (L.V. Smorgunov [24], A.S. Sherstobitov [24], I.V. Miroshnichenko [16], O.V. Mikhailova [15], I.A. Bykov [2], A.N. Kulik [13]). Such studies have become a conceptual shift in the research on e-government towards the analysis of the role of civil society in public policymaking – through e-democracy and e-participation.

The concepts of e-governance and e-participation represent an attempt of institutional design, which is understood as a deliberate change in the formal and informal rules in a society. In political science the value of the institutional approach to study such phenomena are emphasized in the works of W. Wong, A. Welch, E. Klijn, J. Koppenjan, V.M. Polterovich, A.I. Volynskiy [19]. The study of e-participation within the rational choice new institutionalism seems a promising direction of research. According to this approach, the actions of actors are rational within the existing social and political institutions, which simultaneously are the limitations and the sources of information. From this point of view, e-participation is an institution, a complex of "rule of the games" in the interaction between the citizens and the authorities.

3   Research Design

The research was carried out within the neoinstitutional approach and the concept of J. Scott [23]. According to the chosen framework, there are regulatory, normative, and cognitive sources of institutions. These sources, together with related activities and resources, provide stability for social life. The study was concentrated on detection the differences on e-participation perceptions. The detected difference could shed a light to the institutionalization of the new "rules of game" in C2G interaction.

For the survey a special questionnaire was developed. The poll took place in May 2020. There were two purposes. First, to identify the level of social trust in new technologies in public sector among residents of St. Petersburg. Second, is to conduct a comparative analysis with the results of the 2019 survey.

The survey in 2019 was conducted by interviewers in the course of a personal survey. The survey of respondents was conducted in the 6 places of public services provision - multi-functional centers (MFCs) [29]. 600 respondents participated in the survey on the first stage (the sampling error was no higher than 4%, the level of reliability reached 95%).

In 2020 the survey was conducted using an online platform Anketolog for collecting the answers from respondents. The change in the survey format was dictated by the global pandemic of COVID19 and the closure of multifunctional centers and any other crowded places. The sample is representative by age and sex composition of the general population of Saint Petersburg from 18 y.o. and older. The research team used official statistic data published openly at the official website. The sample size was increased to 800 respondents while maintaining the minimum margin of error and reliability. The sample structure is presented at Table 1.

Table 1. The survey sample structure.

Age	Male		Female	
	%	No. of respondents	%	No. of respondents
18–30	22,0	81	22,0	95
31–40	29,3	108	29,2	126
41–50	28,8	106	29,2	126
51–64	16,8	62	17,4	75
65+	3,0	11	2,3	10
Total		**368**		**432**

Differentiation of the respondents by level of education is as follows: higher or incomplete higher education - 77%, incomplete secondary/general secondary - 5%, secondary specialized - 18%. Most of the respondents are employees/specialists (51%), businessmen, top/middle managers (14%), as well as workers, security guards and drivers (11%).

The questionnaire was compiled in the form of 74 question-statements about personal experience in using information technologies for communication in following areas: government, society, economy, healthcare, education, security, information and news, platform economy and quarantine and self-isolation measures. To gradate the answer options, the Likert scale was used, allowing respondents to express their degree of agreement with statements.

The government block consisted questions about citizens trust in getting electronic public services, contacting with authorities via electronic channels and electronic participating in government decisions, including the following statements:

- The Internet helps people like me to be better informed about the activities of public authorities.
- The Internet helps people like me to better understand the management decisions of public authorities.
- As the Internet spreads, people like me get more real opportunity to influence management decisions.
- Thanks to the Internet, politicians and civil servants become more attentive to the problems of citizens, responsive to the opinions of citizens.
- Thanks to the Internet, public authorities really take into account the opinion of citizens when developing management decisions.
- In general, I trust the interaction with state and municipal authorities when receiving public services or submitting applications to authorities via the Internet.
- I assess the possibilities of conducting electronic voting (government issues, elections, etc.) in our country as an effective.
- I use alternative voting resources.

A comparative analysis was carried out by comparing the answers of respondents to identical questions in 2019 and 2020.

4   Findings

4.1   User ICT Skills

According to survey results, most of the respondents are active users of the Internet (81%). Only 1% of respondents did not identify themselves as active users. At the same time, only 42% defines themselves as advanced Internet users. Compared to the results of the 2019 survey, the percentage of active Internet users increased by 15%, while the percentage of advanced users remained unchanged (42%) (see Fig. 1).

The survey results showed that the motivation for using Internet resources is more dependent on confidence in data security (55%) and significant time savings compared to the offline procedure (27%). Similar results were obtained as a result of a survey in 2019. Least impact on motivation to use the Internet respondents noted resource recommendation from relatives, friends, colleagues (1%).

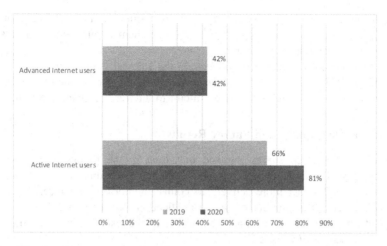

Fig. 1. The percentage of active and advanced Internet users, 2019–2020.

4.2 Trust in Public Sector

During the study, the level of respondents' trust in communicating with city authorities was assessed. 26% of respondents rust the regional and municipal authorities of St. Petersburg.

According to the survey results, 65% of respondents actively use the Internet to obtain state and municipal services (for example, through the Portal of State Services). 49% actively use the Internet to contact authorities through e-mail, specialized portals and other channels. 64% of respondents rate their experience of receiving state and municipal services via the Internet as positive, and 58% had a positive experience for contacting the authorities.

More than half of the respondents (55%) consider the exchange of data via the Internet with the authorities safe and secure. 65% of respondents trust the available means of electronic identification when receiving electronic services.

70% of the respondents noted that the Internet helps people to be better informed about the activities of public authorities. 54% of respondents noted that the Internet helps to better understand the management decisions of government bodies. However, only 32% agreed that at the same time people get more real opportunity to influence management decisions. 35% of respondents believe that thanks to the Internet, politicians and government officials have become more attentive and responsive to the problems of citizens.

Not very optimistic assessment was received regarding the real consideration of citizens' opinions in the development of management decisions (only 28% agreed with this statement).

52% of respondents noted that they generally trust interaction with state and municipal authorities when receiving public services or submitting applications to authorities via the Internet. 34% of the respondents noted that they trust communication with state and municipal authorities through social networks.

The respondents did not give a very high assessment to the possibility of conducting electronic voting in Russia: only 37% rate them as effective, and 28% use alternative resources related to voting.

43% believed that the safety of citizens on the Internet is the prerogative of government bodies. 33% considered the measures taken by the state in the field of Internet security to be sufficient. 41.1% found it difficult to answer the given question.

4.3   Comparative Analysis of Survey Results

The results of the 2020 survey showed that trust in the regional and municipal authorities of St. Petersburg decreased by 3%. At the same time, city residents have begun to use the Internet more actively to contact authorities and receive state and municipal services. The number of online applications to the authorities has almost quadrupled (increased by 36%), and the number of requests for state and municipal services increased by 30% (see Fig. 2).

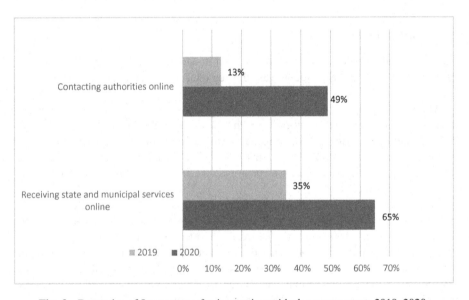

Fig. 2. Dynamics of Internet use for interaction with the government, 2019–2020.

The percentage of respondents who rate the experience of receiving state and municipal services via the Internet as positive has increased by 17%; the percentage of residents who have positive experience of online appeals to the authorities has increased by 21% (see Fig. 3).

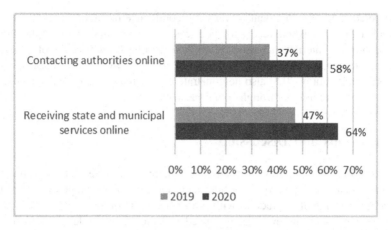

Fig. 3. Dynamics of positive experience of Internet use for interaction with the government, 2019–2020.

The percentage of users who consider the exchange of data via the Internet with the authorities to be secure, as well as who trust electronic identification, increased equally by 13%.

The percentage of respondents who believe that the Internet helps people to be better informed about the activities of public authorities has increased by 18%. The share of respondents who positively assess the influence of the Internet on the attention of the authorities to the problems of the population has increased by 9%. The percentage of respondents who believe that the use of the Internet allows influencing government decisions has slightly increased (by 3%) (see Fig. 4).

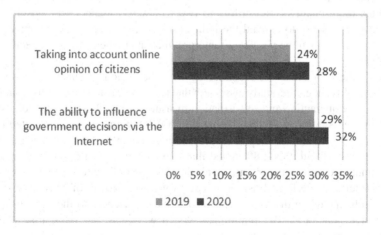

Fig. 4. Dynamics of the level of trust in the ability to influence government decisions online, 2019–2020.

The percentage of respondents expressing confidence in interaction with state and municipal authorities when receiving public services or submitting applications to authorities via the Internet increased by 15%. According to the results of 2019, 37% expressed confidence in such interaction, and in 2020 just over half of the respondents (52%). Research data in 2020 also demonstrated an increase in citizens' confidence in interacting with authorities through social networks (by 9%).

5   Conclusions and Discussion

This paper brings an overview of trends and dynamics in citizen's trust in new form C2G communications. The growth of Internet usage determines the possibility of using new electronic forms of interaction with government authorities.

On the one hand, survey results showed a decrease in the level of trust in the regional and municipal authorities of St. Petersburg. At the same time, residents of St. Petersburg began to actively use state and municipal services in electronic form, as well as interact with government representatives online. As the study has shown, the number of citizens who assess the experience of such interaction as positive is also growing.

The results of the survey showed that citizens began to trust more in electronic identification and security of interaction with the government via the Internet. Trust in interacting with authorities through social media has also increased compared to the results of the 2019 survey.

During the research period, an average rate of trust in G2C communication has grown. However, this tendency is more related to the receipt of state and municipal services in electronic form or submitting online applications. Trust in the ability to influence government decisions via Internet has slightly increased, but still remains at a low level.

The limitations of the study are related to the fact that the study sample was constructed representatively according to two parameters: gender and age. In further studies, it makes sense to expand the indicators of representativeness by another 1–2 parameters. Thus, it will be possible to interpret the data in the context of specific social groups.

Also, some limitations were connected with the period of survey conduction in 2020. From this side, the study assessed the level of trust in technology after the introduction of quarantine and self-isolation measures. According to respondents, 52% said they were using IT more than before the COVID19 pandemic. 37% noted that IT provided an opportunity to keep their jobs during quarantine measures, while 31.8% strongly disagreed with this. 38% noted that they began to trust IT more for personal use (communication, entertainment, training), 36% trust IT more for their work tasks. Such tendencies of the forced use of IT can explain the growth of active use of IT in various fields, including the assessment of positive experience. At the same time, with the extensive penetration of communications, new threats and risks arise that may become the subject of further study.

Acknowledgements. The study was performed with financial support by the grant from the Russian Foundation for Basic Research (project № 18-311-20001): "The research of cybersocial trust in the context of the use and refusal of information technology".

References

1. Ates, H., Bozali, S.: Public administration in the information age: towards an informatised bureaucracy. Kocaeli Universitesi Sosyal Enstitusu Dergisi **10**(2), 46–68 (2005)
2. Bykov, I.A.: Network political communication: theory, practice and research methods, p. 200. St. Petersburg State University of Technology and Design, St. Petersburg (2013). [in Russian]
3. Chugunov, A.V.: The concept of "smart city": the functioning of feedback mechanisms in the context of electronic participation of citizens. Inf. Resour. Russ. **6**, 21–27 (2019). [in Russian]
4. Chugunov, A.V.: The interaction of government and citizens in the institutional environment of electronic participation. Power **25**(10), 59–66 (2017). [in Russian]
5. Dmitrieva, N.E., Styrin, E.M.: Open public administration: tasks and prospects in Russia. Issues State Munic. Adm. **1**, 132–135 (2014). [in Russian]
6. Dyakova, E.G., Trakhtenberg, A.D.: E-Government and Citizens: the Results of a Comprehensive Sociological Study in the Urals Federal District. Publishing House of the Ural University/, Yekaterinburg (2010). [in Russian]
7. Filatova, O., Kabanov, Y., Misnikov, Y.: Public deliberation in Russia: deliberative quality, rationality and interactivity of the online media discussions. Media Commun. **7**(3), 133–144 (2019)
8. Filatova, O.G., Chugunov, A.V.: Electronic interaction between society and government: the formation of a concept and implementation practice in Russia. Manage. Consult. **8**(56), 57–67 (2013). [in Russian]
9. Frissen, P.H.A., Snellen, I.T.M.: Information strategies in public administration. Organ. Stud. **14**(1), 192–202 (1993)
10. Grönlund, Å., Hatakka, M., Ask, A.: Inclusion in the e-service society – investigating administrative literacy requirements for using e-services. In: Wimmer, M.A., Scholl, J., Grönlund, Å. (eds.) EGOV 2007. LNCS, vol. 4656, pp. 216–227. Springer, Heidelberg (2007). https://doi.org/10.1007/978-3-540-74444-3_19
11. Irkhin, Y.: Modern network analysis and blockchain: teria, methodology, problems. Quest. Polit. Sci. **1**, 15–24 (2018). [in Russian]
12. Kabanov, Yu.A.: Electronic authoritarianism. Institute for Electronic Participation in Non-Democratic Countries. Politics: Analysis. Chronicle Forecast **83**(4), 36–55 (2016). [in Russian]
13. Kulik, A.N.: Governance 2.0: the evolution of government models in the internet age. Polit. Sci. **1**, 12–27 (2013). [in Russian]
14. Kurochkin, A.V.: Institutions and technologies of innovative public policy. In: Smorgunova, L.V.M. (ed.) Public Policy: Institutions, Digitalization, Development. Collective Monograph, p. 349 (2018). [in Russian]
15. Mikhailova, O.V.: Networks in politics and public administration. M.: KDU. p. 330 (2013). [in Russian]
16. Miroshnichenko, I.V.: The network landscape of Russian public policy. Krasnodar: Enlightenment - South, p. 295 (2013) [in Russian]

17. Pavlyutenkova, M.Y., Chernyshova, T.M.: Information and communication technologies in the election process of Russia. Pro Nunc. Modern Political Processes (2006). [in Russian]
18. Pavroz, A.V.: The effectiveness of a pluralistic model of policy formation: a classic rationale and modern interpretations. Moscow University Herald. Series 12. Political Sciences vol. 4, pp. 7–23 (2015) [in Russian]
19. Polterovich, V.M.: Institutional Reform Strategies, or The Art of Reforms. M.: HSE. p. 24 (2007). [in Russian]
20. Porshnev, A.V., Lyachina, K.G.: Electronic petitions of the portal Russian Public Initiative (2013–2017): what the dynamics of public priorities indicate. Bulletin of public opinion. Data. Analysis. Discussions **129**(3), 103–113 (2019). [in Russian]
21. Radina, N.K., Krupnaya, D.A.: Opportunities for digital political participation: electronic petitions of non-state digital platforms (based on Change.org) Polis. Polit. Res. **6**, 113–127 (2019). [in Russian]
22. Scherer, K.R., Shuman, V., Fontaine, J.R., Soriano, C.: The GRID meets the wheel assessing emotional feeling via self-report. Components of Emotional Meaning, pp. 281–298 (2013)
23. Scott, J.: Institutions and Organizations, p. 178. Sage Publications, Thousand Oaks (1995)
24. Smorgunov, L.V.: Political Networks: Theory and Methods of Analysis: A Textbook for Students of Higher Educational Institutions Studying in the Direction of Preparation of Higher Professional Education 030200. In: Smorgunov, L.V., Sherstobitov, A.S. (ed.) Political Science, p. 318. M.: Aspect Press (2014). [in Russian]
25. Sokolov, A.V.: Electronic communications in the social activity of citizens. Power **3**, 67–71 (2015). [in Russian]
26. Trachtenberg, A.D.: E-government: will the "invention of the state again" take place? Scientific Yearbook of the Institute of Philosophy and Law of the Ural Branch of the Russian Academy of Sciences **12**, 285–297 (2012). [in Russian]
27. Trutnev, D.R., Chugunov, A.V.: The development of electronic services and methods of "electronic control": issues of evaluating the effectiveness of project implementation. Inf. Resour. Russ. **5**, 5–10 (2014). [in Russian]
28. Vertlib, V.A., Farkhadov, M.P., Petukhova, N.V.: E-government as an automated system of public services, p. 148. M.: MAKS Press (2018). [in Russian]
29. Vidiasova, L.A., Vidiasov, E.Y., Tensina, I.D.: A Study of Social Trust in Information Technology in the Provision of Electronic Public Services and the Use of Electronic Participation Portals (Case Study of St. Petersburg, Russia). Monitoring of Public Opinion: Economic and Social Changes **5**, 43–57 (2019). https://doi.org/10.14515/monitoring.2019.5.03
30. Volodenkov, S.V.: Internet communications in the global space of modern political governance. Moscow State. un-t them. M.V. Lomonosov, Fak. political science, p. 269. M .: Publishing house of Moscow University (2015). [in Russian]

A Multidimensional Model of Cybersocial Trust: Evidence from St. Petersburg, Russia

Yury Kabanov[1,2]($\boxtimes$) and Lyudmila Vidiasova[2]

[1] National Research University Higher School of Economics,
St. Petersburg, Russia
ykabanov@hse.ru
[2] ITMO University, St. Petersburg, Russia
bershadskaya.lyudmila@gmail.com

Abstract. Although trust is considered a crucial driver of online human behavior, its conceptualization often poses a challenge to scholars, due to the multidimensional nature of the phenomenon and the variety of online contexts in which trust manifests itself. While many studies have been performed to reveal the dimensions of trust in certain online domains, little has been done to build a holistic model that describes trust relations across the domains. This study aims to address this by building an empirical multifactor model of cybersocial trust. Using data obtained via the public opinion survey in St. Petersburg, Russia, and exploratory factor analysis, we have revealed six key factors of online trust, each reflecting different forms of interactions with people, organizations, or institutions. Implications of this multidimensional model and further steps for research are also discussed.

Keywords: Trust · Internet use · Online trust · Factor analysis · St. Petersburg

1 Introduction

Trust appears to be a crucial factor in people's use of various technologies [13, 26]. However, it is not always clear what trust is; particularly when discussing the Internet. Many scholars emphasize its multidimensional nature, which makes online trust a set of several perceptions, rather than a single and stable attitude towards cyberspace [33]. As this set of attitudes varies from one sphere of online interaction to another [10], the more digital activities a citizen is engaged in, the more difficult it is to conceptualize online trust in its entirety. Although many studies explore the peculiarities of online trust in different spheres, like e-commerce [1, 13, 24, 33], e-government [3, 4] or e-participation [2, 26], there are still few attempts to view this phenomenon holistically.

This paper attempts to address this research gap. It presents the interim results of a project that aims at exploring the multidimensional nature of the so-called *cybersocial trust,* understood as a "user's confidence in the predictability of the 'behavior' of software and hardware systems (digital technologies), their reliability, which is manifested in the willingness to delegate several tasks to various software and hardware systems" [31].

© Springer Nature Switzerland AG 2020
A. Chugunov et al. (Eds.): EGOSE 2020, CCIS 1349, pp. 205–215, 2020.
https://doi.org/10.1007/978-3-030-67238-6_15

The main research question of this project is what cybersocial trust is, and what *cyber* and *social* features it has. The answer to these questions will allow us to further explore the drivers and determinants of trust in online environments.

Our approach towards cybersocial trust is largely inductive and data driven. The main goal of this paper is to build an empirical model of cybersocial trust and reveal its key dimensions across several domains of human online activity. This is achieved using data obtained via the survey held in St. Petersburg, Russia. This paper expands on some previous results of the project [14].

The remainder of this paper is structured as follows. First, we present a brief background on the topic, with an emphasis on the multidimensionality of online trust. Secondly, we explain the research design, data, and methods we use. Thirdly, we present our findings, obtained with the Principal Component Analysis (PCA), and describe the factors (components) we have revealed. This paper concludes with a discussion of the results and future steps.

2 Background: Dimensions of Online Trust

Though the interest in trust in the context of information technologies is growing in the academic literature [23], there is neither a single definition nor a unified classification of online trust [1]. However, there are certain characteristics of trust many scholars agree on. Firstly, it is its contextual character, when "the trust … is inextricably tied to a specific context, representing the specific action or service performed and the safeguards which are present" [18, p. 88]. Secondly, trust is dynamic: it "varies over time as the factors which influence trust for the party vary" [18, p. 88]. Or, as noted by Urban et al., "trust is developed over a process of repeated visits to a site" [29, p. 182]. Thirdly, trust is multidimensional: it usually consists of several components (attitudes, perceptions) about the trustworthiness of an object or a person [33].

This complexity has provoked a plethora of works dedicated to the dimensions of online trust. In general, it consists of three main aspects: "trust in individuals through technology, trust in quasi-humans… and trust in a technology itself" [23, p. 207]. These three basic attitudes may be decomposed further, in relation to particular spheres of online interaction. E-commerce seems to be the most popular area in this regard, as trust is crucial for consumer loyalty [5]. However, the principles and methods of classification vary greatly. For example, Wang and Emurian focus on the web interface design features that increase consumer trust [33], while Chen and Dillon, as well as Oliveira et al., highlight similar characteristics of consumers, vendors, website, and interaction as important sources of trust in e-commerce [7, 24].

Nowadays, however, online interactions are not limited to e-commerce, which itself is undergoing serious transformations due to social media and recent innovations [23]. In other domains, new factors of online trust can be more profound. For instance, trust in government is vital for e-government and e-participation [2, 6, 9, 34]. The sphere of e-health is another evolving domain of trust research [27], where trust in online health information is a most important aspect [12, 17, 30]. Other emerging areas of interaction include online education [32] and platform economy [15, 19–21].

What the above-mentioned studies have in common is the in-depth approach that explores citizens' trust in certain online technologies, services, or content. This trust is usually decomposed into attitudes towards elements of this service (e.g. website, counterparty etc.), which together represent a certain algorithm by which a person is meant to decide on if a website or service is trustworthy.

Our research is focused on a higher level of abstraction, where cybersocial trust itself is viewed as a generalized attitude towards the Internet, which is then decomposed into trust to online spheres of interaction. While separate domains have their specific features, there might be some more generic (latent) factors that may unite these attitudes, which can then be further explored in detail. Thus, we aim at developing a model that considers the dimensions of cybersocial trust cross-sectionally: from e-government and e-commerce to e-health, social media etc.

3 Research Design

3.1 Empirical Data

Our main source of the empirical data is the opinion survey we conducted among the residents of St. Petersburg, Russia in Spring 2020. The previous waves of the survey were carried out in the multifunctional centers of the city [31], which became impossible due to the COVID-19 pandemic. Hence, this survey was conducted online, and the sample was calculated based on the size, age, and gender composition of St. Petersburg. Overall, 800 respondents took part in the survey.

Although the sample is valid (the sampling error does not exceed 4%), there are certain limitations. First, while conducting a survey online we limit the scope to Internet-users only, who might initially have more trusting online communications. However, this limitation does not invalidate the survey completely, as its aim is to explore several attitudes a respondent has in various spheres. In other words, some Internet users may be active in using e-banking, while having never used online education websites. Secondly, the findings that we have are mostly valid for St. Petersburg, which is an advanced megalopolis in terms of IT-development and Internet penetration [31]. Hence, the results cannot be fully extrapolated to other cities and countries. At the same time Russia and St. Petersburg, in particular, is a new case for online trust research and a promising context in which test the results of other surveys organized in other countries.

The survey questionnaire consists mostly of statements that respondents agree or disagree with, according to the 5-point Likert scale. Citizens were asked about their perceived Internet capabilities, demographic and socio-economic status, as well as their experience in and trust of several online spheres. The full list of questions, related to cybersocial trust, is presented in Table 1. The questions were selected in order to cover the major spheres of human activities online, related to using the services of e-government, e-participation, online banking, e-commerce, e-health, online education etc. While we kept all the questions from the previous face-to-face surveys, there are several new areas covered (marked with * in the table), including a set of questions related to platform economy. We asked whether the citizens generally trust the platforms that provide taxis, food delivery, foodstuffs, and goods delivery. Furthermore, the questionnaire was expanded to include the trustworthiness of information citizens obtain online via social media and websites. Overall, we had twenty questions covering various aspects of cybersocial trust.

Table 1. The list of variables describing cybersocial trust.

Source: Authors' elaboration

Question	Variable code
When getting e-services I trust the means of electronic identification	TrustEIdentification
In general, I trust online communication with the government when getting e-services or submitting e-complaints	OnlineTrustGov
In general, I trust other people when communicating via the social media	SocMediaTrustPeople
In general, I trust the government when communicating via the social media	SocMediaTrustGov
In general, I trust the online payment transactions	OnlineTrustPayment
I think that medical treatment and healthcare information available on the Internet is trustworthy	HealthInformationInternetTrustworthy
In general, I trust the online interaction when getting telemedicine services	EhealthTrust
In general, I trust the online interaction when getting educational services	EeducationTrust
In general, I trust my Internet – provider	TrustProvider
In general, I trust the Russian e-commerce companies	TrustRusCompanies
In general, I trust the foreign e-commerce companies	TrustForeigncompanies
In general, I trust the administrators of the Russian social media	TrustRusSocMedia
In general, I trust the administrators of the foreign social media	TrustForeignSocMed
In general, I trust the Internet interaction when getting taxi-services*	TrustTaxi
In general, I trust the Internet interaction when getting food delivery from the restaurants*	TrustFood
In general, I trust the Internet interaction when getting foodstuffs delivery from the supermarkets*	TrustProducts
In general, I trust the Internet interaction when purchasing goods on the platforms*	TrustGoods
In general, I consider the information I receive via the social media, trustworthy*	TrustInformationSocMed
In general, I consider the information I receive via the news websites, trustworthy*	TrustInformationWebsites
In general, I consider the information I encounter with online trustworthy	TrustOnlineInfoGeneral

3.2   Method

In our preliminary study, we used exploratory factor analysis (EFA), using the *psych* package of the R software. In the previous studies we used Principal Component Analysis (PCA). However, this is less suitable for revealing latent factors than EFA [11]. Based on the scree-plot and eigenvalues (Fig. 1), we have extracted six factors, which give a satisfactory level of variance coverage. The factor analysis is conducted using the maximum likelihood method and the Oblimin rotation. Since the variables of online trust correlate quite significantly with each other, we suppose that the correlation of factors is also to be expected.

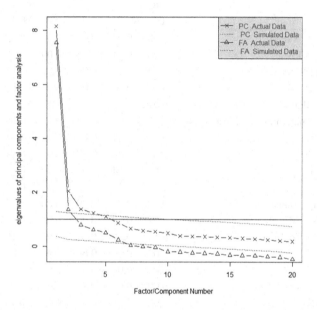

Fig. 1. Parallel analysis scree plots. Source: calculated in R (*psych* package).

4   Findings

It should be noted first that most of the respondents consider themselves active and mostly advanced Internet users. However, at the same time, the level of trust in all domains of online interaction is rather moderate and often did not exceed the average value of 4 out of 5. Online payments seem to be the most trustworthy, while trust in interactions with government via social media is one of the lowest. The reasons for such disproportions may be due to the usage frequency of different services (online payment services seem to be much more actively utilized than communication with the government). On the other hand, it may be explained by some general perceptions of the counterparty (companies and authorities).

The pattern matrix of cybersocial trust is presented in Table 2. The values of the variables that are significant for each factor are in bold. Altogether the six chosen factors explain 64 per cent of the variance, which is a reliable result. To assess the adequacy of the data we refer to the Kaiser – Meyer - Olkin (KMO) and Barlett's tests. Both tests allow us to proceed with the further analysis (KMO is 0.9, Barlett's test is significant). The root mean square of the residuals (RMSR) is 0.02, which is an acceptable score. The Tucker-Lewis Index (TLI) is 0.907, which is also acceptable. The RMSEA index is 0.073, which is a bit higher than needed and hence requires some further testing. The graphic representation of the factor model is presented in Fig. 2.

Table 2. Factor matrix.

Source: Authors' Calculations.

Variables	Factors					
	ML1	ML2	ML3	ML4	ML5	ML6
TrustEIdentification	0.08	0.07	0.03	0.00	0.05	0.72
OnlineTrustGov	0.10	−0.04	0.06	0.09	0.28	0.58
SocMediaTrustPeople	0.02	0.23	0.04	0.27	0.39	−0.04
SocMediaTrustGov	0.06	0.07	0.05	0.09	0.68	0.18
OnlineTrustPayment	0.02	0.18	0.10	0.14	−0.13	0.49
HealthInformationInternetTrustworthy	0.73	0.03	−0.02	0.15	−0.08	−0.03
EhealthTrust	0.98	−0.02	0.00	−0.04	−0.01	0.01
EeducationTrust	0.67	0.06	0.07	−0.03	0.11	0.05
TrustProvider	0.05	0.54	−0.08	0.09	0.10	0.15
TrustRusCompanies	−0.01	0.75	0.03	0.04	−0.01	0.10
TrustForeigncompanies	0.00	0.77	0.09	0.00	−0.15	0.04
TrustRusSocMEdia	0.07	0.59	−0.06	0.07	0.28	−0.01
TrustForeignSocMed	0.11	0.66	0.05	−0.01	0.10	−0.15
TrustTaxi	−0.07	0.06	0.66	−0.01	0.01	0.12
TrustFood	−0.02	−0.03	0.90	0.02	0.04	−0.09
TrustProducts	0.09	−0.02	0.81	0.01	0.02	−0.01
TrustGoods	0.02	0.15	0.64	0.01	−0.13	0.18
TrustInformationSocMed	0.00	0.01	0.04	0.77	0.11	−0.10
TrustInformationWebsites	0.02	−0.02	0.02	0.71	0.03	0.10
TrustOnlineInfoGeneral	0.02	0.02	0.00	0.83	−0.10	0.03

The first major finding is that the factor structure revealed in our previous analysis [14], though obtained using different data and methods, remains quite stable, which is a good indication of the validity of the results. However, since the new variables were added, three new factors have been revealed.

The **first factor** (ML 1) was revealed previously, which is that trust in e-health and online education have the highest loadings. Although in our last analysis it was conceptualized as information trust, now we interpret this factor as *trust in services*, implying at the same time that it is related both to the quality of particular services and the content. Trust in telemedicine services here are highly related to the perceived trustworthiness of online health information, which is crucial for the e-health domain [12, 17, 30]. For trust in e-learning, the quality of information is also an important factor [32], which may determine the interrelation of these two spheres.

The **second factor** (ML 2) groups the variables denoting trust towards particular actors in the cyberspace: Internet providers and companies operating online, as well as administrations of social media services. We refer to this factor as *institutional trust*, i.e. the trust towards organizations on the Internet. Our conceptualization here is similar to the common understanding of institutional trust, as the "perceived reliability of a system or institution involved" [18, p. 89]. According to Kim et al., institutional dimension of trust involves trust to the third parties, which should have certain "reputation, accreditation, authentication, approvals" etc. [16, p. 786].

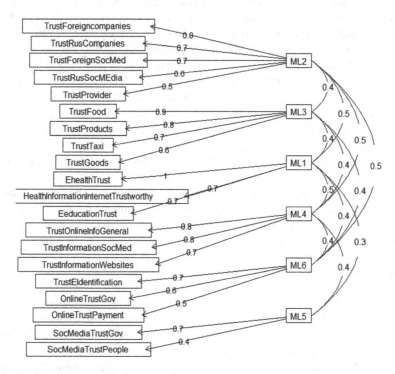

Fig. 2. The factor model of cybersocial trust. Source: calculated in R (*psych* package).

The **third factor** (ML 3), which is new, groups the variables that are related to platforms offering the services of taxi booking and goods delivery. All these services constitute the platform economy, an increasingly developing sector of the digital economy [15], which has become more popular due to the COVID-19 lockdowns. We conceptualize this trust as *platform trust*. It can be understood as trust in the platform as a principle of economic transactions, ensured by trust-building mechanisms pertinent to sharing economy platforms [19]. At the same time, this might also be trust in the platform holders that groups these variables.

Citizens may prefer to use different services from one vendor (e.g. Yandex.Taxi for taxi services and Yandex.Eda and Yandex.Lavka for meals and foodstuffs, accordingly). In other words, trust here is related to loyalty to a particular platform owner and spills over from one sphere to another. As noted by Möhlmann and Geissinger, "[t]he sharing platform provider is an enabler for interpersonal trust, while at the same time being dependent on being perceived as a trustworthy institution itself" [21, p. 29].

In the **fourth factor** (ML 4), which is also new, the variables with the highest factor loadings are associated with trust in the information obtained via the Internet, including both via websites and social media. The possible label for this factor may be *information trust,* which would deal mostly with "attributes that determine the trustworthiness of web-contents" [16, p. 786]. This information component is again cross-dimensional, as it manifests itself in relation to services, as in the first factor, as well as in consuming news from social media, news outlets and information websites [25, 28].

The **fifth factor** (ML 5) in the matrix, also found previously, merges variables such as trust in electronic identification, online interaction with the government and online payments. All these activities seem to involve the exchange of information in obtaining a service, which implies a transfer of personal and financial data to the government or a vendor. We hence conceptualize this form of trust as *transaction trust.* For the sphere of e-commerce and banking, security and transparency of transactions seems crucial [16], but it is also important in the case of e-government, where citizens are no less concerned about their data safety [22].

Finally, in the **sixth factor** (ML 6), the variables with the highest factor loadings are associated with social media: these are trust in interacting with government and people in social media. Apart from the common environment (which is the medium for other dimensions of trust under analysis), the possible ground for these variables is communication. Following Cheng et al., we may assume different forms of online communication in social media – *interpersonal, group* and *mass communication,* having different counterparts and drivers of trust [8]. Hence, we refer this factor to as *communication trust;* the capacity to trust the online communication between a person and a counterpart, be it another citizen, a community, or the government.

It should be noted that all six factors are interrelated, which can be seen on Fig. 2. In general, our exploratory factor analysis has revealed six latent factors that may explain the variance of trust attitudes of the citizens of St. Petersburg. These are *trust in services, institutional, platform, information, transaction,* and *communication trust.* All these types of trust do not necessarily relate to any particular sphere. Rather, they describe the forms of trust which underline various activities citizens are engaged in online. They might have different trustees and trust-building mechanisms, and, hypothetically, different factors that impact the level of trust.

5   Discussion and Conclusion

This is an ongoing study and the results presented in this paper are to be considered as exploratory and preliminary. We intend that our survey results will be further theoretically elaborated and tested empirically. Yet, there are several important conclusions to be drawn at this stage.

Firstly, this research contributes to the understanding of the multidimensionality of trust [14, 16, 33] by shifting the focus of analysis from a particular sphere to cyberspace as a diverse area of online activities. In theoretical terms, it has allowed us to build a conceptual model of cybersocial trust, as a result of different trust attitudes and perceptions to institutions, organizations, processes, and information. Also, the EFA has helped to structure the obtained data and reveal several key dependent variables for further analysis. Thus, this research contributes to the general research on trust in information systems [23], which combines the findings from different spheres of interest, e.g. e-commerce, e-health, e-government etc.

Secondly, this paper distinguishes the forms of trust which hypothetically might have different trust-building mechanisms. This finding can be of practical interest to organizations and decision-makers aimed at building online trust with people as citizens or consumers.

Thirdly, the results of this study are especially relevant to St. Petersburg, giving an overview of the cybersocial trust level among its residents, useful for social scientists, companies, and government agencies. Compared to our previous findings, the revealed patterns of online trust seem stable and invariant to the sample and period of study, and thus seem valid for further analysis and decision-making.

Of course, this study is still ongoing and has certain limitations. Due to the survey-based statistical analysis, the findings are context-dependent. The number of questions asked in the pilot survey were limited, hence some possibly important items were not included. The limitations of the statistical analysis should also be considered: as we employed the exploratory factor analysis, the confirmatory factor analysis is also to be carried out to prove the validity of the given factor composition.

In general, this study reiterates the importance of examining trust in online environments and opens some new avenues for further research, especially the synthesis of findings made within different spheres of online interaction.

The next step for this project is to build up causal models, using statistical inference, that can explain the variance of trust among citizens. The conceptual multidimensional model of cybersocial trust is to be further tested using confirmatory factor analysis and structural equation modeling, to highlight a theoretical contribution to this study area.

Acknowledgment. The study was performed with financial support by the grant from the Russian Foundation for Basic Research (project № 18-311-20001): "The research of cybersocial trust in the context of the use and refusal of information technology".

References

1. Aiken, K.D., Mackoy, R., Liu, B.S.C., Fetter, R., Osland, G.: Dimensions of internet commerce trust. J. Internet Commer. **6**(4), 1–25 (2007). https://doi.org/10.1080/15332860802086136
2. Alarabiat, A., Soares, D.S., Estevez, E.: Predicting citizens acceptance of government-led e-participation initiatives through social media: a theoretical model. In: Proceedings of the Hawaii International Conference on System Sciences (2017). https://doi.org/10.24251/hicss.2017.345

3. Alsaghier, H., Ford, M., Nguyen, A., Hexel, R.: Conceptualising citizen's trust in e-government: application of Q methodology. Electron. J. e-Gov. **7**(4), 295–310 (2009)
4. Alzahrani, L., Al-Karaghouli, W., Weerakkody, V.: Analysing the critical factors influencing trust in e-government adoption from citizens' perspective: a systematic review and a conceptual framework. Int. Bus. Rev. **26**(1), 164–175 (2017). https://doi.org/10.1016/j.ibusrev.2016.06.004
5. Bauman, A., Bachmann, R.: Online consumer trust: trends in research. J. Technol. Manage. Innov. **12**(2), 68–79 (2017). https://doi.org/10.4067/S0718-27242017000200008
6. Carter, L., Bélanger, F.: The utilization of e-government services: citizen trust, innovation and acceptance factors. Inf. Syst. J. **15**(1), 5–25 (2005). https://doi.org/10.1111/j.1365-2575.2005.00183.x
7. Chen, S.C., Dhillon, G.S.: Interpreting dimensions of consumer trust in e-commerce. Inf. Technol. Manage. **4**(2–3), 303–318 (2003). https://doi.org/10.1023/A:1022962631249
8. Cheng, X., Fu, S., de Vreede, G.J.: Understanding trust influencing factors in social media communication: a qualitative study. Int. J. Inf. Manage. **37**(2), 25–35 (2017). https://doi.org/10.1016/j.ijinfomgt.2016.11.009
9. Colesca, S.E.: Understanding trust in e-government. Eng. Econ. **63**(4), 1–9 (2009). http://www.inzeko.ktu.lt/index.php/EE/article/view/11637
10. Costante, E., Den Hartog, J., Petkovic, M.: On-line trust perception: what really matters. In: Proceedings of the First Workshop on Socio-Technical Aspects in Security and Trust, STAST 2011, Milan, Italy, 8 September 2011, pp. 52–59. IEEE (2011) https://doi.org/10.1109/stast.2011.6059256
11. Costello, A.B., Osborne, J.: Best practices in exploratory factor analysis: four recommendations for getting the most from your analysis. Pract. Assess. Res. Eval. **10**(1), 7 (2005)
12. Daraz, L., et al.: Can patients trust online health information? A meta-narrative systematic review addressing the quality of health information on the internet. J. Gen. Int. Med. **34**(9), 1884–1891 (2019). https://doi.org/10.1007/s11606-019-05109-0
13. Gefen, D., Karahanna, E., Straub, D.W.: Trust and TAM in online shopping: an integrated model. MIS Q. **27**(1), 51–90 (2003). https://doi.org/10.2307/30036519
14. Kabanov, Y., Vidiasova, L.: Online trust and ICTs usage: findings from St. Petersburg, Russia. In: Charalabidis, Y.; Cunha, M.A., Sarantis, D. (eds.) Proceedings of the 13th International Conference on Theory and Practice of Electronic Governance (ICEGOV2020). 23–25 September 2020, Athens, Greece. ACM Press, New York (2020) (forthcoming)
15. Kenney, M., Zysman, J.: The rise of the platform economy. Iss. Sci. Technol. **32**(3), 61 (2016)
16. Kim, D., Song, Y., Braynov, S., Rao, R.: A B-to-C trust model for on-line exchange. In: AMCIS 2001 Proceedings, p. 153 (2001). https://aisel.aisnet.org/amcis2001/153
17. Kwon, J.H., Kye, S.Y., Park, E.Y., Oh, K.H., Park, K.: What predicts the trust of online health information? Epidemiol. Health **37**, e2015030 (2015). https://doi.org/10.4178/epih/e2015030
18. Li, F., Pieńkowski, D., van Moorsel, A., Smith, C.: A holistic framework for trust in online transactions. Int. J. Manage. Rev. **14**(1), 85–103 (2012). https://doi.org/10.1111/j.1468-2370.2011.00311.x
19. Messe, M., Dann, D., Braesemann, F., Teubner, T.: Understanding the platform economy: signals, trust, and social interaction. In: Proceedings of the 53rd Hawaii International Conference on System Sciences, HICSS-53, pp. 5139–5148. IEEE (2020). https://doi.org/10.24251/hicss.2020.631
20. Mittendorf, C.: The implications of trust in the sharing economy–an empirical analysis of Uber. In: Proceedings of the 50th Hawaii International Conference on System Sciences, HICSS-50, pp. 5837–5846. IEEE (2017). https://doi.org/10.24251/hicss.2017.703

21. Möhlmann, M., Geissinger, A.: Trust in the sharing economy: platform-mediated peer trust. In: Davidson, N., Finck, M., Infranca, J. (eds.) The Cambridge Handbook of the Law of the Sharing Economy, pp. 27–37, Cambridge University Press, Cambridge (2018). https://doi.org/10.1017/9781108255882.003

22. Navarrete, C.: Trust in e-government transactional services: a study of citizens' perceptions in Mexico and the US. In: 2010 43rd Hawaii International Conference on System Sciences, HICSS-43, pp. 1–10. IEEE (2010). https://doi.org/10.1109/hicss.2010.487

23. Öksüz, A., Walter, N., Distel, B., Räckers, M., Becker, J.: Trust in the information systems discipline. In: Blöbaum, B. (ed.) Trust and Communication in a Digitized World. PI, pp. 205–223. Springer, Cham (2016). https://doi.org/10.1007/978-3-319-28059-2_12

24. Oliveira, T., Alhinho, M., Rita, P., Dhillon, G.: Modelling and testing consumer trust dimensions in e-commerce. Comput. Hum. Behav. 71, 153–164 (2017). https://doi.org/10.1016/j.chb.2017.01.050

25. Rowley, J., Johnson, F.: Understanding trust formation in digital information sources: the case of wikipedia. J. Inf. Sci. 39(4), 494–508 (2013). https://doi.org/10.1177/0165551513477820

26. Scherer, S., Wimmer, M.A.: Conceptualising trust in E-Participation Contexts. In: Tambouris, E., Macintosh, A., Bannister, F. (eds.) ePart 2014. LNCS, vol. 8654, pp. 64–77. Springer, Heidelberg (2014). https://doi.org/10.1007/978-3-662-44914-1_6

27. Sillence, E., Briggs, P., Harris, P.R.: Revisiting the issue of trust in E-Health. In: Web-Based Behavioral Therapies for Mental Disorders, pp. 241–259. IGI Global (2018). https://doi.org/10.4018/978-1-5225-3241-5.ch009

28. Sterrett, D., Malato, D., Benz, J., Kantor, L., Tompson, T., Rosenstiel, T., et al.: Who shared it?: deciding what news to trust on social media. Digit. J. 7(6), 783–801 (2019). https://doi.org/10.1080/21670811.2019.1623702

29. Urban, G.L., Amyx, C., Lorenzon, A.: Online trust: state of the art, new frontiers, and research potential. J. Interact. Market. 23(2), 179–190 (2009). https://doi.org/10.1016/j.intmar.2009.03.001

30. Vega, L.C., DeHart, T., Montague, E.: Trust between patients and health websites: a review of the literature and derived outcomes from empirical studies. Health Technol. 1(2–4), 71–80 (2011). https://doi.org/10.1007/s12553-011-0010-3

31. Vidisova, L., Tensina, I., Bershadskaya, E.: Cyber-social trust in different spheres: an empirical study in Saint-Petersburg. In: DTGS 2020, Proceedings of the 5th International Conference on Digital Transformation and Global Society (2020) (forthcoming)

32. Wang, Y.D.: Building student trust in online learning environments. Dist. Educ. 35(3), 345–359 (2014). https://doi.org/10.1080/01587919.2015.955267

33. Wang, Y.D., Emurian, H.H.: An overview of online trust: concepts, elements, and implications. Comput. Hum. Behav. 21(1), 105–125 (2005). https://doi.org/10.1016/j.chb.2003.11.008

34. Zolotov, M.N., Oliveira, T., Casteleyn, S.: E-participation adoption models research in the last 17 years: a weight and meta-analytical review. Comput. Hum. Behav. 81, 350–365 (2018). https://doi.org/10.1016/j.chb.2017.12.031

Digital Data: Data Science, Methods, Modelling, AI, NLP

City Information Modeling: Designing a Conceptual Data Model

Sergey A. Mityagin[1(✉)] , Vitaly Vlasov[1], Olga Tikhonova[1],
Lada Rudicova[2], and Alexandr I. Repkin[1]

[1] ITMO University, Saint Petersburg, Russia
mityagin@itmo.ru
[2] Yanka Kupala State University of Grodno, Grodno, Belarus

Abstract. The article considers an approach to the design of a universal upper level conceptual model of urban data and its application for the formation of a relational database for development and landscaping projects. The conceptual model of urban data is designed to solve the problem of fragmentation and fragmentation of urban data in the context of the need for urban specialists in data prepared for specific applications. The problem of data fragmentation is caused by the presence of different data sources that produce data according to their internal standards, but there are no requirements for structuring and ordering data at the top level. The conceptual model of urban data should solve this problem. The urban data model is based on the representation of the city as a system formed by the urban planning environment, people with the characteristics of their behavior in the city, as well as providing urban infrastructures. The article shows that the proposed approach can be used as a basis for designing a database for the applied problem of modeling the loyalty of citizens.

Keywords: Data model · System approach · City digital model · Urban environment · Structural methodology · Conceptual model · Data base

1 Introduction

Modern cities produce a huge amount of data, which is used, among other things, for the management and development of cities, the urban environment, and improving the quality of life of citizens. Modern approaches to the management of the territory require high-quality data. At the same time, each application task imposes specific requirements for data quality, which makes it difficult to create universal data banks. Part of the problem of data quality and completeness is being addressed by diversifying data sources. However, this entails problems in ensuring their connectivity and integrity.

The article suggests an approach to creating a meta-model of the city to describe data taking into account the urban environment, population and its activity. And applying this meta-model to form a specific structured base for an applied solution – the loyalty of citizens estimation [1].

In modern research the forms of representation of knowledge about the city in the logic of semantic structures of urban objects are considered [2, 3]. The application of

© Springer Nature Switzerland AG 2020
A. Chugunov et al. (Eds.): EGOSE 2020, CCIS 1349, pp. 219–231, 2020.
https://doi.org/10.1007/978-3-030-67238-6_16

this approach is justified by the development of BIM/CIM technologies (BIM – Building Information Model or Modeling, CIM – City Information Model), which involve the digitization of urban objects in the new technological cycle of territory development. This approach, on the one hand, requires a significant level of detail when describing the urban environment [4], but, on the other hand, allows you to build semantic knowledge bases about the city.

2   Theoretical Basis and Related Works

Smart cities today represent a new paradigm of sustainable social and economic growth in cities. Smart cities make intensive use of information and communication technologies, which, however, are determined by the political, economic, and cultural context. One of the main needs of smart cities is to integrate data from different sources for planning and decision support. Technologies and approaches of the "semantic Web", proposed at the time by the Creator of the Internet Tim Berners-Lee [23] are suitable for solving this problem. Now a whole stack of technologies and a large community of developers allows you to implement a variety of solutions for data integration and knowledge management. The authors of this development use an ontological approach as the basis of the conceptual model.

Caglioni, M., & Rabino in paper [5] proposes three levels of observation, which represent three different areas used in the construction of urban ontology: *the physical level*, which includes all structures, networks, and artifacts in the territory: *socio-economic level*, which is related to all actions performed by people in the city and their relationships with other people; and *the mental level*, relating, for example, to the concepts of ethics and aesthetics, or to consciousness.

Authors of this work also decided to use the first two levels in the design of the conceptual model of urban data as the basic entities on which the information model of the city is based: 1) *physical objects*, 2) *people and organizations* as Agents. The number of agents, for example, includes groups and segments of the population. People assign certain functions to physical objects, which are described through a special layer called Functional Objects.

Urban ontologies in smart city modeling are used in a technological and conceptual context. At the technological level, they provide connectivity between different databases and reengineering existing databases (in our solution we suggest to use ontologies for data integration and collaborative work with current relational database). At the conceptual level they provide a common language for interaction between specialists from different subject areas [6].

In [7] Catalogue of ontologies (datasets) about smart cities and energy efficiency is presented. On the web-site smartcity.linkeddata.es 19 datasets are presented that are not all ontologies but cover different important areas: 1) weather data provided by government organization since 2014 and contain historical values; 2) transportation data presented by 3 datasets (vehicle traffic data, parking data stream and urban public routes; 3) housing data presented by 2 datasets with information about Houses in UK and Housing Market Indicators; 4) energy data have a huge value for this catalogue and included 7 datasets with information from private companies and government. Also authors suggested a way for collecting and updating new data, provide additional meta-data about datasets: language, domains, kind of license, machine-readable format, etc. Unfortunately, some of datasets are not available now and doesn't support by data provider. Having historic data is very important for future Smart Cities development.

Another important issue of using ontologies to describe urban entities is its practical application. The following cities either use an ontological approach directly, or similar solutions in Dubrovnik Smart City [8], Amsterdam [9], Helsinki [10] or Tokyo [11].

In addition to the above, there are specific implementations of urban ontologies that are often used to describe knowledge about the city. Urban Morphology Ontology (SUMO) [12] is designed to support decision-making by urban experts. Ontology development is based on a formal representation of the main types of knowledge: taxonomy, meronomy (hyponymy), spatial relations with a formalized topology, and the shape and size of elements. The OWL 2-LBS ontology [13] aims to describe land use. 4CitySemantics, a GIS-Semantic Tool for Urban Intervention Areas, has been created on its basis.

Smart City Ontology [14] presents nine super classes derived from the analysis of smart city definitions. This project uses some existing ontologies: SKOS (to describe production activities in accordance with NACE codes), "Good Relation" ontology (a more accurate description of urban companies and their functions in the city: products, services, offers, etc.), Organizational ontology, FOAF.

Among the well-developed urban ontologies, we should also mention the KM4CITY projects [15]. Project has been started on the wave of popularity of Open Data Concept and mentioned dramatically bad situation with quality of government data. In 2014 situation with Smart City Data was in the beginning of standardization and popularization and authors discussed data management issues, identifying models, data reconciliation and reasoning. They are relied more on road graph, services available on the roads, traffic sensors and etc. physicals components of city infrastructure more then socio-economic and population data. They created infrastructure as for static the same as for real-time data.

In the area of increasing loyalty of citizens to their cities there are some new publications. More and more researchers consider about balance between technologies and design patterns that can help citizens to be involved in development of the cities via such events like "hackathon" when citizens can meet web developers, data scientists, designers, urban planners; participatory projects and practices in real urban environment. For these goals may help development User Engagement Protocols (UEP) d escribed in this book [26] or common language for better interaction between professionals and non-professionals in Urban Studies and Design via design templating [25].

3   Conceptual Data Model Design

The design of this model is based on objects that have a physical representation in the urban environment. The model is based on the premise of an open world – no subclasses are exhaustive unless the opposite is stated. In other words, it is assumed that the model is incomplete and should expand as new information becomes available or new data needs to be integrated to reflect new characteristics of the city. The model is based on the principles of Linked Data [16]: 1) data connectivity; 2) unique identification of each model object using the Unified Resource Location concept; 3) it is based on an ontological approach and the use of widely used technologies for storing and describing data in OWL/RDF format and the SPARQL query language.

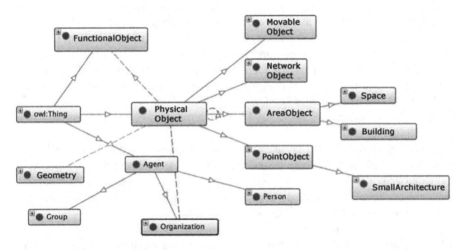

Fig. 1. Top-level classes of the conceptual data model.

To implement queries that depend on geo coordinates, GeoSPARQL [17] technology is used, as well as the Virtuoso server. The current version of the model is published in a publicly available repository [18] and could be retrieved from the website [24].

The top-level classes (Fig. 1) are exhaustive in the current version of the Concept Model. However, as it develops, they will, of course, be updated. Currently, the Model is being expanded by adding new subclasses, refining existing ones, and forming relationships between objects.

At the top level, the model consists of three interconnected classes ("Agent – Physical Object – Functional Object" triad). As well as the geometry service classes *Geometry* (contains the object geometry as a set of geographical coordinates) and directories. The triad describes real-world objects and links them to non-material entities that are necessary to describe the domain. "*Physical object*" is a key class that contains specific physical objects (for example, structures or buildings). Several types of relationships can be formed between classes: inheritance (subclass of) and dependency (depends on). Class attributes are also written via relationships and are of two types: Object Properties and Data Properties (each of which in turn can also have a complex hierarchical structure).

Each physical object can have a *hasFunction* attribute that forms a link to the Functional object. Developed naming styles for classes, attributes, and instances of classes. All data is stored in the format of so-called "triplets" (N-triples) (Fig. 2):

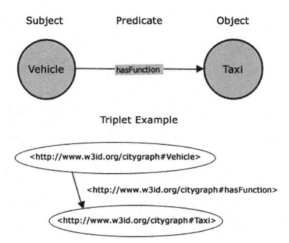

Fig. 2. Triplet is the basis for storing model data.

The key class of the model is a Physical object (*PhysicalObject*). This class is intended for storing urban items in the form they are shown on the map:

- If a city item is represented by an area (polygon) on the map, then this item must be part of one of the subclasses of an Area item (*AreaObject*). For example, a specific building will be included in *CapitalConstruction* Object, and a *Park* will be included in the *Land*.
- Objects represented by lines on the map, such as rivers or roads, will be included in the subclasses of the Network object (*GeoObject*). This class is also used to describe graphs (for example, the graph of the road network, heating networks, electric transmission lines, etc.).
- Objects represented by a point on the map (for example, small architectural forms, traffic lights, trees) are subclasses of a Point object (*PointObject*).
- A *MovableObject* is intended for non-stationary objects (for example, cars, public transport, and other moving equipment).

All Physical objects can be nested within each other. Such objects are linked by the *hasNestedObject* relation and must have the geometry attribute via the *hasGeometry* property. Its spatial coordinates are written to this object.

An important place is given in the Model to administrative division, the system of addressing buildings, cadastral registration of land plots, and in General, various classifiers from state information systems and legislation are widely used. A special *AdministrativeUnit* class is allocated for administrative divisions. it is a subclass of *AreaObject* and includes the following subclasses: *Country, Region, District, Municipality*. The administrative division is a complex hierarchical structure, but the chosen approach allows you to describe all cities, towns, and villages in accordance with the law. Figure 3 shows a variant of the administrative division model.

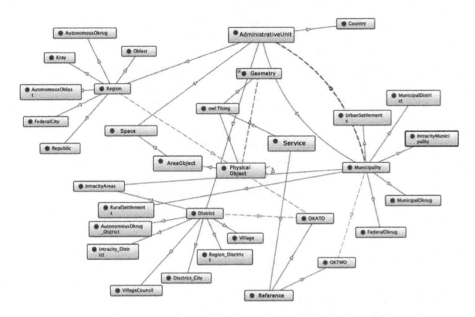

Fig. 3. Ontology of an administrative division (Example Of The Russian Federation).

Buildings are an important part of urban infrastructure. It is in them that residents live, all the main city institutions are located, and they are often the main points of attraction. All buildings in the city are represented using the following class hierarchy. Buildings as physical objects are instances of the *Building* class. Buildings in fact have an important characteristic – it is a category of non-visible property and are located on the ground. Buildings may or may not have foundations (capital construction projects vs garages and temporary structures). Buildings are often associated with a land plot (*Land* class) and have a cadastral number (*CadastreNumber* class). Building has the following subclasses: *TemporaryBuilding*, *Garage*, and *CapitalConstruction*. The list of attributes of this class is shown in the Table 1.

As mentioned above, each building can have a function, for example, a Residential building. To do this, the physical object must be associated with one of the instances of the *Function* class. In this case, it will be the *LivingObject* class. Accordingly, most of the attributes in this class describe the property's properties related to the quality of living (heating, etc.). All characteristics are contained in a separate subclass of hasLivingObjectParameter characteristics. It has the following subclasses: *TallMultyApt, Apartment, Multiapthouse, Townhouse, House.*

To fill in this type of objects, we used data from the government of Saint Petersburg published on the city open data Portal in the form of Technical and economic passports of houses [19], filled with location information from OSM. The ontology of houses is shown in Fig. 4.

Table 1. Properties of building class.

Name	Type	Description
hasHeight	Integer	Building height
hasYearConstuction	DataTime	Year of building construction
hasStairsAmount	Integer	Number of stairs in the building
hasLiftAmount	Integer	Number of elevators
hasAddress	String	The address of the building
hasYearRepair	DataTime	Last year of repairs
hasFloors	Integer	Number of floors
hasMajorRenovation	Object (MajorRenovation)	Link to information about major repairs
hasLand	Object (Land)	Connection to the land plot
hasCadastralNumber	Object (CadastreNumber)	Cadastral number
hasFailureStatus	boolean	Is the structure an emergency

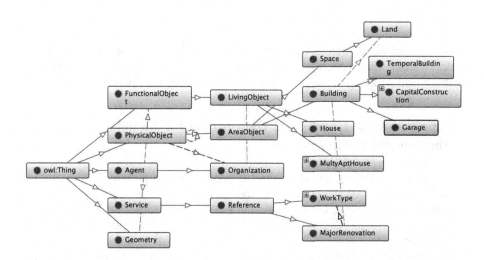

Fig. 4. A fragment of the model in the part of the ontology of residential buildings.

Public SPARQL end-point allows executing requests to part of the stored city data. E.g.: Getting the list of all houses with major repairs (define the type), excluding those in which major repairs were done before 2000.

```
PREFIX cg: <http:. Inwww.w3id.org/citygraph-core#>
SELECT ?Street ?h_number ?WorkTypeTitle ?year
  WHERE
    {
      ?x a cg:CapitalConstruction;
        cg:hasAddressObj [cg:hasStreet [cg:hasTitle ?Street]];
        cg:hasAddressObj [cg:hasHouseNumber ?h_number].
      ?x cg:hasMajorRenovation ?MR.
      ?WorkType cg:hasTitle ?WorkTypeTitle FILTER (?WorkTypeTitle = "Ремонт
    фасада").
      ?MR cg:hasWorkType ?WorkType ;
        cg:hasMajorRenovationDate ?year MINUS
          {
            ?MR cg:hasWorkType ?WorkType ;
            cg:hasMajorRenovationDate ?year FILTER (?year < 2000).
          }
    }
```

This is typical question that can help to city officials to plan capital reconstruction works. Making this request became possible because we integrated several open databases and structured this data. Working with analysis of population is the same.

4 Application of Conceptual Data Model for Modeling the Loyalty of Citizens

Assessing and predicting the loyalty of the population is a non-trivial task, since it requires taking into account on the one hand the needs of the population, which differ for different social groups, life situations and values. At the same time, values peculiar to different generations can significantly change the loyalty of citizens to the same living conditions.

On the other hand, this task requires taking into account the capabilities of the urban environment, to meet the needs of citizens at the expense of existing services and functions.

At the same time, it is necessary to take into account that citizens can be in several social groups and life situations at the same time, which determines some complexity in forming the structure of their requirements for the urban environment. It should also be taken into account that the same objects in the urban environment can perform several functions simultaneously. For example, a Park can perform an ecological or recreational function, as well as serve as a point of attraction, a tourist center, or a place of sports or cultural leisure.

These features make it necessary to use the approach described in the article to design databases in public loyalty management systems. For this purpose, information models of the subject area were formed [20], based on the provisions of the approach described in Sects. 1, 2, 3 of this article. Diagrams of the subject area are shown in Fig. 5.

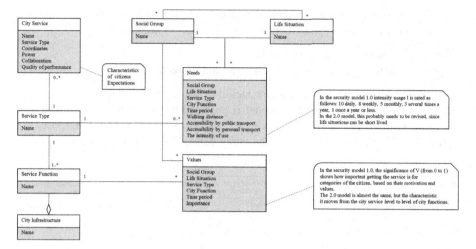

Fig. 5. ER-diagram of model the loyalty of citizens.

Loyalty of a certain group increases if the measures taken increase the security of this social group in at least one of the life situations. And the loyalty of a social group decreases when its security decreases in some of the life situations.

Based on this simplified model of the subject area, a database model for the subject area of population loyalty modeling is formed, shown in Fig. 6.

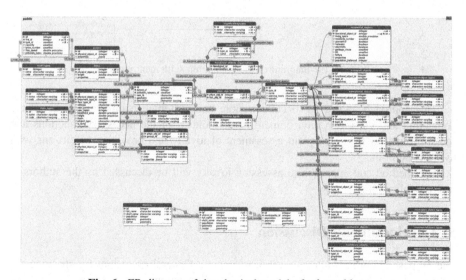

Fig. 6. ER-diagram of the physical model of urban objects.

It should be noted that the proposed database model provides storage of information about urban physical infrastructure, including such objects as:

- buildings, road network, green areas;
- territorial items that include administrative and cadastral divisions.

In addition, functional infrastructure facilities that provide services to the population. Population accounting in this model is provided by "settling" the population in residential buildings in a structure close to the existing one. For this purpose, the population settlement model is used, the entity diagram of which is shown in Fig. 7.

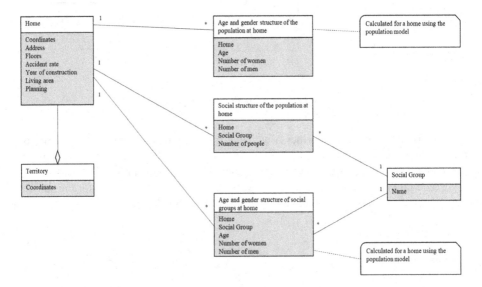

Fig. 7. ER-diagram of the population settlement model.

This approach allows us to collect, store and systematize information about the population and the urban environment in the context of the necessary functions and social groups for the subsequent assessment of loyalty and provision of citizens with living conditions.

The method and approach to assessing loyalty will be discussed by the authors in future publications.

5   Conclusion and Discussion

The proposed approach allows us to implement a General procedure for studying the territory when identifying requirements for its development in the framework of four directions:

First, the description of the study area at the restriction level. Most often, the territory is characterized by the polygon of its borders [22], and its characteristics are determined by the use, taking into account regulatory and regulatory requirements.

Secondly, the description of the urban planning system formed at the local level. In this case, the urban environment formed on the territory under study is subject to analysis. It includes an assessment of the composition and condition of urban objects, the level of their interaction.

Third, a description of the stakeholders in terms of territory development. At the same time, interested parties can be both citizens and business representatives, as well as tourists and persons temporarily staying in the city.

Fourth, it describes the forms of interaction between citizens and the urban environment in terms of addressing the functions of urban objects. In fact, the result of the analysis of the urban environment is to identify the ability of the composition and quality of urban objects and their functions to meet the needs of citizens. The fifth step is to create requirements for the development of the urban environment. However, requirements may include the following types:

- Requirements and restrictions imposed at the level of infrastructure and legislation.
- Requirements for the composition of objects determine the need for an appropriate type of object to ensure the appropriate activities of people on the territory. The composition of objects must not contradict the requirements for types of security.
- The placement requirements determine the preferred geographical location of objects relative to the territory and to each other, taking into account the parameters of interaction between objects. The placement requirements must not contradict the requirements for the types of security of the territory and the requirements for the composition of objects.
- Requirements for the parameters of objects determine the necessary physical properties and features of objects in the urban environment to ensure the appropriate activities of people. These requirements must not contradict the requirements for the types of security of the territory and the requirements for the composition and placement of objects.
- Requirements for the performance of urban objects or non-functional requirements characterize the consumer properties of objects that are not directly related to their use. For example, this may be requirements for the design or architectural performance of the urban environment.

Requirements for the development of the urban environment are naturally placed in a hierarchy according to the levels of decomposition. However, the requirements of higher levels cannot contradict the requirements of lower levels. In some cases this may lead to a contradiction. The digital model of the city is a tool for resolving contradictions and taking into account the predicted effects of following linear requirements [4, 21]. The digital model of the city is considered, on the one hand, as a way to describe the city and urban data, and, on the other hand, as a way to organize and describe knowledge about the city.

Acknowledgements. This research is financially supported by The Russian Science Foundation, Agreement #20-11-20264.

References

1. Psyllidis, A., Bozzon, A., Bocconi, S., Titos Bolivar, C.: A platform for urban analytics and semantic data integration in city planning. In: Celani, G., Sperling, D.M., Franco, J.M.S. (eds.) CAAD Futures 2015. CCIS, vol. 527, pp. 21–36. Springer, Heidelberg (2015). https://doi.org/10.1007/978-3-662-47386-3_2
2. Chen, Y., Sabri, S., Rajabifard, A., Elijah, M.: Computers, environment and urban systems an ontology-based spatial data harmonisation for urban analytics. Comput. Environ. Urban Syst. **72**, 1–14 (2018)
3. Simonelli1, L., Amorim, A.L.: City information modeling: general aspects and conceptualization. Am. J. Eng. Res. **7**(10), 319–324 (2018)
4. Stojanovski, T.: City information modelling (CIM) and urban design – morphological structure, design elements and programming classes in CIM. In: CITY MODELLING & GIS, vol. 1, pp. 507–516 (2019)
5. Caglioni, M., Rabino, G.A.: Theoretical approach to urban ontology: a contribution from urban system analysis. In: Teller, J., Lee, J.R., Roussey, C. (eds.) Studies in Computational Intelligence, vol. 61, pp. 109–119. Springer, Heidelberg (2007). https://doi.org/10.1007/978-3-540-71976-2_10
6. Falquet, G., Métral, C., Teller, J., Tweed, C.: Ontologies in Urban Development Projects, vol. 1, pp. 139–152–152. Springer, London (2011). https://doi.org/10.1007/978-0-85729-724-2
7. Poveda-Villalón, M., García-Castro, R., Gómez-Pérez, A.: Building an ontology catalogue for smart cities. In: eWork Ebus. Architecture Engineering Construction – Proceedings of 10th European Conference Product and Process Modelling ECPPM 2014, pp. 829–836 (2014)
8. Dubrovnik Smart City case. https://Incityos.io/dubrovnik
9. Base data city of Amsterdam. https://Inamsterdamsmartcity.com
10. The open data portal Helsinki with examples of applications in the framework of the concept "city as a service". https://Inhelsinkiasaservice.com. https://Inhri.fi/en_gb/
11. Concept Society 5.0 Tokyo
12. Berta, M., Caneparo, L., Montuori, A., Rolfo, D.: Semantic urban modelling: knowledge representation of urban space. Environ. Plan. B Plan. Des. **43**(4), 610–639 (2016)
13. Montenegro, N., Gomes, J., Urbano, P., Duarte, J.: An OWL2 land use ontology: LBCS. In: Murgante, B., Gervasi, O., Iglesias, A., Taniar, D., Apduhan, Bernady O. (eds.) ICCSA 2011. LNCS, vol. 6783, pp. 185–198. Springer, Heidelberg (2011). https://doi.org/10.1007/978-3-642-21887-3_15
14. Komninos, N., Bratsas, C., Kakderi, C., Tsarchopoulos, P.: Smart city ontologies: improving the effectiveness of smart city applications. J. Smart Cities **1**(1), 31–46 (2016)
15. Bellini, P., Benigni, M., Billero, R., Nesi, P., Rauch, N.: Km4City ontology building vs data harvesting and cleaning for smart-city services. J. Vis. Lang. Comput. **25**(6), 827–839 (2014)
16. Tim Berners-Lee: Linked Data - Design Issues (2006). Retrieved May 2020. https://www.w3.org/DesignIssues/LinkedData.html
17. GeoSPARQL - A Geographic Query Language for RDF Data. Retrieved May 2020. https://www.opengeospatial.org/standards/geosparql
18. The current version of the conceptual model in OWL. Retrieved May 2020. https://Ingithub.com/iduprojects/cityont/blob/master/city-data-conceptual-2.owl
19. Technical and economic passports of apartment buildings. Retrieved May 2020. http://Indata.gov.spb.ru/opendata/7840013199-passports_houses/

20. Rudikova, L.V.: Database design: studies. student manual higher studies. Institutions in the field of "Software Information Technologies", "Economic Cybernetics, "Applied Mathematics". In: Rudikova, L.V. (ed.) Information. systems and technology (in economics)", p. 352, ITC Ministry of Finance, Minsk (2009)

21. Stojanovski, T.: City information modelling (CIM) and urban design: morphological structure, design elements and programming classes in CIM. In: eCAADe Conference, Lodz University of Technology, Lodz, Poland, 19–21 September 2018, pp. 507–516 (2019)

22. Rodoman, B.B.: Districting as a way of possessing space. Region. Res. Russ. **8**(4), 301–307 (2018). https://doi.org/10.1134/S2079970518040081

23. Berners-Lee, T., Hendler, J., Lassila, O.: The semantic web. Sci. Am. **284**(5), 34–43 (2001)

24. St. Petersburg city graph web-site. http://Incitygraph.onti.actcognitive.org/

25. Wolff, A., Barker, M., Hudson, L., Seffah, A.: Supporting smart citizens: design templates for co-designing data-intensive technologies. Cities **101**, 102695 (2020)

26. Stelzle, B., Jannack, A., Holmer, T., Naumann, F., Wilde, A., Noennig, J.R.: Smart citizens for smart cities. In: Auer, M.E., Tsiatsos, T. (eds.) IMCL 2019. AISC, vol. 1192, pp. 571–581. Springer, Cham (2021). https://doi.org/10.1007/978-3-030-49932-7_54

Neural Network Processing of Natural Russian Language for Building Intelligent Dialogue Systems

Danila Parygin[1]([⊠]) [ID], Nikolay Matyushin[2], Anton Finogeev[3],
Natalia Sadovnikova[1] [ID], Tatyana Petrova[4], and Ekaterina Fadeeva[1]

[1] Volgograd State Technical University,
Lenina Ave. 28, 400005 Volgograd, Russia
dparygin@gmail.com, npsnl@ya.ru, kween2@mail.ru
[2] Skolkovo Innovation Center, Bolshoy Blvd. 2/1, 121205 Moscow, Russia
dolphinn@bk.ru
[3] Penza State University, Krasnaya Street 40, 440026 Penza, Russia
fanton3@ya.ru
[4] Volgograd State Socio-Pedagogical University,
Lenina Avenue 27, 400005 Volgograd, Russia
modest63@yandex.ru

Abstract. Currently chatbots, dialogue systems and intelligent assistants increasingly found in an equipment of everyday life, used in technical support of commercial organizations and in entertainment services. Systems for the English language have good groundwork. However, the process of "recognition" of a natural language associated with a number of difficulties caused by the need to have a significant initial database of dialogues, explore various architectures of neural networks, solve problems of the perception and morphology of the Russian language. In this regard, the purpose of this study is the development of a neural network model for natural Russian language processing, capable of becoming an open platform for the development of specialized dialogue systems. For this, design and training of dialog models of neural networks based on modifications of the Transformer architecture are proposed. Own parsers for extracting and post-processing dialogues in natural Russian from the Otvet@-mail.Ru portal and public chat rooms in the Telegram messenger for training neural networks were developed. The data set, prepared with their help and now publicly available on the Internet, contains more than 22.5 million question-answer pairs in natural Russian language. The prepared data set in various configurations applied when training a number of neural network models designed by modifying the Sequence2Sequence, Transformer and text2text architectures. The final version of developed neural network model generates answers to any user message up to 200 characters and is integrated into a dialogue system implemented using the client-server architecture for user interaction with the chat bot.

Keywords: Neural network · Natural language · Russian language · Intelligent assistant · Dialogue system · Chat bot · Telegram-bot · Transformer model

A. Chugunov et al. (Eds.): EGOSE 2020, CCIS 1349, pp. 232–244, 2020.
https://doi.org/10.1007/978-3-030-67238-6_17

1 Introduction

Modern workflows are associated with the management of a complex of sophisticated and intelligent equipment. The constantly increasing speed of the appearance of tasks requiring an objective assessment of the situation, the adoption of quick and adequate decisions, determines the need to organize effective human-machine interaction. But not only production issues require the formation of appropriate control interfaces. A new level of comfort for human life conditions, provided by high-tech gadgets, leads to the search for means of control channels integration in an "intuitive" format [1].

Currently, chat bots, dialogue systems and intelligent assistants are increasingly found in everyday life [2]. Every modern mobile operating system has its own intelligent assistant. Such a program allows to interact with a computer using natural language, for example, to find out the weather, use an Internet search, call a friend, send a message, and much more.

In some cases, dialogue systems and chat bots allow to completely solve a client's problem without involving staff. However, most of these systems only support English, which is a limiting factor for a Russian speaking person. In addition, such solutions often work on the basis of predefined patterns. The advantage of this approach is that the response of the dialogue system can be predicted in advance with very high accuracy. However, this approach has significant drawbacks, the main of which are the uniformity of responses, which is especially critical for a chat bot, and thematic limitations, since the dialogue system will answer only those questions for which the patterns have been predefined. These aspects determine the relevance of using machine learning to build dialogue systems. And in this regard, it becomes necessary to solve the scientific problem of intellectual communicative support of a person when solving a wide range of issues of life activity in a natural language dialogue form.

2 Analysis of the Current Level of Development and Approaches to the Construction of Intelligent Dialogue Systems

The popularity and scope of intelligent dialogue systems are expanding. The growth has been particularly noticeable with the development of machine learning and neural networks [2]. There are several main types of dialogue systems. First of all, these are personal assistants that have received mass distribution, helping to solve a person's everyday tasks. Interaction with them occurs in natural language, as a rule, using voice commands converted into textual representation. Examples of such systems are Alexa [3] and Cortana [4]. They are capable of both responding according to predefined patterns and conducting a casual dialogue with the user. However, these systems do not support Russian.

Another type is the so-called dialogue QA-systems for advising clients. The tasks of the first line of technical support, as well as the functions of presenting goods and services, are delegated to chatbots by up to 20% of companies in some sectors of the economy [5].

There are already well-established companies on the market that are developing solutions for building human-computer interaction interfaces according to given patterns in Russian [6].

Platforms for developing applications that process English texts or speech in natural language, such as Wit.ai, api.ai, LUIS.ai, Kore.ai and others, have also become widespread [7]. These platforms make it possible to recognize user phrases and extract "intents" from them, which are user intentions received in a computer-friendly format. Complex intents can be recognized, but the developer must register all sorts of situations and answers to them to expand the dialog field.

At the same time, several basic machine learning models are used in the construction of intelligent dialogue systems. The main idea of the "encoder-decoder" model is that the encoder compresses some input into the distributed representation, and each time it is fed to the input of the neural network, which works as a decoder. A kind of semantic representation for the entire sentence is built using this architecture [8]. The main drawback of the encoder-decoder architecture is that the entire sentence has to be "collapsed" into a fixed-dimensional vector, so a long sentence will always be more difficult to collapse and expand.

Dialogue in the model of the hierarchical recurrent encoder-decoder "HRED" is considered as a two-level system that includes a sequence of statements, consisting of a sequence of words. Developing modified versions of this architecture allow reducing the number of training parameters by 25%–30%, and training time by more than 50%, without degrading the quality [9].

The Transformer model uses an attention mechanism [10], the idea of which is to extract the most important part from an array of input data. The Google Brain Team introduced the Tensor2Tensor model, which is based on attention mechanisms and is presented as "One model for learning everything": voice, text, images, translation, etc. Such a model will expand the possibilities of processing various kinds of content in dialogue systems. However, this model requires more GPU and memory for training, especially for large data sets [11].

Thus, the choice of a suitable initial neural network architecture is associated with the need for empirical research [12]. But, in addition, the tasks of teaching dialogue models are still associated with a number of problems of understanding information that is natural for human perception. So the problem of resolving anaphora is related to understanding what a particular pronoun refers to in the text [8]. Another important problem of dialogue models is the assessment of their quality, taking into account many parameters, while the concept of a "correct" answer is not unambiguous for almost all open questions. The work [13] presents the results of using such quality metrics as BLEU, METEOR, etc. in the context of evaluating model responses in a dialogue and draws conclusions about the need to continue searching for adequate metrics. The complexity of the morphology of the Russian language with many different word forms complements the picture of critical problems [14]: the verb "read" has more than 40 forms in Russian ("читает", "читаем", "читаю", "читаешь", "читать", "читал", etc.), and only 3 main forms differing in spelling in English (read, reads, reading).

An analysis of the current situation shows that the level of technology development allows training dialogue models of neural networks that are capable of "recognizing" the natural language of a person and offering the most frequent answers. However, such models are not yet able to understand the essence and generate meanings. And even the learning process itself is associated with great difficulties caused by the need to have a significant conversational database. For example, about 30,000 question-answer pairs, the preparation of which is difficult for many organizations and individuals, necessary for recognize of 200 answers [5]. In this regard, the purpose of this study is to develop a neural network model for processing the natural Russian language that can become an open platform for the development of specialized dialogue systems.

3 Development of a Dialogue Neural Network Model

It was decided to use the software library of machine learning TensorFlow to build and train a neural network model [15]. The TensorFlow library is cross-platform, written in C++, and the Python programming language is used to build models. However, prepared data [16] containing question-answer pairs are necessary to start training a conversational neural network. Moreover, these couples had to be in Russian in accordance with the intended objectives of the project.

3.1 Preparing Data for Training a Neural Network Model

The required data was not publicly available at the time of the study. Based on this, it was decided to form a data set from open sources. The "Ответы@Mail.Ru" portal [17] and public chats in the Telegram messenger [18] were used as such sources of initial data. Parsers written in Python have been developed to extract data [19].

The Telegram parser accepts a list of Telegram chats at the input, and unloads the message history for each chat into a separate JSON file. Data upload is carried out using a separate Telegram account. The created Telegram parser uses the pyrogram and tgcrypto libraries to interact with the Telegram server via the mtproto protocol. The resulting JSON file contains the message ID (message_id), the message date (date), the quoted message ID (reply_message_id), the user ID (user_id) and the message text (text).

The parser of the "Ответы@Mail.Ru" portal saves all available information into one JSON file. Data unloading occurs through a non-public API located at https://otvet. mail.ru/api/v2/question?qid=n, where 'n' is the id of the question. A high-performance streaming JSON parser in C is additionally written using the yajl library to process the resulting JSON file.

Post-processing is performed on the received raw data. It consists in filtering and transforming the initial data into a format convenient for further processing by the neural network. The program for post-processing of the initial data filters all messages according to the algorithm presented in the block diagram (see Fig. 1). The program has the ability to set the data processing mode depending on a specific source, Telegram chats or the "Ответы@Mail.Ru" site.

Only messages citing other messages are selected when processing data received from Telegram chats. This allows to explicitly highlight user dialogues in the general message flow and exclude spam messages, which ultimately improves the quality of the sample.

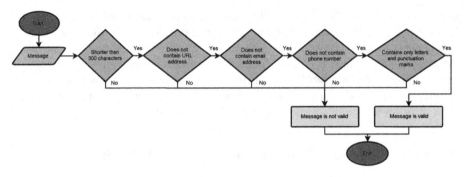

Fig. 1. Message validation algorithm.

The text of the message must be additionally processed when working with data received from the "Ответы@Mail.Ru" site. It is necessary, for example, to remove HTML tags. In addition, the program should exclude questions that do not have confirmed answers.

In total, at this stage, texts were extracted from 177 Telegram chats and 15 million questions from the "Ответы@Mail.Ru" website with a total volume of 120 GB of raw data. 10.5 million pairs of processed messages from Telegram and 12 million pairs of processed messages from "Ответы@Mail.Ru" were received as a result of post-processing. Prepared data sets are openly available for free use by links:

- On MEGA: https://mega.nz/#F!odRXBKQa!CbYInd-mROOSeeWLxd_1Dw
- On Kaggle: https://www.kaggle.com/dolfik/datasets

3.2   Neural Network Design and Training

It was decided to conduct initial tests on the prepared sample on the Sequence2Sequence model, which is a recurrent neural network with a symbol-by-symbol Embedding layer at the input [20]. Each cell of the recurrent network consists of several sequentially located GRU cells (Gated recurrent unit). A data set of 500,000 question-and-answer pairs was used to train the model. The complete training of the model took 12 days. The resulting model learned to correctly build sentences and place punctuation marks as a result of training. However, the sentences were often incoherent and disconnected from the question asked. The only exceptions were greetings, goodbyes, and other messages that were often found in the original data set. As a result, it was concluded that the model was under-trained, but in addition, it turned out to be excessively cumbersome and poorly trained.

It was decided to investigate the applicability of the Transformer neural network model as an alternative. Library tensor2tensor [10], which is a wrapper over the Transformer model, was used for training. It allows to solve various kinds of problems, including natural language processing problems. The text2text model [21] was taken as a basis and modified for the conditions of the original data set and the problem being solved: the vocabulary size has been increased to 219, the subtoken length limitation has been removed, the input data loading has been redesigned, and the training to evaluation ratio has been changed to 9 to 1 accordingly.

A data set of 125,000 phrase pairs was chosen for the first neural network training. The training was carried out on the graphics accelerator NVidia Tesla P100 of the computing cluster of VSTU [22]. The training took 2 h 30 min with transformer_base_single_gpu and batch size equal to 2048.

The trained model showed much better results than the Sequence2Sequence model, even with a smaller data set. The value of the loss function reached 0.7 as a result of training, which is an acceptable result for such a task (see Fig. 2), proves the efficiency of the applied neural network model and its applicability for research purposes.

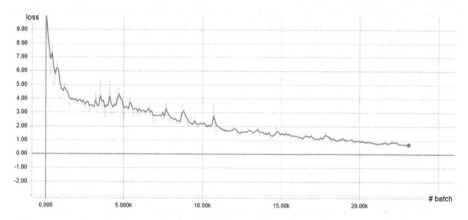

Fig. 2. Graph of change in the loss function value.

The next step was to increase the amount of training data to 500,000 phrase pairs. The loss function stops between 5.0 and 6.0 regardless of the training time when training a neural network on such a data set. The analysis showed that an increase in the amount of data requires a decrease in the size of the batch. In this case, the batch size was reduced to 512. At the same time, the quality of training in the Transformer model is sensitive to the size of the batch [11], since the attention mechanism needs to "see" a large amount of data at each time point.

Attempts were made to improve the result by changing the training settings, as well as using the transformer_base_multistep8 model, which emulates training on 8 accelerators. This only slightly improved learning outcomes, but the trained model responded to almost all messages with the word "Yes". In this regard, it was decided to further use the model trained for 125,000 message pairs.

4 Development of a Dialogue System on the Telegram Platform

It was decided to integrate the developed neural network model into the dialogue system. This will make it possible to effectively test the created model itself, and will also become the basis for conducting experiments on the development of specialized intelligent assistants on a single basis. A chat bot was chosen as the format for building the system.

Chatbots are based on a platform, which can be a messenger with an appropriate API. WhatsApp, Viber and Telegram are in the top three in popularity among such messengers in Russia [23]. WhatsApp, which is the leader in the rating, does not have a free and open API for developing bots. Only Telegram and Facebook Messenger have the most complete and functional API, which partly confirms the comparison of the dynamics of search queries (see Fig. 3). Thus, Telegram is currently the most promising platform for developing and using bots.

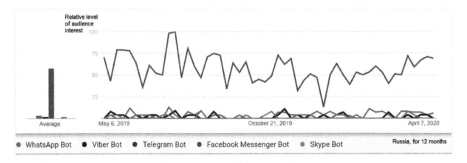

Fig. 3. Popularity of search queries for messengers with the word "bot" [24].

The developed system uses a client-server architecture (see Fig. 4) for user interaction with the chatbot. The Telegram application installed on the user's device acts as a software client. The interaction between the Telegram bot and the trained model is carried out using the REST API, via the HTTP protocol. The ability to host a Telegram bot and a trained model on physically different servers has been implemented. Telegram bot interacts with the user through the Telegram Bot API.

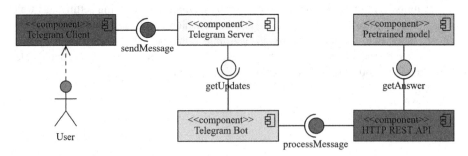

Fig. 4. Architecture of intelligent conversational system.

The HTTP server is developed in Python using the "falcon" library. Python was chosen to facilitate interaction with the trained model, as it is the standard for the TensorFlow library. The server accepts POST requests to the address/send/message. The request body must contain a JSON string with a single field – "message". If the request is successfully processed, then the server responds with a 200 code and a JSON string in the response body with two fields – "message" and "answer", which respectively contain the original message and response. The HTTP server interacts with the trained neural network model and returns the processing result to the Telegram bot.

4.1 Telegram-Bot Implementation

Telegram bot communicates with Telegram server via HTTP REST API. The program sends a request containing a text message of the user to the HTTP server when receiving a message from the user. The received response is sent to the user.

The user has the opportunity to assess the response received, depending on the bot settings for a particular chat. This response is saved to the database for further analysis.

The F# programming language and the Funogram library [25] are used to develop a Telegram bot. This choice is due to the compactness of the syntax of the F# language. The LiteDB embedded file database is used to store the neural network model response scores. The Akka.Net library with the F# Akkling wrapper [26] is used to build the actor architecture.

There are four main actors ("updates", "chats", "storage", "outputGate") and "n" secondary actors, where "n" is equal to the number of chats the bot has ever been in:

- The updates actor is the input actor of the program and accepts all updates coming from the Telegram Api.
- The chats actor is a persistent actor and stores a key-value dictionary, where the key is the chat ID and the value is a reference to the corresponding actor (this actor forwards all messages to the chat actor; if there is no such actor, then it is created).
- The storage actor has access to the database context (it receives an asynchronous function with one argument, database context, in a message, and starts execution by passing the database context).
- The chat/n actor is also persistent, and is able to store chat information and setting flags for a given chat (this actor processes all messages sent by the user to this chat).
- The outputGate actor is a gateway to Telegram Api and forwards all received messages to the Telegram server.

4.2 Results of Dialogue System Testing

The developed chatbot @TrittBot was launched for testing, which was carried out on random dialogues in the Telegram messenger. Quite a lot of false positives (at least 50% for difficult questions) are present in the studied dialogues, while in the chatbot's responses, one can record the presence of logical coherence.

Up to 90% of the answers corresponding to the question posed can be received in the dialogues of welcome and clarification of interests. However, it is clearly possible to highlight the problem of loss of connection in the chain of questions, which occurs due to the absence of a context layer in the created neural network model.

The correct processing of commands by the Telegram bot was checked in the Telegram X messenger for Android, version 0.21.3.1036-arm64-v8a. Available commands are displayed when enter the "/" (Fig. 5a) –/toggle_rating and/toggle_bot, which trigger the message evaluation (Fig. 5b) and the messages from the bot themselves. The bot showed stable performance in personal (Fig. 5c) and group dialogues (Fig. 5d). The neural network model generates responses to any user message up to 200 characters long. The bot responds with a text message to every text message that is not a command. The "typing" request processing status is displayed while the response is being generated. The bot responds only to those messages that were addressed to it when working in group chats.

In general, the developed solution has a distributed, fault-tolerant architecture. The absence of a response from one of the components does not lead to an abnormal system termination. Situations like this are handled correctly.

Docker [27] is used to host parsers, an HTTP server and a Telegram bot, which greatly speeds up application deployment and eliminates problems with incorrect versions of dependencies (for example, the Python interpreter), since all dependencies are supplied with the container. Docker also has the ability to combine multiple containers into one network. This feature is used to combine an HTTP server container and a Telegram bot.

The project code is available at https://github.com/Dolfik1/Thesis.

5 Discussion

The results obtained allow to look optimistically at the solution of many key problems in the development of e-government. The technologies that underlie the concepts of a smart city, open government and key aspects of the information society, in one way or another, target society and people as the main beneficiaries. And the receipt of information benefits for each individual includes communication as an integral component of digital services.

The use of the developed model within the framework of the created bot or in the form of an integrated component can contribute to the formation of a structured picture of the relationship between individual profiles, groups and social problems for solving problems of municipal or state management, between similar interests in the distribution of funds, for example, in proactive budgeting. Dialogue communication close to a person will allow organizing the accounting of the mood of the population for the implementation of smart city technologies, monitoring the state of society in terms of social tension, when used within social networks and instant messengers, for the automated creation of focus groups when implementing e-government technologies.

However, arriving in the euphoria of technological progress, it is necessary to remember the dangerous aspects of humanizing intelligent technologies. The natural language and competent responses of the neural network model in criminal goal-setting can have an informational and psychological impact aimed at destabilizing the internal political and social situation.

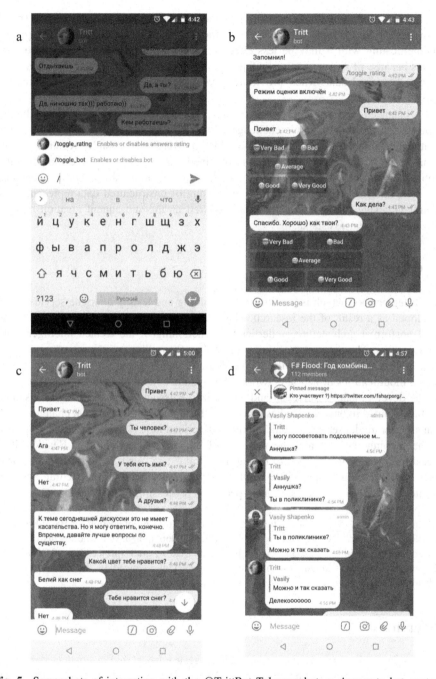

Fig. 5. Screenshots of interaction with the @TrittBot Telegram-bot: a. Access to bot control commands; b. Work in the mode of evaluation bot messages; c. Personal dialogue with the bot; d. Group chat with bot.

The threat of communicating with a developed bot that is able to correctly respond to the text, while skipping the context of the internal emotional state of the person communicating with it may be less effective at first glance, but therefore more dangerous because of its latent spread. Objective lack of empathy in a robot can aggravate the psychological state when providing psychological assistance or in pedagogical work.

A balanced appraisal of the risks and benefits of technology is undoubtedly important in meeting society's challenges. But only further study and use of already created developments will make it possible to overcome possible negative consequences. The application of the results obtained can be used to solve the scientific problem of automatic classification of dialogue texts to establish similar semantic schemes, interrelated presentation and processing of unstructured data represented by natural language dialogue constructions, as well as the subsequent creation of specialized intelligent assistants.

6 Conclusion

The Telegram bot, which is a platform for building and testing dialogue services, was developed as a result of the research. The trained neural network model, designed on the Transformer architecture, underlies the functioning of the created intelligent dialogue system. The data set containing more than 20 million question-answer pairs in natural Russian and placed in the public domain was prepared for training the investigated modifications of neural networks. The results obtained are the information base for the development of universal and specialized Russian-language dialogue systems.

It is planned in ongoing studies to explore the potential for additional changes to the Transformer model settings, including those described in [11], while increasing the size of the training data set and the memory of the graphics accelerator. Besides, it is necessary to check the variants of the ratio of "train" and "eval" data. Adding a context layer looks extremely promising, but such an adjustment to the neural network architecture will require revision and special preprocessing of the training data.

Acknowledgments. The reported study was funded by Russian Foundation for Basic Research (RFBR) according to the research project No. 18-37-20066_mol_a_ved. The results of part 3 were obtained within the Russian Science Foundation (RSF) grant (project No. 20-71-10087). The authors express gratitude to colleagues from UCLab involved in the development of UrbanBasis.com project.

References

1. Parygin, D.: Implementation of exoactive management model for urbanized area: real-time monitoring and proactive planning. In: SMART-2019, Proceedings of the 8th International Conference on System Modeling and Advancement in Research Trends, pp. 310–316. IEEE (2020)

2. Ryzhikova, A.: Zapisat'sya k vrachu i kupit' aviabilety: chem polezny chat-boty [Sign up for a doctor and buy air tickets: what chat bots are useful for]. https://bloomchain.ru/fintech/zapisatsya-k-vrachu-i-kupit-aviabilety-chem-polezny-chat-boty/. Accessed 15 Mar 2020 (in Russian)
3. Alexa. https://developer.amazon.com/alexa. Accessed 19 Mar 2020
4. Cortana – Your intelligent assistant across your life. https://www.microsoft.com/en-us/cortana. Accessed 19 Mar 2020
5. Issledovaniye R-Style Softlab: razvitiye chat-botov [Research R-Style Softlab: the development of chat bots]. https://www.softlab.ru/upload/iblock/4f1/issledovanie_perspektivy-razvitiya-chat_botov.pdf. Accessed 09 Apr 2020. (in Russian)
6. Nanosemantika [Nanosemantics]. https://nanosemantics.ai/. Accessed 20 Mar 2020. (in Russian)
7. A Comparative Analysis of ChatBots APIs. https://activewizards.com/blog/a-comparative-analysis-of-chatbots-apis/. Accessed 20 Jan 2020
8. Nikolenko, S., Kudrin, A., Arkhangelskaya, E.: Glubokoye obucheniye, pogruzheniye v mir neyronnykh setey [Deep learning, immersion in the world of neural networks], St. Petersburg (2018). (in Russian)
9. Wang, C.C., Jiang, H.: Simplified hierarchical recurrent encoder-decoder for building end-to-end dialogue systems. https://www.groundai.com/project/simplified-hierarchical-recurrent-encoder-decoder-for-building-end-to-end-dialogue-systems/. Accessed 18 Nov 2019
10. Vaswani, A., et al.: Attention is all you need. https://papers.nips.cc/paper/7181-attention-is-all-you-need.pdf. Accessed 27 Nov 2019
11. Popel, M., Bojar, O.: Training tips for the transformer model. Prague Bull. Math. Linguist. **110**, 43–70 (2018)
12. Donchenko, D., Sadovnikova, N., Parygin, D.: Prediction of Road Accidents' Severity on Russian Roads Using Machine Learning Techniques. In: Radionov, Andrey A., Kravchenko, Oleg A., Guzeev, Victor I., Rozhdestvenskiy, Yurij V. (eds.) ICIE 2019. LNME, pp. 1493–1501. Springer, Cham (2020). https://doi.org/10.1007/978-3-030-22063-1_157
13. Liu, C., Lowe, R., Serban, I.V., Noseworthy, M., Charlin, L., Pineau, J.: How NOT To Evaluate Your Dialogue System. In: Proceedings of 2016 Conference on Empirical Methods in Natural Language Processing, Austin, 1–5 November 2016, pp. 2122–2132 (2016)
14. Boiko, D., Parygin, D., Savina, O., Golubev, A., Zelenskiy, I., Mityagin, S.: Approaches to Analysis of Factors Affecting the Residential Real Estate Bid Prices in Case of Open Data Use. In: Chugunov, A., Khodachek, I., Misnikov, Y., Trutnev, D. (eds.) EGOSE 2019. CCIS, vol. 1135, pp. 360–375. Springer, Cham (2020). https://doi.org/10.1007/978-3-030-39296-3_27
15. Golubev, A., Sadovnikova, N., Parygin, D., Glinyanova, I., Finogeev, A., Shcherbakov, M.: Woody plants area estimation using ordinary satellite images and deep learning. In: Alexandrov, D.A., Boukhanovsky, A.V., Chugunov, A.V., Kabanov, Y., Koltsova, O. (eds.) DTGS 2018. CCIS, vol. 858, pp. 302–313. Springer, Cham (2018). https://doi.org/10.1007/978-3-030-02843-5_24
16. Velichko, A.N., Budkov, V.Y., Karpov, A.A.: Analytical survey of computational paralinguistic systems for automatic recognition of deception in human speech. Informatsionno-upravliaiushchie sistemy, no. 5, pp. 30–41 (2017)
17. Otvety@Mail.Ru [Answers@Mail.Ru]. https://otvet.mail.ru/. Accessed 29 Apr 2020. (in Russian)
18. Telegram. https://telegram.org/. Accessed 29 Apr 2020

19. Donchenko, D., Ovchar, N., Sadovnikova, N., Parygin, D., Shabalina, O., Ather, D.: Analysis of comments of users of social networks to assess the level of social tension. Procedia Comput. Sci. **119**, 359–367 (2017)
20. Solving NLP task using Sequence2Sequence model: from Zero to Hero. https://towardsdatascience.com/solving-nlp-task-using-sequence2sequence-model-from-zero-to-hero-c193c1bd03d1. Accessed 22 Dec 2019
21. text2text. https://github.com/google/text2text. Accessed 20 Dec 2019
22. Mnogoprotsessornyy vychislitel'nyy kompleks (klaster) [Multiprocessor computing complex (cluster)]. http://evm.vstu.ru/index.php/labs/hpc-lab/about-hpc. Accessed 12 May 2020. (in Russian)
23. Rossiyskaya auditoriya mobil'nykh prilozheniy messendzherov [Russian audience of mobile applications of instant messengers]. https://www.rbc.ru/technology_and_media/13/04/2019/5caf56bb9a7947f245247621. Accessed 13 Apr 2020. (in Russian)
24. Google Trends. https://trends.google.ru/. Accessed 21 Apr 2020
25. Funogram: F# Bot Api library. https://github.com/Dolfik1/Funogram. Accessed 02 Feb 2020
26. Akkling Wiki. https://github.com/Horusiath/Akkling/wiki. Accessed 04 Feb 2020
27. Docker. https://www.docker.com/. Accessed 09 Mar 2020

Data-Driven Government in Russia: Linked Open Data Challenges, Opportunities, Solutions

Yurii Akatkin and Elena Yasinovskaya[✉]

Plekhanov Russian University of Economics, Moscow, Russia
{u.akatkin, elena}@semanticpro.org

Abstract. The trend of data-driven Government sets the priority of a data-centric paradigm for the development of digital government. It also maintains the use of linked open data as the basis for information sharing. Even though today when many countries have made a significant breakthrough, this task has turned out to be rather challenging for most of them and for Russia as well. Following the key criteria highlighted and proved for our assessment in 2018 we re-consider the results revealing Russian e-government readiness for the digital transformation basically in linked open data production. New challenges posed by the implementation of recently accepted data strategies in Russia set the objective of this research to check how the situation changed over the past two years. Due to the role of statistics in Open Government Data we give the review existing international practice in Linked Open Statistical data and shortly present ongoing research initiatives of The Russian Federal State Statistics Service. Expanding our previous recommendations, we advise to consider the competence gained in existing research and development and use it for implementing the state strategies with the focus on LO(S)D.

Keywords: Data centricity · Data-driven government · Semantic interoperability · Linked open data · Linked open statistical data · Sematic assets

1 Introduction

In 2019, the Government of the Russian Federation approved the Concept for the creation and operation of National Data Governance System (hereinafter referred to as the System) [22], developed to implement the objectives of the federal project "Digital Government Management" as a part of the national program "Digital Economy of the Russian Federation"[1]. The goal of the System is to increase the efficiency of government data creation, collection and use for the delivery of public services at the state and municipal levels, implementation of state and municipal functions, and the provision of access to the information in accordance with the needs of citizens and business [22].

---

[1] http://government.ru/info/35568/.

© Springer Nature Switzerland AG 2020
A. Chugunov et al. (Eds.): EGOSE 2020, CCIS 1349, pp. 245–257, 2020.
https://doi.org/10.1007/978-3-030-67238-6_18

The Concept authors plan to achieve this goal by "ensuring the completeness, relevance, consistency and coherence of government data". The task of regulatory legal and methodological framework development sets the requirement to establish "the rules for creating the government data model based on the principles of continuous development, gradual filling, and consistency, including the development of descriptions and relations of entities as well as their formats". According to the definition this government data model is "the totality of government data descriptions, organizational and technological rules and standards used to manage government data, including the description of relations between data types, as well as between the objects defined by them" for the purposes of cross-agency information exchange (interaction). Among the declared functions of the System we can distinguish the feature "to maintain government data model, including the description of the structure, contents and relations of government data, their suppliers and users, ensuring the historicity and versioning of the model, as well as the management of government data lifecycle" [22].

However, the Concept Road Map does not contain any action focused on the development of such government data model. This obviously contradicts to one of the System principles "to ensure the ontological unity of government data contained in the information resources of public sector bodies and organizations" [22].

Many researchers agree that the lack of accessible ontologies and standards inhibits the process of government data development as well as the achievement of the fifth level in the 5-star model [4]. Proposed by Tim Berners-Lee this model serves for OGD maturity assessment in Europe [18]. 5-star model defines all government data should be open, linked and published in a machine-readable format, providing the context to the data consumers [4]. This means that for "maintaining the government data model" it is necessary to develop and implement methods and tools for creating and reusing such ontologies (and other semantic models). It is also important to support the collaboration of experts working on domain models which will form the basis for the future government data model. The life cycle management should cover not only the data, but also the models describing them [1]. Unfortunately, the Concept and its Road Map do not declare such functions or actions.

Nevertheless, according to the Concept "the linking of government data in various information systems" serves to achieve significant economic effects: increasing the accuracy of planning and forecasting, the speed and quality of government decisions made within the framework of public administration tasks due to the use of "big data" tools and machine learning technologies.

In 2018 we conducted the first round of this research aimed to answer "if Russia is ready for digital transformation of e-Government" [2]. We suggested assessment methodology based on a detailed review showing the importance of Linked Open Data (LOD) for the establishment of data-centric and model-oriented paradigm in the achievement of new e-government maturity levels and its changing over to data-driven digital government [2]. This year new challenges posed by the implementation of recently accepted data strategies in Russia have motivated us to focus mostly on linked open data and to check how the situation changed over the past two years.

The task to reach data-centricity through LOD has become complicated not only in Russia, but also in other countries. This challenge arises even though open government data has long been recognized as a stimulating driver for innovative public services and increasing the level of public value. The driver, which changes the approach to the public services development and provides the possibility of proactive delivery in accordance with the demand and expectations of consumers.

Government organizations produce and publish many open datasets. Some of them do this only to fulfill regulatory requirements and perform their direct functions. But the majority hopes that the customers will effectively use published data for analysis, visualization, and/or application to new digital services. But, unfortunately, many researchers agree this potential has not yet been realized at the expected level. Among the most common barriers that impede the use of OGD they name the "lack of quality, lack of license and lack of technical know-how" [16, 19]. According to our previous review and practical experience in OGD dissemination and reuse there are some other significant barriers: (1) the absence of models for the preparation and interpretation of data such as semantic assets of various levels (ontologies, thesauruses, glossaries, dictionaries) providing the data with semantic annotation; (2) the lack of methods and tools for the development and distribution of these models, as well as for the collaboration of domain experts. To ensure semantic interoperability in a heterogeneous information environment of e-government with lots of inherited systems and services is not enough just to assign URIs to the concepts describing data. It is necessary to set all the relations sufficient to unambiguous data interpretation and reuse, and not to lose or distort their meaning in the process of machine processing.

Given the acceptance of this new National Data Governance System Concept in Russia we consider rather important to make the second round of our research and renew the assessment results. The main objective of this paper is to reexamine Russian e-government readiness for digital transformation in terms of data-centricity using the same criteria to ensure comparability of results.

Among the ways to overcome the barriers mentioned above and get the expected value from the open government data produced by public administration the experts suggest the use of Linked Open Statistical Data (LOSD) and open cubes [3, 16, 21]. Indeed, most OGD have close connection to statistics: demographic (for example, census data), economic or social indicators (for example, the number of new enterprises, unemployment rate) [9]. Open multidimensional statistics is one of the main OGD domains. It provides an important basis for accelerating socio-economic development by creating new socially significant public services and innovative projects using disruptive technologies. In Russia Digital Analytical Platform for providing statistical data will be the part of National Data Governance System with the aim to improve statistical data production and dissemination [22]. Due to the importance of this topic we give the review of existing approaches to Linked Open Statistical data and the use of ontologies (i.e. semantic models) in this field, which serve to support current Rosstat's initiatives and ongoing research on LOSD implementation for statistics in Russia.

2 Methods

The study of digitalization experience in Russia and abroad conducted in 2018 [2] represented a detailed review and put the ground to identify the following criteria characterizing the data-centric and model-oriented approach to the development of data-driven e-government:

- Linked open government data publication (use of semantic models).
- Application of information exchange models to achieve semantic interoperability.
- Use of open data model standards [2].

This year in the second round of assessment we used the same methodology to ensure the comparability of current research results. Therefore, we have conducted a comparative analysis of results (2018-2020), based on the previously identified criteria, showing the level of digital transformation in Russia in:

1. *Information sharing practice.* We again used the 5-star model [4] to measure the maturity of Open Data published on Russian Portal[2] and EU OD Portal[3], and then compared these results with the previous round of research (Sect. 4.1). The use of 5-star model is relevant to the existing methods of open data quality evaluation [4, 18].

2. *Preconditions to the establishment of data-centric and model-oriented paradigm in digital government.* Guided by the fact that such prerequisites are usually reflected in academic papers we used Google Scholar to reveal the works devoted to the digital transformation in public sector of Russia and abroad. We took 2019-2020 as a new publication period and compared achieved results to make the conclusion (Sect. 4.2).

According to expert opinion, linked OGD sets play an important role in the development of new public services development providing the data layer for innovative applications [16]. Moreover, a number of works devoted to the development of linked open statistical data [14, 15, 20] proves how LOSD (and LOD in general) projects supported by the groundwork of semantic models and standards [2] are able to bring new life to disparate sets of open government data and significantly increase their value for the development of new digital public services and data-driven government. We represent the review of the existing practice in LOSD and the application of such semantic models as ontologies (Sect. 3). We consider this approach necessary for the implementation of linked open statistics in Russia.

3 Review

In 2018 we conducted the first round of this research to study if Russia was ready for digital transformation of public sector. We represented rather detailed analysis and review to prove the role of data-centricity supported by models in digital transformation. That time we highlighted the needs to take effort and move towards a data-centric paradigm to achieve the goals of Russian Digital Economy program. The first review

---

[2] https://data.gov.ru/.

[3] https://www.europeandataportal.eu/en.

set the basis both for the developed research methods and for the identified assessment criteria, but it did not focus on the experience and the role of LOD in statistics.

In statistics Linked Open Data provides a comprehensive analysis of disparate and isolated datasets. In fact, many national statistical institutes and public agencies already actively follow the linked paradigm in publishing statistical data on the Internet [15]. Many standard vocabularies have been already proposed in this domain (for example, QB, SKOS, XKOS), and necessary semantic models have been developed (for example, in the LOD2 project[4]) [1]. Within the framework of the European Statistical System LOSD ESSnet has been recently established to collect and analyze best practices for publishing Linked Open Statistical Data implemented by statistical organizations of various levels (National Institutes, Eurostat). Pan European programs (for example, already mentioned ISA (see Footnote 2)) also support and encourage LOSD development.

In the process of LO(S)D creation developers feel the demand to significantly expand existing semantic standards to meet the requirements and reflect various statistical concepts classification and management specific features. The management of statistical concepts requires the use both hierarchies (e.g. in statistical classifications) and associations because they are more informative. At the same time, common (standard) relations are not sufficient to description of statistical concepts since it is necessary to determine either cause-effect or temporal interconnections. Thus, to remove SKOS[5] restrictions, for example, in 2013 UNECE and Eurostat proposed to use eXtended Knowledge Organization System (XKOS) [8]. Another example of SKOS extension is Japan Open Data Project providing an expanded set of external dictionaries and models.

Ontologies, successfully used over many years in the less formalized Semantic Web environment, provide naming, definition, and description of domain concepts, as well as various relations between these concepts. In official statistics, there are also some vocabularies, ontologies, or other semantic models, but as a rule they have no formal representation as well as they are usually not consistent with each other. Being one the leaders in digital transformation of public sector the United Kingdom pays great attention to the development of ontologies for government data, including statistics domain[6]. The Italian National Institute of Statistics (Istat) also reports on the use of ontologies for the integration and dissemination of statistical data. They follow Ontology-Based Data Management approach (OBDM) proposed to integrate several heterogeneous data sources. Italy has applied this experience on Istat Linked Open Data Portal[7].

The High-Level Group for the Modernization of Official Statistics is responsible for the implementation of ontologies at UNECE. It includes a special group formed to support standards and find the ways to develop, improve, integrate, and promote their implementation necessary for modernizing statistics. This group has operational responsibility for maintaining and developing the General Model of Activities for Statistical Organizations (GAMSO) [10], General model of statistical business

---

[4] http://aksw.org/Projects/LOD2.html.

[5] https://www.w3.org/2004/02/skos/.

[6] https://ukparliament.github.io/ontologies/.

[7] https://www.istat.it/en/ontology.

processes (GSBPM), General Model of Statistical Information (GSIM) [12] and Common Statistical Production Architecture (CSPA) [6].

The important activity for LOSD development is the creation of Core Ontology for Official Statistics (COOS) which began in November 2018. Its main objective is solving the problem of heterogeneity and fragmentation inherent for existing semantic models in statistics. Additionally its indirect, but important task is to bring together the expert community interested in developing ontologies for statistical data [7].

Following this review, which proves the importance of LOD supported by semantic models in statistics, we extended our research with a brief study of the initiatives taken in Russia in LOSD production and dissemination.

4 Results and Discussion

4.1 Information Sharing Practice

Experts widely use the 5-star open data deployment scheme [4] to evaluate the maturity level of open data.

Table 1 demonstrates aggregated statistics showing OGD publication in Russia (criterion 1) during the first assessment (2018) and at present time (2020) during our research.

In May 2020, the number of data sets available on the official Russian Federation Open Data Portal[8] remains minimal. 23,775 sets have been published over the entire period. This is 9 times less than in the USA[9] (211,000 sets) and 46 times less than on the European Data Portal (1,086,559 sets). Thus, the "open data available on the web (whatever format)", is still catastrophically small in Russia. Over the past two years, no more than 3,000 datasets were added. From this aspect Russian OGD is still at the 1st level of 5-star model. However, over 60% of OGD is available in CSV, and it maintains the position corresponding to the 3rd star. We should note that over this period not a single new dataset in RDF format has been published, and those 5 existing datasets have not been updated since 2016–2018. It confirms the fact, in Russia there is still no practice in LOD publication and development.

The study of open data registry[10] shows no positive changes in datasets updating. In 2020 from 15,234 datasets published under the tag "State" only 705 have the status "updated". Totally there are 2036 datasets updated since 2018. Many datasets have the reference to the data structure. It is represented in the card, describing the dataset. However, it remains difficult to get an idea what kind of data this dataset contains and how it can be interpreted.

It is not possible to identify the datasets with linked open data. There is no special section or signified tag in the Open Data Portal of Russia. Despite the regulatory requirements there are also no signs of pilot projects on official web sites representing "linked open data sets with the possibility of visualization" [17].

---

[8] https://data.gov.ru/.

[9] https://data.gov/.

[10] https://data.gov.ru/opendata/export/xls.

Table 1. Russian OGD Publication in 2018 vs 2020.

Format	Quantity of OGD sets May 2018	% of OGD sets May 2018	Quantity of OGD sets May 2020	% of OGD sets May 2020
Total	20,309		23,775	
CSV	12,187	60,01	15,250	64,14
XML	6,397	31,50	6,386	26,86
JSON	973	4,79	1,251	5,26
ZIP	71	0,35	111	0,47
XLS	55	0,27	70	0,29
XLSX	32	0,16	52	0,22
GZ	31	0,15	33	0,14
RDF	5	0,025	5	0,021

We must admit LOD creation is rather difficult not only for Russian e-government but also for many other countries. For example, the analysis of data available in European countries in accordance with the requirements of the 5-Star Open Data model [4] is represented in EU Open Data Maturity Report [18]. It reveals that most data (above 50%) on the national data portals is available according to the requirements of the first three stars. In 68% of countries more than 90% of the data still only corresponds to 1*. 64% of countries achieved 3* level with 50–90% of data. However that data according to four and five stars - the use of Uniform Resource Identifiers (URIs) (4*) as well as linking data so that a person or a machine can explore the web of data (5*) is not common in in the public sector open data of Europe yet. Only in 7% of countries most data (50–90%) correspond to 4*, and 96% of countries do not have open data at level 5*.

Nevertheless, the European Union considers the implementation of LOD as a crucial objective for the development of OGD. It is one of the maturity indicators confirming data quality. Unfortunately, Russia uses neither the 5-star model adopted in many countries (and we followed its requirements in this and previous work), nor any other measurable indicators to evaluate the quality of open data (Fig. 1).

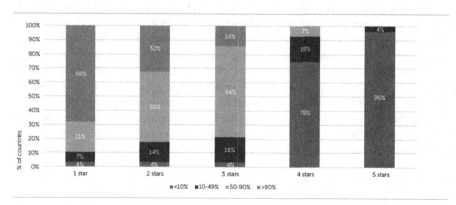

Fig. 1. The percentage of EU data provided in conformity to the 5-Star model [18].

Therefore, these updated research results cast doubt on the possibility to follow a data-centric paradigm in Russian e-government without changing the attitude to OGD publication together with linking data for its interpretation. Published datasets do not gain any special interest either from experts, press or business. Using open data for the benefit of the state and society has not become essential and has not even come to practice. That is why there is no "customer demand" for the data quality, as well as for its relevance and availability. Conversely, while data customers do not use (linked) open data constantly, data providers do not see the need to save the unique and correct meaning for further information sharing. At the same time, tracing the requirements of new conceptual documents, regulating data governance in Russia, it is impossible to identify the continuity of the existing Open Government legacy resources and their correspondence to the future systems and services developing within the framework of the National Data Governance System.

4.2   Preconditions to the Establishment of Data-Centric and Model-Oriented Paradigm in Digital Government

The volume of research papers published in the areas outlined in Sect. 2 is a good indicator for checking the relevance and practical significance of the studies in semantics for digital government. They aim to provide the effective information sharing and digitalization of the public sector. Thus, we consider it important to re-analyze recently published academic papers using the same keywords and search requests refining the query as we highlighted in our previous study [2]. We use Google Scholar (GS) as a source again sticking to the same indexing system, to maintain the integrity of this study and the comparability of its results.

To determine the relevance of the publications obtained as a result of a search request, we make an expert evaluation of the first thirty papers in order to understand how relevant they are to the chosen topic and criteria, using the same approach as at the previous study. The group of experts included specialists in semantic interoperability, LOD, domain models and programming from the community of our Center for Semantic Integration[11]. Table 2 presents comparative results for both periods.

Table 2 shows a significant growth of Russian academic studies dedicated to the application of open standards, open models (ontologies) and especially LOD to overcome the challenges of digitalization (Fig. 2). Thus, we should point not only the increase of this topic relevance and applicability. We can also determine that by 2020, Russian academic community, finally, has formed the prerequisites to establish a data-centric and model-oriented e-government, expressed via a wide range of research works. The current trend also proves the establishment of academic basis and the availability of experts actively working in this direction. It means their potential competence can and should be used in the implementation of the Concept.

Nevertheless, we must again highlight the lack of studies describing the experience of implementing the developed models and the actual use of LOD in Russian e-government. The relevance of search results retrieved for these requests in Russian is

---

[11] http://csi.semanticpro.org/

Table 2. Search results (GS).

Criteria	Queries	2017–2018				2019–2020				Growth	
		Total		Relevant from first 30, %		Total		Relevant from first 30, %		Total, %	
		en	ru	en	ru	en	ru	en	ru	en	ru
Open Standards	Open standards in digital government	17,900	1100	100	83	18800	1,530	93	80	5	39
	Open standards in e-government experience	5,100	2040	100	16	5,850	1,910	47	23	15	–6
Data Models, Semantics, Ontologies	Domain ontology in digital government	7,680	82	70	50	9,490	150	67	83	24	83
	Domain data models in e-government	4,870	2030	73	16	5,400	2320	63	33	11	14
	Semantic interoperability in e-government	5,120	26	70	50	739	25	83	50	–86	–4
Linked Open Data	Linked open data in e-government	4,700	415	90	13	5,020	645	93	23	7	55
	LOD e-government	77	27	100	10	84	19	93	0	9	–30

extremely low. Therefore, it brings us to the conclusion that there are no papers describing LOD pilot projects fulfilled in accordance with the roadmap [19] or they have not been presented to the academic community or to the practitioners yet. The lack of new research shows that these pilot projects have not received any continuation and the development of LOD in Russia is still rather complicated.

On the other hand, we point just a slight increase (by 6%–7%) in the number of academic papers published in English at the "Open Standards" and "Linked Open Data" criteria, as well as a significant decrease (by 13%) in the criterion "Data Models, Semantics, Ontologies". Until 2018, there were much more publications, especially obtained at searching "semantic interoperability". Apparently, the reason for this dynamic is the accomplishment of academic work in this area (its peak was in 2010–2016), while even its practical implementation is already at the final stage. Indeed, for example, in Europe the achievement of interoperability has been regulated over 10 years by the ISA program established by European Commission. This year the second stage of the program comes to the end, leaving a good basis, formed of implemented strategies, developed architectures, accepted standards, and applied models. LOD creation is also the task of a practical level. In accordance with "Open Data Maturity Report" the availability of LOD indicated open data quality [18].

Among the papers published in Russian for the entire search period, we found just a little more than fifty works using the query "semantic interoperability in e-government". Their relevance is only 50%. The reason for that is rather obvious. The state level does not support any research on this topic, despite its importance in e-government development and only a few enthusiasts continue their work.

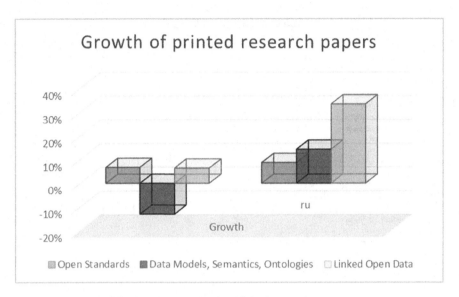

Fig. 2. The growth of published research papers.

4.3 Linked Open Statistical Data Initiatives in Russia

Statistics domain in Russia represents the effective implementation of international open standards for open government data. The Federal State Statistic Service uses object models, including SDMX and DDI[12] to improve customer understanding of data and increase the interoperability of statistical information systems. However, object models do not have the ability to deepen and extend. They are not interconnected, do not form multidimensional structures of concepts, as well as they do not reflect the variability of relations and associations that are essential for representing real-world entities. The effective reuse of open statistics is rather hampered. The primary reasons for that are (1) the heterogeneity of open statistical data environment, (2) data fragmentation and (3) the lack of the possibility to get meaningful interpretation [11, 13].

Semantic Web technologies (SW) serve to overcome these challenges. In accordance with SW principles data is presented in a standard form covering the data associations and relations. Semantic annotation allows both people and machines to determine a unique meaningful interpretation of data using semantic models (ontologies, thesauruses, glossaries, and dictionaries), which have no restrictions on complexity, coherence, and variation. These "embedded semantics offer significant advantages such as reasoning over data and operating with heterogeneous data sources" [5].

In Sect. 4.2 we place emphasis on a small percentage of LOD published among other datasets on OGD portals in Russia. We suppose the certain reason for that is the considerable effort required to complete this task. First, it is necessary to create and disseminate semantic models and then to use them for linking data as well as for adding

---

[12] https://sdmx.org/, https://ddialliance.org/.

the semantic annotation. This is rather complicated, labor-consuming, and multi-aspect work fulfilled only due to the significant joint efforts of IT specialists and domain experts. At the same time, these efforts invested in "linking" the data will get the reward by reaching a new level of statistical analysis using visualization tools and providing the opportunity to take full advantage of knowledge and context generated through the application of the semantic approach towards the development of data-driven government.

In September 2020 Russian Federal State Statistics Service together with Plekhanov Russian University of Economics started the research with the aim to develop the concept and the roadmap for the production and dissemination of linked open statistical data based on the study of international experience in terms of applied regulatory, methodological and technological approaches. This initiative is the first step to LOSD in Russia and representing its results will be the objective for our future work.

5 Conclusion and Recommendations

Within this research we put the aim to reexamine the readiness of Russian e-government and public sector in general for the digital transformation with the focus on LOD development and to compare it to the results obtained in 2018. Following three main criteria [2] we re-analyzed datasets published on official government open data portals, searched for the academic studies on semantic interoperability, the application of data models, as well as the experience of Linked Open Data development. Since statistics is one of the key cross-sector domains of OGD we give a review of existing practice in Linked Open Statistical data. The analysis of current LOSD initiatives both at the strategic and practical levels is rather useful for further research on LOSD implementation in Federal State Statistics Service.

This study shows the academic level in Russia has already provided rather solid background for the establishment of data-centric paradigm in digital government. The number of studies relevant to this topic has significantly increased since 2018. There are some papers, describing projects devoted to the development of semantic models in the public sector and other domains.

However, at the state level, there are still no conditions for data-centricity, despite the newly adopted conceptual documents. At the present time neither the existing international experience, nor the competencies of Russian experts, acquired over the past 10 years, come into account. The concept of "Government as platform", fundamentally important for digitalization, is often replaced by the "platforms for the government" development, as well as the implementation of data-driven government is reduced to data governance.

To achieve the objectives of the Concept for the creation and operation of National Data Governance System, in particular "to provide the ontological unity of government data contained in the information resources of public sector bodies and organizations" [22] we propose to focus on the building of the groundwork for data-driven government, realized in the development, distribution and reuse of semantic assets (ontologies, thesauri, dictionaries and other semantic models) necessary for the semantic annotation of data and sustainable information sharing. Encouraged by academic and expert community we expand the recommendations given earlier [2] and suggest to organize at the state level the collaboration of domain experts and IT specialists for LOD production and dissemination, improving the quality of government data. Within the joint Center of competence among other things they could work on:

- cataloging and managing of semantic assets, providing their dissemination and reuse.
- development and dissemination of information exchange models for cross-sector interaction in distributed heterogeneous information systems of e-government.
- LOD implementation for the comparison, analysis, and visualization of government data.
- providing the informational, methodological, organizational, regulatory, and legal support to the expert community in the field of semantic integration and semantic analysis.

References

1. Akatkin, Y.M., Laykam, K.E., Yasinovskaya, E.D.: Linked open statistical data: relevance and prospects. Voprosy statistiki. **27**(2), 5–16 (2020). (in Russia). https://doi.org/10.34023/2313-6383-2020-27-2-5-16
2. Akatkin, Y., Yasinovskaya, E.: Data-centricity as the key enabler of digital government: is russia ready for digital transformation of public sector. In: Chugunov, A., Misnikov, Y., Roshchin, E., Trutnev, D. (eds.) EGOSE 2018. CCIS, vol. 947, pp. 439–454. Springer, Cham (2019). https://doi.org/10.1007/978-3-030-13283-5_33
3. Attard, J., et al.: A systematic review of open government data initiatives. Gov. Inf. Quart. **32**(4), 399–418 (2015). https://doi.org/10.1016/j.giq.2015.07.006/
4. Berners-Lee, T.: 5-Star Open Data, Homepage. http://5stardata.info/en/
5. Chung, S.-H.: The MOUSE approach: mapping ontologies using UML for system engineers. Comput. Rev. J. **1**(1), 8–29 (2018). ISSN 2581-6640
6. Common Statistical Production Architecture (CSPA) and ESS Vision 2020 SERV. ESTP training course Item **7**(1), 21–22, Luxembourg, November (2017). https://ec.europa.eu/eurostat/cros/system/files/07a._validation_services_developed_in_the_ess_-_cspa.pdf
7. Cotton, F.: Core ontology for official statistics. In: Conference of European Statisticians. ModernStats World Workshop, pp. 26–28. Geneva, Switzerland, June (2019). https://www.unece.org/fileadmin/DAM/stats/documents/ece/ces/ge.58/2019/mtg2/MWW2019_COOS_Cotton_Abstract.pdf
8. Cotton, F., Cyganiak, R., Grim, R., Gillman, D.W., Jaques, Y., Thomas, W.: XKOS: an SKOS extension for statistical classifications. In: Proceedings 59th ISI World Statistics Congress (Session CPS203), pp. 25–30 August 2013, Hong Kong (2013). https://www.researchgate.net/publication/280740700_XKOS_An_SKOS_Extension_for_Statistical_Classifications
9. Cyganiak, R., Hausenblas, M., McCuirc, E.: Official statistics and the practice of data fidelity. In: Wood, D. (ed.). Linking Government Data https, pp. 135–151. Springer-Verlag, New York (2011). https://doi.org/10.1007/978-1-4614-1767-5

10. Economic commission for europe. In: Generic Activity Model for of Statistical Organisations (GAMSO) Conference of European Statisticians Geneva, pp. 15–17 June (2015). https://www.unece.org/fileadmin/DAM/stats/documents/ece/ces/2015/12-Generic_Activity_ Model_for_Statistical_Organisations_HLG.pdf
11. Hassani, H., Saporta, G., Silva, E.S.: Data Mining and Official Statistics: The Past, the Present, and the Future. Big Data. **2**(1), 31–43 (2014). https://doi.org/10.1089/big.2013.0038
12. High-level workshop on modernization of official statistics. In: Generic Statistical Information Model (GSIM). Nizhni Novgorod, Russian Federation, pp. 10–12 (June 2014). https://www.unece.org/fileadmin/DAM/stats/documents/fund.principles/2014/2-Generic_Statistical_Information_Model_EN.pdf
13. Janssen, M., Charalabidis, Y., Zuiderwijk, A.: Benefits adoption barriers and myths of open data and open government. Inf. Syst. Manage. **29**(4), 258–268 (2012). https://doi.org/10.1080/10580530.2012.716740
14. Kalampokis, E., Tambouris, E., Tarabanis, K.: A classification scheme for open government data: towards linking decentralised data. Int. J. Web Eng. Technol. **6**(3), 266–285 (2011). https://www.inderscience.com/
15. Kalampokis, E., Zeginis, D., Tarabanis, K.: On modeling linked open statistical data. J. Web Semant. **55**, 56–68 (2019). https://doi.org/10.1016/j.websem.2018.11.002
16. Mcbride, K., Matheus, R., Olesk, M., Kalvet, T.: The Role of Linked Open Statistical Data in Public Service Co-Creation. In: ICEGOV'18, Galway, Ireland, April (2018). https://doi.org/10.1145/3209415.3209446, https://www.researchgate.net/publication/322235606_The_Role_of_Linked_Open_Statistical_Data_in_Public_Service_Co-Creation
17. Open Data Council, the Governmental Commission for the Coordination of the Open Government Activities, Meeting Protocol, No. 1, Methodical recommendations on the organization and planning of activities in the field of open data. (2018). http://opendata.open.gov.ru/opendata/documents/, (in Russian)
18. Open Data Maturity Report 2019. In: European Data Portal, ISBN: 978-92-78-42052-9 ISSN: 2600-0512 (2019) https://doi.org/10.2830/073835, https://www.europeandataportal.eu/sites/default/files/open_data_maturity_report_2019.pdf
19. The Government Commission for the Coordination of the Open Government Activities, Action Plan, Open Data in Russian Federation, Meeting protocol 25.12.2014 No 10 (2014). http://rulaws.ru/goverment/Plan-meropriyatiy-Otkrytye-dannye-Rossiyskoy-Federatsii/, (in Russian)
20. Toots, M., Mcbride, K., Kalvet, T., Krimmer, R.: Open data as enabler of public service co-creation: exploring the drivers and barriers. In: International Conference for E-Democracy and Open Government, pp. 102–112 (2017)
21. Zuiderwijk, A., Janssen, M.: Open data policies, their implementation and impact: a framework for comparison. Gov. Inf. Quart. **31**(1), 17–19 (2014). https://doi.org/10.1016/j.giq.2013.04.003
22. Распоряжение Правительства РФ от 03.06.2019 № 1189-р «Об утверждении Концепции создания и функционирования национальной системы управления данными и плана мероприятий («дорожную карту») по созданию национальной системы управления данными на 2019–2021 годы». http://static.government.ru/media/files/jYh27VIwiZs44qa0IXJlZCa3uu7qqLzl.pdf

Intelligent Legal Decision Support System to Classify False Information on Social Media

Arsenii Tretiakov$^{(\boxtimes)}$, Elizaveta Kobets$^{(\boxtimes)}$, Natalia Gorlushkina,
Viktor Kumpan, and Alexandra Basakina

ITMO University, Saint-Petersburg, Russia
ars.tretyakov@gmail.com, www.kobets@yandex.com

Abstract. In the study, a decision support system for governance in the field of law was developed and the existing decision making model to conduct linguistic expertise of inaccurate public information in online media and social networks was improved, taking into account the human factor. The results of the proposed system are presented in a set of the formed recommendations, based on which the user makes a decision. The specific feature of the decision support system (DSS) is that it works with several types of false information in accordance with the Russian legislation against "fake news" addressed in the study. The adapted algorithms of Bayes classification were studied and built for effective work of the decision-making and classification module of false information. These algorithms were implemented in the system and a computational experiment on text classification was performed. The study examined the features of the Russian legislation on false information dissemination, and described the components and functionality of the proposed intelligent legal DSS, as well as its efficiency. This solution implies a widespread use of systems, application packages, special software and legal support for analytical work, obtaining forecasts and conclusions on the processes under study based on databases and expert judgment, considering the human factor and active influence of the controlled system on the governance process.

Keywords: Decision support system · Social media · Linguistic expertise · Fake news · Text classification · Legal decision support system · Law

1 Introduction

The rapid dissemination of "fake news" is facilitated by a huge flow of news information; limited time and attention that users can devote to watching the news feeds and choosing what to share [1]. The structure of social networks makes it possible to share links quickly, including through users' trust in each other [2]. The post-truth environment is characterized by blurring the boundaries between objective information and false news. The content of false information is often not completely inaccurate, but it can be misleading and mixed with real facts [3]. Other news is published to manipulate the market or gain certain advantages in economic activity and to discriminate against people.

© Springer Nature Switzerland AG 2020
A. Chugunov et al. (Eds.): EGOSE 2020, CCIS 1349, pp. 258–272, 2020.
https://doi.org/10.1007/978-3-030-67238-6_19

"Fake news is distinguished by its stylistically marked vocabulary and its rich metaphorization, so expressions play a much more important role than content [4]. But unfortunately "fake news" is too general a designation, so it was decided to analyze this type of information from the point of view of laws.

The increase in the number of legal cases on crimes related to the freedom of information abuse, honor and dignity protection or falsification of documents demonstrates the interest of people and companies as plaintiffs, public authorities and pre-trial bodies in such cases. Particular attention is paid to the regulation of such cases and legislation. In the Russian Federation in 2019, amendments [5] to Article 153 of the Federal Law "On Information, Information Technologies and Information Protection" were made, and the wording "unreliable socially significant information disseminated disguised as reliable messages …" was added. In April 2020, the Code of Administrative Offenses (CAO) [6] was amended in part 10 of Article 13.15 (abuse of mass media freedom), introducing fines for disseminating inaccurate socially significant information. Individuals, media officials and legal entities as subjects of responsibility can be a subject of abuse [7]. Statistics on cases related to false information dissemination are shown in Table 1 and demonstrate the interest in such cases.

Table 1. Statistics on cases related to false information dissemination.

Code and article	Period	Number of cases processed	Number of convicts
13.15 CAO	2019	682	377
13.15, 13.16 CAO	2018	590	456
	2017	319	208
	2016	66	42

Source: Legal Information Agency [8]

Article 128.1 paragraph 2 of the Criminal Code of the Russian Federation for libel in a "publicly displayed work or mass media" is punishable by fines. The Federal Law No. 100 of April 1, 2020 of the Criminal Code of the Russian Federation was supplemented [9] with Articles 207.1 and 207.2, which provide criminal punishment for "public dissemination of deliberately false information disguised as reliable messages about circumstances posing a threat to life and safety of the citizens" and entailing harm to human health. The law was introduced to control false information dissemination about the COVID-19 pandemic [10].

In connection with the expansion of the legal framework in judicial office work, new problems and tasks have emerged, namely, the need to ensure the quality of the definition of reliable and unreliable socially significant information. The linguistic analysis of the texts "containing credible models of reliable news reports makes it possible to investigate the semantic status of the speech acts, which have not been subject to forensic examination so far" [11]. It is necessary to determine how to use style to pass false information as true.

Based on these facts, the task of governance in the field of law is set to qualitatively determine false socially significant information. The result of this problem is the adoption and implementation of a competent management decision in a short time span. Thus, there is a need to develop a decision-making system that is not only capable of identifying unreliable socially significant information, but conducting an automated linguistic examination of the published news information, which the court, pre-trial authorities or government departments may consider as "unreliable information", "libel" or "abuse of mass media freedom".

2 Characteristics of Legal Regulation in Russia

Article 4 of the Mass Media Law of the Russian Federation uses the term "abuse of mass information freedom". If a publisher is caught in mass information freedom abuse twice during the year, then this becomes the reason for the termination of the mass media status. Abuse of media freedom is a form of deviant legally significant behavior, defined as a legal complex of media freedom performed by mass communication participants (individuals and media officials, including journalists) for the purpose of deliberately causing harm to the jural subjects. Table 2 provides a brief overview of Russian laws regarding false information dissemination.

Table 2. Legal measures in Russia against false information dissemination in news and social networks.

Code and article	Violation	Penalty measures
152 Civil Code	Protection of honor, dignity and business reputation	Fine
207.1 Criminal Code	Public dissemination of deliberately false information about circumstances that endanger the lives and safety of citizens	Fine, compulsory/corrective labor, restriction of freedom
207.2 Criminal Code	Public dissemination of deliberately false public information with grave consequences	Fine, compulsory/corrective labor, restriction of freedom
128.1 Criminal Code Part 2	Libel	Fine, restriction of freedom
13.15 CAO Parts 9, 10	Abuse of mass media freedom	Fine

If an individual defends their honor and dignity, then they apply to a court of general jurisdiction. However, if an individual is aggrieved by any activity related to making a profit, then the plaintiff applies to the arbitration court. If false information causes economic damage to a legal entity (a company, state corporation, public organization or a regional executive committee), then it applies to an arbitration court against an individual (a journalist, blogger, public person, private person) or another legal entity (mass media, a company). For a successful decision in favor of the plaintiff in court, the information can be considered both inaccurate and abusive to honor and dignity or business reputation, since inaccurate information is an inevitable component for satisfying such a claim. The media in case of losing the case are obliged, for example, to publish a refutation. Such suits are often used as a method of pressure.

A variety of options for determining inaccurate information, its possible damage to an individual, business, or economy, pose an acute problem of unambiguous interpretation of information reliable in court proceedings.

The definition of this interpretation is often subjective, which is expressed in human factor errors. Special attention is given to the regulation of false information dissemination cases and legislation. The development of intelligent legal decision support systems can increase the level of training and qualifications of lawyers, support risk and information management ensuring their efficiency, and also reduce the cost of legal services [12].

3   Related Work

Scientists from various fields of knowledge are engaged in solving this problem, which confirms the need to develop legal decision support systems, especially when working with inaccurate information, namely, the experience of detecting "fake news". A group of researchers from Kazan Federal University [13, 14] used DSS tools in the field of law to accurately determine the type of document on a test sample for several classes of claims in an arbitration process. Thus, it is possible to recommend the most likely litigation outcomes or mark important places to pay attention to in procedural actions using text analytics tools. The study [15] demonstrates the need to significantly increase the level of information of basic operations implemented in jurisprudence. Automated detection and assessment of the reliability of news information is discussed in [16–18], which present automation models, machine learning methods for detecting fake news in Facebook Messenger chat. Research groups, when detecting "fake" information in Russian news and social networks with machine learning methods, received an accuracy of 84.3% by analyzing posts on the social network VKontakte [19] and 92.5% in news and Twitter posts [20].

All the works reviewed show the relevance of the problem described, but do not provide a solution. The need to create a legal DSS is also due to the fact that decision-making is based on compliance with legislation, as well as predicting the legal consequences of the proposed actions, and the consequences of changes in legislation, as well as analyzing and conducting cases [21]. Detection of false information is a multi-criteria process, complex and largely dependent on the human factor.

Legal DSS, unlike other intelligent systems, are capable of flexible situation modeling, extraction and integration of database, knowledge base and models, a short list of key results and obtaining alternative solutions [22]. The system covers data processing algorithms aimed at identifying trends, models, relationships, and prospects for the development of decision-making processes. For example, using the multicriteria method, knowledge calculation of the algorithmic method allows decision makers to be more confident in the decisions offered by decision support systems. In current DSSs, mining methods are the logical result of various analytical tests [23].

Soft computing techniques, fuzzy logic and neural networks contribute to the development of intelligent systems for supporting legal decision-making. A research group [24] reviewed the Split-Up and IFDSSEA projects, which show how statistical and symbolic methods provide more effective decision-making in knowledge-based systems based on inaccurate data. Legal DSSs in corporate governance [22] were also considered, focusing on the most effective economic solutions.

The related works stress the importance of solving the problem, although they do not give the solution in the field of qualitative determination of unreliable and false information.

4 Methodology

When working with the identification of unreliable socially significant information, the presented decision support system in the field of law solves the main tasks of optimizing the search for information and ordering possible solutions based on a set of criteria and rules by which possible solutions can be evaluated and compared in the future [25]. To analyze and develop DSS proposals, independent data marts, methods of information retrieval, data mining, and neural networks are used. By its type, the proposed system is closer to decision-making systems based on knowledge (Knowledge Driven Base), since it includes expert and machine-derived assessments. The system relies heavily on expert knowledge as a central element in the knowledge base formation. The purpose of building a knowledge base is practical application of expert knowledge of the highest order for solving complex and non-standard applied problems. Within the framework of DSS development, a prerequisite is to access metadata for the subsequent operation with the available information.

The knowledge base (KB) uses a combined knowledge representation model, which includes a semantic network, production rules and frames. Usually, a legal DSS knowledge base contains the rule-based or the case-based or a hybrid base [22]. The combined knowledge representation model adequately corresponds to the specific properties of the displayed tasks and the capabilities of a decision maker, and also provides more efficient knowledge processing. The semantic network reflects the distributed nature of the tasks being solved, the frame slots reflect the states of the model parameters, and the system of production rules reflects the logic of the expert's actions in choosing the method.

The knowledge base is a set of statements and their application rules. The peculiarity of the legal sphere is that statements are short-term, usually volatile, and are expressed in determinable facts that need to be identified [26]. The developed knowledge base is used for expert assessment and creation of an expert subsystem for the development and formation of several solutions and descriptions of criteria, values, and weights [22] in the analyzed documents. For example, it determines the type of false information, the type of law violation, and the context of the document. The knowledge quality and completeness in KB is ensured by:

- experts with unique empirical and theoretical knowledge from various industries;
- professional examples and data;

– research in the field of law.

After the required minimum amount of knowledge and general principles regarding the identification and classification of inaccurate information are identified, a procedure for knowledge presentation and its display within the system is performed. For these purposes, each parameter is assigned a certain criterion to optimize the work with KB.

Within the framework of the current research, it was required to use database systems [27, 28] to accumulate information. By database (DB) all the data stored are meant. The database itself was introduced into an intelligent computing system for storing and processing document examples, as well as for effective document classifier training and identifying stylistic and contextual patterns containing inaccurate information in DB texts. The database used for training the model consists of sample texts that were obtained from cases of court decisions under Article 152 of the Civil Code "Protection of honor, dignity and business reputation". Materials of court decisions contain materials of publications in the mass media or social networks, through which the lawsuits took place. Fragments of such publications were used. According to one of the research experts, this article of the civil code is more suitable for training the model and classification due to the long history of its use, the elaboration of the article and the adequacy of the court decisions.

Table 3. Experts (Table 3) were recruited from various professional fields

№ Expert	The level of education	Professional field	Diploma work experience (years)	Total experience (years)
Expert 1	Higher, full-time, PhD	Applied and Mathematical linguistics, Forensic linguistic examination	33	33
Expert 2	Higher, full-time, the degree of specialist	Mass Media, Jurisprudence	20	20
Expert. 3	Higher, full-time, master's degree	Mass Media, Jurisprudence Infocommunication Technologies	14	14
Expert 4	Higher, full-time, master's degree	Economics, Infocommunication Technologies	3	4
Expert 5	Higher, full-time, the degree of specialist	Economics, Infocommunication Technologies	16	16
Expert 6	Higher, full-time, the degree of specialist	Infocommunication Technologies	11	14
Expert 7	Higher, full-time, the degree of specialist	Infocommunication Technologies	12	14
Expert 8	Higher, full-time, master's degree	Infocommunication Technologies	3	3

These data were marked and the connections between the constituent parts of the data were determined and structured. When designing DB to automate the search for false information in publications, processes, objects and users were studied. This database must contain texts of various types (classes) of inaccurate and false information in accordance with legislation and judicial practice.

In addition, to improve the classification accuracy and identify inaccurate and false information and the relevance of DSS itself, DB should be regularly updated by increasing the examples of texts containing false information. Unlike the Knowledge Base, the Database stores the texts themselves, which contain already identified and established inaccurate or false information.

As a result, the formed database structure ensured the effective search and data processing. The performance metric used is the accuracy of the classification of the analyzed documents (texts). The Bayesian algorithm was applied to classify documents and identify inaccurate information. Thus, it is possible to increase productivity in the development of this DSS. Based on DSS and KB, a logical conclusion or a solution is obtained.

Since the proposed system performs several functions, such as determination of originality degree, text tonality, the type of unreliable information, and degree of information reliability, it is necessary to use the model base (MB), which includes a set of model blocks, modules and procedures. These models mathematically represent various decision-making actions based on the built-in analytical tools [29]. The MB aims to transform data from a database into information required for decision making. This allows users to manipulate models to solve a specific problem, depending on the request and input data. The presented MB includes models that take advantage of quantitative (Gray relational analysis (GRA)) and qualitative (the analytic hierarchy process (AHP)) criteria.

In the decision-making process, a decision maker can involve experts to obtain the necessary assessments [30]. The person making the decision becomes the main user of the system in a corporate management system. Also, the user can be an internal or external expert of the organization who evaluates the system-issued solution. In the system under consideration, the decision maker may be a private or legal entity that is interested in identifying false information and the possibility of filing claims in court. They may also be a lawyer (specialist in the field of law) considering applications in such cases. In the system under consideration, the decision maker may be a private or legal entity that is interested in identifying false information and the possibility of filing claims in court. They may also be a lawyer (specialist in the field of law) considering applications in such cases.

As part of development and creation of the model and software infrastructure of the intellectual legal decision support system for further use in the field of law, flexible project management methods were applied. These methods are:

- Scrum method [31],
- Kanban method [32],
- Eisenhower's principle [32, 33],
- method of planning by G. Gantt [34].

The application of these methods made it possible to achieve a reduction in the work timing, improve work quality, optimize the resources used, adapt to the team in the face of time pressure, formalize the competencies of each participant, clearly assign roles and set individual boundaries of responsibility, as well as visualize the relationships between participants, and within iterations transparently display current tasks, predict expected tasks and evenly distribute the workload in the team.

The main task of the system is to perform a global search, monitor and verify the validity of legal norms governing the disputed legal relations. For this, the system conducts a linguistic examination of publications (based on the provided initial data from "fake news" database) that may fall under the categories of "unreliable socially significant information", "libel" and "abuse of mass media freedom", "false information dissemination."

5   Intelligent Legal Decision Support System

The study proposes a DSS structure to classify false socially significant information, which is based on the experience of developing [35] similar systems in the legal field [36] and the technology of risk-based audit, "providing a well-grounded decision, as at the stage control the auditor acts as an expert" [37]. The result of the proposed system is a set of recommendations for a user to make a decision considering expert's recommendations. The developed DSS is a cooperative and dynamic system [38]. It allows the decision-maker to change the decisions that the system offered. Considering the nature of the proposed system and the tasks solved in the study, DSS includes a knowledge base, database, decision-making module with a data analysis unit and a control unit, output results, user interface, a user, and expert evaluation of the decision. Figure 1 shows the DSS architecture.

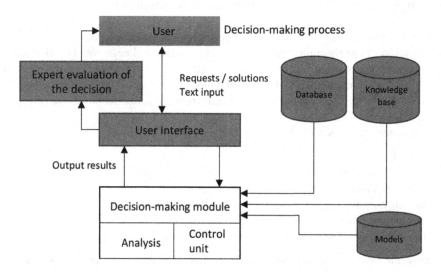

Fig. 1. Intelligent legal decision support system to classify false information.

The system has extended functionality, since according to the presented DSS architecture, the user enters the necessary query in the form of a text or keywords (for reference monitoring and the global search for publications in online mass media and social networks) about the subject of the analysis into the interface. Based on this request, data streams from the database and knowledge driven base are transformed in accordance with the requirements of the decision-making module. Based on the data available, the module analyzes risk patterns and classifies the resulting query result. Depending on the problem, the system uses a specific model, since each model type has its own unique characteristics. The interface includes a software system for managing a dialogue between a computer, a user, and an expert. When analyzing the data received at the input, the decision-making module analyzes a text based on databases, knowledge and trained models, detects false information and classifies it by the type of crime, depending on the style, content and context of the analyzed document (publication). The task of training the classifier was to consider positive and negative word or text connotation. The criteria initially set by an expert during the web material search were considered.

The system solutions are of a recommendation nature in the tasks of legal sphere governance. These recommendations help to automate the process of linguistic analysis and classify false information in publications in news and social networks. It is important to take into account the user's knowledge, supporting instructions and reference data that must be present in the system. Instructions and reference data issued by the system at the user request are usually not standard, but depend on the problem context. The decision-making module output results are sent for further analysis, detecting risk patterns based on the data, and are converted into a set of decisions when analyzing the published text for its reliability. The output results are sent back to the user interface and passed on to the end users.

6 Applying the Bayesian Document Classification

Before using the Bayes' algorithm in the considered model, the selected news articles and social media publications were divided into positive and negative. The division of these articles was carried out by experts according to certain criteria at the stage of search and selection of material when creating a database. Experts (Table 3) were recruited from various professional fields: infocommunication technologies, jurisprudence, and economics.

All experts identified the following criteria:

- text fidelity score;
- text originality score
- sentiment analysis;
- classification the type of inaccurate and false information;
- information truthfulness in mass media and social media;
- publication dissemination and original source.

Initially, the experts manually performed the search and demonstrated: how to perform the search, how the materials are selected, what criteria are followed and why, they also provided feedback on the stages and the results of the search. At the abstraction level, from a whole set of data search elements, as part of the decision-making process, the necessary sets were selected. This interaction made it possible to generalize expert experience and formulate search and analysis algorithms.

The following four-staged search algorithm is proposed both for searching by keys and by texts:

- receiving keys and/or texts from experts;
- entering keys and/or texts into the database;
- getting results;
- result output to the interface.

Followed by the search algorithm is the analysis algorithm (Fig. 2), which consists of six stages:

1. defining keys and/or texts;
2. determination of criteria for data evaluating;
3. entering keys and/or texts of the search;
4. receiving a data array for the subsequent processing;
5. selection of materials from the database that match the criteria,
6. result output to the interface.

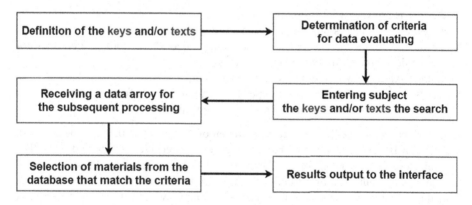

Fig. 2. The analysis algorithm

The first three stages are conducted manually and the last three are automated. Based on the data, the system automatically identifies fragments of the analysed text and classifies it as a possible violation of law. In accordance with this, the system then automatically offers an assessment of the text being analysed, and the expert manually decides whether to accept the proposed decision. The expert also gives his assessment of the text based on the proposed decision. Then, based on this analysis, an algorithm model (see Fig. 3) was built and the working algorithms of various systems that work automatically were analyzed. The automated search is based on news web-sites and social media. As a result, a search algorithm for keywords and expert search texts has been formulated and developed.

Also, a software implementation for automated analysis based on open sources has been performed. The results obtained are presented in the form of text publications with references to the specified keywords to classify inaccurate information by type.

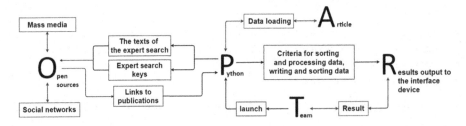

Fig. 3. The algorithm for automated search and sorting of publications.

This made it possible to develop a sequence to solve publication classification task during technical development of intelligent DSS. The structure of work by tasks included both standard operations and non-standard ones. As part of text preprocessing task using natural language processing, it was required to remove stop words that do not carry a semantic load to obtain a high-quality training of the classification model:

- the text is converted to lowercase;
- all punctuation marks and other symbols are removed;
- words that do not carry a semantic load are excluded (these words are constant for any model training and are in open sources);
- lemmatization of words in the text is carried out;
- words from a sentence are sent to a positive array if they are from a positive text, or to a negative array if they are from a negative sentence.

In a situation, where there is a certain amount of the analyzed material, the next task is to train a Bayesian forecasting model based on the received words and texts. The algorithm proposed is ideal for this task, since it does not require a large amount of data, and as a result, it allows to obtain a high prediction rate of about 98.32%. This algorithm is based on the Bayes formula. For example, weight is assigned to certain keywords in the learning process; if a certain word occurs in the expert word array, then its weight immediately increases by n%.

The next step was the clustering of unknown/new publications based on the already trained text corpus. For the classification of the unknown publications (documents), text processing was performed: the words are not arranged in random order, but are in the same order in which they were originally in the sentences. The limits of application of the Bayesian algorithm by the authors in the research are related to the use of the Bayesian network approach. It was suggested to use a modified Bayesian network for calculations to provide feedback in the model upon receipt of data.

7   Discussion and Future Work

The study attempted to demonstrate the structure of the main model related to the field of linguistic and legal analysis. The main result of the presented study is the development of a decision support system for the legal governance and the improvement of the existing models and methods to increase the efficiency and reliability of classifying false social significant information considering the human factor. The system can also be used to improve and complement the existing methods for detecting fake news and checking facts in online media and social networks. The algorithms of the Bayes classification were adapted and built for an effective decision-making module to classify false information. These algorithms were implemented in the system and a computational experiment on text classification was performed.

The results obtained can be used in software development for implementation in public organizations, public and private enterprises as a legal decision support system when working with false socially significant information published in media and social networks. Even though the proposed DSS does not solve the problem of fake news dissemination, it helps to classify the writing style that is not inherent in true news with 98% accuracy. In combination with other available methods, such as crowdsourcing, classification of sources and authors, fact checking and other types of text analysis, this approach can give a maximum level of result accuracy with low resource costs.

Further research in developing methods for false information identification in the field of law will improve legal measures against false information dissemination in news and social networks. In addition to the base model developed and presented in the study, individual internal models are being developed, which together have interaction with the base model and among themselves. The subsequent application of this model is possible in the field of justice within the DSS model framework for the European Union and other countries.

The development of individual internal models is essential to the smooth functioning of each individual tool in the process of analyzing the structure and constituent elements of texts and documents. Aspects of contact with texts in open sources of information on the Internet are related exclusively to the study of jurisprudence, legal norms and requirements of individual codes, federal laws, structure of documents and messages, grammar, word formation.

As a result, the principle of transparency, impartiality and reliability [39] is ensured regarding the analysis of posted documents and texts in open sources on the Internet. The application and practical use of this basic model will allow authors who post texts in open sources to check the texts for compliance with legal requirements and comply with the established norms and laws on the Web. This is socially significant for more ethical online behavior through the use of artificial intelligence. Then the user is a conscious participant in the communication and he consciously controls the information posted and published by him.

References

1. Klinkova, D.A.: "Fake News" in social networks: problems and solutions. In: collection: Modern Technologies: Current Issues, Achievements and Innovations. Collection of articles of XII International Scientific and Practical Conference. In 2 parts. Under the General Editorship of G.Y. Gulyaev, pp. C. 233–235 (2017). (in Russian)

2. Magallón Rosa, R.: Desinformación en campaña electoral. Telos. FUNDACIÓN TELE-FÓNICA.   https://telos.fundaciontelefonica.com/desinformacion-en-campana-electoral/. Accessed 15 May 2020. (in Spanish)

3. Vivar, J.M.F.: Inteligencia artificial y periodismo: diluyendo el impacto de la desinformación y las noticias falsas a través de los bots. Doxa Comunicación. Revista interdisciplinar de estudios de Comunicación y Ciencias Sociales, pp. 197–212 (2019). (in Spanish)

4. Koretskaya, O.V.: Fake News as an object of study of media linguistics (on the material of English-speaking mass media). Philological sciences. Questions of theory and practice, № 9-1 (75), pp. 118–120 (2017)

5. Federal law from 2019/03/18 № 31-FL About making changes to the article 15-3 of the Federal law: «On information, information technologies and information protection» . http://kremlin.ru/acts/bank/44084. Accessed 29 May 2020. (in Russian)

6. Veretennikova, K., Makutina, M., Rozhkova, E., Galanina, A.: The disease waited for urgent corrections. Ksenia Veretennikova, Maria Makutina, Elena Rozhkova, angelina Galanina. "KommersantKsenia Veretennikova, Maria Makutina, Elena Rozhkova, angelina Galanina. "Kommersant", №58, p. 3, April 2020. (in Russian)

7. Guryanova, V.V.: Abuse of freedom of mass information: concept, features and types. In: Legal Culture and Legal Standards of Interaction Between the Legal and Journalistic Communities: Multimedia Trends, pp. 19–34 (2017). (in Russian)

8. The legal information agency is registered by the Federal service for supervision of communications, information technologies and mass communications, certificate no. FS 77-63321. http://апи-пресс.рф (the domain in the zone.RF) or, http://legalpress.ru (the domain in the zone .RU), Accessed 01 June 2020. (in Russian)

9. Federal law of April 1, 2020 N 100-FL « About modification of the Criminal code of the Russian Federation and articles 31 and 151 of the Criminal procedure code of the Russian Federation » . « Russian newspaper » . Federal issue 72(8126) from 2020/04/03. https://rg.ru/2020/04/03/uk100fz-dok.html. Accessed 29 May 2020. (in Russian)

10. Mislivskaya, G.: Sovfed approved laws on punishment for fakes about coronavirus. Galina Mislivskaya. «Rossiyskaya Gazeta» from 2020/03/31. https://rg.ru/2020/03/31/sovfed-odobril-zakony-o-nakazanii-za-fejki-o-koronaviruse.html. Accessed 29 May 2020. (in Russian)

11. Galyashina, E.I.: The phenomenon of "fake" in the aspect of forensic linguistic expertise. In: Actual Problems of Criminalistics and Forensic Examination, pp. 26–31 (2019). (in Russian)

12. Zeleznikow, J.: Building Intelligent Legal Decision Support Systems: Past Practice and Future Challenges. In: Fulcher, J., Jain, L.C. (eds.) Applied Intelligent Systems. Studies in Fuzziness and Soft Computing, vol. 153, pp. 201–254. Springer, Heidelberg (2004). https://doi.org/10.1007/978-3-540-39972-8_7

13. Alekseev, A., Katasev, A., Kirillov, A.: Prototype of classifier for the decision support system of legal documents. In: CEUR Workshop Proceedings, vol. 2543, pp. 328–335 (2020)

14. Alekseev, A.A., Katasev, A.S., Khassianov, A.F., Tutubalina, E.V., Zuev, D.S.: Intellectual information decision support system in the field of economic justice. In: CEUR Workshop Proceedings, vol. 2260, pp. 17–27 (2018)

15. Yakutko, V.F.: Decision support systems in law. V. F. Yakutko. The legal life of modern Ukraine: materials of Intern. Sciences. Conf. Prof. and graduate student. Responsible for the release V. M. Dremin; NU OYA, Southern region. The Center national Academy of legal Sciences of Ukraine. Fenix, Odessa, vol. 2, pp. 562–564 (2014). (in Ukraine)
16. Shu, K., Sliva, A., Wang, S., Tang, J., Liu, H.: Fake news detection on social media: a data mining perspective. ACM SIGKDD Explor. Newsl. **19**(1), 22–36 (2017)
17. Popat, K., Mukherjee, S., Strötgen, J., Weikum, G.: Credibility Assessment of Textual Claims on the Web. In: Proceedings of the 25th ACM International on Conference on Information and Knowledge Management, pp. 2173–2178. Indianapolis, Indiana (2016)
18. Vedova M.L., et al.: Automatic online fake news detection combining content and social signals. In: 22nd Conference of Open Innovations Association (FRUCT), pp. 272–279. IEEE (2018)
19. Vychegzhanin, S., Kotelnikov, E.V.: Stance detection in russian: a feature selection and machine learning based approach. In: AIST (Supplement), pp. 166–177 (2017)
20. Lozhnikov, N., Derczynski, L., Mazzara, M.: Stance Prediction for Russian: Data and Analysis. In: Ciancarini, P., Mazzara, M., Messina, A., Sillitti, A., Succi, G. (eds.) SEDA 2018. AISC, vol. 925, pp. 176–186. Springer, Cham (2020). https://doi.org/10.1007/978-3-030-14687-0_16
21. Waterman, D.A., Paul, J., Peterson, M.: Expert systems for legal decision making. Expert Syst. **3**(4), 212–226 (1986)
22. Mikštienė, R., Keršulienė, V.: Legal decision support system application possibility in corporate governance. In: 9th International Scientific Conference «Business and Management» (2016)
23. Trakhtengerts, E.A.: Computer systems for management decisions support. Prob. Manag. **1**, 13–28 (2003). (in Russian)
24. Zeleznikow, J., Nolan, J.R.: Using soft computing to build real world intelligent decision support systems in uncertain domains. Decis. Support Syst. **31**(2), 263–285 (2001)
25. Starodubtsev, A.A.: Actual problems of aviation and cosmonautics. Decis. Support Syst. **2**(12), 99–101 (2016). (in Russian)
26. Muromtsev, D.I.: Introduction to expert systems. ITMO, St. Petersburg. pp. 8–86 (2005). (in Russian)
27. Date, C.J.: An Introduction to Database Systems. 8th edn. Williams, Moscow (2005). ISBN 5-8459-0788-8
28. Connolly, T.M., Begg, C.E.: Database Systems: A Practical Approach to Design, Implementation, and Management, 6th edn. (2015)
29. Pitchipoo, P., Venkumar, P., Rajakarunakaran, S.: Modeling and development of a decision support system for supplier selection in the process industry. J. Ind. Eng. Int. **9**(1), 1–15 (2013). https://doi.org/10.1186/2251-712X-9-23
30. Kravchenko, T.K.: Expert decision support system. Open Educ. **6** (2010). (in Russian)
31. Kniberg, H., Skarin, M.: Kanban and Scrum - making the most of both. C4Media, Publisher of InfoQ.com (2010)
32. Anatolyevna, K.O., Rimovna, G.D.: Organization of time: from personal effectiveness to the development of the company. Vestnik SUSU. Series: Education. Pedagogical sciences chapter 2 (2014). (in Russian)
33. Batalov, D.A., Sergeevna, M.S.: Methods and tools of operational and strategic controlling. Sci. J. KubGA **67**(03), 1–19 (2011). (In Russian)
34. Brcic, M., Mlinaric, D.: Tracking predictive gantt chart for proactive rescheduling in stochastic resource constrained project scheduling. J. Inf. Organ. Sci. Chap. **42**(2), 179–192 (2018)

35. Khan, I., et al.: Conversion of legal text to a logical rules set from medical law using the medical relational model and the world rule model for a medical decision support system. In: Informatics Multidisciplinary Digital Publishing Institute, vol. 3, No. 1, p. 2 (2016). https://doi.org/10.3390/informatics3010002

36. Zuev, D.S., Marchenko, A.A., Khasyanov, A.F.: Application of tools for intellectual analysis of texts in jurisprudence. In: CEUR Workshop Proceedings, vol. 2022, pp. 214–218 (2017

37. Massel, A.G., Gaskova, D.A.: Ontological engineering for the development of an intelligent system for threat analysis and risk assessment of cyber-security of energy facilities. Des. Ontol. **92**(2(32)), 175–179 (2019)

38. Haettenschwiler, P.: Neues anwenderfreundliches Konzept der Entscheidungsunterstützung. Gutes Entscheiden in Wirtschaft, Politik und Gesellschaft. Zurich: Hochschulverlag AG, pp. 189–208 (1999)

39. European Union, Report/Study, Ethics guidelines of April 8, 2019 «Ethics guidelines for trustworthy AI». https://ec.europa.eu/digital-single-market/en/news/ethics-guidelines-trustworthy-ai. Accessed 29 May 2020

Factors of Open Science Data Sharing and Reuse in the COVID-19 Crisis: A Case Study of the South Korea R&D Community

Hanna Shmagun[1], Charles Oppenheim[2], Jangsup Shim[3],
Kwang-Nam Choi[1], and Jaesoo Kim[1(✉)]

[1] Korea Institute of Science and Technology Information (KISTI),
Korea University of Science and Technology (UST), Daejeon, South Korea
hanna.shmagun@gmail.com, {knchoi,jaesoo}@kisti.re.kr
[2] Robert Gordon University, Aberdeen, Scotland, UK
c.oppenheim@rgu.ac.uk
[3] Korea Advanced Institute of Science and Technology (KAIST),
Daejeon, South Korea
sjshlliit@gmail.com

Abstract. Semi-structured interviews with South Korean experts were conducted to explore enabling and limiting factors influencing open commutation of scholarly outputs and data in public health emergencies, such as the COVID-19 outbreak. The study provided a set of contextual/external, institutional/regulatory, resource, and individual/motivational factors with some relevant examples. The results revealed the highest importance of institutional/regulatory factors in such situations. The findings might be useful for a country's comprehensive Open Science policy development as a component of future outbreak preparedness.

Keywords: Open science · Data sharing · Scholarly communication · Public health emergency · COVID-19 pandemic · South Korea

1 Introduction

While states have closed their borders in response to the COVID-19 outbreak, science has in contrast opened up well beyond research communities by disseminating key research results. The aim of this paper is to identify those enabling and limiting factors, which affect Open Science (OS) practices (that is, online sharing and reuse of research data and outcomes) in a pandemic crisis. These include both pandemic-specific and broader factors related to national R&D information infrastructure put in the South Korean context. The study has been driven by an acknowledgement of the rapidly increased practical value of OS for society at large, and particularly for combatting public health emergencies. The ongoing coronavirus pandemic is the main focus of this study.

In recent months, numerous OS initiatives and collaborative platforms have been set up by different institutions around the world. The leading scholarly publishers, such as Elsevier, Springer and Wiley, have granted open access to some of their coronavirus-related subscription-based content from high-impact journals, including The Lancet

© Springer Nature Switzerland AG 2020
A. Chugunov et al. (Eds.): EGOSE 2020, CCIS 1349, pp. 273–290, 2020.
https://doi.org/10.1007/978-3-030-67238-6_20

and British Medical Journal. The European Commission has recently launched a research data sharing and reuse portal to facilitate coronavirus research and to encourage research collaboration. UNESCO has called on governments to reinforce scientific cooperation and integrate OS into their strategies to mitigate the global pandemic. South Korea, in particular, has improved the user-friendliness of its previously developed national R&D information sharing and reuse services by providing COVID-19 Special Issues on multiple platforms.

However, many of the OS initiatives launched during the pandemic are seen as ambiguous, serving at best as a temporary reaction rather than a permanent policy change. For instance, international scholarly publishers are expected to return to their traditional subscription-based services as soon as the pandemic is over. It means that if later on, some researchers make new discoveries about COVID-19 or other coronaviruses, which might be helpful for future outbreak preparedness, much of the scientific evidence will no longer be available free of charge.

In practice, efficiently communicating scientific information has yet to become the norm, even within South Korea, which had already invested a significant effort to set up its national OS policies and practices before the pandemic. It is hoped that our results might offer helpful insights for the institutions planning to improve their general R&D information sharing and reuse policies and services, on the one hand, and to develop specific mechanisms for responding to both current and possible future pandemics, on the other hand.

2 Related Work

The current pandemic has encouraged a general awareness of the concept of OS, which aims to transform traditional science by making research more open, global, collaborative, creative and closer to society. It is about the way research is carried out, disseminated, deployed and transformed by digital tools and networks [1]. OS data can be defined as any scientific information resources (e.g., pre-registration plans, research data, scholarly outputs, research software codes, etc.), which are produced at each stage of an open-research life cycle, vigorously verified according to the respective academic fields' requirements towards the shared praxis, and are findable, accessible, interoperable and reusable both by machines and by people [2].

A number of previous studies have examined the factors influencing scientists' data sharing and/or reuse behaviour in general [3] or within particular disciplines – for example, in health and life sciences [4], food science and technology [5], and astrophysics [6]. A widely cited study (co)-authored by Y. Kim argues that all factors can be categorised into four groups: (1) *institutional factors*, including funding agency's policy; (2) *resource factors*, including data repositories; (3) *individual factors*, including researchers' perceived efforts, benefits, and risks; and (4) *other organisational and environmental factors* [7].

A few studies have partially examined the enabling factors or barriers of OS data sharing and reuse in public health emergencies [8–11]. There have also been studies on the topic conducted by international organisations. For example, in response to the previous SARS, MERS-CoV, Ebola and Zika outbreaks, the Global Research

Collaboration for Infectious Disease Preparedness (GloPID-R), an international consortium of research funding organisations, commissioned a study about policies, practices, and infrastructure supporting pathogens data sharing in public health emergencies [12]. The Research Data Alliance (RDA) COVID-19 Working Group has developed guidelines on data sharing under the present COVID-19 circumstances, focusing primarily on Omics, Clinical, Epidemiology, and Social Sciences research domains [13]. OECD has published an opinion piece "Why Open Science is critical to combatting COVID-19", where some enablers and barriers of OS in the crisis context are drawn up and some policy actions are recommended [14]. However, in our opinion, the results of these and other studies have not been sufficient to provide comprehensive policy recommendations on the issue.

3   Methodology

In order to achieve the aim of the study, we used a single-case research strategy by conducting semi-structured interviews with eleven experts from the South Korea R&D community. A case study based on semi-structured interviews is a well-established method of undertaking qualitative research. Such an approach is useful for investigating a complex contemporary phenomena within its real-life context, which require holistic and in-depth examination [15].

Interview questions were developed by the authors using NVivo software for open, axial, and selective coding of the literature following a systematic literature review. The PRISMA protocol [16] was used for identification, screening, and inclusion/exclusion of literature from Web of Science and SCOPUS databases. From an initial collection of 375 papers, we finally selected 40 papers for NVivo qualitative analysis.

Using a purposive (expert/judgmental) sampling technique [17], we selected researchers and practitioners from Biomedical and Health Sciences as well as researchers from the S&T policy and OS/Open Access fields. The interviewees represent different generations, have different levels of career experience, and were affiliated with the following organisations: the Korea Institute of Science and Technology Information (KISTI), the Korean Bioinformation Center (KOBIC), the Korea Research Institute of Chemical Technology (KRICT), the Korea Institute of Science and Technology (KIST), Science & Technology Policy Institute (STEPI), the Republic of Korea Navy Marine Corps (Medical Service), and Chungnam National University.

The interviews were conducted between May 11 and May 24, 2020 using face-to-face interviews, telephone interviews, and email exchanges as appropriate. All interviews were transcribed and analysed using NVivo following the same coding procedure as it was used for a systematic literature review.

4   Findings

This study defined a set of factors affecting OS practices in public health emergencies, such as the COVID-19 crisis. Multiple factors, first identified from the literature review and then tested/supplemented by interviews, were designated to four groups using Kim's typology noted above. These are *contextual or external factors* (political and socio-economic context, including public health emergency circumstances); *institutional and regulatory factors* (regulatory regime and leadership; interdisciplinary and cross-sector partnerships; and research communities' norms); *resource factors* (ICT[1] infrastructure, financial and human resources); and *individual and motivational factors* (perceived personal efforts; perceived risk of negative consequences; perceived extrinsic and intrinsic benefits; multiple dimensions of trust related to OS practices).

4.1   Contextual or External Factors

Emergency Management Experience. All interviewees agreed that a public health emergency situation itself extremely encourages OS development and can be considered as its possible contributing factor. As it was stated by an interviewee, "In facing a public health crisis, which has great impact on everything from a small retailer to a national government, everyone feel urgency to overcome it. It leads people, who are capable of handling this crisis, to cooperate. Those multiple cooperations would accelerate OS data sharing practices and it would enable researchers to achieve their goals faster for overcoming the crisis." Additionally, another interviewee added that emergency experiences (its success stories and failures) become long-lasting and heightened memories. In a post-pandemic world, countries such as South Korea that used OS as a tool for combatting COVID-19, can become a model for other nations to implement OS for non-emergency and emergency situations.

Globalisation of Open Science. Another factor, which the majority of participants talked about, is globalisation and global interdependence. OS along with Open Data have become global trends. Some participants mentioned that Korea started its path towards transforming traditional scholarly communication via OS after the concept had become globally recognised and some initiatives had been adopted in Europe, the US, and other regions: "OS is a global idea, trend and we are trying to follow it as other countries do."

Political Openness and Open Science. The interviewees shared the position that in a pandemic outbreak global scholarly communication, based on OS principles, is highly dependent on a country of origin of a novel pathogen. At the beginning of the current pandemic, China, a country of origin of COVID-19, failed to provide the global scientific community with timely, transparent, and trustworthy information about a novel coronavirus. One interviewee gave an example – Chinese officials reported that the first confirmed case came from the Huanan Seafood Market in Wuhan in December 2019, but later research [18] provided evidence that the market was not the very source of

---

[1] Information and Communication Technologies

origin and that a new coronavirus was likely to appear earlier than it was reported. Due to such misinformation, the global scientific community wasted time striving to understand the virus' unique characteristics and its pathogenesis. Some participants linked it with a communist political regime in China and concluded that in non-democratic countries there are usually less space for OS practices. In contrast, the South Korea's democratic regime, combined with its deep-rooted collectivist culture, was characterised as generally favourable for OS.

Impact of Conflicts. The COVID-19 has also demonstrated that any international or internal socio-political conflicts is a limiting factor for effective scholarly communication during the outbreak. One of the interviewees gave an example of the current tension between the US and China triggered by a coronavirus: "The conflict between the US and China over COVID-19 slows down the global cooperation process, which can also challenge OS practices. We can see a lot of recent international OS initiatives and crowdsourcing projects. But there is some backlash caused by this conflict. So any kind of conflicts between countries can badly affect international cooperation, including cooperation on OS."

Competition in Science. Global scientific competition to develop a coronavirus vaccine was seen as another external limiting factor of OS. It can prohibit sharing pre-clinical animal data and data from human clinical trials of candidate vaccines. As one interviewee said, "There are not only commercial reasons to withhold vaccine R&D data but also a risk to the country's reputation in case of low-quality evidence."

Level of Economic Development. Interviewees also stated that it is difficult to implement OS in developing countries with low-resource settings. Such countries have an investment demand for more basic necessities to improve people's standard of living and cannot afford additional expenses in scientific infrastructure and services. "Not only government agencies but also the general public can be against OS expenses. In such countries, there is usually a low status of science and there is a general opinion that scientists live off the state's generosity by not producing qualitative outcomes," said an interviewee.

Digital Divide. Some participants expressed a concern that the digital divide – inequalities in ICT access and skills between developed and developing countries and between different social groups – can be a barrier to practice OS in both non-emergency and emergency situations: "Research should be carried out and disseminated in both ways (offline and online). We cannot totally replace traditional science by OS. It is only a supplement to a traditional scholarly communication, otherwise the minority groups, such as senior researchers or the disabled, can be discriminated."

Government-Citizen Collaboration. Interviewees saw government-citizen collaboration as a factor that has positively influenced Korea's general response to COVID-19 and OS data sharing practices in particular. "Korean people are very collaborative with government, especially in any crisis. We feel a duty to follow government policy. Even people who have different political views support the government in a crisis. For example, 20 years ago during the IMF crisis in Korea many people supported government policy and initiatives to overcome the crisis, the same as they did in the COVID-19 outbreak now."

4.2 Institutional and Regulatory Factors

Regulatory Regime and Leadership. In general, there were two kinds of interviewees' responses about OS legislation, regulation, and policies. Some interviewees (mostly from Biomedical and Health Sciences) did not know much about these issues: "Scientists generate data, do research, and publish their outputs in international journals… I don't think national regulations affect much scientists' daily activities. So I can't say much about it."

The others, partly involved in OS policy-making, said that Korea has not properly developed yet a strong legal and regulatory framework for R&D data and outcomes sharing: "Korea has a strong Open Government Data policy…but we don't have a well-developed, coherent OS policy, such as in the European Union. It is an ongoing process in Korea." Some interviewees commented that the Korean government, research funders, and researchers themselves still do not fully understand the importance, advantages of OS. Thus, having an agency, such as the Korea Institute of Science and Technology Information (KISTI)[2], with a strong leadership to promote and coordinate national OS policy across multiple actors is a crucial enabler for further improvements in this area.

Flexibility of Regulation. All participants agreed that a "top-down" mandatory approach with legally binding instruments and enforcement mechanisms for government-funded research projects – such as the submission of Data Management Plans (DMP), research reports, and relevant research data and outcomes required by funding agencies – is effective to promote OS practices, especially in a public health emergency. At the same time, many participants argued that overregulation can be a burden and demotivation for scientists to carry out government-funded research. Some interviewee stated that these days the Ministry of Science and ICT of the Republic of Korea has started to think about a flexible regulatory approach to OS, which should provide some freedom for researchers and develop multiple incentive structures rather than to impose very strict rules on researchers. An example of such flexibility is that not all government-funded researchers have to submit a DMP: "In Korea, DMP applies in a selective manner… According to the amendments to the Article 25 of the Regulations on the Management, etc. of National Research and Development Projects[3] adopted in 2019, each ministry is responsible for deciding which research project/programme needs DMP… Usually these are projects of high national importance."

Special Emergency Measures. Some participants added that "in times of a crisis, the central and local governments obtain emergency power (extra-legal power) so that they can do anything from banning outdoor gathering, closing clubs to cross-domain data sharing mandates," "it is kind of control tower which oversees everything, what is needed more urgently and … thus they can direct projects, initiatives to fulfil necessities they encounter." Thus, in a crisis such as COVID-19, governments can set up special measures, including those related to scholarly communication, which are not

---

[2] https://www.kisti.re.kr/eng/

[3] http://www.law.go.kr/법령/국가연구개발사업의관리등에관한규정

typical for non-emergency situations. As many participants stated, the most important requirement for scholarly communication in a pandemic is to "get the right information as soon as possible." The examples of the 'fast track' mechanisms, which should be implemented in such a situation, are liberalisation and expediting of regular bureaucratic procedures involved in a research life cycle (i.e. data production, sharing of preliminary findings, data and final results publishing), simplification and speeding up of the budgeting and funding processes, etc. In particular, the interviewees commented that in the COVID-19 pandemic, local Korean journals and research communities have not been ready enough for expedited peer-reviewed publication, though some domestic preprint services have been newly developed (e.g., preprint service on the Korea Open Access platform for Researchers (KOAR)[4], launched in March 2020). Another example of special measures, adopted by the Korean government during the current pandemic, is releasing some privacy-sensitive data – movement data of confirmed or potentially infected individuals, obtained from telecommunication and credit card companies and CCTV (closed-circuit television video surveillance). These data are anonymised; analysed to identify movement patterns; and then delivered to the public via Emergency Mobile Alerts in order they can avoid the infected premises and places. However, as some interviewees mentioned, all these special measures and mechanisms should be rather flexible and should accommodate uncertainty and changing nature of an emergency. It is more likely that such procedures should not be implemented on a permanent basis, but until the end of the emergency situation, for example, until the development of a vaccine.

Balance Between Collective and Individual Interests. Another important issue raised by the interviewees is how to protect individual interests while facilitating open scholarly communication based on data sharing. One of the interviewees said: "No matter how good is the intention, government bodies or research groups shouldn't force data sharing if it is harmful, disadvantageous to researchers or human research subjects." Many of the interviewees noted that, ideally, it should be legal mechanisms balancing collective interests (open data-driven public health, economy, innovation, security) with individual interests (protection of intellectual property and personal data). However, a few participants argued that in a time of a catastrophic public health emergency, public health interests can sometimes be prioritised on the condition that a social consensus is reached. "The urgency of getting information for the sake of public health interest may have greater priority than privacy concerns," said a respondent. A similar position was shared by representatives of the World Health Organisation in response to the previous outbreaks [10, p. 4]. This has been demonstrated in the above-mentioned example of a Korea's special measure related to the release of people's movement patterns during COVID-19. As some of the participants mentioned, this measure has been taken despite the fact that South Korea's Personal Information Protection Act[5] is recognised as "one of the world's strictest privacy regimes"[6].

---

[4] https://www.koar.kr/

[5] http://www.law.go.kr/개인정보보호법(16930,20200204)

[6] It was recognised by the International Association of Privacy Professionals (IAPP): http://overseas. mofa.go.kr/be-ko/brd/m_7601/view.do?seq=1337611&srchFr=&amp.

Interdependence Between Science and Public Policy. The interviewees also spoke about the inextricable link between science and public policy in a public health emergency. Nonetheless, one participant noted that "in such a crisis, government and political groups shouldn't make the key policy decisions without consultations with the relevant expert groups, scientists..." In addition, some participants drew attention to the high interdependence of scientific, government, and clinical information in such a crisis and the importance of developing relevant policies, technical standards, and specifications on cross-sector information sharing and convergence. One of the interviewees gave an example of how the public policy of the Korean government agencies supports the creation of scientific knowledge in the pandemic by opening de-identified nationwide clinical data to researchers. According to the *#opendata4Covid19* project of the Ministry of Health and Welfare of Korea and Health Insurance Review and Assessment Service of Korea[7], domestic and foreign researchers can apply for accessing all COVID-19 tested cases and historical data of patient medical service by submitting a research proposal (scientific rationale of the data use) for the peer-review process. Among the terms of service requirements is publishing research products, produced as a result of use of these data, in open access.

Interdisciplinary and Cross-Sector Partnerships. Many interviewees stated that fostering an interdisciplinary R&D and cross-sector (e.g., government, research institutes, hospitals, industry) collaborative activities, based on technology and data/knowledge fusion, can accelerate the process of finding an innovative solution to a complex social problem, such as COVID-19. This also has a direct impact on the development of OS and Open Data culture. The interviewees explained: "The more interaction patterns between multiple actors are developed – the greater the demand in society for some open access data hubs." However, some of the participants mentioned that multi-actor partnerships also involve "more complicated decision-making ... because one has to acquire more approvals from other partners" and "more complex interests towards jointly produced outcomes." That is why it is important, especially in a crisis situation, to have a mediator to initiate, support, and monitor scientific and other related partnerships in a country. "In Korea this kind of responsibility mostly lies on the government side, but in the Western culture non-profit organisations also can run joint initiatives and partnerships," said one participant.

The majority of participants said that partnerships and collaborative research with the private sector investments are more likely to impose restrictions to sharing of research data and outcomes, since the primary goal of industry is technology commercialisation. However, the participants added that such collaborative projects are different from public procurement contracts for private companies to participate in the construction of a public service, such as an OS data platform. In the latter case, the industry involvement cannot challenge OS data sharing practices.

Research Communities' Norms. In the context of the COVID-19 pandemic, OS practices of different research communities should be taken into account for developing a multi-disciplinary solution to the problem. Many participants mentioned that disciplines

---

[7] https://hira-covid19.net/

which produce a large volume of data are more likely to share it for reuse. For example, such data-intensive fields as Biomedical Science (particularly genomics), Astronomy, Earth Science, and High-Energy Physics (Particle Physics) were said to have a long tradition of OS practices all over the world. Biomedical Science was said as one of the leading areas of OS in Korea.

Some of the interviewees stated that the complexity of procedures and the amount of resources required to undertake a research in a particular field have an impact on OS data sharing practices: "In Social Sciences we don't need much money to carry out a research. But in Natural Science they need a lot of money for data collection and data processing. In short, in Social Sciences a research process is more simple, but in Natural Science – very complicated and expensive. Therefore, researchers from Natural Science need more material benefits in return to opening up their research data and findings, but researchers from Social Sciences might feel scholarly altruism."

One of the participants referred to the results of the previously conducted interviews with Korean researchers and noted that "researchers who are in applied science, they are more likely to withhold their ideas and data, but researchers in basic science like Mathematics and Life Science are more willing to share their data and outcomes." Another participant added that some research communities of Social Sciences and Humanities can be against OS principles because of the ethical concerns over privacy protection of human research subjects.

Many interviewees stressed that despite some OS traditions in particular research communities, at the individual level, the majority of Korean researchers are not ready to change their habits and routine towards a new, disruptive way of doing research. But the interviewees noted that this problem might also be relevant to many other countries.

4.3   Resource Factors

ICT Infrastructure for Open Science. All of the interviewees argued that having a world-leading ICT infrastructure has had a tremendous impact on OS practices in South Korea. The basic ICT infrastructure includes, for example, a high-speed 5G and other advanced technologies, the world 14th fastest supercomputing resources, etc. Korea has also started to develop ICT infrastructure for scholarly communication: "We have collected and opened variety of scientific content on different OS data platforms before the crisis… Otherwise it would not have been possible to share it during COVID-19. We cannot start suddenly from zero in a crisis like this…" However, national ICT infrastructure for OS was characterised as still being at the early stage of development.

Open Science Data Platforms and Channels for Sharing Scientific Information. Some interviewees said that in Korea there are two main types of OS data platforms, which currently provide coronavirus-related research data and outcomes. The first type is national multi-disciplinary OS platforms, operated by KISTI, such as (1) the National Science & Technology Information Service/NTIS (www.ntis.go.kr) for research outcomes from government-funded projects, i.e. research papers, patents, research reports, (2) the Korea Open Research Data Platform/DataOn (dataon.kisti.re.kr) for research data from government-funded projects, and (3) the Korea Open Access platform for

Researchers/KOAR (www.koar.kr) for open access articles published by Korean scholars locally and internationally.

The second type is domain (discipline)-specific or problem-based repositories, which provide a quick, single point of access to the outbreak related scientific content. Some of the interviewees agreed that in the COVID-19 crisis there is probably a slightly greater demand for such kind of OS data platforms rather than for multi-disciplinary ones. The interviewees gave an example of the Korean Bioinformation Center (KOBIC)'s COVID-19 research data portal (www.kobic.re.kr/covid19/go_data_view), released in March 2020 to provide worldwide data on corona-related genome sequences, protein structures, drug development, etc. Another example is the Korean Society of Infectious Disease (KSID)'s data platform (www.ksid.or.kr/ncov/index.php) to access important announcements and the findings (summaries) from the most relevant, recently published, highly-cited international scientific articles on coronavirus infectious disease. In addition to local data platforms, some researchers said that they also use such global platforms, as the U.S. National Institutes of Health's PubMed database for biomedical journal literature (pubmed.ncbi.nlm.nih.gov) and the GISAID database for genomic data of influenza viruses and the novel coronavirus (www.gisaid.org).

Many interviewees stressed that COVID-19 showed the importance and increased the popularity of sharing preliminary results in preprint repositories. However, they added that local preprint services are not much popular among Korean researchers. Only a few participants mentioned KISTI's preprint service on KOAR platform, opened up during the pandemic. "Korean researchers prefer to use international pre-print repositories, such as bioRxiv.org, especially in the pandemic situation, when the global visibility of research outcomes is critical," said one of the participants.

In addition to the above-mentioned OS data sharing platforms, a few participants stressed the necessity to develop Citizen Science/Living Labs interactive platforms, mobile applications (e.g., as municipal initiatives): "The general users and researchers, experts can find problems raised on a platform, then discuss them in order to propose ideas and find a solution together." Such communication and cooperation during an outbreak will help researchers better understand the behaviour, problems, and concerns of citizens, while citizens will become more knowledgeable about how to protect themselves.

The interviewees also talked about social media as an additional channel for sharing scientific information. They all agreed that this channel is not appropriate or sufficient for scholarly communication between researchers, but it can be very effective to rapidly disseminate up-to-date information to the general public. However, some participants expressed concerns about the reliability and accuracy of content delivered to the general public by social media. They suggested the use of official social media accounts of research institutes and other relevant organisations in order to provide any scientific information or redirect a user to a specialised OS platform. Other concerns were that "in Korea, social media would be useful channel only for young people. For old people – SMS would be more suitable to deliver important emergency-related information" and "there are different tastes… some people like Facebook, some – Twitter, another – KakaoTalk… the same content should be delivered on different social media platforms in order to avoid discrimination of any kind."

Infrastructural Interoperability. Many interviewees mentioned the interoperability problem that hinder effective and rapid (meta)data exchange between heterogeneous OS data platforms: "In the future we need to think about how to connect all different scientific information systems in Korea," "it can be, for example, a hierarchical structure, which has one top-level national information system and some sub-systems attached to it." Some of the interviewees noted that in 2020, KISTI has been working to develop links between NTIS and DataOn information services: OAI-PMH (Open Archives Initiative Protocol for Metadata Harvesting) based API is used to provide DataOn metadata to the NTIS platform and RESTful (Representational state transfer) based API is likewise used to provide NTIS metadata to the DataOn platform. It has been also planned to link DataOn platform with institutional, domain(discipline)-specific research data repositories. In addition, it was said that the current pandemic has demonstrated a need to ensure interoperable data exchange not only between scientific information systems but also between different sectors (government agencies, hospitals, research institutes, companies).

Legal Compliance and User-Centered Service Design. Some participants felt that in the future it is necessary to embed some advanced technologies, such as blockchain or intelligent software agents, in scientific information systems in order to protect intellectual property rights and privacy-sensitive information by ensuring the legitimate, transparent, and controlled use of OS data. In addition, a participatory design with researchers was indicated as an effective but time-consuming approach to develop or improve scientific information services tailored to the user's needs.

4.4   Financial Resources

Maintenance Costs. All the respondents reported that the OS related ICT infrastructure is usually developed and maintained by the public sector and, thus, is highly dependent on government funds. As one said, "The pandemic situation is some kind of helpful to remind Korean government officers of the importance of scientific data sharing. So later on the investment on such infrastructure will be increasing." Some interviewees pointed out that in a public health emergency situation the government agencies can minimise and share the costs for some OS initiatives and projects by using crowd-funding mechanisms and taking advantage of global crowdsourcing efforts.

Emergency Funding and Budgeting. There was a consensus among participants that COVID-19 has revealed a gap, at least in Korea, between the regular and emergency budget, on the one hand, and the real financial needs to respond to the pandemic, on the other. One participant explained: "In general, the national budget cycle is one year. In the pandemic situation, this system does not work... Since the Sewol ferry disaster, occurred on the 16 April 2014 in South Korea, the government has started to prepare some emergency fund, but it has been not enough for COVID-19. From now on, they will start to save more for future emergency needs." Nonetheless, another interviewee added: "The emergency fund usually go not for science and researchers, but rather to support ordinary citizens, hospitals, patients..." One interviewee shared the experience of their research institute's budget deficiency in the pandemic: "In this pandemic we had to use our own, very limited budget to rapidly launch a data service related to the outbreak... There is a complicated procedure, money cannot easily flows from the government to public research institutes, and the allocated budget should be used by an institute only for a particular predetermined purpose. So the government should think about some mechanisms in the future."

Access Costs to Databases/Repositories. Some of the interviewees stated that much relevant scientific information from all over the world has been paywalled, despite the COVID-19 outbreak, and that subscription-based access to international databases is costly: "Domestic scientific information services, which are free of charge, do not cover everything. Korean researchers also need global data to do research. My research institute purchased subscriptions to some international databases (chemical compounds, advanced materials, etc.), but our budget is limited..."

4.5 Human Resources

Open Science Education. "We need to promote an OS culture among researchers, government agencies, ordinary people. They should start thinking about the importance of OS and Citizen Science for safe and comfortable living in a society. It can be done by providing some trainings and delivering specific information." The majority of interviewees said that Korean researchers have the ICT skills to use generic information systems and web services, but "the problem is that researchers do not know much about OS data services: where to upload my data, where to access other researchers' data and why I should do it..." "We are not trained on OS practices – how to make our data available and understandable to other people. I personally need such kinds of specialised training programmes," said one of the interviewees. As some participants reported, many research institutes provide some very basic assistance to researchers in sharing/reuse of their data and outcomes. However, the participants agreed that there is an obvious need to create a help desk channel on each of the OS data platforms, such as NTIS and DataOn, to provide better assistance to researchers.

Fast-Track Peer-Review. Many participants stressed that inaccurate and low-quality information can bring much more negative consequences in an emergency than it can bring in normal, non-emergency situations. That is why the emergency-related information sharing should be preceded by a solid fact-checking and scientific peer-review process, but performed at high speed. Some participants felt that additional expert groups, accompanied with advanced technologies such as artificial intelligence, are needed to achieve this purpose.

Evidence-Based Popular Science Content. Despite the general belief that non-experts are expected not to have interest and sufficient knowledge to consume scientific information, this pandemic has demonstrated the ordinary people's enhanced desire for scientific information in facing a life-threatening risk. "The general public wants to know how the virus transmits, what kind of conditions are favorable for and what conditions are hostile to it...From the very beginning of the outbreak, such information was not delivered to people. But there was very limited knowledge on it...," said one of the interviewees and continued, "In order that ordinary people pay attention to scientific information, understand it, and benefit from its use in daily life, such information should be really interesting and easy to understand. It can be, for example, infographics, summary of research findings in a story-writing style, Q&A interviews with researchers." Another participant argued: "I don't think this is a job of research institutes or researchers themselves. The job of researchers is to do research, but not to advertise their activity to the public. The government should support alternative organisations and professionals, such as science journalists, who are much more capable to create popular science content and communicate it to the public."

4.6 Individual and Motivational Factors

Perceived Personal Efforts. The majority of interviewees argued that the greater the effort (intellectual work, cost, time) to produce, share and reuse data/outcomes, the more reluctant researchers are to practice OS. "Researchers are very busy, they have to undertake government-funded research projects... OS activity is a highly time-consuming work," "it is an additional effort to share their data with others, because they should guarantee some data quality, scientific data should be standardised in order others understand it. Also there are some rules, instructions, administrative burden like DMP," "especially researchers will perceive this effort if a platform does not work well, not user friendly," said participants. However, the researcher's perceived effort was seen to be mitigated in case it is properly recognised and rewarded.

Perceived Risk of Negative Consequences. There are three types of the perceived risks (demotivation for OS data sharing practices), which the participants most discussed. The first issue, the majority of participants are concerned about, is the privacy protection and compliance with a strict personal data protection law ("people are reluctant to reveal their data to the public, because they will be blamed in case the revealed data has any kind of privacy issues. So people tend to avoid such kind of risk," "on the one hand, many of daily activities are digitised in Korea, people are active users of advanced technologies, on the other hand, people are too worried about the privacy"). The second most discussed risk is the concern of being "scooped", which means that one's unpublished ideas, data, or results are stolen and first published by another researcher. With this regard, all interviewees, who talked about this risk, argued that researchers are reluctant to open up information, which has not been yet published, for example, in a peer-reviewed scholarly journal. One of the interviewees stressed that in a crisis such as COVID-19, science is exceptionally competitive: "Time is more important than everything, and being the first to publicise some scientific evidence on a crisis-related topic would have more impact than in normal circumstances." Finally, some respondents pointed out the researchers' fear that many people will find mistakes in their shared work and, as a consequence, they can lose reputation or will have to spend additional time for a remedy. However, the same as with the perceived efforts, the respondents said that the perceived risks will be diminished if researchers are properly benefited.

Perceived Extrinsic and Intrinsic Benefits. All respondents agreed that extrinsic benefits (financial incentives and academic rewards/recognition) are the most important motivation for the majority of researchers to share their data and outputs, however, such incentive structures are found not to be properly developed. Only a few respondents said that some researchers, and themselves in particular, can be driven by intrinsic altruistic motives: "The most important motivation for me, as a scientist... We do not follow money much, we think more about general science development, good science," "if researchers consider their data can be used for public benefits and it will be really helpful, they are willing to share their data." The most important extrinsic benefits for researchers were seen as follows: citation of research data and published results ("citation of research data is not common in Korea, not in a global domain as well"); reputation building via research visibility; inclusion of OS activities and items (e.g., open access paper, shared research data, preprints) in the research performance evaluation process in research organisations; inclusion of OS activities in the researcher's working hours (no extra work); promotion opportunities; increased chances to get research funds; feedback from a scientific community for research improvement, etc.

One of the interviewees argued that all OS related practices to some extent benefit researchers extrinsically through scholarly recognition: "The visibility of open research data and outcomes helps build some reputation in the field and increases the chances to get research funds from the government or industry..." Another interviewee highlighted that this is especially true in the situation of the COVID-19 crisis: "The COVID-19 crisis increases national and international visibility of research far beyond scientific communities... Thus this situation by default, without any actions aimed at developing specific incentives, gives researchers motivation for data and outcomes sharing, such as the increased visibility and reputation building." However, beyond this, the other above-mentioned extrinsic incentives need to be developed.

4.7 Trust in Open Science

Trust in Open Science Service Providers. The respondents talked about trust in the OS data service provider (institution) by which they understood the feeling of reliance on the trustworthiness of an organisation/sector collecting diverse scientific information, providing open access to it, managing such information, and offering other relevant services. Many participants said that, especially in an emergency, they only trust in the government to provide such services: "I trust only in government platforms, because there are different evaluation and quality monitoring mechanisms embedded in them... Sometimes the private sector's platforms may be useful. But they can be biased in favour of the company profit. They do not pursue public interest..."

Trust in Open Science Data Platforms. The participants also discussed the issue of trust in the OS data platform based on the overall user experience of a service (user-friendliness and functionalities). "Different platforms – different user experience, even though they are developed by the same organisation. The user experience with KISTI's National Science & Technology Information Service (NTIS) can be different from the experience with KISTI's National Digital Science Library (NDSL). Frustrating experience make me away from a platform," said one participant.

Trust in Open Science Data Quality. Trust in quality of OS data within a platform was found as an important factor influencing reusers' judgments. This is related to the intrinsic data quality (e.g., scientific rigor and validity associated with good quality research) and the extrinsic data quality (data reusability properties, including quality of metadata). As one interviewee said, "If I am not satisfied with the quality of research data or outcomes on a particular platform, I will go to another one, which will provide better quality data." Many participants noted that they are more likely to trust in OS data quality if they are aware that the data is properly curated and peer-reviewed.

Trust in Open Science Researchers. Some interviewees also found research community as a source of trust in OS. It refers to researcher's reliance on shared experiences within his scholarly community, peer evaluation of OS practices and open scientific content itself. For example, one interviewee said: "Local research community can persuade its members to use a platform, it can help build trust in a platform. Community members know each other… if the community members have had a good experience in using a data platform, so I will use it as well."

Trust in Open Science Reciprocity. One participant stated: "Before opening my data I should be confident that any kind of action or reward will be in return to my efforts." Another participant added that systematic incentive mechanisms should be properly developed and embedded in the OS data sharing system, and researchers should be aware of them ("to know the rules of the game… the same as everybody knows the rules of the journal publication system").

5   Discussion

The study identified a range of diverse factors influencing OS data sharing and reuse in public health emergencies, such as the COVID-19 pandemic. We have systematically classified all identified factors into four groups (*contextual or external, institutional and regulatory, resource, individual and motivational* factors) and illustrated them with relevant real-world examples and suggestions provided by the experts from the South Korea R&D community. In addition, during the interviews we asked the respondents to rank the four identified groups of factors according to their importance in public health emergencies. The *institutional and regulatory* factors were named as the most important group, followed by the *contextual or external* group of factors. Two other groups comprising *resource factors* and *individual and motivational* factors were ranked as least important. However, one of the eleven interviewees assigned the same degree of importance to all the identified factor groups not being able to discriminate between them and arguing that OS is dependent on different combinations of all factors.

The institutional/regulatory issues as primary factors that influence sharing of publicly funded research data and outcomes are also acknowledged in other studies [19]. Regulative pressures by government bodies, funding agencies, journal publishers and research communities' norms can significantly foster or hamper scientists' behaviour to share their research materials. Although OS data sharing and reuse practices are technically feasible with the Internet and ICT, multiple legal and ethical barriers still continue to exist [20]. In public health emergency situations, it is additionally important to ensure co-ordination between OS and Emergency Management policies with regard to dissemination of outbreak-related research findings and related information. As a response to the COVID-19 crisis, the OECD emphasises the need to strengthen regulatory frameworks for publicly funded research data exchange and open-access publishing, including co-ordination, interoperability, accountability, and safeguards mechanisms [14]. This corresponds to the interviewees' opinion that Korea needs reinforcement of OS legal and regulatory framework in a comprehensive way to close the gaps identified during the current pandemic, especially the lack of proper inter-sectoral co-ordination policy, based on the pre-defined roles and responsibilities.

While the pandemic has accelerated the process of globalisation, our research reveals a range of competing interests that still challenge the openness of scholarly communication. Many respondents have argued that the COVID-19 crisis significantly increases the impact of contextual/external factors (global and national political and socio-economic context) on OS development. These were overlooked in the previous research, despite the fact that public health emergencies, such as Zika virus, were identified as an intervening factor for research data communication [8].

Finally, the respondents reported resource factors together with individual/motivational factors as the least influential. It can be explained by the fact that the allocation of ICT, financial, and human resources is largely dependent on institutions' consistent, co-ordinated policies and commitment to OS development. Besides, in public health emergencies, researchers' individual perceptions and motivations are expected to have less influence on the dissemination of publicly funded research findings in comparison with the impact of relevant laws, regulations, and policies.

6   Conclusion

Our study has found that there has been significant impact of COVID-19 on the actualisation of OS. We hope that the results of this study will contribute to a clearer understanding of the multifaceted issue of OS policy development that can be relevant to other countries. The main lesson to learn from the Korean case is the importance of the country's pre-crisis commitment to OS development. A national OS-based scholarly communication system cannot be built within a short period of time in sudden crisis situations, especially in low-resource settings – even though some of its elements and tools can be hastily constructed during the crisis, for example, through crowdsourcing initiatives. Many such initiatives have been launched nationally and globally in the wake of the pandemic aiming to achieve either the rapid deployment of the already established data service and computational tools or the provision of new ones. As Jevin West, a data scientist at the University of Washington [21], argues "It's hard to change [scientists'] way of information foraging and searching within a pandemic… It's like going into an emergency room and giving the doctors a different scalpel and saying: 'This is actually better.' It's going to take some time to get people to change their habits." Indeed, the normative structures of OS are changing a way slower than the technologies that help communicate research data and outcomes. The lack of the adequately developed norms and mechanisms for striking the right balance between opening scientific data and the protection of intellectual property rights is a significant barrier for smooth communication of scientific evidence, especially at the time of a public health emergency.

One of the major limitations of the study is the relevance of the results beyond South Korea, as not all Korea's lessons might be universally applicable for other nations. The South Korean government has earned sufficient trust among the population in its emergency management policies. Both scholars and citizens feel sufficiently confident that data collected in the pandemic will only be used to deal with the pandemic. Other nations may not enjoy the same level of public trust [22].

At the next phase of the research we aim to expand the interview sample to invite experts from other countries and from more diverse fields covering, for example, epidemiologists, research funders, and publishers. The semi-structured interviews will be also supplemented by other methods, such as a policy content analysis and structured questionnaires. In addition to analysis of factors, we will examine in more detail support mechanisms that can enable OS data sharing and reuse in the most efficient manner. Our ultimate aim is to build a coherent conceptual framework of an ideal national OS ecosystem for scholarly communication in public health emergency and non-emergency situations. The framework will be based on Ostrom's Institutional Analysis and Development (IAD) analytical framework [23] by integrating the four groups of factors identified in this paper as the input factors.

References

1. European Commission. Shaping Europe's digital future. Open Science. https://ec.europa.eu/digital-single-market/en/open-science. Accessed 01 July 2020
2. Shmagun, H., Oppenheim, C., Shim, J., Kim, J.: The uptake of open science: mapping the results of a systematic literature review. In: Proceedings of the International Online Conference on ICT Enhanced Social Sciences and Humanities (ICTeSSH 2020), ITM Web of Conferences (2020). https://doi.org/10.1051/itmconf/20203301001
3. Tenopir, C., et al.: Data sharing, management, use, and reuse: practices and perceptions of scientists worldwide. PLoS ONE 15(3), e0229003 (2020)
4. Park, J., Gabbard, J.L.: Factors that affect scientists' knowledge sharing behavior in health and life sciences research communities: differences between explicit and implicit knowledge. Comput. Hum. Behav. 78, 326–335 (2018)
5. Melero, R., Navarro-Molina, C.: Researchers' attitudes and perceptions towards data sharing and data reuse in the field of food science and technology. Learn. Publish. 33(2), 163–179 (2020)
6. Zuiderwijk, A., Spiers, H.: Sharing and re-using open data: A case study of motivations in astrophysics. Int. J. Inf. Manage. 49, 228–241 (2019)
7. Kim, Y., Stanton, J.M.: Institutional and individual factors affecting scientists' data-sharing behaviors: a multilevel analysis. J. Assoc. Inf. Sci. Technol. 67(4), 776–799 (2016)
8. da Costa, M.P., Leite, F.C.L.: Factors influencing research data communication on Zika virus: a grounded theory. J. Doc. 75, 910–926 (2019)

9. Modjarrad, K., et al.: Developing global norms for sharing data and results during public health emergencies. PLoS Med. **13**(1), e1001935 (2016)

10. Ribeiro, C.D.S., et al.: How ownership rights over microorganisms affect infectious disease control and innovation: a root-cause analysis of barriers to data sharing as experienced by key stakeholders. PLoS ONE **13**(5), e0195885 (2018)

11. Chretien, J.P., Rivers, C.M., Johansson, M.A.: Make data sharing routine to prepare for public health emergencies. PLoS Med. **13**(8), e1002109 (2016)

12. Pisani, E., Ghataure, A., Merson, L.: Data sharing in public health emergencies. A study of current policies, practices and infrastructure supporting the sharing of data to prevent and respond to epidemic and pandemic threats. Wellcome Trust, London (2018). https://wellcome.figshare.com/ndownloader/files/10506073. Accessed 01 July 2020

13. RDA COVID-19 Working Group: Recommendations and Guidelines on data sharing. Research Data Alliance (2020). https://doi.org/10.15497/rda00052

14. OECD Policy Responses to Coronavirus (COVID-19). Why open science is critical to combatting COVID-19. http://www.oecd.org/coronavirus/policy-responses/why-open-science-is-critical-to-combatting-covid-19-cd6ab2f9/. Accessed 01 July 2020

15. Yin, R.K.: Case Study Research. Design and Methods, 5th edn. Sage Publications, Thousand Oaks (2014)

16. Moher, D., et al.: Preferred reporting items for systematic reviews and meta-analyses: the PRISMA statement. PLoS Med. **6**(7), e1000097 (2009)

17. Pickard, A.J.: Research Methods in Information, 2nd edn. Facet Publishing, London (2013)

18. Satellite data suggests coronavirus may have hit China earlier: Researchers. https://abcnews.go.com/International/satellite-data-suggests-coronavirus-hit-china-earlier-researchers/story?id=71123270. Accessed 01 July 2020

19. Lämmerhirt, D.: PASTEUR4OA briefing paper: disciplinary differences in opening research data. Zenodo (2016). https://doi.org/10.5281/zenodo.51856

20. Hashim, H.N.M.: Developing a model guidelines addressing legal impediments to open access to publicly funded research data in Malaysia. Data Sci. J. **18**, 27 (2019)

21. Scientists are drowning in COVID-19 papers. Can new tools keep them afloat? https://www.sciencemag.org/news/2020/05/scientists-are-drowning-covid-19-papers-can-new-tools-keep-them-afloat. Accessed 01 July 2020

22. Trust in UK government and news media COVID-19 information down, concerns over misinformation from government and politicians up. https://reutersinstitute.politics.ox.ac.uk/trust-uk-government-and-news-media-covid-19-information-down-concerns-over-misinformation. Accessed 01 July 2020

23. Ostrom, E., Hess, C.: A Framework for Analyzing the Knowledge Commons. Understanding Knowledge as a Commons: From Theory to Practice. MIT Press, Cambridge (2011)

Generating Social Environment for Agent-Based Models of Computational Economy

Aleksandra L. Mashkova[1,2(✉)] ⓘ, Ivan V. Nevolin[2,3] ⓘ,
Olga A. Savina[1] ⓘ, Maria A. Burilina[2,3] ⓘ,
and Evgeniy A. Mashkov[1] ⓘ

[1] Orel State University named after I.S. Turgenev,
Komsomolskaja St. 95, 302026 Orel, Russian Federation
[2] Central Economics and Mathematics Institute Russian Academy of Sciences,
Nakhimovsky Av. 47, 117418 Moscow, Russian Federation
[3] State Academic University for the Humanities,
Maronovskiy Pereulok, 26, 119049 Moscow, Russian Federation
aleks.savina@gmail.com

Abstract. The article is devoted to methods of simulating population and social environment in agent-based computational economy models: the agent model of the spatial development of the Russian Federation and the model of anemia dynamics among Russian population. We present structure of the models and their databases. Information support of the model is based on statistical yearbooks, SPARK-Interfax database, RLMS survey results and websites of the ministries, including demographic structure of the population, production, import, export, employment, financial characteristics of organizations and households and other parameters. Since this information is presented in different sources, it is necessary to convert it to the structure that matches the input tables. For this task we use iterative proportional fitting algorithm; as an example we show sequence of iterations for aggregating information about the regional labor market. The model database is filled with the objects, which are generated using initial modeling data; all required interrelations are set among them. Simulation results show objects that have been created in the Russian Federation and in a separate region.

Keywords: Agent-based model · Iterative proportional fitting · Spatial development · Anemia dynamics · RLMS

1 Introduction

At the present stage of information technologies evolution, big data and its applications to decision support in various areas of planning and management are becoming increasingly important. In particular, large volumes of open data can be used in predicting processes of socio-economic development of territories, implementation of new technologies, population dynamics and health.

Currently, an approach to forecasting socio-economic processes is actively developing, based on agent-based computational economy models (ACE), which reproduce

A. Chugunov et al. (Eds.): EGOSE 2020, CCIS 1349, pp. 291–305, 2020.
https://doi.org/10.1007/978-3-030-67238-6_21

structure of the system and evaluate various options for controlling influences on it. To ensure maximum similarity between the model and the real system, and consequently high forecast accuracy, it is necessary to load large volumes of data reflecting the current state of the system in ACE-model. In this type of models population is connected with organizations and institutions, which provides possibility to simulate socio-economic policy at regional and federal levels.

In this article we present methodology, algorithms, initial modeling data structures and sources for simulating population and social environment in agent-based computational economy models.

2 Literature Review

In our study we implement methods of agent-based computational economics (ACE) [1, 2]. Comparing to other widespread approach to building computer models of economy, known as dynamic stochastic general equilibrium (DSGE) or computational general equilibrium (CGE), ACE models have a few features that define their capability of simulating complex socio-economic processes:

1. Heterogeneity of agents and their characteristics, which leads to different patterns of behavior.
2. Direct interactions among the agents that influence their decisions.
3. Bounded rationality of the agents based on limited information adaptive expectations.
4. Emergence of complex phenomena from a bottom-up perspective as a result of the features described above.

In this context ACE models may be considered as a tool for estimating economic and social consequences of the applied policies. This class of models is used in industrial dynamics, environmental regulation, traffic management, etc. In the context of macroeconomic policies there are agent-based models of fiscal policy [3, 4], monetary policy [5, 6], macroprudential policy [7, 8] and labor market policy [9].

In K+S model [4] Keynesian theories of demand-generation and Schumpeterian theories of technology-fueled economic growth are combined. K+S model consists of heterogeneous agents: firms, consumers, workers, banks, and a public sector.

Alternative monetary strategies are studied in [6]. Depending on its strategy, the Central Bank in the model uses a fixed parameter rule or a changing according to a genetic algorithm rule to regulate interactions of firms and workers.

Different labor-market regimes are studied in [9]. For each regime wage flexibility, labor mobility, minimum wage and unemployment benefits are set. The model simulates labor market, unemployment and wage dynamics.

One of the most complex ACE models is EURACE simulator – an agent-based model of multiple-market economy of European Union countries. In [10], EURACE model simulates regional local labor markets where workers have heterogeneous skills. Simulation results show how policies influence on skills of workers, innovations of firms, inequality dynamics and economic convergence. While EURACE incorporates crucial connections between the real economy and the credit and financial markets, it operates with abstract data and does not refer to any particular European country [11, 12].

It is still considered an ambitious objective to fill the ACE models with real data. This task is partly solved in the regional management models, for instance, in the model for Leeds City Council [13] (the United Kingdom) and the model 'Governor' (Leningrad region, the Russian Federation) [14]. The model for Leeds City Council is used to predict future trends in health of population and composition of households. Based on this information impact of policy interventions at the local level can be estimated [13]. In the regional model "Governor" there are agents of the following types: residents; organizations; municipal areas. At each step of the simulation agents consume goods and services; contribute to social production and receive a salary depending on their qualifications [14]. Since these models are regional-scaled, all federal policy measured are considered uncontrollable, as well as world trade and financial markets [15].

3   Methodology of Case Study

The methodology used by our team for forecasting socio-economic processes is based on agent-based models of computational economy, which reflect key elements of the explored system and its state at the current time. We assume that key elements of each model of this class are population, economy, education system and state administration, in this case, the detail of each element is determined, firstly, by formulation of the task, and, secondly, by availability of initial data. Initial data is the crucial part of our research, as it enables to reproduce the current state of the system in geographical and socio-economic context, thereby increasing accuracy of the forecast and expanding possibilities of its interpretation to control the real system. The methodology includes three main steps:

1. Generation. At this stage we reconstruct population and social environment of the model based on available data about initial state of the system.
2. Dynamic simulation. This step reflects dynamics of the system, as a result of its individual components actions and relationships between them. In particular, dynamics of population, economic and educational system is simulated.
3. Simulation of control actions. At this step, functions of the administration system are simulated: various options for control actions are set, and it is estimated how they affect dynamics of the system.

The key principles of the presented methodology are scalability, interactivity and modularity. Scalability in this context implies that on the basis of a general methodology and modeling tools, it is possible to simulate dynamics of the system at the regional, federal or international extent. Interactivity is implemented through scenario calculations, in which various parameters of the external environment are set by the user. Modularity of the models distinguishes demographic, educational, financial processes, production and consumption in separate modules, which makes it possible to detail the processes under study to varying degrees and expand the functionality of the models by including additional modules.

The presented methodology is implemented by combining the following methods:

- reproduction of demographic structure of population and composition of households within each region;
- simulation of agents' decision-making taking into account their bounded rationality;
- integration of the input-output balance into an agent-based imitation model to reflect the existing financial and economic relationships in the economy;
- adaptation of budgetary and accounting system in the model, which provides analysis of the output simulation data similarly to government statistics.

In the following paragraphs we will consider data structures and algorithms used for generation of social environment at the first stage in more detail.

3.1   Key Elements of Computational Economy Models

At the moment, our team is developing two agent-based models of computational economy: model of the spatial development of the Russian Federation (SDRF model) and model of anemia dynamics among Russian population (ADRF model). Despite the significant difference in the research tasks, both of these models consist of key elements mentioned above: population, economy, education system and state administration. Specification of each element varies in each model. United modeling scheme for both models is presented in Fig. 1.

Population in both models is reproduced taking into account its regional affiliation, age, gender and distribution among households. Migration processes play a significant role in the SDRF model, while health status of various groups of population is significant in the ADRF model. Simulation of population dynamics is discussed in more detail in [16].

The economic system is more deeply detailed in the SDRF model: it reproduces production of various industries, property of organizations, as well as regional infrastructure (roads, energy and communications) and the financial system. These issues are discussed in more detail in [17]. In the model of anemia dynamics, the main emphasis is on agriculture, food production, their price and availability in various regions.

Employment and consumption are basic connection links between the population and the economy. As employees (or businessmen) agents get wages and profits; as consumers they buy commodities. In the SDRF model general frame of household consumption of products and services is reflected; in the model of anemia dynamics, food consumption is simulated with a greater degree of detail: the number of cereals, meat, fish, dairy products, vegetables and fruits consumed by households is taken into account.

Education system is significant for the SDRF model, as it creates qualified personnel necessary for the economy (more details are presented in [18]). In the ADRF model, education system acts as an auxiliary channel for maintaining health through students playing sports and organizing balanced school meals.

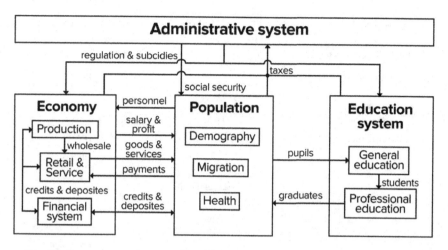

Fig. 1. Components of computational economy models of the Russian Federation.

Administrative influences in the SDRF model are infrastructure projects, subsidies and tax incentives for production in the key industries. In the ADRF model, subsidization and tax stimulation of food production, regulation of their exports and imports are simulated. The main channel for implementing control actions in both models is the budget system; its structure and algorithms are presented in [19].

3.2   The Model Database

Figure 2 shows structure of the integrated database for models the Russian Federation spatial development and anemia dynamics in the Russian Federation. Common for them are tables "Agent", "Household", "Region", "Organization", "Workplace" and "Educational place" presented on the right. These objects reflect population and key structures of social environment in both models. Data structures in the SDRF model are presented in [17].

To simulate dynamics of spread of anemia, additional information is required on the current state of public health (which is displayed in the "Anemia stage" field in the table "Agent"), household food consumption ("Food consumption pattern" and "Menu" tables), content of valuable nutrients in food and recommended daily allowance of their consumption (tables "Product" and "Nutrition pattern"). Probabilities of transition from the current stage of anemia to more or less serious, depending on the quality of nutrition, are stored in the table "Health Dynamics".

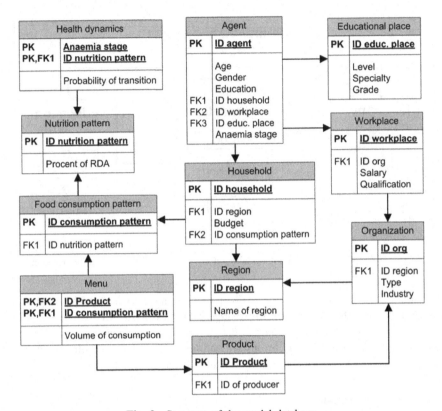

Fig. 2. Structure of the model database.

3.3 Initial Modeling Data

For information support of agent-based computational economy models data on population, production, infrastructure and education is required, which can be found in various sources: statistical yearbooks, open data of ministries, specific databases and surveys. So far as structure of this information is variegated it is necessary to convert it to the structure that matches the input tables of the models. Table 1 presents the basic tables of input data used in the creation of objects.

Information content of the tables is based on the collections of All-Russian Population Census [20], Federal State Statistics Service [21], SPARK-Interfax database [22] reports of Ministry of Economic Development [23], the Central Bank [24] and Ministry of Education and Science [27] open data. For some issues (such as consumption of food) we use survey results [25, 26], since this information is not detailed in official sources. All-Russian Population Census data is very well structured and detailed and we use it with minimal corrections. Information presented in other sources needs some processing. Particularly, we need to integrate information about employees, equipment and credits of organizations (Table 1) which is presented in different perspectives: sectoral and regional.

Table 1. Initial modeling data structure.

Initial modeling data tables	Available open data	Data sources
Population	Regional distribution and gender-age sex structure of the population; composition of households	All-Russian Population Census of 2010 [20]
Production	Regional product structure Information about organizations	Federal State Statistics Service website [21] SPARK-Interfax [22]
Equipment	Equipment in the regions	Federal State Statistics Service website [21]
	Equipment in the economic activities	
Export & Import	Export - import structure	Report of Economic Development Ministry [23]
Credits & Deposits of organizations	Total volume of credits of organizations in different regions	Federal State Statistics Service website [21]
	Total volume of credits of organizations of different economic activities	The Central Bank website [24]
Sales & Supply	Input-output table	Federal State Statistics Service website [21]
Credits & Deposits of households	Total volume of credits of households in different regions	The Central Bank website [24]
	Average credit size in different regions	Survey results [25]
Employment	Employees in the regions	Federal State Statistics Service website [21]
	Employees in the economic activities	
Consumption	Structure of money income and expenditures of population	Federal State Statistics Service website [21]
	Food consumption of households	RLMS [26]
Education	Organizations carrying out training under education programs	Report of Ministry of Education and Science [27]

We use iterative proportional fitting algorithm (IPF) to solve this problem. Further we illustrate how IPF works for aggregating information about employees. Initial data includes L_r – employees in the region r (table "Employees in the regions") and L^e – number of employees in economic activity e (table "Employees in the economic activities") [21]:

$$L = \sum_{r=1}^{82} L_r = \sum_{e=1}^{15} L^e \qquad (1)$$

where $L = 68838,2$ thousand persons – number of employees in Russia [21].

At the first iteration of the IPF algorithm we calculate preliminary number of employees in economic activities in each region $L_r^e(prel)$. At iteration 1 we calculate variation of preliminary number of employees in regional scale v_r; maximal variation is

232% in Ivanovsky region. Since variation is very high, we recalculate L_r^e applying $v_r(i1)$ as correcting coefficient:

$$L_r^e(i1) = L_r^e(prel) * v_r(i1) \tag{2}$$

At iteration 2 we calculate variation of number of employees in the aspect of economic activities v^e. Maximal variation is 22% in economic activity "Agriculture and Forestry". Repeating iterations, on the fourth we get a zero deviation in regional scale and 0.4–2.5% in economic activity scale.

Data from the Federal State Statistics Service are not detailed enough to be implemented in agent-based model to calculate production and consumption. All the data are available as set of separate tables. For example, one can observe distribution of households on size, on income, on food consumption. But, these are three independent tables and researchers have no opportunity to generate contingency tables that are crucial while initializing agents. As so, we rely on side databases to fill gaps in our model.

To model production side we involve data on economic activity at microeconomic level. Russian database SPARK-Interfax [22] is recognized as a source of valid information about national companies: registration data, affiliated entities, financial reports, legal cases and etc. Approaching the food industry in the context of anemia we focus on sub-industries producing the meal affecting disease: fruits and vegetables, nuts; meat and meat byproducts (offal, organ meats); poultry; milk, cheese and fermented milk products; fish and seafood.

Closer look at the initial data reveals outliers: revenue and return on assets as well as return on sales are enormous for some enterprises. General source for financial statements is public agency responsible for data audit and handle. All the companies in Russia fill strict forms and officially report assets and cashflow in thousands of Russian rubles. But, SPARK-Intarfax database stores data in Russian rubles – three orders less then in original documents. Suppose, this difference could result in misprints in data imports and entail enormous values mentioned. Without access to the initial documents from the public agency we can only omit outliers and correct the data at the level of firms to fit the macroeconomic data of the Federal State Statistics Service.

SPARK-Intarfax data cover producers in the all sub-industries from the above. And many of them have negative operating profit as return on sales (ROS) and return on assets (ROA) demonstrate. Further, we should correct them according to the officially reported activity in these sub-industries to implement in the model. As we see small variation in the effectiveness of companies in terms of returns, we focus solely on revenue as the proxy of production volumes and size of the firm.

While neglecting outliers we can involve distribution of enterprises on revenue to the model. Consider revenue distribution for milk production as an example (Fig. 3). Officially reported production amounts 29,4 bln. RUR in the Central Federal district (average price of 24 thousands per tonne multiplied by 1206 thousand tonnes in 2018). SPARK-Interfax reported 34 firms in this sub-industry for the Central Federal district with 24 of them explaining 19,9 bln. RUR revenue in 2018. Note, that for some of them SPARK provided no financial information, so the data are missing and do not present in histogram. Suggest, the Fig. 3 gives correct picture for revenue distribution.

Consequently, we generate agents-firms for the model to meet sample distribution, production volumes and the number of producers.

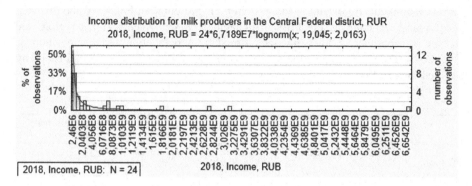

Fig. 3. Income distribution of income with fitting curve.

To model consumption side we involve longitude survey of households – The Russia Longitudinal Monitoring Survey, RLMS [26]. This survey suggests different questionnaires for households, adults, children. As the model operates at both individual and household levels RLMS is useful source of data to initialize agents. First, consider questionnaire for adults. It covers age, gender, education, employment and health issues that fit our database. Special question clearly reveals anemia disease and longitude survey makes space to track changes of the state for person. Second, the survey assigns each person to the household. At the level of households answers about income, consumption, size and the place of living are available. Problems arise while using RLMS data for regional models. Sample of the survey represents the Russian population at the country level – not regional dimension. As so, we have to employ special procedure to generate data for our model that is regional one.

Consider income and consumption data for households. Given the representative sample at the country level we build contingency tables: household size vs income, household size vs products consumption. We should further add some regional variation. Following official statistics, we observe income and structure of expenses for main categories of food products. Income distribution is available as the ratio between 10% top and 10% bottom for the country and in regional dimension. Calculate joint income-household size distribution using iteration procedure analogous to the case of labor above. Assume the distribution of households on income from RLMS to be the same for the fixed region.

Consider expenses. This is the case where we rely on data provided by the Federal State Statistics Service at the side of consumption. We know the distribution among main categories of food products per capita in dimension of regions. So, joint distribution in the simplest case is defined by multiplication of costs per capita on the size of households.

3.4   Algorithm for Generating Synthetic Population and Organizations

Generation of population and social environment for the models of experimental economy is aimed at creating objects in the model database and setting interconnections among them. Algorithm of this procedure is presented in Fig. 4. At the first step geographical structure of the Russian Federation is set. Agents in the regions are created in accordance with gender-age structure of population and composition of households. Details of population synthesis for the models of experimental economy are presented in [28].

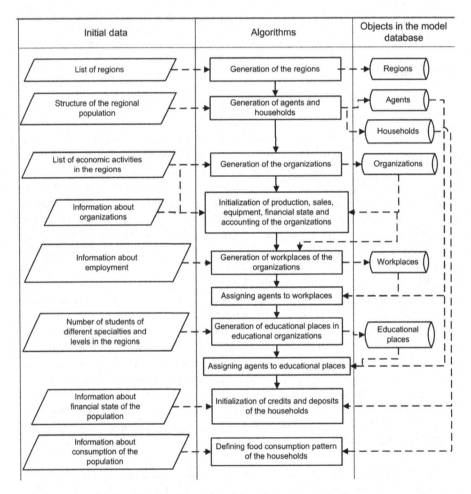

Fig. 4. Algorithm of social environment generation.

Economic system in the SDRF model consists of aggregated organizations, each of those represents collection of regional organizations belonging to one industry. For the ADRF model, organizations of sectors "Agriculture" and "Food production" are detailed using data obtained from the SPARK database. The order of data processing is considered in [17]. For each organization in the model employees, financial liabilities, accounting and supplies are set.

Education system in the model consists of educational organizations, to which educational places are assigned. While school is obligatory for all children in Russia, secondary vocational and higher education is free available within set rates for applicants with best results in Unified State Examination and paid for others. In the model we create set number of educational places for different specialties and levels and assign agents of the appropriate age to them.

For each household we set its financial state. Having information on the total household credits [24] and the average credit size [25] in each region, we assign credits to individual households in the region so that the monthly loan payment does not exceed half of the total income of agents in the household. Similarly, we assign deposits to households so that the deposit does not exceed the total household income for 5 years. Assumptions made at the initialization of the financial state of households are quite strict due to the insufficient detailing of available information in official sources [21, 24, 25].

At the final step of the social environment generation procedure in the model of anemia dynamics we set structure of food consumption by households based on data from the RLMS survey [26].

4   Empirical Analysis of the Case

Both SDRF and ADRF models are programmed in Microsoft Visual Studio. Figure 5 shows the sequence of data processing in the model. The generation procedure is divided into several stages, because available data about population and economy relates to different time periods. The most detailed information about the population structure is presented in 2010 population census; sectoral structure of economy – in

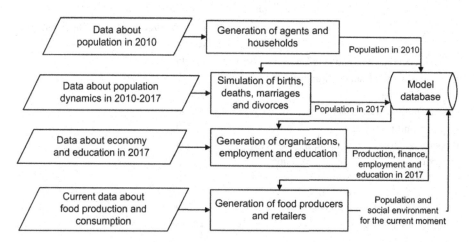

Fig. 5. Data processing in the model.

2017 input-output balance; particular organizations – in SPARK-Intarfax database for the current moment. For this reason, at first we create agents and households, then simulate their dynamics at a given time interval, after that we create organizations and establishes their relationship with agents.

Table 2 presents the main objects and characteristics of the generated society in the country as a whole and in a particular region (Belgorod) reproduced for 2017. To cope with computational complexity of generating synthetic population of such a huge country we reduce number agents (100 to 1) and aggregate organizations of each economy sector in one region. We change number of students and employees accordingly.

Table 2. Simulation results (The Russian Federation and Belgorod region).

Parameter	The Russian Federation	Belgorod region
Agents	1469000	15499
Households	545600	5870
Organizations	4672	57
Employees.	688382	7911
Schoolchildren	142201	1439
Students on secondary vocational education programs	7690	85
Students on higher education programs	6419	54

Details of the population synthesis for the SDRF model and algorithms of its dynamics are presented in [16, 28]. Table 3 presents more detailed parameters for a separate aggregated organization, Agriculture in Belgorod region.

Table 3. Simulation results for an organization.

Parameter		Organization: Agriculture in Belgorod region
Year production, thousand standard units (tons)		6895
Average price for a standard unit, RUR		29442
Year supply, million RUR		93681
Credits, million RUR		54293
Deposits, million RUR		6889
Property, plant and equipment, million RUR		89568
Number of employees	Higher education	783
	Secondary vocational education	2859
	Unqualified	3349
Average official salary, RUR		13076

For the year production accountancy we use standard units, which retain quantitative correlation during transition of currency rates and allow to assess impact of private and federal investment programs on the dynamics of output in various industries.

5 Discussion of Results

The main methodological result of our research is modeling framework for interconnected socio-economic processes based on the agent approach and implementing principles of scalability, interactivity and modularity. Key elements of such a model are population, economy, education system and state administration, detailed depending on the purpose of simulation.

Information support of the model consists of datasets that match required structure and are checked for completeness and consistency. The main data sources for this task are results of the population census, SPARK-Intarfax database, statistical yearbooks, websites of the Central bank and the ministries. As we gained this information from official collections, we faced the problem of its scaling for regions and economic activities, whereas spatial simulation requires taking into account both of these components. In order to merge these arrays of information the iterative proportional fitting technique was implemented. Data from SPARK-Intarfax database and Russia Longitudinal Monitoring survey results were also converted to the structure that matches the input tables.

The overall result of the generation stage is the model database, which reflect characteristics and interconnections of population and social environment. The database was generated within assumed aggregation: one agent in the model corresponds to 100 inhabitants and each model organization integrates organizations belonging to a certain industry within a separate region. The assumed degree of detail allowed generation of social environment of the models within 10 min on a stationary computer, the size of the database on the hard disk is 8 Gigabyte.

6 Conclusions

Reconstruction of population, economic structures and social institutions was the aim of the first step in the implemented research methodology. For this task diverse information sources were used. Complexity of data processing was connected with incompleteness on the one hand (especially about financial condition of organizations and population), and excessive aggregation of data on the other. The obtained data arrays were converted into the database objects applying the developed algorithms and data structures for generating population and social environment, so that it could be used within scenario calculations.

The next stage of the study is simulation of agents' behavior and organizational decision-making. This stage includes integration an artificial component into the model agent and so that the agent would be able to make a number of decisions based on his knowledge of the environment and ability to communicate with other agents. Within the framework of the spatial development model, we consider decisions in education, employment and migration, which seriously influence on processes of the agents' resettlement. For the model of anemia dynamics the main decision area is consumption of different products. Both these models would become platforms for modeling various control actions of the federal policy on the spatial development and health of the population.

Acknowledgments. Data processing and program implementation of production and education simulation algorithms was funded by Russian Foundation for Basic Research according to the research project №18-29-03049. Processing of data from SPARK and RLMS databases, defining food production and consumption, was funded by Russian Foundation for Basic Research according to the research project №19-57-80003.

References

1. Tesfatsion, L.: Agent-based computational economics: a constructive approach to economic theory. In: Handbook of Computational Economics, vol. 2, chap. 16, pp. 831–880. Elsevier (2006). https://doi.org/10.1016/S1574-0021(05)02016-2. http://www.sciencedirect.com/science/article/pii/S1574002105020162

2. Lebaron, B., Tesfatsion, L.: Modeling macroeconomies as open-ended dynamic systems of interacting agents. Am. Econ. Rev. **98**, 246–250 (2008). https://doi.org/10.1257/aer.98.2.246

3. Fagiolo, G., Roventini, A.: Macroeconomic policy in DSGE and agent-based models redux: new developments and challenges ahead. J. Artif. Soc. Soc. Simul. **20**(1), 1 (2017). https://doi.org/10.18564/jasss.3280. http://jasss.soc.surrey.ac.uk/20/1/1.html

4. Dosi, G., Napoletano, M., Roventini, A., Treibich, T.: Micro and macro policies in Keynes +Schumpeter evolutionary models. J. Evol. Econ. **27**(1), 63–90 (2016b). https://doi.org/10.1007/s00191-016-0466-4

5. Raberto, M., Teglio, A., Cincotti, S.: Integrating real and financial markets in an agent-based economic model: an application to monetary policy design. Comput. Econ. **32**(1), 147–162 (2008). https://doi.org/10.1007/s10614-008-9138-2

6. Delli Gatti, D., Gaffeo, E., Gallegati, M., Palestrini, A.: The apprentice wizard: monetary policy, complexity and learning. New Math. Nat. Comput. **1**, 109–128 (2005b). https://doi.org/10.1142/s1793005705000068

7. Alexandre, M., Lima, G.T.: Combining monetary policy and prudential regulation: an agent-based modeling approach. J. Econ. Interact. Coord. (2017). https://doi.org/10.1007/s11403-017-0209-0

8. Popoyan, L., Napoletano, M., Roventini, A.: Taming macroeconomic instability: monetary and macro prudential policy interactions in an agent-based model. J. Econ. Behav. Organ. **134**, 117–140 (2017). https://doi.org/10.1016/j.jebo.2016.12.017

9. Dosi, G., Pereira, M., Roventini, A., Virgilito, M.E.: The effects of labour market reforms upon unemployment and income inequalities: an agent based model. Socio Econ. Rev. **16**(4), 687–720 (2018). https://doi.org/10.1093/ser/mwx054

10. Dawid, H., Harting, P., Neugart, M.: Economic convergence: policy implications from a heterogeneous agent model. J. Econ. Dyn. Control **44**, 54–80 (2014b). https://doi.org/10.1016/j.jedc.2014.04.004

11. Cincotti, S., Raberto, M., Teglio, A.: Credit money and macroeconomic instability in the agent-based model and simulator EURACE. Econ. Open-Access Open-Assess. E-J. **4**(25) (2010). http://dx.doi.org/10.5018/economics-ejournal.ja.2010-25. https://ssrn.com/abstract=1726782

12. Dawid, H., Neugart, M.: Agent-based models for economic policy design. East. Econ. J. **37**, 44–50 (2011). https://doi.org/10.1057/eej.2010.43
13. Ballas, D., Kingston, R., Stillwell, J.: Using a spatial microsimulation decision support system for policy scenario analysis. In: Van Leeuwen, J.P., Timmermans, H.J.P. (eds.) Recent Advances in Design and Decision Support Systems in Architecture and Urban Planning, pp. 177–191. Springer, Dordrecht (2004). https://doi.org/10.1007/1-4020-2409-6_12
14. Sushko, E.: Multi-agent model of the region: concept, design and implementation. Technical report Preprint WP/2012/292, CEMI RAS (2012). (in Russian)
15. Ballas, D., Kingston, R., Stillwell, J., Jin, J.: Building a spatial microsimulation-based planning support system for local policy making. Environ. Plan. A **39**, 2482–2499 (2007). https://doi.org/10.1068/a38441
16. Mamatov, A., Mashkova, A., Novikova, E., Savina, O.: Reproduction of dynamics of population of Russian regions using agent modeling. Inf. Syst. Technol. (2(112)), 48–55 (2019). (in Russian)
17. Mashkova, A.L., Savina, O.A., Banchuk, Y.A., Mashkov, E.A.: Using open data for information support of simulation model of the Russian Federation spatial development. In: Chugunov, A., Misnikov, Y., Roshchin, E., Trutnev, D. (eds.) EGOSE 2018. CCIS, vol. 947, pp. 401–414. Springer, Cham (2019). https://doi.org/10.1007/978-3-030-13283-5_30
18. Mashkova, A., Savina, O.A., Mamatov, A.: Integrating artificial agent in the simulation model of the Russian Federation spatial development. In: Adamov, A., Abzetdin, A. (eds.) The IEEE 12th International Conference on Application of Information and Communication Technologies/AICT 2018: Conference Proceedings, pp. 344–349. Institute of Electrical and Electronics Engineers Inc., Almaty (2018)
19. Mashkova, A.L., Novikova, E.V., Savina, O.A., Mamatov, A.V., Mashkov, E.A.: Simulating budget system in the agent model of the Russian Federation spatial development. In: Chugunov, A., Khodachek, I., Misnikov, Y., Trutnev, D. (eds.) EGOSE 2019. CCIS, vol. 1135, pp. 17–31. Springer, Cham (2020). https://doi.org/10.1007/978-3-030-39296-3_2
20. All-Russian population census 2010 official website. http://www.gks.ru. Accessed 22 Mar 2020
21. Russian Federation Federal State Statistics Service. http://www.gks.ru. Accessed 10 June 2020
22. SPARK web sites. https://www.spark-interfax.ru/. Accessed 25 Mar 2020
23. Ministry of economic development of the Russian Federation official website. http://economy.gov.ru/minec/main. Accessed 22 Mar 2020
24. The Central Bank of the Russian Federation official website. http://www.cbr.ru/eng/. Accessed 22 Apr 2020
25. National credit bureau official website. https://www.nbki.ru/company/news/. Accessed 16 May 2020
26. Russia Longitudinal Monitoring survey of Higher School of Economics, RLMS-HSE web sites. http://www.cpc.unc.edu/projects/rlms-hse. Accessed 12 Feb 2020
27. Ministry of science and higher education Russian Federation official website. https://minobrnauki.gov.ru/. Accessed 21 Dec 2019
28. Novikova, E., Mashkova, A.: Creation of the initial generation of agents in the computer model of the Russian Federation industrial development. In: VII International Scientific and Technical Conference "Information Technologies in Science, Education and Production" (ITSEP-2018): Conference Proceedings, pp. 313–318 (2018). (in Russian)

Russian Text Corpus of Intimate Partner Violence: Annotation Through Crowdsourcing

Ekaterina Mitiagina⬛, Marina Borodataya⬛, Elena Volchenkova⬛,
Nina Ershova⬛, Marina Luchinina⬛, and Evgeny Kotelnikov$^{(\boxtimes)}$⬛

Vyatka State University, Kirov, Russia
mityagina2004@yandex.ru, m.luchinina@yandex.ru,
m.borodatay@gmail.com, kotelnikov.ev@gmail.com,
lena_volc@mail.ru, nina.ershova.59@bk.ru

Abstract. The problem of intimate partner violence (IPV), which has become more acute under quarantine during the COVID-19 pandemic, affects millions of people and families around the world. It is extremely difficult for victims to disclose their experience of IPV and seek help from the relevant services. They prefer to search for help from people of their kind, on the Internet, in particular. Nevertheless, the forms, types of violence, people's stance and the sentiment of opinions regarding violence are particularly diverse.

The paper proposes a method for creating an annotated corpus of texts through crowdsourcing. Using the methodology of the crowdsourcing study by M. Sabou et al., the authors expand and supplement it with important points specific to burning social problems, such as compiling search queries, describing data processing, as well as evaluating the relevance of the data obtained. The key result of the study is the first Russian annotated IPV text corpus.

The main type of crowdsourcing presented in the paper is volunteer crowdsourcing, based on the annotators' loyalty to the problem under study. Despite the fact that the possibilities of its application are increasingly expanding, the scientific community still lacks a set of guidelines similar to traditional and expert methods for creating annotated corpora.

Keywords: Crowdsourcing · Annotated corpus · Intimate partner violence · Relevance of messages · Keyword search

1 Introduction

In the 2018 World Bank's report on *Woman, Business and the Law* [1], Russian women are considered the most vulnerable from violence in the world: the Russian Federation scored zero points in the legislation to protect women's rights since the country has not adopted laws on domestic violence and harassment in the workplace, there is no article on sexual violence at work in the Criminal Code, and, in 2017, the article *Battery* was transferred to the category of administrative offences.

As a result, Russia was included in the list of countries which are not protected from family violence along with Armenia, Afghanistan, Haiti, the Federated States of Micronesia, Myanmar and Uzbekistan.

The original version of this chapter was revised: The author's last name in the reference 10 has been corrected as "Haddadian". The correction to this chapter is available at https://doi.org/10.1007/978-3-030-67238-6_24

© Springer Nature Switzerland AG 2020, corrected publication 2022
A. Chugunov et al. (Eds.): EGOSE 2020, CCIS 1349, pp. 306–321, 2020.
https://doi.org/10.1007/978-3-030-67238-6_22

The problem of IPV has become particularly acute in the context of the global COVID-19 pandemic when people's daily lives have changed dramatically [2]. These changes have brought about plenty of new challenges, including physical and psychological health risks, isolation and loneliness, the shutdown of many schools and businesses, economic vulnerability, and job losses. As a result, more and more people are becoming IPV victims, both in Russia and worldwide.

It is difficult for IPV victims to disclose information about their experience and seek help from the relevant sources, and the percentage of victims seeking support from relevant professionals and organizations, including the police and medical workers, remains extremely low. In addition, experts claim that 56% of domestic violence victims who seek help from law enforcement agencies and psychological and legal services are not satisfied with their performance [3]. The victims prefer to search for help on the Internet where there are plenty of online communities to support them. People apply to these resources anonymously in order to make sure that their own situation is typical or atypical and get a possible solution to their problem.

The study of online messages and comments should become an additional source of information about the specific character of IPV, the types and forms of its implementation, and the extent of its spread. Such corpora allow analyzing the current situation with domestic violence and develop methods for automatic data collecting and processing, e.g., based on machine learning.

There are English annotated text corpora on domestic violence [4–8]. G. Karstianis et al. [4] studied the police reports of domestic violence events. The authors manually labelled 300 reports, created syntactical pattern rules and then applied this approach to a large set of police reports. A. Sánchez-Moya [5] explored 472 posts from online forums available for IPV survivors with the help of the text analysis software tool LIWC (Linguistic Inquiry and Word Count). N. Schrading et al. [6] collected corpus of tweets dedicated to one event: Ray Rice assault scandal in 2014. This corpus contains 33,628 tweets, but only 1,000 tweets were annotated manually by the authors. Then the machine learning models were constructed to classify the tweets as "pro" or "contra" with relation to the decision of victim to stay and support her abuser. N. Schrading et al. [7] gathered the posts about domestic abuse from Reddit. Afterwards, the classification per two classes was made – "abuse" and "non-abuse". But only 101 posts were annotated manually by the authors. S. Subramani et al. [8] collected the posts about domestic abuse and child abuse from Facebook. These posts were labelled automatically according to their key search terms and were classified into "abuse" and "general" using machine learning techniques. Total number of posts is equal to 4,239 (1,821 abuse posts and 2,418 general posts).

In general, existing English corpora on domestic violence have few manually annotated posts (from 100 to 1,000) collected from one type of source (e.g. Reddit or Facebook). The number of annotated classes is limited to two (e.g. "abuse" vs. "non-abuse").

Besides, to date, there are no Russian text corpora of IPV, which makes it difficult to automatically analyze Russian texts within this topic, as well as to apply statistical methods to analyze IPV data.

The contribution of this paper is twofold. Firstly, we created the first Russian annotated IPV text corpus. This corpus differs from the corresponding English corpora in number of texts (10,291 manually annotated messages), in number of sources (more than 20 social media sources of 9 types), in number of annotation classes (7 categories including forms and types of violence, type of offender, etc.). These differences make it possible to increase the performance of machine learning models, to extend the coverage of social media platforms, and to conduct a deeper analysis of text content.

Secondly, we propose a method for creating an annotated IPV corpus, including the compilation of search queries, the description of data processing and annotation criteria, as well as the evaluation of the data obtained.

2 Study Description

2.1 Study Methodology

In the paper, the crowdsourcing approach to the corpus annotation is applied. Crowdsourcing is the use of time, intellectual or other resources of a large number of people to solve a task, generate ideas or solutions. Initially, crowdsourcing appeared in commerce [9]. Currently, the advantages of obtaining linguistically annotated text corpora through crowdsourcing are the subject of much study [10, 11]; the number of crowdsourcing platforms is increasing, *Amazon Mechanical Turk, CrowdFlower, GATE, Zooniverse,* and others are particularly popular among them.

Currently, three main types of crowdsourcing are widely used: paid work, games with a purpose, and volunteer activities [12, 13]. In the first approach, the practitioners get small tasks through crowdsourcing platforms like Amazon Mechanical Turk. If the task is completed, the practitioner gets micro-payment. This approach has a simple setup, convenient platforms, and a large base of workers. But the tasks should be easy and do not need long training process. The annotation of the big corpus is very expensive and the final labeling requires careful quality evaluation.

In the game-based crowdsourcing approach, the annotation tasks are designed to entertain the annotators during the task. The main motivation of participants is fun and this is an important factor of good quality annotation. But the recruitment of the annotators and the creating of the platform are very difficult.

The third approach – volunteer activities – is altruistic, it does not need any payment. The annotators make their job for the feeling of their valuable contribution to the important project. In contrast to other approaches, volunteer crowdsourcing can be applied to non-trivial complicated tasks.

In our view, the latter approach, based on the annotators' loyalty to the problem under study, which has become more acute during the COVID-19 pandemic, is considered to be the most preferable approach for creating a corpus of IPV texts. Volunteer crowdsourcing allows reducing costs and makes the study more dynamic. Crowdsourcing makes it possible not to use annotators' expensive services.

However, a number of problems arise when it is applied: motivation of volunteers, ensuring the reliability of results, quality control of work, problems of screening out unscrupulous participants and even direct spoilers. Also, the scientific community still lacks a list of instructions and guidance with specific examples.

In this paper, the crowdsourcing approach proposed in M. Sabou et al. [13] was used to obtain the annotated IPV corpus.

M. Sabou et al. [13] propose the following crowdsourcing steps to get an annotated corpus:

1. Project Definition: choosing a problem and a crowdsourcing approach; decomposing the problem into tasks; designing a crowdsourcing task.
2. Data Preparation: collecting and pre-processing texts; creating a user interface for annotators; performing pilot studies.
3. Project Execution: recruitment of volunteers; training and support of volunteers; managing and monitoring the crowdsourcing tasks.
4. Data Evaluation and Aggregation: annotation evaluation and aggregation; evaluation of the overall corpus of characteristics.

In the method proposed within this paper, each of the above stages is supplemented or transformed considering the need to obtain the annotated corpus on acute social and multidimensional issues.

Important additions, taking into account the specific character of the topic, are:

– using a specific genre of volunteer crowdsourcing, based on the annotators' loyalty to the problem under study;
– combining volunteer crowdsourcing with expert markup as it was impossible to use the crowdsourcing approach only to get the annotation since, at the pilot stage of the study, it was obvious that the authors of the posts and their commentators, as well as the annotators, who marked up the corpus, understand the topic of violence ambiguously;
– using advanced keyword search to reduce the number of texts found that are not relevant to the topic of IPV;
– increasing the significance and number of pilot stages for annotation.

A detailed description of each stage and additions to them will be provided in the corresponding paragraphs.

2.2 Project Definition

This stage involves three subtasks: 1) choosing a problem and a crowdsourcing approach; 2) decomposing the problem into tasks; 3) designing a crowdsourcing task.

The problem of IPV has been decomposed into a set of simple crowdsourcing tasks that can be understood and performed by student volunteers with minimal training. The experience of expert markup shows that the annotators should choose from no more than ten, ideally, seven categories [14]. The instruction for volunteers includes seven categories:

– relevance (relevant/irrelevant message);
– form of violence (physical, sexual, psychological, economic);
– type of violence (systemic violence, control; resistance, defense; situational violence, provocative violence, relationship breakdown);
– type of offender (male, female, mixed type);

- sentiment (positive, negative, contradictory, neutral);
- stance (condemning violence, justifying violence, supporting the victim, neutral stance, contradictory stance);
- type of support in the comments, if available (informational, emotional).

The markup consisted of two stages: first, binary markup for the "relevance" category, and second, markup of relevant messages for the other categories. In this paper, the analysis of markup results was performed only on the example of relevance as a key category. A message was considered relevant if it referred to a specific case of IPV (i.e., violence between spouses, inmates, intimate partners, etc.), or expressed an opinion about the experience of IPV or IPV in general.

2.3 Data Preparation

The data preparation stage involves: 1) collecting and pre-processing texts; 2) creating a user interface for annotators; 3) performing pilot studies.

The text messages containing cases and opinions about IPV on the Internet were collected automatically using *Kribrum*[1], a cloud-based automated social media monitoring system. Based on the search query, this tool collects mentions of a given object from Russian Internet resources: social networks, online media, blogs, thematic and regional forums, and others. The result is a composite matrix of posts, comments, reposts, and images with the specified parameters (sentiment, geography, sources, tags, and comments, etc.).

From 1 February to 11 March 2020, *Kribrum* collected 27,596 messages related to the cases of IPV or opinions about it. Most often, people use social networks to describe the case of IPV or express their opinion about it. According to the study, this is 82% of all Internet messages: vk.com (63%), instagram.com (7.8%), odnoklassniki.ru (6.7%), facebook.com (4.5%), and others. Significantly fewer messages are found in microblogs (twitter.com), online media (skoronovosti.ru, kavkaz-uzel.eu etc.), forums (woman.ru etc.), videos (youtube.com) and blogs (zen.yandex.ru) – the aggregate percentage is 9.8%, of which microblogs constitute 7.2%, Internet media – 5.3%, videos – 1.3%, and forums – 2%. The total share of thematic portals (otvet.mail.ru), messengers (telegram.org) and review sites (otzyvru.com) takes less than 1% (Table 1).

Apart from the source (*Vkontakte, Facebook*, etc.) and the type of source (social networks, microblogs, etc.), *Kribrum* returns such characteristics as the date of publication, its author, categories, tags, sentiment, etc. However, it should be noted that automatic assigning certain characteristics to messages in *Kribrum* causes errors (e.g., when specifying the sentiment), which requires additional manual re-checking.

The search queries in *Kribrum* were based on the classification of IPV forms (physical, psychological, sexual, economic) and the type of offender (male or female as intimate partners). A form of violence was defined as a characteristic that described the external manifestations of violence; a type of offender was considered a person who committed violent acts against his/her partner.

---

[1] https://www.kribrum.ru/.

Table 1. Main data sources.

Source type	Source example	Number of messages	Percentage
Social networks	vk.com, instagram.com, odnoklassniki.ru, facebook.com	22,638	82.0
Microblogs	twitter.com	1,994	7.2
Internet media	skoronovosti.ru, kavkaz-uzel.eu	1,452	5.3
Forums	woman.ru	563	2.0
Videos	youtube.com	356	1.3
Blogs	zen.yandex.ru	334	1.2
Thematic portals	otvet.mail.ru	180	0.7
Messengers	telegram.org	61	0.2
Review sites	otzyvru.com	10	0.1
Total		**27,588**	**100.0**

The most common IPV forms are physical, sexual, and psychological violence [15]. They refer to the use of physical force to cause pain, injury or physical suffering to the victim, an attempt to obtain a sexual act, forcing a partner to perform sexual acts [16] that he/she considers humiliating and offensive, blackmail or verbal abuse [17]. Financial or economic abuse is a rarer form of IPV on the Internet. They stand for the constant monitoring of a person's ability to acquire and use their own money and resources. The abuser can prevent the victim from earning his/her own money, make him/her sabotage job interviews, receive social security benefits instead of the victim, forbid to use his/her money without consent, etc. [15].

The messages were sought using keywords and the maximum possible number of synonyms and wordforms. The keywords «бить» ("to beat") and «драться» ("to fight") (+53 synonymous wordforms) were chosen as the basis for identifying physical violence, «угрожать» ("to threaten") and «унижать» ("to humiliate") (+40 synonymous wordforms) – for psychological violence, «насиловать» ("to rape") and «принуждать к сексу» ("to force sex") (+20 synonymous wordforms) – for sexual violence, «отбирать деньги» ("to denude of money) and «запрещать работать» ("to forbid somebody to work") (+82 synonymous wordforms) – for economic violence. To get a relevant corpus of messages, as well as to identify the partner, these keywords with synonyms were specified, and afterwards a search query was compiled. For instance, for the word «бить» ("to beat"), which is a marker of physical violence, the following synonyms were used: *хватать (to grab), душить (to strangle), избивать (to beat), замахнуться (to aim a blow), толкать (to push), истязать (to torture), колотить (to batter), пороть (to give a spanking), лупить (to flog), пинать (to kick). Сожитель (inmate), муженек (hubby), благоверный (better half), супруг (spouse), хахаль (lover), ненаглядный (beloved), мой парень (my boyfriend), сожительница (inmate), женушка (wifie), благоверная (better half), супруга (spouse), невеста (bride)*, ненаглядная *(beloved)*, моя девушка *(my girlfriend)* were used as synonyms to define the type of rapist.

The examples of messages are: «*Здравствуйте, мне так больно. Мой муж издевается надо мной, ни о чем не думает, играется с утра до вечера в телефоне, курит какую непонятную фигню, любит людям портить жизнь, ... когда хочет может ругать меня даже причины не надо. Не знаю, что делать. Помогите*»[2] (*"Hello, I'm in so much pain. My husband mocks at me, does not think about anything, plays on the phone from morning till night, smokes some strange stuff, likes to spoil people's lives, ... he can scold me without any reason if he wants. I don't know what to do. Help me"* (the keywords «издеваться» (to mock), «ругать» ("to scold"), «портить жизнь» ("to spoil one's life") indicate psychological violence); «*Мне муж, уже бывший, запрещал работать, куда-то ходить, разговаривать с мужчинами. Это было ужасно. Сейчас у меня в отношениях свобода и это кайф*» (*"My husband, who was already my ex-husband, forbade me to work, go somewhere, talk to men. It was awful. Now I have freedom in my relationship and this is a bliss"*) (the phrase «запрещал работать» ("forbade me to work") indicates economic violence, the phrase «запрещал куда-то ходить, разговаривать с мужчинами» ("forbade me to go somewhere, talk to men") indicates psychological violence).

Further work with the messages found, including the corpus pre-processing and markup, was performed in the desktop version of *Microsoft Excel*. The advantage of this software tool, in comparison with the specialized ones, is its popularity and ease of use. The annotators were not required special training to work in *Microsoft Excel*, which is especially important in the context of crowdsourcing markup. The software tool makes it possible to preliminarily prepare texts (remove duplicates and long messages). In addition, to simplify the process, the volunteers were provided with so-called selection tasks when it is needed to select one option from the list of possible categories (*Microsoft Excel* makes it easy to create pop-up lists). The main drawback of this program when organizing crowdsourcing markup is the insufficient integrity control and the lack of monitoring of changes to the tables – the user may accidentally or intentionally enter erroneous data in them.

Pre-processing of the corpus included removing duplicates and messages that exceeded the specified threshold. When longer documents are being annotated, one needs to decide whether to put the entire document into one task, to split it up into smaller parts – one per crowdsourcing task (e.g. paragraphs or sentences), or to avoid including any documents above a certain size in the corpus. It was decided to exclude messages exceeding 5,000 characters from the corpus since such messages contained information not only about IPV.

Thus, the corpus was reduced to 14,000 messages, which was 50.7% of the original one, of which 90% of the reduction was due to the removal of duplicates.

The reason for the high number of duplicates is the media's interest in the topic of violence. The news about the case of violence with severe consequences, especially murder, is replicated by many media outlets.

---

[2] All the examples in the paper are given with the author's spelling and punctuation preserved.

The pilot stage is an important part of crowdsourcing markup, which is necessary to prepare and correct instructions for annotators. In case of study on a complex and ambiguous topic, the pilot stage is also needed to train experts. The authors of this paper, who are specialists in social work with various groups of the population who find themselves in a difficult life situation, acted as experts, and students of socially oriented training areas acted as volunteers-annotators. In total, 60 annotators and 5 experts took part in the message markup.

Within this study, the pilot phase was conducted in three stages, but even in this case, the degree of consistency of the five experts on the relevance criterion differed significantly from 100%. At the end of the first stage, it was 60%, the second – 95%, the third – 80%. We attribute the decrease in the level of expert agreement at the third stage to the increase in the COVID-19 pandemic, which led to a sharp increase in media interest in the topic of IPV, which in turn most likely affected the experts' understanding of IPV. It should be noted that the marked-up messages had been received before the lockdown was announced in Russia.

Anyway, we were not able to reach a consensus on whether to classify a particular message as relevant or irrelevant. This once again proves the complexity and ambiguity of the topic of IPV, its constant transformation.

The following messages are the examples that caused difficulties for experts: «В Тверской области жена угрожает усыпить собаку больного мужа» ("In the Tver region, the wife is threatening to put down her sick husband's dog") or «Муж нервный в последнее время, новая работа… Я уже давно с ним не контактирую, чтоб скандалов лишних не было. Думала, может наладится… У дочки начала спрашивать, что будем делать, она говорит не знаю, мол что хочешь то и делай!» ("My husband has been nervous recently, a new job… I haven't been in contact with him for a long time, so that there won't be any unnecessary scandals. I thought it might get better… I started asking my daughter what we would do, she says she doesn't know, that I can do whatever I want!").

2.4   Project Execution

This stage involved: 1) recruitment of volunteers; 2) training and support of volunteers; 3) managing and monitoring the crowdsourcing task.

When recruiting volunteers, motivation is of primary importance. The first motive was a conversation on statistical data on the problem of violence in Russia, which showed the importance of the study on the problem from the scientific point of view and revealed the aim and tasks of the project. It was also essential for the volunteers to take part in the major study with the team of scholars they trust.

We organized training sessions to prepare and support the annotators. The training was carried out on the basis of the pre-developed instruction. The annotators were introduced to its content, and the coordinator (an expert) gave detailed examples of how to conduct annotation. It took us 3 h on average to train a group of 10 annotators. The greatest difficulty in training was caused by the categories of sentiment and stance.

In order to form the necessary skills, the volunteers received 100 messages to make the pilot markup. Besides, the pilot markup allowed us to determine the time interval that the annotator spends on a single message – one minute on average. Consequently, three weeks were allocated for annotation of 1,000 messages (50-60 messages per day).

The annotators encountered a number of difficulties in the course of work. Firstly, it was hard for them to analyze the reported cases of IPV due to their relatively brief life experience. The students (average age – 20 years) and the experts (average age – 45 years) perceived the messages differently, which affected the markup results. Secondly, some annotators experienced IPV in their families, thus, dealing with such a topic was considered psychologically challenging for them. Due to these difficulties, as well as personal qualities and lack of motivation, 6 out of 60 annotators dropped out.

The work organized in this way allowed us to obtain the crowdsourcing markup in time to compare it with the experts' markup.

2.5 Data Evaluation and Aggregation

This stage included: 1) annotation evaluation and aggregation; 2) evaluation of the overall corpus of characteristics.

In this section, data evaluation and aggregation will be shown using the example of one category – "relevance". Evaluation of the corpus as a whole will be given in Sect. 3.

Various authors suggest using different numbers of annotators to mark up a single message related to an expression of opinion or a description of a fact. The minimum number of annotators is three [18], and the maximum number is five to seven [14]. Within this study, every thousand messages were marked up by 3 or 4 volunteers. Due to the limited number of experts, each expert marked up only 250 out of 1,000 messages. As a result, 14,000 messages were marked up, with 250 messages marked up by the expert and annotators in each thousand, and 750 messages marked up by annotators only. Some of the messages were marked up by three annotators, and some – by four of them. The difference in the number of annotators is explained by the chosen method of markup – volunteers' performance in which some of the annotators, as mentioned above, were unable to complete the work, and some of the work performed was not in accordance with the instructions.

The marked-up data obtained were analyzed in two ways, depending on the expert's opinion: taking the expert opinion into account ($250 \times 14 = 3,500$ messages) and without taking the expert opinion into consideration ($750 \times 14 = 10,500$ messages).

The concept of *a reference opinion* was introduced, i.e., the opinion of an expert which coincided with the opinion of the majority of annotators. Within the first method of analysis (taking the expert opinion into account, 3,500 messages), the reference opinion was considered to be the opinion of an expert, in case it coincided with the opinion of the majority of annotators. Within the second method of analysis (without taking the expert opinion into account, 10,500 messages), a student annotator performed the expert role, their opinion most often coincided with the reference opinion determined in accordance with the first method. The messages for which a reference opinion could not be found were removed from the corpus.

Initially, it was planned to use the expert's opinion as a reference opinion within the first method, and within the second method – the opinion of the student annotator, whose opinion most often coincided with the expert's opinion. However, this idea had to be abandoned in the course of work as the pilot stage showed that even experts in the subject area do not always manage to reach a consensus.

Schemes for determining the reference opinion for a message with two, three, and four annotators are presented in Tables 2, 3, and 4, respectively. The plus sign in the tables refers to the case when the expert's and the annotator's opinions coincide; the minus sign is used to show that the annotator's opinion does not coincide with the expert's opinion. In the absence of an expert opinion (the second method), the expert is a student annotator whose opinion most often coincides with the reference opinion determined in accordance with the first method.

Table 2. Message markup by an expert and two annotators.

Expert	A1	A2	Decision
+	−	−	Remove the message
+	+	−	Remove the message
+	+	+	Reference opinion

Table 3. Message markup by an expert and three annotators.

Expert	A1	A2	A3	Decision
+	−	−	−	Remove the message
+	+	−	−	Remove the message
+	+	+	−	Reference opinion
+	+	+	+	Reference opinion

Table 4. Message markup by an expert and four annotators.

Expert	A1	A2	A3	A4	Decision
+	−	−	−	−	Remove the message
+	+	−	−	−	Remove the message
+	+	+	−	−	Remove the message
+	+	+	+	−	Reference opinion
+	+	+	+	+	Reference opinion

It should be noted that the increased number of annotators increases the probability of classifying messages as relevant/irrelevant and reduces the probability of their removing.

Table 5 shows the number of messages removed from each thousand if three or four annotators are involved. The average number of removed messages with three annotators involved is 345 messages, and with four of them – 205 messages.

Table 5. Number of removed messages from each thousand.

Number of thousand	3 annotators	4 annotators
1	–	145
2	–	236
3	–	186
4	351	–
5	327	–
6	233	–
7	–	284
8	283	–
9	549	–
10	–	199
11	–	174
12	–	179
13	327	–
14	–	236
Total removed	2,070	1,639
Removed per one thousand on average	345	205

3   Results and Discussion

3.1   Characteristics of Relevant and Irrelevant Messages Received

As a result of the aggregation procedure described in previous subsection, 3,709 messages were removed from the total corpus (14,000 messages), which reduced the annotated corpus to 10,291 messages, 6,140 (60%) of which are considered irrelevant, 4,151 (40%) – relevant. The main form of violence in relevant messages is physical violence (81%), followed by psychological violence (15%). Sexual (3.5%) and economic (0.5%) violence account for less than 5% of all the relevant messages. We can draw an intermediate conclusion that violence related to the use of physical force occupies a key position in the minds of Internet users. Women are more likely to be victimized (72%); however, men can be victims (28%) as well. Although it should be noted that if the victim is a man, most often it is a mixed form of violence when the woman committed the criminal act in response to male violence.

The majority of relevant messages were found in vk.com (2,362, 56.9%). In other social networks and sources, the number of messages is significantly lower: instagram.com (444, 10.7%), twitter.com (262, 6.3%), facebook.com (209, 5.0%), youtube.com (111, 2.7%) woman.ru (83, 2.0%), odnoklassniki.ru (82, 2.0%), zen.yandex.ru (49, 1.2%), etc.

The analysis of irrelevant messages allowed us to identify the following characteristics, according to which the message was classified as not relevant to the topic of IPV.

1. The message content. A number of messages touched upon violence, but not IPV («*Житель Республики Хакасия получил 14 лет колонии за то, что пьяным <u>забил до смерти</u> маленького пасынка*») ("*A resident of the Republic of Khakassia got 14 years in prison for <u>beating</u> a young stepson <u>to death</u> while being drunk*"), or markers of violence («*бьет*» ("*beats*"), «*пытает*» ("*tortures*"), «*унижает*» ("*humiliates*"), etc.) were mentioned in the message in another context, e.g., in a figurative sense («*Очень вовремя наткнулась на пост. Мой муж как раз сейчас меня <u>пытает</u>, как ему за кожей ухаживать. Спасибо за пост*» ("*I came across the post just in time. My husband is "<u>torturing</u>" me right now how to take care of his skin. Thank you for the post*"); «*Если не поставлю лайк то меня Женя <u>побьет</u>, поэтому поставлю*» ("*If I don't leave a like, Zhenya <u>will "beat"</u> me, so I'll do it.*"); «*Людка в каких то дешевках, видать развод с мужем <u>ударил</u> по карману, а вот баб Шура ни в чем себе не отказывает на пенсии*» ("*Lyudka wears cheap things, perhaps, the divorce from her husband <u>hit</u> the pocket, but Baba Shura does not deny herself anything in retirement*")).

2. The crime scene. The messages describing cases of violence that occurred outside the Russian Federation were considered irrelevant. We focused on the language of the message (e.g., «*кад бих нашла неког сличног Андрији Милошевићу замолила бих га да ме ожени и била бих добра жена*» – Serbian language), the country/city discussed in the message («*Рим: Домашний любимец спас россиянку, которую пытался убить ее муж-итальянец*») ("*Rome: a pet saved a Russian woman who her Italian husband tried to kill*"), the names of participants mentioned («*Актер Джонни Депп в переписке с друзьями говорил о том, что утопит и сожжет бывшую супругу, актрису Эмбер Херд, после чего ... ее труп*» .) ("*In correspondence with his friends, the actor Johnny Depp said that he would drown and burn his former wife, the actress Amber Heard, then ... her body.*").

3. Violence mentioned in anecdotes, jokes, horoscopes, e.g.: «*Переговоры полиции по рации: – Вы по вызову подъехали, что там? – Да бытовуха, муж пришёл домой, прошёл по только что вымытому полу, в грязной обуви. Жена <u>ударила</u> его пять раз сковородкой. Насмерть. – Орудие убийства изъяли? Труп сфотографировали? – Тут это... Пол не высох ещё, мы в подъезде ждём*» ("*Police radio conversations: – You came on a call, what's up? – Yes, a domestic crime, the husband came home, walked on the newly washed floor in dirty shoes. His wife hit him with a frying pan five times. To death. – Was the murder weapon removed? Was the body photographed? – Well... The floor is not dry yet, we are waiting in the entrance.*")

4. The description of situations of violence in works of fiction, both in prose and in verse («*Синий кит глотает души, Дно заменит колыбель. Муж жену в угаре <u>душит</u>...*») ("*the Blue whale swallows souls, the Bottom will replace the cradle. The husband <u>is strangling</u> his wife blinded...*"), in annotations and film reviews («*...и я смотрела в оригинале, понимая с пятого на десятое. Сюжет прост: стоматолог Сьюзан устав от мужа, который её всячески <u>унижал</u>, забирает двоих детей и уезжает в новые апартаменты. Только вот в её апартаментах живёт призрак. Который не знает, как туда попал*») ("*...and I watched in the original, understanding from the fifth to the tenth. The plot is simple:*

Susan's dentist is tired of her husband, who <u>humiliated</u> her in every possible way, takes her two children and leaves for a new apartment. But there's a Ghost in her apartment. Who doesn't know how he got there").

5. Limited /inaccurate information. A message was considered irrelevant if it was impossible to make a clear conclusion about the case of violence from its content. Ambiguity, incompleteness of the message (*«Илья, он не любит, когда его там <u>унижают</u>, он же все еще ищет там себе жену)* (*"Ilya, he does not like <u>to be</u> <u>humiliated</u> there, he is still looking for a wife there),* assumption (*«Игорь, в каком смысле он «нормальный дядька»? Он <u>унизил</u> многих женщин, а, значит, <u>унижает</u> жену и дочь»)* (*"Igor, in what sense is he a "normal uncle"? He <u>humiliated</u> many women, which means that he <u>humiliates</u> his wife and daughter")* or a question (*«Денис, тебя жена побила»; «Сергей, пожалуйста, ответьте, как будет время... Что по-вашему донос/стукачество? Вот примеры: жену бьет муж, она обращается в полицию с заявлением. Донос?»)* (*"Denis, did your wife beat you?"; "Sergei, please answer as soon as possible... What do you think is snitching? Here are examples: a wife is beaten by her husband, and she goes to the police with a statement. Denunciation?")* did not allow us to identify the case of violence or to isolate the author's opinion on the problem.

These features of irrelevant messages, with the exception of the message language, are usually not taken into account when collecting automatically, which confirms the complexity of the topic of IPV, as well as the inability to organize an absolutely accurate automatic search for relevant messages.

3.2 Evaluation of the Corpus

The evaluation of the developed corpus is usually carried out by computing inter-annotator agreement within annotators and/or with an annotation of the experts; and also through machine learning techniques [13]. We evaluated the IPV corpus in these two ways: with the help of computing inter-annotator agreement and using machine learning classifier.

We compute inter-annotator agreement using Fleiss' kappa statistical measure [19]. It is calculated as the ratio of the degree of annotators' agreement actually attained above what would be predicted by chance and the degree of agreement attainable above chance. This measure was calculated for resulting corpus in two ways: for the annotations of annotators alone and for the annotations of annotators together with experts (the whole annotation of the corpus). For the first case the Fleiss' kappa is equal to 0.753 and for the second case – 0.770. In accordance to [20], these values are appropriated for such a complicated domain as intimate partner violence and coincide with the measures from [6, 7].

We also did some preliminary research and built a machine learning model – gradient boosting from scikit-learn machine learning library [21] – to classify annotated messages as "relevant" and "non-relevant" to IPV. We found the normal forms of all the words, selected the words with frequency not less than 10 in the corpus (we got 13,298 normalized words). For the text representation, the TF.IDF model was used. The evaluation of the model is performed through 5-fold cross-validation. The average accuracy was equal to 0.765 (±0.023). These results are comparable with the results for English corpora. For example, in [6] the accuracy was 0.700 (±0.020) for LinearSVM classifier.

Thus, the quality of the resulting corpus is enough for future research.

4 Ethical Issues

Ethical issues are considered to be important within the topic of IPV. These issues are always relevant when using publicly available data to study various social phenomena. This study follows international ethical criteria related to social media data collection and analysis; in particular, we followed the ethical guidelines for social media study supported by the European Commission [22]. At all stages of data processing, the principles of confidentiality were observed. We are aware of the risk of harm and absolutely guarantee the anonymity of users, using only public information, without identifying any user. The data were appropriately coded, anonymized, and protected to avoid the possibility of tracking users.

5 Conclusion

The main result of the study is the first Russian-language corpus of texts on IPV, the extremely important topic in modern Russia. It differs from English corpora not only in the language, but also in a number of texts, the variety of types of social media sources, and the diversity of IPV classifications associated with its forms, types of violence, types of offenders, sentiment and stance of the authors in relation to the victim. The resulting corpus will allow, on the one hand, using machine learning methods to automate the rapid detection of violence-related messages, on the other hand, applying statistical methods to obtain information on IPV, and analyzing stances of the society to this issue.

The contribution of this work also lies in the proposed method of volunteer crowdsourcing to obtain texts on acute social issues. This method can help scholars who implement crowdsourcing projects and developers of platforms to automate crowdsourcing tasks.

The study revealed a number of features of the proposed method. First, we recommend using volunteer crowdsourcing in conjunction with expert markup, it will improve the accuracy and consistency of the annotators. Second, the loyalty of annotators in volunteer crowdsourcing, on the one hand, makes it possible to attract the necessary number of volunteers, on the other hand, it can distort the results and cause inconsistencies between the markup developers. Volunteers can have experience of domestic violence, their own vision of the problem related to their age, gender, and social status. Therefore, pilot stages of research, high-quality instructions, training, as well as evaluation and aggregation of the obtained data are fundamentally important. Third, the quality of markup improves if the number of annotators increases. This paper shows how fundamental the differences are when a message is marked up by three and four annotators.

References

1. Women, Business, and the Law 2018 (Russian). http://documents.worldbank.org/curated/en/927271534918263759/Women-Business-and-the-Law-2018. Accessed 2020/06/07
2. Bradbury-Jones, C., Isham, L.: The pandemic paradox: the consequences of COVID-19 on domestic violence. J. Clin. Nurs. **29**(13–14), 2047–2049 (2020)
3. Parlamentskaya Gazeta. IPV statistics. https://www.pnp.ru/social/eksperty-predstavili-v-gosdume-statistiku-po-domashnemu-nasiliyu.html. Accessed 7 June 2020
4. Karystianis, G., Adily, A., Schofield, P.W., Greenberg, D., Jorm, L., Nenadic, G., Butler, T.: Automated analysis of domestic violence. police reports to explore abuse types and victim injuries: text mining study. J. Med. Internet Res. **21**(3), e13067 (2019)
5. Sánchez-Moya, A.: Corpus-driven insights into the discourse of women survivors of intimate partner violence. Quaderns de filología. Estudis lingüístics **22**, 215–243 (2017)
6. Schrading, N., Alm, C.O., Ptucha, R., Homan, C.M.: #WhyIStayed, #WhyILeft: Microblogging to Make Sense of Domestic Abuse. In: Proceedings of the Human Language Technologies: The 2015 Annual Conference of the North American Chapter of the ACL, pp. 1281–1286, Denver, Colorado (2015)
7. Schrading, N., Alm, C.O., Ptucha, R., Homan, C.M.: An analysis of domestic abuse discourse on reddit. In: Proceedings of the 2015 Conference on Empirical Methods in Natural Language Processing, pp. 2577–2583, Lisbon, Portugal (2015)
8. Subramani, S., Wang, H., Islam, M.R., Ulhaq, A., O'Connor, M.: Child abuse and domestic abuse: content and feature analysis from social media disclosures. In: Wang, J., Cong, G., Chen, J., Qi, J. (eds.) ADC 2018. LNCS, vol. 10837, pp. 174–185. Springer, Cham (2018). https://doi.org/10.1007/978-3-319-92013-9_14
9. Howe, J.: The rise of crowdsourcing. Wired Mag. **14**, 1–5 (2006)
10. Masoumi, V., Salehi, M., Veisi, H., Haddadian, G., Ranjbar, V., Sahebdel, M.: TeleCrowd: A Crowdsourcing Approach to Create Informal to Formal Text Corpora (2020). https://arxiv.org/abs/2004.11771
11. Ohman, E.: Challenges in annotation: annotator experiences from a crowdsourced emotion annotation task. In: Proceedings of the Digital Humanities in the Nordic Countries 5th Conference, pp. 293–301, Riga, Latvia (2020). https://researchportal.helsinki.fi/en/publications/challenges-in-annotation-annotator-experiences-from-a-crowdsource
12. Wang, A., Hoang, C.D.V., Kan, M.-Y.: Perspectives on crowdsourcing annotations for natural language processing. Lang. Resour. Eval. **47**, 9–31 (2013). https://doi.org/10.1007/s10579-012-9176-1
13. Sabou, M., Bontcheva, K., Derczynski, L., Schar, A.: Corpus annotation through crowdsourcing: towards best practice guidelines. In: Proceedings of the Ninth International Conference on Language Resources and Evaluation (LREC 2014), pp. 859–866, Reykjavik, Iceland (2014)
14. Hovy, E.: Annotation. In: Proceedings of the 48th Annual Meeting of the Association for Computational Linguistics (ACL 2010), Tutorial Abstracts, Uppsala, Sweden (2010)
15. Ali, P., McGarry, J.: Domestic Violence in Health Contexts: A Guide for Healthcare Profession. Springer, Cham (2020). https://doi.org/10.1007/978-3-030-29361-1
16. García-Moreno, C., Jansen, H., Ellsberg, M., Heise, L., Watts, C.: WHO multi-country study on women's health and domestic violence against women: initial results on prevalence, health outcomes and women's responses. World Health Organization, Geneva (2005). https://www.scirp.org/reference/ReferencesPapers.aspx?ReferenceID=1704948. Accessed 7 June 2020

17. Follingstad, D.R., DeHart, D.D.: Defining psychological abuse of husbands toward wives: contexts, behaviors, and typologies. J. Interpers. Violence **15**(9), 891–920 (2000)
18. Sayeed, A.B., Rusk, B., Petrov, M., Nguyen, H.C., Meyer, T.J., Weinberg, A.: Crowdsourcing syntactic relatedness judgements for opinion mining in the study of information technology adoption. In: Proceedings of the 5th ACL-HLT Workshop on Language Technology for Cultural Heritage, Social Sciences, and Humanities, pp. 69–77, Portland, OR, USA (2011)
19. Fleiss, J.L.: Measuring nominal scale agreement among many raters. Psychol. Bull. **76**(5), 378–382 (1971)
20. Artstein, R., Poesio, M.: Inter-coder agreement for computational linguistics. Comput. Linguist. **34**(4), 555–596 (2008)
21. Pedregosa, F., Varoquaux, G., Gramfort, A., Michel, V., Thirion, B., et al.: Scikit-learn: machine learning in python. J. Mach. Learn. Res. **12**, 2825–2830 (2011)
22. Ethics in Social Science and Humanities (2018). European Commission, https://ec.europa.eu/research/participants/data/ref/h2020/other/hi/h2020_ethics-soc-science-humanities_en.pdf. Accessed 7 June 2020

Conspiracy Theories Dissemination on SNS Vkontakte: COVID-19 Case

Konstantin Platonov[1](✉) and Kirill Svetlov[2]

[1] Center for Sociological and Internet Research, Saint Petersburg State University, St. Petersburg, Russia
konplatonov@gmail.com
[2] Laboratory for Research of Social-Economic and Political Processes of Modern Society, Saint Petersburg State University, St. Petersburg, Russia
k.svetlov@spbu.ru

Abstract. COVID-19 crisis has caused the growth of popularity of conspiracy theories disseminated by opinion leaders as well as anonymous actors via social media. This trend poses a danger because supporters of fake agendas contribute to spreading disinformation, deny the real risks, break the rules, and even undertake some unlawful actions. Since March 2020 Russian Federal Service for Supervision of Communications, Information Technology and Mass Media (Roskomnadzor) initiated blocking fake news about coronavirus on social media but some of them remained available to the public. In our study, we considered the agenda on conspiracy theories presented in the posts on the most popular Russian SNS VKontakte. The initial database contained 2342689 posts published between March 30 and May 12, 2020.

After the interpretation of the results of topic modeling, we found that conspiracy-related posts comprised a small share among all popular COVID-related posts on VKontakte. Content analysis showed that only about a half of the posts with information on conspiracy theories about COVID-19 was devoted to the promotion of conspiracy arguments but the sufficient share related to the debate on alternative versions or criticism. It was revealed that the most popular theory presented in posts on Vkontakte can be described as "anti-vax/politicized" version of "the chipping theory" which found the link between coronavirus and "planned chipping" of population via "mass vaccination".

The structure of the agenda on COVID-related conspiracy theories is described. The key features of the analyzed agenda on conspiracy theories and practical applications are discussed.

Keywords: Social media · Conspiracy theories · COVID-19 · Vkontakte · Denialism · Russia

1 Introduction

Global crises often provoke an increase in dissemination of unverified information and rumor mongering. The complex and controversial information available on coronavirus has given rise to heterogeneous denialism movement and a lot of conspiracy theories. By MARCH 2020 the number of sites propagating fakes and conspiracy theories about

© Springer Nature Switzerland AG 2020
A. Chugunov et al. (Eds.): EGOSE 2020, CCIS 1349, pp. 322–335, 2020.
https://doi.org/10.1007/978-3-030-67238-6_23

COVID-19 reached a record 52 million [1]. According to the polls, 29% of Americans believe in the artificial origin of the virus [2], also only 38% of Russians trust the information on pandemic from the official media [3].

Today, some political leaders [4] and governments [5] still tend to understate the risks related to the COVID-19 outbreak. As an example, Turkmenistan banned the word "coronavirus" in media and prohibited wearing masks in public [6]. Denialism often gives rise to varying alternative versions of current events.

The made-up link between COVID-19 and vaccination conspiracy is one of the widespread hypotheses among denialists in Russia. Some celebrities become proponents of such ideas including film director Nikita Mikhalkov [7], tennis player Marat Safin [8], and many others. Exposing the relationship between unrelated phenomena is a common trick used by conspiracy theorists [9:1]. Another hypothesis claims a connection between spread of the virus and 5G cellular technology [10]. These rumors caused arsons of cell towers in UK [11].

Other fake theories assume artificial origin of COVID-19 and claim the possibility of treatment with vitamin C or garlic [1]. A significant part of denialists' theories developed political connotations. Various arguments are already being used as a political instrument and have political consequences. Particular cases show fake news inflaming distrust against the official agenda and provoke tensions in society [12]. Misinformation is used for political manipulation and pressure [13, 14]. Social media is one of the key resources for replication of fakes and influence on mass audience.

Despite the great struggle against the propagation of fake information, conspiracy theories still leaked in the Russian social media. However, it is still unclear how widespread this phenomenon has become and which particular theories related to COVID-19 have become the most popular. In this article, we investigate data retrieved from the most popular social network in Russia, VKontakte, in order to understand to what extent and how exactly conspiracy theories have manifested themselves in the published content under the conditions of fake content blocking by Roskomnadzor.

Based on described issues we formulate the following research questions.

- How are the popular conspiracy theories (related to COVID-19) represented in the posts on SNS VKontakte?
- How does the subtopic of content related to conspiracy theories about COVID-19 on VKontakte affect the user's engagement?

In order to address the objectives of the study, we refer to related research on conspiracy theories in general and in social networks in particular, justifying the place of our work in the context of the issues relating to COVID-19. In the following sections we describe the data acquisition and sampling procedures used in this study, as well as the main methods employed, such as topic modeling and content analysis. This is followed by a presentation of the results and conclusions about the spread of conspiracy theories, distribution of their varying versions, and the audience engagement on the content on various subtopics. In conclusion, the perspectives of practical application of the presented research are proposed.

2 Related Work

Popular COVID-related conspiracy theories started from the denial of official information. Denialism can lead to disastrous consequences, especially in the hands of decision-makers who have an impact on population. Some HIV-related cases can be named as vivid examples [15]. Diethelm and McKee formulate 5 key features of denialism: conspiracy theories, fake experts, selectivity, exaggerated expectations of research opportunities, and mistakes as well as logical errors [16]. Denialists are characterized by pulling ideas and facts out of context and generalizations [9:2]. Online communication became a breeding ground for the spread of conspiracy theories [17]. The level of anonymity [18] and the echo chamber effect [19] can be identified among the typical reasons for people's involvement in propagation of conspiracy theories, in particular sharing fake news. The tendency to share unverified information is also influenced by information overloads and propensity for trusting online publications in general without any fact checking [20]. In social media, the dissemination of fake information manifests itself in a wave-like manner, and people often do not even think about the quality of the information they share with subscribers.

Experimental studies show that the percentage of people willing to share information about COVID-19 is significantly higher than the percentage of those willing to believe in it [21]. In a large-scale study aggregating a number of outlets from Twitter, Instagram, YouTube, Reddit and Gab, Cinelli et al. have shown that only 1837 of the 2637 sources of the information related to COVID-19 is reliable [22]. Empirical studies show that Twitter bots are active in publishing politicized conspiratorial content [23] more than other users. Adherence to a certain political ideology influences behavior regarding COVID-19, for example, conservatives in the USA tend to underestimate health risks and are less willing to comply with social distancing [24].

Conspiracy theories and denialism on Russian social networks remain an insufficiently researched issue. This problem becomes even more urgent under the conditions of coronavirus infodemic. The spread of such theories seems to be a common knowledge, but we still know little about the contents of their dissemination and thematic landscape, in particular on VKontakte, the most influential social media for the Russian speaking audience. Using the COVID-19 case as an example, firstly, we present the methodology of mining the content relating to conspiracy theories and, secondly, we describe its thematic landscape as well as the levels of the audience engagement.

3 Data

Studies covering issues connected with propagation of information on COVID-19 use a number of data sources such as Twitter [20, 25], Facebook [26], YouTube, and many others [7]. The present research is based on data acquired from the most popular social network in Russia "VKontakte" (monthly reach over 65%) [27]. The database was obtained using request "coronavirus" (analog in Russian) to VK API.

The initial set contained 2342689 posts (DB_0) published between March 30 and May 12, 2020 (the period of the official self-isolation in most of the Russian regions), as well as information on key metrics such as the numbers of comments, likes, reposts and views.

In order to filter relevant content, we carried out following procedures.

1. We selected posts with relatively high popularity based on formal metrics. Thus, we excluded all the posts which did not meet at least one of the following criteria.

   - At least 100 likes.
   - At least 10 comments.
   - At least 1000 views.
   - At least 10 reposts.

2. All texts were lemmatized using MyStem [28]. As a result, we obtained database containing 476876 posts (DB_1).

3. We used abstract keywords "coronavirus + {deception, fabrication, disclosure}" (analogs in Russian) to reveal the words which typically had been used to query to popular search engine Yandex with the above mentioned terms via WordStat [29]. Then, we collected all unique words from the Wordstat results (LIST_1).

4. At the next stage, we filtered the database obtained on step 1 (DB_1) using the words from step 2 (LIST_1), then we calculated the frequency of occurrence in posts for each word. New list of words was compiled by excluding common words (frequency of occurrence >1%). Then during manual expert assessment other 15 terms were excluded as irrelevant. Final list contained 74 keywords (LIST_2).

5. Finally, we filtered the database obtained on step 1 (DB_1) using the reassembled wordlist compiled on step 3 (LIST_2) to the resulting database contained 69971 posts (DB_2).

The distribution of the number of posts per day reveals some downward trend during April. The same trend is also present in DB_1 and DB_2 (Fig. 1).

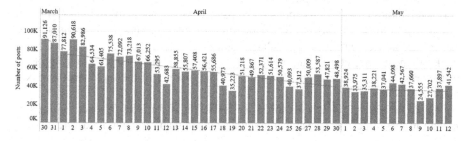

Fig. 1. The number of posts per day during the research period. (DB_0).

In contrast, the level of engagement has remained stable during the research period (Fig. 2). We calculated engagement rate using simple formula that represents the ratio of the number of activities to the reach multiplied by 1000 (similar formulae are used for Facebook [30]).

$$ER = ((likes + comments)/views) * 1000$$

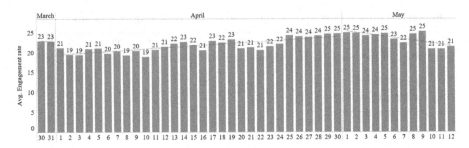

Fig. 2. Average engagement rate for posts per day during the research period. (DB_0)

4 Methods

In research related to COVID-19 on SNS, different methods and approaches are used, such as cluster analysis [20, 25], mathematical modeling and regression [22], machine learning [31], and content analysis [26].

The data for the present study were obtained and processed with social media mining methods. For topic modeling we implemented LDA algorithm. After extraction, qualitative content analysis was conducted to interpret and summarize the data [32].

4.1 Topic Modeling

One of the effective tools for analyzing text data is probabilistic topic modeling [33]. Topic modeling allows to obtain the main topics in a text corpus, as well as to assign the distribution of topics to each document. Thus, topics of interest are attributed to the documents automatically. Topic modeling performs the task so called soft clustering [34]. The studies note that this approach helps to solve the problems of homonymy and synonymy [35]. Synonyms are found in similar contexts, while homonyms are presented in different semantically unrelated topics.

From the mathematical point of view, the problem of topic modeling is the problem of factoring the term-document P matrix into the product of the topic-term matrix Φ and the topic-document matrix Θ.

Let D be a set of documents for analysis and let W be a set of tokens (words, n-grams) in these documents. Several assumptions are made in topic modeling.

- Hypothesis of the existence of topics. It is assumed that the occurrence of the token $w \in W$ in the document $d \in D$ is related to some topic t from the finite set T.
- Hypothesis of a bag-of-words. It is assumed that the document $d \in D$ represents a multiset of tokens $w \in d$, each of which occurs n_{dw} times. Accordingly, the order of the tokens in the document becomes unimportant.

- The hypothesis of conditional independence, according to which the probability of meeting the token w in the document d on topic t does not depend on the document, that is

$$p(w|d,t) = p(w|t)$$

Taking into account the above hypotheses, let us consider the distribution of tokens in a document d. The probability of finding a token w is equal to

$$p(w|d) = \sum_{t \in T} p(w|d,t)p(t|d) = \sum_{t \in T} p(w|t)p(t|d) = \sum_{t \in T} \varphi_{wt}\theta_{td}$$

Thus, the matrix $P = \{p(w|d)\}_{w,d}$ with size $|W| \times |D|$ decomposes into a product of matrices $\Phi = \{\varphi_{wt}\}_{w,t} = \{p(w|t)\}_{w,t}$ with size $|W| \times |T|$ and $\Theta = \{\theta_{td}\}_{t,d} = \{p(t|d)\}_{t,d}$ with size $|T| \times |D|$. For a given matrix P, matrices Φ and Θ are need to be restored. The LDA model (Latent Dirichlet allocation) makes an additional assumption about the distribution of columns φ_t и θ_d. They are considered to be vectors of random variables satisfying the Dirichlet distribution with the parameters $\alpha \in R^{|T|}$ и $\beta \in R^{|w|}$.

Often, all components of α and β are taken equal [36], their possible choice being $\alpha_1 = \frac{1}{|T|}$ and $\beta_1 = 0.1$.

We used the standardized procedure for text preprocessing for all the text data in this study. This consists of the several steps including deleting links, non-letter characters, punctuation and numbers, stop words as well as replacing emojis with special codes [37] and some other procedures.

For definition of topics in DB_2 we used the Gensim library [38] implementation of LDA algorithm and also pyLDAvis [39] library for visualization of results. Gensim library operates with a dictionary of terms which would be then used in training. Into the dictionary used in the present study, we included words and bigrams that have been found in at least 20 documents, but no more than in 50% of the entire collection. Then, the model was put through 10 epochs of training on the whole collection of the documents represented as bags-of-words with the number of topics set to 40. This number of topics was selected on the basis of the following principle. The selected number of topics was chosen as the minimum number of overall topics required to distinguish most clearly the topic related to conspiracy theories. In order to find the optimal number of topics, five analyses were conducted starting with 30 with step of 5 up to 50. Afterwards, filtering out irrelevant content analysis was implemented.

4.2   Content Analysis

We developed two code schemes for qualitative data analyses. **Code scheme 1**. After exploratory analysis, the following categories of posts were identified as the most prominent.

1. **Conspiracy theories.** Actually, posts containing arguments and ideas of conspiracy theories, denialism, sensationalism, including copy-paste.

2. **Debate on conspiracy theories.** News related to conspiracy and denialism, posts on combating fakes, also neutral reviews of conspiracy versions of some events and incidents related to the activity of their supporters.
3. **Criticism of conspiracy theories.** Texts containing arguments against alternative theories, appeals to ignore fakes.
4. **Other.** Content of low relevance, indirectly connected with the subject.

Code Scheme 2. This scheme determines subcategories for the code «**Conspiracy theories**» from the previous classification. Preliminary analysis allowed to determine the most significant subcategories.

1. **Chipping.** The version of global conspiracy, operating on the ideas of "global vaccination conspiracy", "coercive chipping program founded by organizations financed by Bill Gates". The most popular versions of this theory presented by celebrities received their unique subcodes: **"Mikhalkov"**, **"Safin"**, **"Icke"**.
2. **Anti-globalism.** The group of more abstract «enemy above» [40] theories proposes COVID-19 link with global conspiracy and global state or World empire. This type of theories is often connected with some elements of "Chipping theory" but do not represent it in its pure form.
3. **Anti-vax.** The criticism of vaccination and in some cases discussion of "global vaccination conspiracy" but without any mentioning of "chips" and "chipping".
4. **"Russian conspiracy".** The versions related to criticism of the authorities, Russian state bodies and healthcare. These texts often contain accusations against the Government of hiding real statistics and concealing true information.
5. **Sensationalism.** The versions which erratically use different elements of other theories including bold speculations, such as involvement of "Masonry" or "satanic cults".
6. **Other**

5   Results

The key topic ("topic_33") found by the LDAVis visualization tool closely related to denialism and conspiracy theories was characterized by top-10 terms such as *"Gates"*, *"vaccine"*, *"global"*, *"population"*, *"Bill"*, *"world"*, *"virus"*, *"conspiracy"*, *"pandemic"*, *"theory"* (Fig. 3).

As we can see the most popular versions of conspiracy propagated on VKontakte tend to be based on the "link" between Gates, vaccines and COVID-19 pandemic.

For the following analysis we filtered out from DB_2 the posts which contained less than 25% of "conspiracy topic". As a result, we obtained new database (DB_3) contained 1570 posts. The following graph shows the co-occurrence of terms (LIST_2) in posts (DB_3) (Fig. 4). Size of each node corresponds to its degree, weight of each edge corresponds to PMI between two words, and color shows the class of modularity.

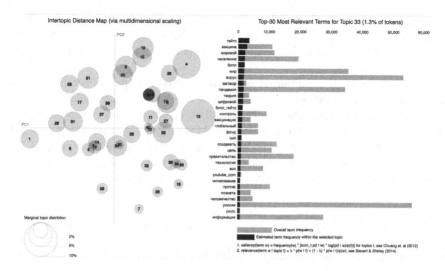

Fig. 3. Results of LDAVis visualization tool.

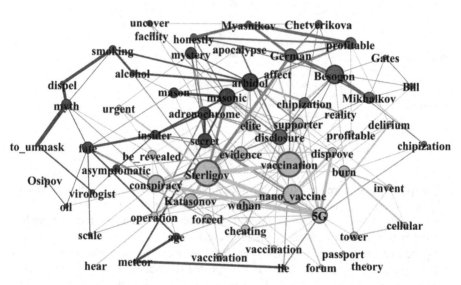

Fig. 4. Co-occurrences of keywords (LIST_2, Yifan Hu layout with label adjustment).

We built the co-occurrence graph using the NetworkX package [41] and the visualization tool Gephi [42]. Its nodes are keywords used in DB_2 (LIST_2). Edges were built based on PMI [43] values.

$$PMI(word_1, word_2) = \log_2 \frac{p(word_1, word_2)}{p(word_1)p(word_2)}$$

between these keywords based on the posts from "conspiracy topic". If $PMI > 0$ the corresponding $word_1$ и $word_2$ nodes will be joined by an edge with the corresponding weight. In visualization of this graph, only 20% of the edges with the highest weights are displayed.

After that, we made a subsample containing 500 random posts from DB_3 using coding schemes described previously. We used weighted measures which were calculated as ratios of metrics (the numbers of likes, comments, reposts) to the number views then multiplied by 1000 (by analogy with ER formula). At first, notice that, only about a half of the posts relates to the main topic «Conspiracy theories» (Fig. 5). The topic «Debate on conspiracy theories» is presented in slightly more than a quarter of the relevant texts. There are far fewer posts with critical remarks.

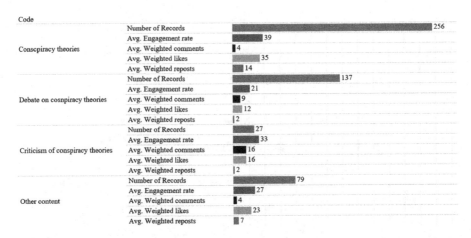

Fig. 5. Key metrics for different types of posts in DB_3.

- The posts directly related to «Conspiracy theories» and also «Criticism on conspiracy theories» received higher engagement rate comparing to other.
- The publications related to «Criticism on conspiracy theories» had the highest number of weighted comments among the categories.
- The texts actually promoting conspiracy theories received more likes comparing to other posts and were more likely to be reposted by users or other communities.
- The average number of reposts for a typical conspiracy post was about 35 times higher comparing to the average post simply containing the key "coronavirus" (DB_0).

The most widespread conspiracy theory in posts, as it should be expected, was the theory of chipping, presented in the form of interpretations by anonymous authors or celebrities, which, however, have no connection with medicine or epidemiology. First of all, it was already mentioned film director Nikita Mikhalkov, tennis player Marat Safin, anchorwoman Victoria Bonya, businessmen German Sterligov. Also, the posts often referred to the conspiracy episode in the popular program "Man and the Law" on Channel One. All interpretations operated on the same system of ideas, but the details differed, for example, Bonya's version focused on the COVID-19 and 5G link, and Sterligov's concept was more of an anti-vax theory. In addition to the most frequently cited celebrities, there are also a number of other opinion leaders who were often mentioned in posts, such as economist Sergei Katasonov, public figure Nikolai Starikov, English conspiracy theorist David Icke and others.

There was also "soft denialism" in the posts when the author recognizes the danger of the virus and the general provisions of the official (epidemiological) agenda, but claimed that the problem (in some aspects) was "artificially inflated" and exploited for political purposes. Some types of conspiracy ideas could be found quite rarely, for example, theories about the spread of COVID-19 through tests, connections between chipping and QR-codes issued as passes during quarantine in Moscow, Big Pharma theories, 5G influence or the creation of the virus to cover the economic crisis.

- It is worth mentioning that, for instance, Mikhalkov's version of chipping theory had comparatively high engagement rate but primarily the same theory presented by not so influential (in Russian context) Safin or Icke was not so involving (Fig. 6).
- The most popular versions of conspiracy theories were the most commented (taking in account the effect of reach). But «Anti-vax» version had the highest average number of weighted likes (Fig. 7).

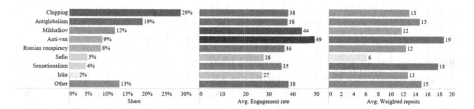

Fig. 6. Average engagement rates and average weighted reposts for the posts representing different versions of conspiracy theories.

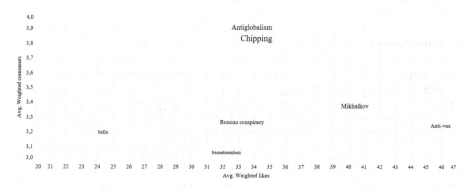

Fig. 7. Average weighted likes and comments for the posts representing different versions of conspiracy theories.

6 Discussion

Using social media mining approach, we described the structure of representation of conspiracy theories related to COVID-19 on VKontakte. To summarize, we can say that it is neither a united system of ideas nor a disparate set of statements. The first element in this structure is the main theory related to "chipping and vaccination". The second one is represented with interpretations by opinion leaders who often can be classified as "fake experts". The third element includes additional versions of theories which often use particular pieces of the main theory but emphasize some aspects or shifts to local agenda, denialism, sensationalism and so on. This core in surrounded by the other elements as well as criticism and debate on conspiracy theories and this content is quite popular too.

As a result of content analysis we have confirmed that almost all of the conspiracy versions are connected with each other and inherit certain ideas from the main "enemy above" theory.

Our algorithm of multi-stage filtering and subsampling allows to obtain relevant content on topic of interest regardless of the presence of spam. Such approach can be effective in presence of high level of information noise.

Bot activity analysis is beyond the scope of our study. However, in general, it should be taken into account that the impact of bots publishing content on COVID-19 is quite high. For example, on Twitter it was found that artificial accounts were spreading «sensationalistic headlines» about the laboratory origin of the virus and the use of the infection as a «globalist biological weapon» [44].

Limitations. In our research we used data from only one SNS that is considered the most representative for Russian online media agenda. The database was also limited to the period from March 30 to May 12, 2020. Another factor which could have influenced our sample was the fact that Roskomnadzor had ordered all social media to take down all « fake news » on March 20, in other words before the period of official self-isolation began [45]. Consequently, it is obvious that VKontakte use some inner algorithms to filter out content related to conspiracy and denialism which provide significant decrease in «suspicious» texts propagation.

7 Conclusion

The results have shown the variety and narrowness of conspiracy theories about COVID-19 presented on VKontakte. In general, it should be noted that popular posts related to conspiracy theories, and furthermore promoting conspiracy versions, were not so common in our sample of popular posts. In the process of filtering the relevant content, the initial database of 2342689 entries shrank to the dataset of 1570 posts.

We revealed that content related to conspiracy theories represented in posts on SNS VKontakte includes not only the promotion of alternative versions but a sufficient amount of texts devoted to debate on this topic, in some cases, critical. Only a half of the posts in subsample contained conspiracy arguments or claims to support sensationalism or denialism. The main alternative theory presented in relevant posts on

VKontakte was the chipping theory connected with the idea about "global collusion" and anti-vax movement in combination with the denial of a natural origin (or spreading) of COVID-19. Besides, in some posts, the other sensationalistic concepts were presented such as Big Pharma influence, a link between COVID-19 and 5G, the willful spread of COVID-19 through tests, and so on.

According to calculations, the posts promoting conspiracy arguments provided a higher level of engagement rate and were more likely to be reposted in comparison with the other types of content such as criticism or debate on conspiracy theories. In other words, "conspiracy arguments" made posts more viral. Critical texts, in turn, on average, were the most commented. Accordingly, the reactions to COVID-19 conspiracy differed depending on qualities of the texts, in other words, the particular subtopic mattered.

Therefore, the conspiracy content was in demand comparing to the general flow of posts about coronavirus on VKontakte, moreover, posts directly promoting conspiracy theories caused a positive response from the audience, ensuring high user engagement, as well as a high repost rate, which promoted infodemic of misinfomation.

This work presents the method for mining the information related to conspiracy theories which can be used for description of thematic landscape of propagated agenda in SNSs. Our classification and subsampling method can be applied to a methodological framework for developing anti-fake algorithms for newsfeeds. The analysis of representation of conspiracy theories can be implemented to counteract « andemic populism» [26] which is hindering an adequate response to COVID-19 outbreak.

Further Work. In the future we plan to expand our design adding the analysis of comments. In addition, we intend to reveal the patterns of online discussion on COVID-19. Further research is also needed to determine key trends in the amount of supporters and opponents which can be estimated using comment classification.

Acknowledgement. We would like to thank our colleagues from the Center for Sociological and Internet Research of Saint Petersburg State University for guidance and support.

References

1. Mian, A., Khan, S.: Coronavirus: the spread of misinformation. BMC Med. **18**(1), 1–2 (2020)
2. Pew Research Center. Knowledge and perception surrounding COVID-19. https://www.journalism.org/2020/03/18/knowledge-and-perception-surrounding-covid-19/. Accessed 15 June 2020
3. Levada Center. Coronavirus pandemic 26.03.2020. https://www.levada.ru/2020/03/26/pandemiya-koronavirusa/, Accessed 15 June 2020
4. The Atlantic. The Coronavirus-Denial Movement Now Has a Leader 27.03.2020. https://www.theatlantic.com/politics/archive/2020/03/bolsonaro-coronavirus-denial-brazil-trump/608926/, Accessed 15 June 2020
5. The Guardian. As the rest of Europe lives under lockdown, Sweden keeps calm and carries on. 28.03.2020. https://www.theguardian.com/world/2020/mar/28/as-the-rest-of-europe-lives-under-lockdown-sweden-keeps-calm-and-carries-on, Accessed 15 June 2020

6. CBS. This Central Asian country will reportedly arrest you for saying the word "coronavirus" 01.04.2020. https://www.cbsnews.com/news/coronavirus-turkmenistan-bans-word-coronavirus-arrest/, Accessed 15 June 2020

7. Russia today. 'Bill Gates seeks to microchip humanity!' Russian Oscar-winning director pushes vaccine conspiracy... loosely-based on REAL patent 3.05.2020. https://www.rt.com/news/487634-mikhalkov-bill-gates-microchip-implants/, Accessed 15 June 2020

8. Russia Today. 'They're preparing people for microchip implants': Tennis legend Marat Safin shares coronavirus conspiracy theory 14.04.2020. https://www.rt.com/sport/485744-marat-safin-coronavirus-conspiracy/, Accessed 15 June 2020

9. Specter, M.: Denialism: How irrational thinking harms the Planet and threatens our lives, p. 294. Penguin (2009)

10. Kaur, H.: The conspiracy linking 5G to coronavirus just will not die. CNN Business 9.04.2020. https://edition.cnn.com/2020/04/08/tech/5g-coronavirus-conspiracy-theory-trnd/index.html, Accessed 15 June 2020

11. Peter, J.: Cellphone towers attacked as conspiracy theory connecting 5G and coronavirus gains steam. USA Today 6.04.2020. https://www.usatoday.com/story/tech/2020/04/06/coronavirus-5-g-conspiracy-theory-cellular-towers/2955557001/, Accessed 15 June 2020

12. Tapia, L.: COVID-19 and fake news in the dominican republic. Am. J. Trop. Med. Hyg. **102**(6), 1172–1174 (2020)

13. Prasad, A.: The organization of ideological discourse in times of unexpected crisis: explaining how COVID-19 is exploited by populist leaders. Leadership **16**(3), 294–302 (2020). https://doi.org/10.1177/1742715020926783

14. Ricard, J., Medeiros, J.: Using misinformation as a political weapon: COVID-19 and Bolsonaro in Brazil. Harvard Kennedy School Misinf. Rev. **1**(2) (2020), https://doi.org/10.37016/mr-2020-013

15. Bateman, C.: Paying the price for AIDS denialism. S. Afr. Med. J. **97**(10), 912–913 (2007)

16. Diethelm, P., McKee, M.: Denialism: what is it and how should scientists respond? Eur. J. Public Health **19**(1), 2–4 (2009)

17. Wood, M.J., Douglas, K.M.: Online communication as a window to conspiracist worldviews. Front. Psychol. **6** (2020). https://doi.org/10.3389/fpsyg.2015.00836

18. Talwar, S., Dhir, A., Kaur, P., Zafar, N., Alrasheedy, M.: Why do people share fake news? associations between the dark side of social media use and fake news sharing behavior. J. Retail. Consum. Serv. **51**, 72–82 (2019)

19. Walter, S., Brüggemann, M., Engesser, S.: Echo chambers of denial: explaining user comments on climate change. Environ. Commun. **12**(2), 204–217 (2018)

20. Laato, S., Islam, A.K.M., Islam, M.N., Whelan, E.: Why do people share misinformation during the Covid-19 pandemic? (2020). arXiv preprint arXiv:2004.09600

21. Pennycook, G., McPhetres, J., Zhang, Y., Rand, D.G.: Fighting COVID-19 misinformation on social media: experimental evidence for a scalable accuracy nudge intervention (2020). https://doi.org/10.31234/osf.io/uhbk9

22. Cinelli, M., et al.: The COVID-19 social media infodemic (2020). arXiv preprint arXiv:2003.05004

23. Ferrara, E.: #COVID-19 on Twitter: Bots, Conspiracies, and Social Media Activism (2020). arXiv preprint arXiv:2004.09531

24. Rosenfeld, D.L., Rothgerber, H., Wilson, T.: Politicizing the COVID-19 pandemic: ideological differences in adherence to social distancing (2020). https://doi.org/10.31234/osf.io/k23cv

25. Ahmed, W., et al.: COVID-19 and the 5G conspiracy theory: social network analysis of Twitter data. J. Med. Internet Res. **22**(5) (2020), https://doi.org/10.2196/19458

26. Boberg, S., Quandt, T., Schatto-Eckrodt, T., Frischlich, L.: Pandemic Populism: Facebook Pages of Alternative News Media and the Corona Crisis. A Computational Content Analysis (2020). arXiv preprint arXiv:2004.02566
27. Mediascope.   https://webindex.mediascope.net/report/general-statis-tics?byDevice= 3&byDevice=1&byDevice=2&byGeo=1&byMonth=202003&id=16571, Accessed 15 June 2020
28. Yandex. MyStem. https://yandex.ru/dev/mystem/, Accessed 15 June 2020
29. Yandex. WordStat. https://wordstat.yandex.ru/, Accessed 15 June 2020
30. Chan, M., Fassbender, K.: Evaluating public engagement for a consensus development conference. J. Palliat. Med. **21**(S1), 20–26 (2018)
31. Shahsavari, S., Holur, P., Tangherlini, T.R., Roychowdhury, V.: Conspiracy in the Time of Corona: Automatic detection of Covid-19 Conspiracy Theories in Social Media and the News (2020). arXiv preprint arXiv:2004.13783
32. Mayring, P.: Qualitative content analysis: theoretical foundation, basic procedures and software solution, p. 143 (2014). https://nbn-resolving.org/urn:nbn:de:0168-ssoar-395173
33. Vorontsov, K., Potapenko, A.: Tutorial on probabilistic topic modeling: additive regularization for stochastic matrix factorization. In: Ignatov, Dmitry I., Khachay, Mikhail Yu., Panchenko, A., Konstantinova, N., Yavorskiy, Rostislav E. (eds.) AIST 2014. CCIS, vol. 436, pp. 29–46. Springer, Cham (2014). https://doi.org/10.1007/978-3-319-12580-0_3
34. Blei, D.M., Ng, A.Y., Jordan, M.I.: Latent Dirichlet allocation. J. Mach. Learn. Res. **3**(Jan), 993–1022 (2003)
35. Sun, R. (ed.): The Cambridge Handbook of Computational Psychology, p. 768. Cambridge University Press, Cambridge (2008)
36. Griffiths, T.L., Steyvers, M.: Finding scientific topics. Proc. Natl. Acad. Sci. **101**(1), 5228–5235 (2004)
37. Svetlov, K., Platonov, K.: Sentiment analysis of posts and comments in the accounts of Russian politicians on the social network. In: 2019 25th Conference of Open Innovations Association (FRUCT), pp. 299–305 (2019)
38. Gensim. https://github.com/RaRe-Technologies/gensim, Accessed 15 June 2020
39. PyLDAVis. https://github.com/bmabey/pyLDAvis, Accessed 15 June 2020
40. Walker, J.: The United States of Paranoia: a Conspiracy Theory, p. 448. Harper Collins, New York (2013)
41. NetworkX. https://networkx.github.io/, Accessed 15 June 2020
42. Gephi. https://gephi.org/, Accessed 15 June 2020
43. Matsuo, Y., Sakaki, T., Uchiyama, K., Ishizuka, M.: Graph-based word clustering using a web search engine. In: Proceedings of the 2006 Conference on Empirical Methods in Natural Language Processing, pp. 542–550 (2006)
44. Ferrara, E.: What types of COVID-19 conspiracies are populated by Twitter bots? First Monday **25**(6) (2020). https://doi.org/10.5210/fm.v25i6.10633
45. The Moscow times. Russian News Outlets Ordered to Take Down 'Fake' Coronavirus News (2020).   https://www.themoscowtimes.com/2020/03/20/russian-news-outlets-ordered-to-take-down-fake-coronavirus-news-a69699, Accessed 15 June 2020

Correction to: Russian Text Corpus of Intimate Partner Violence: Annotation Through Crowdsourcing

Ekaterina Mitiagina⬤, Marina Borodataya⬤, Elena Volchenkova⬤,
Nina Ershova⬤, Marina Luchinina⬤, and Evgeny Kotelnikov(✉)⬤

Correction to:
**Chapter "Russian Text Corpus of Intimate Partner Violence:
Annotation Through Crowdsourcing" in: A. Chugunov et al.
(Eds.): *Electronic Governance and Open Society:
Challenges in Eurasia*, CCIS 1349,
https://doi.org/10.1007/978-3-030-67238-6_22**

In the originally published version of chapter 22, the reference 10 contained an error in the author's last name. The author's last name in the reference 10 has been corrected as "Haddadian".

The updated original version of this chapter can be found at
https://doi.org/10.1007/978-3-030-67238-6_22

Author Index

Printed in the United States
by Baker & Taylor Publisher Services